SELECTED LETTERS OF MALCOLM LOWRY

Other books by Malcolm Lowry

UNDER THE VOLCANO

HEAR ÚS O LORD FROM HEAVEN
    THY DWELLING PLACE

ULTRAMARINE

Malcolm Lowry
at Tlaxcala, Mexico

SELECTED LETTERS OF
Malcolm Lowry

Edited by Harvey Breit & Margerie Bonner Lowry

JONATHAN CAPE
THIRTY BEDFORD SQUARE
LONDON

First published in Great Britain 1967
© 1965 by Margerie Bonner Lowry

Lines from Conrad Aiken's "The House of Dust" are quoted by
permission of Oxford University Press, Inc., from Aiken's *Collected
Poems,* copyright 1953 by Conrad Aiken.

A passage from José Ortega y Gasset is quoted by permission of
W. W. Norton & Company, Inc., from *History as a System, and
Other Essays Toward a Philosophy of History,* copyright 1941,
© 1961 by W. W. Norton & Company, Inc., New York, N.Y.

Verse LXXVI of "Gitanjali" from *The Collected Poems and Plays
of Rabindranath Tagore* is reprinted by permission of The Macmillan Co., the Trustees of the Tagore Estate, and Macmillan & Co.,
Ltd., London, copyright 1918 by The Macmillan Co., renewed 1946
by Rathindranath Tagore.

Printed in Great Britain by
Lowe and Brydone (Printers) Ltd, London
on paper made by John Dickinson & Co. Ltd
Bound by A. W. Bain & Co. Ltd, London

To those who have assisted us in the

compilation of this volume and to those who

esteem the work of Malcolm Lowry

ACKNOWLEDGMENTS

The editors are grateful to the following for permission to reprint certain of the letters that appear in this volume:

Wake (No. 11, 1952, issue): for the letter to Seymour Lawrence dated November 28, 1951.

Les Lettres Nouvelles (July–August 1960 issue): for the letters to Albert Erskine dated January 25 and October 29, 1947; November 7, 1949; and Spring 1953; and the letters to David Markson dated November 1953 and February 5, 1954.

Canadian Literature (Spring 1961 issue): for the letter to Albert Erskine dated Spring 1953.

Prairie Schooner (Winter 1963/64 issue): for the letters to John Davenport dated 1936, Nordahl Grieg dated 1938, and Downie Kirk dated 1951.

Shenandoah (Spring 1964 issue): for excerpts of letters to Albert Erskine dated October 29, 1947; Summer 1948; March 5, 1949; June 5, 1951; 1953 [summer]; Halloween 1953; and July 1955.

The editors are also grateful for permission to publish the letters of James Agee, Jacques Barzun, Jonathan Cape, Robert Giroux, Ralph Gustafson, Christopher Isherwood, Alfred Kazin, Jay Leyda, Harold Matson, Maxwell Perkins, Charles Scribner, Sr., and Frank Taylor to Malcolm Lowry which appear in the Appendices.

INTRODUCTION
By Harvey Breit

To MY MIND, the letters of Malcolm Lowry are remarkable in at least two major ways. They reflect with agonizing completeness the artist at bay, cornered as it were by poverty, the world's indifference, and his apparently savage inclination for alcohol. And they also reflect, to a degree I find unparalleled in any other writer, an awareness, a minute knowledge, of what he was up to in his work.

But this plight and this gift may seem familiar enough: writers are invariably hounded by this or that; and they are, of course, highly conscious of what they are doing. With such a notion I cannot agree. Reality breaks off from this obsolescent or classic sense we continue to hold of the fate and wisdom of the artist. Since the Thirties he has rarely been so harassed as Lowry by a lack of money and an absence of opportunity; and most writers are in truth only partly conscious of the meanings in their work. There are too many times, one will see in the letters, when a five-dollar bill was crucial. And the letter to his English publisher is a document, a masterpiece of self-analysis as well as an extraordinary critique of his own masterpiece, *Under the Volcano*.

Born in England in 1909 and dead in England at forty-eight, Lowry spent most of the last seventeen years of his life as a squatter in Dollarton, near Vancouver, British Columbia. His struggles for some sort of minimum financial equilibrium are unbearably Herculean; and his lucid grasp of the dark elements and bottomless wells in his work I find unique. The letters, individually and cumulatively, will, I believe, establish for most readers this tragic *condition humaine* as well as the exhilarating synthesis the author forged from his complex and elusive visions.

At the very start of Lowry's *Volcano*, two men discuss the fate of the hero. "Poor your friend," Dr. Vigil says, "he spend his money on earth in such continuous tragedies." Though one would be in error to search for a point-to-point correspondence between the created and the creator, the Consul's plight resembles Lowry's. The Consul, sad and great man though he be, is the symbol of man's fall from grace or, to give the screw a turn, his voluntary exile from the Garden of Paradise. Except for the most ephemeral of minutes, the Consul lives in an unrelieved Hell. Lowry falls from grace many times, he knows the experience profoundly, haunted as he was by outer passivity and inner demonism. But his seasons in Hell are interrupted by excursions into more joyous worlds. Perhaps in the end, like the Consul, he ran toward his final Hell, but during his life, as the reader will observe, he continued to sniff an air of hope. And, of course, he created the Consul. He had that advantage and the kind of pleasure that must accrue when achieving such plausible and magnificent doom: some form of catharsis had to be at work for him.

In the letters Lowry reveals so many of the gifts one senses in the Consul, that his hero possessed—and one gets only in brief flashes—in the pre-novel, before his demons took over. Lowry was limited by the tragic points he had to make in his fiction. In the letters he is obviously free, and those intimations of irony, erudition, manners, generosity, independence, humanity and literary taste break out, powerful and substantial gifts in themselves, and that yet make me, at least, marvel at how simply and sensitively and even sparingly he employed them in his fiction. How—if one may say it—correctly he employed them.

Many of the letters are concerned with work, with his plans and projects, with his stops and starts, his revisions, his contrapuntal labors, his designs, his inspiration and bafflement. This overwhelming need to work, together with his staggering consciousness of what he was doing, give the reader a rare opportunity to get inside a writer's workshop. But there are also letters that deal with Lowry's struggles for the merest existence as well as his struggles to maintain dignity. It is something of a square circle he was getting at, yet he does manage somehow. In the midst of the direst dilemma he is concerned with not letting someone down, caught between fulfilling an obligation and the God-awful quest for perfection. Both obsessions, with work and survival, create an impression of a man boxed in by a diabolical combination of inner and outer events. The attempts to break out read a little like a Kafka story.

And yet, as was said, there did exist those journeys out of Hell. He was not only a man who drank too much (a *borracho*); he was not only a man with an intermittent touch of paranoia; he was not only a poor devil of a sub-sub in the literary hierarchy.

He was witty and hopeful. "Cheerfulness was always breaking in," he writes. He was erudite, apparently reading everything and forgetting nothing. He was a self-made naturalist, naming flowers and trees with the ease of a top sergeant naming the parts of his rifle, and even arguing with Melville about sea birds. He was a seaman. He was a carpenter. He had once shot golf in the seventies. He was a swimmer. He was an expert movie-goer. He was a poet and a critic. He had political acumen, a surprising virtue because he avoided politics, preferring to know men, to guess what they struggled toward, and feared and fled from.

He also had three remarkable relationships, with his wife, his editor, and his agent. At certain periods in his life it may have been impossible for him to survive without the help of these three people. Lowry was married to Margerie Bonner for the last eighteen years of his life. She was his confidante, his onetime collaborator, a novelist herself (as the letters will reveal), so close to him that he frequently gave preference to her work over his own as (I would surmise) he gave preference to her life over his own. His relationship with his editor, Albert Erskine, first at Reynal & Hitchcock, then at Random House, was an inspiring one for Lowry: Erskine buoyed him, helped him both materially and spiritually, offered him hard and intelligent criticism, backed him each time and all the time, until toward the end when it became more than impossible. Harold Matson was there, was simply and beautifully there.

These were the good journeys, refreshing but ephemeral. Because dominant, and only too applicable, was Lorca's line:

How tremendous with the final banderillas of gloom.

Though Lowry knew Heaven, he knew Hell best. Though he knew hope, he knew despair better.

Having to make a selection was not an easy task. Mrs. Lowry and I found ourselves in a quandary quite often. Still we believe we have selected the best letters (two-thirds of the available ones), and we also selected with an eye to creating a continuity, so that where there was a choice between two equally interesting letters, we tended to choose the letter that best filled a gap in the history. We have also made use of an Appendix, putting in material we thought of more than usual importance or that complemented or completed an exchange. Because of this commitment, we have had to exclude some fine letters, particularly from Conrad Aiken, John Davenport and James Stern. The typographic treatment of literary titles and foreign expressions has been standardized. However, no attempt has been made to standardize spellings, although misspellings have been corrected. Occasionally, in order to avoid giving pain to the living, we have substituted for a name or omitted sentences. We have not used ellipses to indicate these omissions because we believe that the letters have lost little or nothing, and wish they might be read without those distracting symbols, which tend to exaggerate the excisions.

Since the correspondence too frequently suggests frustration and failure, it is an irresistible pleasure to record the current status of Lowry's work. *Under the Volcano*, first published in 1947, has from the beginning been some sort of underground classic. It is now safe to say that it is no longer subterranean. Very much above ground, the *Volcano* is included in university courses throughout the world and is usually listed as one of the major novels of the twentieth century. The publisher of this volume has restored *Volcano* to hard covers (a tribute to its durability) simultaneously with the appearance of the letters. The novel has enjoyed great success in Europe, where it has appeared in all the obvious foreign languages, as well as Polish, Portuguese and Dutch. Recently it was translated into Spanish for the first time, making its initial entrance (with fear and trembling) into Mexico, the country of the book's *natividad* as well as its tragic and perilous locale.

Ultramarine, Lowry's first novel, is in print. *Hear Us O Lord From Heaven Thy Dwelling Place*, a collection of short novels and stories, mentioned frequently in the letters, finally appeared in 1961. A novella, *Lunar Caustic*, was published in *The Paris Review*. *The Selected Poems of Malcolm Lowry* has been published and a *Collected Poems* is contemplated. Some of the short stories, most of them now together in *Hear Us O Lord*, were printed in various literary magazines.

So Lowry's furious war, almost lost in his lifetime, appears to be won. The aura of genius that clung to him during his lifetime and yet seemed dispelled has now gained substance. Most moving, I feel, is the ultimate corroboration of the author's belief in his tragic novel. He wrote to Jonathan Cape, after Cape had first rejected the *Volcano*: "There is something about the destiny of the creation of this book that seems to tell me it just might go on selling for a very long time."

Let the reader mark the word *destiny* well. Throughout the letters he will come upon a constellation of words revolving around a magical or fatalistic concept: *mystery, talisman, diabolic, cabbala, esoteric, demon, coincidence, luck, infernal, spell* and the *Law of Series*.

Lowry held to some of this, not only as a writer. He was involved, perhaps like Faust or perhaps less nefariously like Melville, with the invisible world. In a remarkable letter to a friend to whom he has sent a book, he cautions the father to keep the book away from the daughter because of its supernatural powers. In one of the most magnificent tours de force, "The Element Follows You Around, Sir" (an excerpt from an unpublished novel, *October Ferry to Gabriola*), Lowry, in a dæmonic spree, develops a series of natural disasters that can only have supernatural causes. They are otherwise inexplicable.

By the very nature of the supernatural—is this a contradiction in terms?—to be immersed in its logic is also to appropriate and possess (or be appropriated and possessed by) some of its mysteries and secrets. Is it too fanciful to conceive the possibility that Lowry's magic, distracted and therefore weakened by life's demands, is operative now, posthumously, with all its concentrated power, to reveal its possessor's remarkable talents? These were so frequently neglected during Lowry's creative life that some form of retribution seems to be at work. It is, of course, Malcolm Lowry himself who is at work. But whether solely *through* the work or hovering just *over* the work is a whimsical and haunting question. For myself, particularly during days of drift, I believe Lowry to be somewhat there, in some questionable shape. For his great novel has magic in it, achieving the fusion of opposites, containing the tranquility of a noble style and the fever of a contemporary vision. He gave us our own Prince Myshkin, the Consul, in whom the past, present and future merge, with all their conflicting memories and desires, contracts and promises, therapies and gaping wounds. Through these letters I think the reader will see that Lowry paid his dues only too well and at great cost.

A BIOGRAPHICAL CHRONOLOGY

JULY 28, 1909	Born in Birkenhead, Cheshire, England
MAY, 1927	Went to sea as cabin boy and traveled to Japan, China, etc.
OCTOBER, 1927	Returned to England
1928	Studied at the English College in Bonn
SUMMER, 1929	Went to Cambridge, Mass., to meet Conrad Aiken
FALL, 1929	Entered Cambridge University
SUMMER, 1930	Made trip to Norway as fireman on Norwegian freighter. Met Nordahl Grieg.
SUMMER, 1932	Graduated from Cambridge with third-class honors in the English tripos, received B.A.
1933	*Ultramarine* published by Jonathan Cape
DECEMBER, 1933	Married Jan Gabrial in Paris
1935	Went to New York alone
1936	Went to Los Angeles alone
NOVEMBER, 1936	Went to Mexico with Jan Gabrial
1936	Began work on *Under the Volcano*
1938	Returned to Los Angeles
JULY, 1939	Went to Vancouver, B.C., Canada
1940	Was divorced
DECEMBER 2, 1940	Married Margerie Bonner
1940	Moved to Dollarton, B.C.
1940	Sent third version of *Under the Volcano* to agent Harold Matson
1941	*Under the Volcano* refused by 12 publishers and withdrawn from agent, fourth version begun
JUNE 7, 1944	House burned down, went East to stay with Gerald Noxon, near Toronto
FEBRUARY, 1945	Returned to Dollarton and started to rebuild house
JUNE, 1945	Finished *Under the Volcano* and sent to agent
FALL, 1945	Went to Mexico

SPRING, 1946   *Under the Volcano* accepted by Reynal & Hitchcock in New York and Jonathan Cape in London the same day

MAY, 1946   Returned to Dollarton, received M.A. from Cambridge University

DECEMBER, 1946   Sailed from New Orleans on a freighter for Haiti

FEBRUARY, 1947   Went to New York, *Under the Volcano* published by Reynal & Hitchcock, returned to Dollarton

SEPTEMBER, 1947   *Under the Volcano* published by Jonathan Cape

NOVEMBER, 1947   Sailed from Vancouver, through the Panama Canal, to France, on French freighter

1949   Returned to Dollarton and began stories in *Hear Us O Lord from Heaven Thy Dwelling Place* and movie script of *Tender Is the Night*

APRIL, 1950   Finished script and continued work on *Hear Us O Lord* and poems

1950–1954   In Dollarton working on *Hear Us O Lord, October Ferry to Gabriola,* poems

AUGUST, 1954   Went to New York and sailed for Genoa on Italian freighter

WINTER, 1954–55   In Taormina, Sicily

JUNE, 1955   Went to England and moved to Ripe, Sussex

JUNE 27, 1957   Died

CONTENTS

PART I: *1928–1940*

To Conrad Aiken*

5 Woodville Road
Blackheath, London S.E.3
[Sometime in 1928]

I have lived only nineteen years and all of them more or less badly.
And yet, the other day, when I sat in a teashop (one of those grubby
little places which poor Demarest loved, and the grubbier the better, and so do I) I became suddenly and beautifully alive. I read
. . . "I lay in the warm sweet grass on a blue May morning, My
chin in a dandelion, my hands in clover, And drowsed there like a
bee . . . Blue days behind me Reached like a chain of deep blue pools
of magic, Enchanted, silent, timeless. Days before me Murmured
of blue sea mornings, noons of gold, Green evenings streaked with
lilac . . ."
I sat opposite the Bureau-de-change. The great grey tea urn
perspired. But as I read, I became conscious only of a blur of faces: I
let the tea that had mysteriously appeared grow clammy and milk-
starred, the half veal and ham pie remain in its crinkly paper; vaguely,
as though she had been speaking upon another continent, I heard the
girl opposite me order some more Dundee cake. My pipe went out.

> . . . I lay by the hot white sand-dunes.
> Small yellow flowers, sapless and squat and spiny,
> Stared at the sky. And silently there above me,
> Day after day, beyond all dreams or knowledge,
> Presences swept, and over me streamed their shadows,
> Swift and blue, or dark . . .†

I paid the bill and went out. I crossed the Strand and walked down
Villiers Street to the Embankment. I looked up at the sea gulls, high

* The American poet and novelist.
† From Aiken's "The House of Dust."

[3]

in sunlight. The sunlight roared above me like a vast invisible sea. The crowd of faces wavered and broke and flowed.

Sometime when you come to London, Conrad Aiken, wilst hog it over the way somewhere with me? You will forgive my presumption, I think, in asking you this.

I am in fact hardly conscious myself of my own presumption. It seems quite fated that I should write this letter just like this, on this warm bright day while outside a man shouts Rag-a-bone, Rag-a-bone. It may not even interest you, my letter. It may not be your intention *ever* to come to London even to chivy up your publishers.

While on the subject of publishers I might as well say that I find a difficulty bordering upon impossibility in getting your "Nocturne of Remembered Spring." Have you got a spare copy of this in Rye that you could sell me? If you have, it would be a good excuse for you to write to tell me so. You could also tell me whether you are coming to London any time, you would have any time to see me. Charing X is only a quarter of an hour away from here. But perhaps this letter has infuriated you so much that you have not read this far.

te-thrum te-thrum
te-thrum te-thrum
Malcolm Lowry

To Conrad Aiken

5 Woodville Road
Blackheath
Tuesday night
[Postmarked March 13, 1929]

Sir. (Which is a cold but respectful exordium.)

It has been said by no less a personage than Chamon Lall, once General Editor of a quarterly of which you were an American Editor that—sorry I'm wrong. It has been said by no less a personage than *Russell Green* (and I don't say that it is an original aphorism because one of his others "Sentimentality is a name given to the emotions of others" is sheer Oscar Wilde) that the only criterion of love is the degree of impatience with which you wait for the postman.

Well, I am a boy and you (respectfully) are a man old enough to be my father, and so again I may not talk of love in the way that

Russell Green intended, but all the same, I may here substitute love for—shall we say—*filial affection* and, to apply the aphorism, since I wrote to you, my attitude towards postmen has completely changed. Once they were merely bourgeoisie beetles carrying their loads. Now they are divine but hopeless messengers. The mirror opposite the foot of my bed reflects the window to the right of the head of my bed (set between two mysterious green curtains) and this window—I cheat myself that this is good for my health—I keep open all night. In the mirror I can also see the road behind me when it is light. Early yesterday morning, it must have been about dawn, when I imagined that I could actually *see,* in the mirror, a long and never ending procession of postmen labouring along this road. The letters were delivered and among a great pile for other people was one for me from you.

I cannot remember what you said. You were pleased that I ended off my letter to you with *te-thrum te-thrum, te-thrum te-thrum;* but I can't remember anything else except your handwriting. Of course it was, as I realised bitterly when I woke up, merely a rose-festooned illusion. You had no intention of writing me. You didn't like the way I asked if you would have time ever to see me in London when you might have *time* but hardly time enough to trouble about having a lunch on someone you'd never seen. I perhaps didn't make it clear enough that I'd go anywhere within my reach from Pimlico to the Isle of Dogs if only there was half a chance of seeing *you*. And then it is possible I should have sent a postal order in anticipation for "Nocturne of Remembered Spring" because even if you hadn't got it I take it even though you would have found it a nuisance you would have sent the postal order back which would have meant at least a cautious letter of some sort. But I'm wandering from the point.

The point is this.

I suppose there are few things you would hate more than to be invested with any academic authority. Well, this I shall say. Next October I am going to Cambridge for three or four years to try and get an English Tripos and a degree. Until October I am more or less of a free lance and a perpetual source of anxiety to a bewildered parent. The bewildered parent in question would be willing to pay you 5 or 6 guineas a week (I should say six personally, but tactily) if you would tolerate me for any period you like to name between now and then as a member of your household. Let me hasten to say that I would efface myself and not get in the way of your inspiration when it comes toddling along, that my appetite is flexible and usually entirely satisfied by cheese, that although I can't play chess and know little of the intricacies of gladioli, I too have heard the sea sound in strange waters—sh-sh-sh like the hush in a conch shell—and I can wield a fair tennis racket.

All I want to know is why I catch my breath in a sort of agony when I read:

> The lazy sea-waves crumble along the beach
> With a whirring sound like wind in bells,
> He lies outstretched on the yellow wind-worn sands
> Reaching his lazy hands
> Among the golden grains and sea-white shells.*

And I want to be in Rye at twilight and lean *myself* by the wall of the ancient town—*myself*, like ancient wall and dust and sky, and the purple dusk, grown old, grown old in heart. Remember when I write like this, remember that I am not a schoolboy writing a gushing letter to Jeffrey Farnol or somebody. (Remember, too, that you must respect me a little for having such an intense admiration for your poetry.)

I know you are a great man in America and that you have your own school of followers, but to me—in the dismal circle in which I move nobody had ever heard of you, my most intellectual moments, such as they are, being spent entirely alone, it was as though I had discovered you and I like to preserve this absurd idea in my childish mind and give myself a great deal of unearned credit for having done so. Well, to continue, I won't weary you by eulogizing what you know yourself to be good (good is quite stupendously the wrong word but I don't want to appear to gush, you understand.)

I know almost before you reply—if you do reply—that you are either away or that you would not have the slightest intention of acting for the shortest period of time as my guardian and/or tutor, but at any rate do you mind reading this letter sympathetically because you must have been pretty much the same as me in heart when you were a kid. And I do want to learn from you and to read your earliest and most inaccessible works and perhaps even your contributions to the *Dial*. I go back home (here is my address—Inglewood, Caldy, Cheshire) next Monday. Nobody reads at home: the only paper we take is *The British Weekly;* there are few books in the house more exciting than *Religions and Religion* by James Hope Moulton (although a careful searcher might find in a somewhat inaccessible region Donne, Chatterton, *The Smell of Lebanon*, Crabbe's *Inebriety* and

* From "The House of Dust."

Blue Voyage) and although I have had a certain amount of youthful success as a writer of slow and slippery blues it is as much as my life is worth to play anything in the house—that doesn't worry me so much—but when they see me writing anything serious they don't exactly discourage me but tell me that it should be subordinate to my real work. What my real work is, heaven only knows, as the only other department that I have had any success in, is in writing seriously and that success rarely meant acceptance but quite often sincere encouragement from people whose opinion could hardly be taken to be humble.

But I don't want to worry you with anything I've written and indeed after reading this rackety incoherence you would probably be extremely averse to being worried in that way. Look here, you don't hate me already, do you? (hate is too dignified a word).

Now if you are in London any time between when you receive this letter and Sunday (inclus) could you let me know, because you see we have put things on somewhat of a business footing?

I could meet you anywhere in London. And anytime. Between now and Montag. If not write to my address in the dismal swamp.

Klioklio,
C. M. Lowry*

To Conrad Aiken

8 Plympton Street†
[Probably 1932]

My dear Conrad:

It was very good of you to write me about the tripeos: as for that I can't tell as yet, but we did our best—we did our best. I wrote a fairly good essay on Truth and Poetry, quoting yourself liberally not to say literally, and Poe and the Melody of Chaos; I was all right on the criticism paper, and I think I bluffed my way through on Literature from 1785 to the present day—I knew my Keats better than I thought I did, for instance—on the whole I have nothing to complain about from the papers (which I'll try and get together and send you),

* Lowry's full name was Clarence Malcolm Lowry.
† Of this letter, Mr. Aiken notes: "Written from St. Catharine's College to me at Rye. The 8 Plympton Street is of course M's joke—it was *my* address in the *other* Cambridge."

and if I have failed, and that's on the cards, I was more stupid at the time than I thought.

Meantime I have been leading a disordered and rather despairing existence, and you can probably guess at the reason why I was incapable of replying promptly. Your telegram, however, brought me to my senses and made me feel rightly ashamed of myself.

My d. & r.d.e. is due to a complexity of melancholy reasons none of which are either particularly complex, melancholy, or reasonable, and I have made up my mind about only one point in this business of living which is that I must, and as soon as possible, identify a finer scene: I must in other words give an imaginary scene identity through the immediate sensation of actual experience etc. This, you say, I may have already done in some part, and is becoming with me a desire for retrogression, for escaping from the subtle and sophisticated: that if it is not deep-rooted in honest transmission at all and has nothing to do with really wanting more experience and to rub off more prejudice, to use more hardship, load myself with finer mountains and strengthen more my reach, than would stopping home among books (even though I shall reach Homer!) but is nothing more than wanting alternately to kill Liverpool and myself: that I am in *truth*—although occasionally straining at particles of light in the midst of a great darkness—"a small boy chased by furies" and you can sympathize with me as such. Well—if t'were so t'were a grievous fault—

I prefer to think sometimes that it is because I really want to be a man rather than a male, which at present I'm not, and that I want to get from somewhere a frank and fearless will which roughly speaking does not put more mud into the world than there is at present. Nonsense.

Then I must read—I must read—I must read! Dostoievsky and Dante: Donne, Dryden, Davenant and Dean Inge. . . . Again, nonsense, but then at the moment I despair of all literature anyway. If I could read Homer—however much he may have roared in the pines, I'm sure I should hate him: Donne means damn all to me now, Herrick is terrible, Milton I can't read and wouldn't if I could: all Restoration comedy and most all Greek tragedy is a bore . . . Tolstoy? My God what a bloody awful old writer he was!

Well, there is Melville and Goethe, you say.

Well, there was the story of Hamlet, I said, and fell into silence—

(By the by, "Experiment" was reviewed in the *Times Lit Sup* of a week or two back, side by side with a review of Martin Armstrong's collected—or are they selected?—unaffected, undetected and well-

[8]

connected poems. I can't remember whether the review was a favourable one or not, I rather fear not—of my own contribution it remarked that it was a kind of prose fugue, with recurring themes, consisting of the rough talk of sailors or something, "effectively contrived"—I can't remember it in detail but I felt quite pleased. I haven't sent you a copy of it because the punctuation, length of dashes and so forth, was all wrongly done and I was sure it would give you a pain in the neck to look at: this is a rather selfish reason, for as a matter of fact the rest of the paper, in my opinion, is well worth reading. So I might send you a copy after all!)

I am delighted to hear that a novel is under way: it is really quite intolerable that I should have been so long sending you the tone dream—

Here it is however. . . .

It occurs to me also, and with some horror, that I have not paid you the £4 I owe you. This has not been because I could not afford to pay it but simply because I have wasted my substance in riotous living —I have just put it off, and off, and there is no doubt whatever but that you could do as well with the four pounds as I could do well without it, but as I write this it so happens I have only a farthing in my pocket: moreover I can never think of the peculiar circumstances under which the debt, or ¾ of it, was accrued, without terror, inchoate flashes of nightmare—and perhaps this procrastination is due in a very small part to the fact that to pay the debt means writing about the circumstances and therefore remembering them. Ho, I am not Mr. Sludge the medium, nor was meant to be. . . . But I wish I knew where the hell that three pounds was all the same.

The reason why I have a farthing, and not a halfpenny or a penny or a half crown, in my pocket is a peculiar one. The other night I was walking outside a Fuller's Cafe, the windows looked something like Selfridges and not very different from any of the other modern buildings erected all over London, or Cambridge, except perhaps in size— all the windows were filled with chocolates or chocolate-coloured cakes —I was in despair, when suddenly I caught sight of myself in the shop window and saw myself murmuring: Can he warm his blue hands by holding them up to the grand Northern Lights? Would not Lazarus rather be in Sumatra than here? Would he not rather lay him down lengthwise along the line of the Equator. . . . When at that moment a small boy suddenly came up to me, a small and very grimy urchin, and said, "Would you like a farthing?" So I replied, "Well why not keep it—it's good luck to have a farthing. Besides I haven't got a penny to give you for it." And he said, "ho, I don't want it, I've given my good luck to you." He then ran away. Strange!

7 A.M.

I am King Elephant Bag
I am King Elephant Bag
from de rose pink mountains.

I enclose you a letter from one Edward O'Brien, all the more mysterious because he failed to take any notice of my reply. . . . Moreover his letter miscarried to *me*—it pursued Noxon* half round Europe—I sent him hopefully my biography (in cameo) as it appears at the back of the letter, at the same time giving away that I was an English writer, not an American. If you have any notion what O'Brien means, meant, or intends, if anything, could you let me know sometime if your brain will function in that direction? I never submitted him any story, and the only story he can have read from *Experiment* is the one about the mickey†, all of which improves the joke.

I can assume only that he did mean to publish the thing in the 1931 volume, American, and have already informed the old man on this score to counteract in part the effect of my (possible) failure in the exam which gawd forbid. O'Brien either ignored or didn't receive a couple of replies so I sent him a wire asking him if he could give me some information "as was going to Peru," and received the answer: "O'Brien in the Balkans—O'Brien." Which seems to me funny. Still, I would like your advice. It is a nice point.

And it's that story,‡ you know, in all its pristine beauty, Conrad, full of "stop it, he muttered's," and "they growled's" and "they howled's" and "there, are you better now's," far away, yo hai's

long ago, yo ho
Malc

* Gerald Noxon, an old friend from Cambridge.
† This eventually became Chapter V in *Ultramarine*.
‡ "Seductio ad Absurdum." *Best British Short Stories of 1931*, edited by O'Brien.

To John Davenport*

Hotel Francia
Oaxaca de Oaxaca, Mexico
[1936]

S.O.S. Sinking fast by both bow and stern
S.O.S. Worse than both the *Morro Castle*
S.O.S. and the *Titanic*—
S.O.S. No ship can think of anything else to do when
S.O.S. it is in danger
S.O.S. But to ask its closest friend for help.
C.Q.D. Even if he cannot come.

John:

My first letter to you was impounded by the police here. It contained both congratulation for you and Clem and commiseration for myself.

Better so, because it was a letter nobody should read. Commiseration = Comisario de Policía.

I have now destroyed this letter but with it also myself. This letter might be prettier too.

No words exist to describe the terrible condition I am in.

I have, since being here, been in prison three times.

No words exist either to describe this. Of course, this is the end of introversion. If you cannot be decent outside you might as well have a shot at being decent in.

Here I succeeded but what shots will be needed now even God would not care to know.

Everywhere I go I am pursued and even now, as I write, no less than five policemen are watching me.

This is the perfect Kafka situation but you will pardon me if I do not consider it any longer funny. In fact its horror is almost perfect and will be completely so if this letter does not reach you, as I expect it will not.

At any rate an absolutely fantastic tragedy is involved—so tragic and so fantastic that I could almost wish you to have a look at it. One of the most amusing features of the thing is that even an attempt to play Sidney Carton has resulted in a farce. I thought he was a good man but now my last illusion is destroyed. It was not that he was not good so much as that he was not allowed to be. Excuse me

* The author and literary critic.

if I speak in riddles but the eyes of the police are polyagnous—is it polyganous? Perhaps polygamous. Finally—I cannot play second fiddle to Harpo Marx. Ah, how the police will try to puzzle this out—they will think I mean Karl! For obvious and oblivious reasons I cannot write to my family; for reasons so obvious they are almost naked I may not write to my wife. I cannot believe this is true; it is a nightmare almost beyond belief. I looked around in the black recesses of what used to be a mind and saw two friends—yourself and Arthur Calder-Marshall. I also saw something else not so friendly: imminent insanity. I have no conceivable idea how you could help me; or anyone else, unless it is by sending money that will be inevitably ill-spent. I can only send greetings from death to birth and go to pray to what in Mexico they call "the Virgin for those who have nobody with."

There is a church here for those who are solitary and the comfort you obtain from it is non-existent though I have wept many times there.

Another complication is that never in my whole life have I been to a place so fantastically beautiful as this, and, in spite of all, it would be difficult for me to leave. It is absolutely as fantastic as the aforementioned tragedy with which I am involved. The people are lovely, gentle, polite, passionate, profound and true. I hope the policemen who read this will believe it. Even they, with reservations, are the same. But—well; just but. . . .

Incidentally I smell.

Nobody but the Oaxaquenians will say a good word for me.

The Spanish detest me; the Americans despise me; and the English turn their backs on me.

If I were able, I would turn my back on myself.

Or wouldn't I?

I scent—(or might if I did not smell so badly myself)—some integrity in all this.

Like Columbus I have torn through one reality and discovered another but like Columbus also I thought Cuba was on the mainland and it was not and like Columbus also it is possible I am leaving a heritage of destruction. I am not at all sure about this but in a Mexican prison you have to drink out of a pisspot sometimes. (Especially when you have no passport.)

But, even without this, I am in horrible danger: and even with it.

Part of this, of course, is imaginary, as usual; but for once it is not as imaginary as usual. In fact danger both to mind and body threatens from all sides.

I am not sure that the danger is not ten times as bad as I make out.

This is not the cry of the boy who cried wolf. It is the wolf itself who cries for help. It is impossible to say that this is less of a cry than a howl.

What is impossible is to eat, sleep, work: and I fear it may rapidly be becoming impossible also to live.

I cannot even remotely imagine that I am writing these terrible words, but here I am, and outside is the sun, and inside—God only knows and He has already refused.

I cannot see Jan now. But for God's sake see she is all right. I foresaw my fate too deeply to involve her in it.

I would like to see you. Whether you would like to see me is up to you. At such a time it is probably impossible, and with such responsibilities as yours: but I fear the worst, and alas, my only friend is the Virgin for those who have nobody with, and she is not much help, while I am on this last tooloose-Lowrytrek.

Malc

To Juan Fernando Marquez*

[Oaxaca, 1937]

Juan:

I am here because there is much hostility in my hotel.

I am trying to do some work here but my life is so circumscribed by your detectives who walk up and down the street and stand at the street corner as though there were nothing better to do than to spy on a man who is unable to do anything anyway and never had intentions of doing anything but be good and love and help where help was necessary that I am rapidly losing my mind. It is not drink that does this but Oaxaca.

Do you wish me to leave with the impression that Oaxaca, the most lovely town in the world and with some of the most lovely people in it, is a town consisting entirely of spies and dogs?

This is unfair to me but it is a hell of a sight unfairer to Oaxaca.

The English are sufficiently stupid but the stupidity and hypocrisy of your detectives and the motives which are behind their little eternal spying—their activities—completely transcend any criminality

* A Oaxaquenian-Zapotecan and a good friend.

[13]

B

and stupidity I have ever encountered anywhere in the world. Have these guys nothing better to do than to watch a man who merely wants to write poetry? As if I had not enough troubles on my mind!

I do profoundly think that the Oaxaquenians are among the most courteous, sweetly gracious, and fundamentally decent people in the entire world. I think this too of your boss and of yourself and of this lovely town.

However, the whole damn thing is being raised to an insane state of suspicion.

People even camp outside my bloody door to see if I am drinking inside, and of course I probably am because it is so difficult or becoming so difficult to drink outside.

If I do not drink now a certain amount there seems no possible doubt that I shall have a nervous breakdown. If I have that, equally I shall find myself in that Goddamn jail to which I seem to be progressing almost geometrically, and as you know, when one goes there sober, one comes out drunk. It seems almost that I have a kind of fixation on the place because, like the novelist Dostoievsky, I have practically a pathological sympathy for those who do wrong (what others are there?) and get into the shit.

What I have absolutely no sympathy with is the legislator, the man who seeks, for his own profit, to exploit the weaknesses of those who are unable to help themselves and then to fasten some moral superscription upon it. This I loathe so much that I cannot~conceivably explain how much it is.

Nor—for that matter—has any man a right to legislate upon a person (who has paid through the nose as I have, who has his house robbed, his wife taken away, in short everything taken away, simply to be in Mexico) for his own Goddamned stupid political reactionary reasons when anyhow it is only a country that he himself—I mean the legislator—has criminally stolen. You know what I mean, of course. Of course it is true that Montezuma—not the beer—may not have been much better than Cortez or Alvarado. However, this is another story.

Malcolm

To Conrad Aiken

[*1937*]

Dear old bird:
Have now reached condition of amnesia, breakdown, heartbreak, consumption, cholera, alcoholic poisoning, and God will not like to know what else, if he has to, which is damned doubtful.

All change here, all change here, for Oakshot, Cockshot, Poxshot and fuck the whole bloody lot!

My only friend here is a tertiary who pins a medal of the Virgin of Guadalupe on my coat; follows me in the street (when I am not in prison, and he followed me there too several times); and who thinks I am Jesus Christ, which, as you know, I am not yet, though I may be progressing towards thinking I am myself.

I have been imprisoned as a spy in a dungeon compared with which the Château d'If—in the film—is a little cottage in the country over-looking the sea.

I spent Christmas—New Year's—Wedding Day there. All my mail is late. When it does arrive it is all contradiction and yours is cut up into little holes.

Don't think I can go on. Where I am it is dark. Lost.

Happy New Year,
Malcolm

To Nordahl Grieg*

[*Los Angeles, 1938*]

Dear Nordahl:
Thanks for your letter of 7 years ago (inst) almost to the day. I read it by the Atlantic—Atlanterhavet!—sitting on a rock in the sun.

Although I have not written you my consciousness has never been far away from you: nor has my friendship. I did not write because I felt myself too deeply lost in a dark purgatory blind.

How did your book on Rupert Brooke go?

I wish I could tell you all the extraordinary coincidences which led up to our meeting. One day I shall. My identity with *Benjamin* even-

* Norwegian novelist and playwright, nephew of the composer.

tually led me into mental trouble. Much of *Ultramarine* is paraphrase, plagiarism, or pastiche from you.

I have finished—apart from other versions—*The Ship Sails On* and I have been faithful to it. I think the U.S. stage would be interested in this. It would be terrific, but I need your formal permission to go ahead. I wish I could see you and we could collaborate on this. I am not thinking of the financial angle of this. It has been my dream to see it on the stage here.

I am sitting here alone and pretty ill trying to finish 2 short stories by Mann. If you would write me a letter it would cheer me up more than I can say—wish me God speed at least—else, like Herman Bang, I shall die of grief, sitting bolt upright in a Pullman car, in Utah, without a country.

I have written a book of poems: *The Lighthouse Invites the Storm*. I will send it to you if I can light on a copy. I think you would approve.

I could not get *The Ship Sails On* in England as I promised you because it was out of print. It is a great book. I hope Edward Thomson is all right.

I have always looked upon you as the greatest of poets. Tell me where you are, where you will be. Remember me. Perhaps because I have difficulty in remembering myself.

I have been married, lost my wife, importuned and been importuned by fascists. I had a terrible sojourn in Mexico. I am but a skeleton— thank God—of my former self. I read with delight your words on Ossietzky: but, while myself disgusted with Hamarm [?] I cannot refrain to repeat as coming from myself that your words storm in me day and night.

> I am now the age you were then but
> Ah, the world must still be very young.

Malcolm Lowry

To Mrs. John Stuart Bonner*

595 W. 19th Ave.
Vancouver, B.C., Canada
October 19, 1939

Dear Mrs. Bonner:

Since I am the cause of your daughter's present stay in Canada I thought I had better write to you; as this country is at war, and I am British, you must be feeling anxiety on her account. First, I want you to set your mind at rest as to her safety. There is no likelihood of this country becoming a battlefield for many years, and no possibility of its being bombed so long as the Monroe Doctrine exists. As for the war itself, although it exists, in spite of its reality, as more or less of a smoky rumor here, it is entirely responsible for any vagueness or complexity about the situation in which Margerie and I find ourselves. As for myself, any definitive future which I myself might have been able otherwise to predict or promise, is alike shrouded in obscurity. I simply do not know, nor does anyone else, what is going to happen. All of which being so, it becomes doubly necessary for oneself to take a firm stand, as to the war, which is a shifting principle that can take any form whatsoever and so effectively block any purpose, if you leave it out of account. The only stand I can take is that I do truly love Margerie, and in spite of whatever adverse circumstances, I feel I can make her happy: the stand which she takes, likewise. We therefore wish to be married as soon as we can. From her point of view, due, as I say, to the utter tentativeness of any given situation during wartime, there is almost every conceivable argument against doing any such thing and, objectively, I have tried to persuade her against it; on the other hand, I love her so deeply that I feel my persuasions are painfully half-hearted, in addition to which I am certain that her own happiness is bound up with being with me, and it is very difficult to persuade a person even objectively to give up their own happiness, whatever material compensations there may be.

All I can say is, that I shall postpone enlistment to the last possible moment which should give her less cause for worry. Had I been able to come to America a few weeks ago, the chances are I would have sailed for England before now, and be already fighting. But though I volunteered for this, I was refused, and the result is I am here. What

* Margerie Lowry's mother.

the future holds, I don't know. Nor do I know now whether, as I write, she may change her mind and return to Hollywood. But this much is certain, that while she is with me she is with someone she loves and who loves her truly, and who has her happiness at heart. Whether that happiness is worth the risk of the kind of grief which war distills, if you are unlucky, is a debatable point; but perhaps a similar risk is always taken anyhow.

I was very sorry not to have had the opportunity of meeting you in Hollywood, and I hope I shall soon. Margerie will be always in touch with you. Meantime, at all events, please be at rest in your mind, for she is happy and well; and we are working together on a book.*

Yours very truly,
Malcolm Lowry

To Conrad Aiken

c/o Sergeant Major Maurice Carey
595 W. 19th
Vancouver, B.C., Canada
[Spring, 1940]

Mein liber alter Senlin Forslin Malcolm Coffin Aiken:†

Since my last bagful of news the situation has become so bloody complicado that if we do not receive some help, and at that immediately, I shall lose what remains of my reason, not to say life. It is all (like everything else) such a complexity of melancholy opposites that, although I expect you to understand it all, I'm not going to attempt to explain it. I shall just hang the more succulent-looking hams of misfortune in the window hoping to entice you in to where the whole pig, that would be cut down, is hanging.

When I returned to Los Angeles (from Mexico)—this journey being at the old man's request—I travelled by the Great Circle too; the railroad, being built by a British concession, paid by the kilometer so it naturally went the most roundabout way, but the train didn't hurry and it is rather farther as you know than from New York to Boston—I practically went to pieces, this being due to illness, partly

---

* Under the Volcano.
† References to works of Aiken.

[18]

to Jan, who went promptly to Santa Barbara, leaving me, a sort of Lear of the Sierras, dying by the glass in the Brown Derby, in Hollywood: I don't of course blame her, I was better off in the Brown Derby, but to continue.

My income was then put into the hands of an amiable fellow with hay fever and some kind of legal rapport with the old man's London solicitors, who paid my bills but gave me no money. After a year alone, I suffered horribly but was taken out of the Brown Derby and despair by a grand gal named Margerie Bonner, but no sooner had this to happen than I was taken suddenly by [the man mentioned above] to Canada. I was taken to Canada on the under-standing that this jaunt here was simply in order to obtain a visa back to the U.S. Here he placed my money in the hands of *two* men whom he scarcely knew, one of whom I believe to be honest enough, but who, being constantly away on Secret Service, was and is unapproachable: the other a member of the Oxford Group. After two months going quietly insane care of this Oxford Group, war was also declared. All might have been well had not this Oxford Grouper discovered that I was in love with Margerie, whom I hope to God you meet and love as you do me, who has stuck by me through thick and thin, mostly thin, sharing conditions with me which make Gorki's *Lower Depths* look like a drawing-room comedy.

. . . At this point I should state more clearly that I left Margerie in Hollywood fully expecting my return, that I lived only for that return, but that a series of circumstances I won't inflict on you had brought me to the verge of a real breakdown, one of the kind with cast-iron whiskers on it. There was not only Margerie, you see, but all my work, in the United States in one port or another. There was the war too, so I didn't expect to finish all the work, but did expect to see you, and appoint you, if you were to be found, a literary executor, and I had accomplished much work. No excuse would wash with the family, though I had volunteered to fight for England in England, and even possessed a return ticket via the *Berengaria,* which, although long since broken up as a fire trap, is still a ship, if only in the memory, and a return ticket is still a return ticket, even if left behind in Mexico. So, Conrad, to make a long story longer, turned back at the dock's edge and knowing how cold the water was I wired Margerie (with what was left of her fare) to come immediately to Vancouver, a distance rather further than that from London to Warsaw, as I needed her. When she arrived she found me in such a state of despair that she wrote back and resigned her job at home to take care of me. Now the setup is this: $2 a week for myself and Margerie in return for which we get one meal a day if we're lucky. There is a family of six, including a loud speaker, a howling wind which rages through the house all day, twins, and a nurse. I forgot the dog, the canary and a Hindoo timber merchant, educated at Corpus Christi—you can't get away from Oxford—who sleeps in the woodpile in the basement, hoping, with his fine Oriental calm, that one day he'll be paid for the wood.

We are, therefore, as you might guess, more or less living in secrecy—we have stoutish hearts too, even if a trifle cracked—because once it is known that Margie is here, she will be deported, since she is by now in Canada illegally, to parts unknown, and ourselves separated. It is not that one day the fear that the more detestable of the twins may be found—there was something appealing in its upturned face as we lifted it tenderly out of the toilet—mysteriously drowned; not that the oversexed Hindoo has an axe downstairs and that we know he intends to use it. Nor that the sound of the radio is like the voices of the damned howling for help, or that——, an ex-sergeant major, has a habit of drilling an imaginary platoon up and down the stairs at three o'clock in the morning; not that Vancouver is like the Portobello Road magnified several thousand times, and is the most hopeless of all cities of the lost; not all the bells and clashes of the night which appall us: it is the thought rather of the absolute injustice of all this, of the misunderstanding, of the hopelessness of communication. For by now you can see that we cannot remain here much longer or God knows what will happen.

Now as to the line, the hook, line and sinker, to use with the old man, if you see fit to take one. Before you take any though, perhaps it is best to know that my relationship with —— is further complicated by the fact that he has written to my father asking to be made trustee for my money here, with the understanding that he would then turn it over to me for a certain cut each month. Being so desperate to be with Margie I agreed to this as at the time he seemed sympathetic—to do him justice he is, sort of, but what with the twins and the Hindoo and all we all have our bloody troubles and have to use certain methods to solve them, not sometimes the real right thing—but he has since proved difficult; and anyhow there is always the terrible fear that Margie may be deported; so you must not say anything about this to the family because if it is impossible for you to help us (and try and realize that your help is not just help, only; I must see you and also owe a duty to you) and we are forced to remain here, we shall have to depend on him. Margie is American, helpless, and utterly without money, and were she deported to Hollywood she would have nothing to live on, and moreover she would be, for many reasons, in an untenable position, and also she could not stand being without me. Anyhow I am very near a mental and nervous collapse, though cheerfulness is always breaking in, and I know that if Margie and I were separated, unless I could feel she were going to you, or a friend of yours, or somewhere where she could be at least near the hope of seeing me again, or near some encouragement of that hope or assuagement of its loss, which she would not have in Hollywood, she would break up because—but why go on?

As to jobs here I would take anything but I cannot because of my status, nor are they taking any more recruits.

It is queer, when all I wish is to be independent, that I should now be placed forcibly in a position where it is virtually impossible, although all this is quite consistent with the pattern of my father's general attitude.

Now you could suggest to my father, if the plan doesn't work by cable (a little long perhaps) which would be better among other things that may occur to you that:

(1) You would be the trustee of my income and my guardian, but that your position would be to try and help me find a position in which I can be independent; in short, you know you can find a job for me, subject of course to the limitations of my status and time.

(2) You certainly would be more likely to expend it—that is, my income, if any—for my benefit than an utter stranger, with whom I'm unsympathetic and who cares nothing for me.

(3) My letter suggests to you that I am desperately unhappy, absolutely alone and without friends in an abominable climate, but particularly unhappy because of the unfairness of not only being rendered unable to finish all my work, but unable to convince England that it exists, or is important, or that the definite understanding was that I should be allowed to go back to America.

(4) They objected to my going east on my own hook before to see publishers because they would not trust me: therefore you must make it plain that I will be under proper supervision: viz, in your home and in your constant care: also that I *have got* publishers who are influential people and who are interested in my work.

(5) That I have made every attempt to enlist here, apparently, but have been turned down either because of health or status, you don't know which, and now they are taking no more recruits. However, if

two birds must be killed with one stone, your own home is only a short journey from eastern Canada, and later, when my work is in the right hands, and they are again taking recruits, I could have another shot from the east. (I may agree with you eventually, Conrad, that there are better institutions than the army but it probably would not be tactful to say this to people who may be being bombed, even as you write.)

(6) Can you make it plain to my father that what he has heard of me has been mostly through other people, and that I am anxious to state my case, through you, who know me better than anybody.

(7) That I feel that my father is being exploited in the present situation (which is intolerable and hopeless) but that as my word is obviously discredited, I feel it useless to make any statement of my own side of the case, which is a matter of constant torment to me, and that you could act as mediator, you, who know and respect both parties.

(8) That injustice is being done to me, that my presence in Canada was none of my own seeking and was not, in the first place, necessary, since my visa would have been extended: or that I am very unhappy about the estrangement and I am appealing to you, desperately, to help me personally adjust the misunderstanding which goes between myself and my mother too. (In spite of the fact that the misunderstanding will always be as complete as ever, of course.)

(9) That above all I am among strangers who do not understand me, and if I am to go to war you would like me at least to have his friendship.

(10) That I am still perfectly willing to go and enlist in England but since they will not pay the fare over, I could earn it with you, and anyhow Boston is the most sensible port to sail from in this hemisphere.

(11) You can say further, that if they are anxious about drink, that if there is still anxiety in that regard any longer on their side, from what you can gather from my letter it is unfounded, but that you'll keep a strict eye on me in that regard. (Here's looking at you.)

(12) If their idea is to cut me off without a penny fairly soon, why not give me enough to live on for some months in Boston anyhow, which you would administer, so that at least I would have a fair chance, having none in Vancouver.

Now the family, as you probably have gathered, are not likely to take kindly to the idea of my marrying again so soon after one marital disaster (though in this connection it should be mentioned that I can't anyhow; having only an interlocutory decree I can't be married for a year), so besides everything else we must keep Margie secret for the time being and you must not mention her in your letter. Nevertheless, my plans for the future must include Margie, as you can well understand; for our devotion to each other is the only thing holding me to life and sanity. We are perfectly adjusted to each other, and perfectly happy: and she is just the kind of gal you always wanted me to have: and you always said I'd be all right if I had the right gal: I do have the right gal, and I'm all right as anybody can be who feels he's just waking from a nightmare, and were it not for this God-awful environment of rain and fear—for although we fear no longer, fear itself is about us, and the war with its smell of dead truth, its first casualty, in our nostrils—we'd both be all right.

I have some other ideas about approach to the family: one, seriously, if it could be afforded by cable, which would suggest that you had heard I was stranded in Vancouver and that Canada was taking no more recruits, that you had seen my publishers who wanted me on the spot, and could I come, because something important had developed for me, and that I could then stay with you: or perhaps put a publisher, or Bernice,* or Linscott,† or even someone wholly imaginary up to sending a cable saying that I was wanted in America for some work, and could it be made possible: or something like that. Any of these things might work. As for the financial end of it, my God, Conrad, you know as well as I that you are far more my father than my own father and that once I was on the spot *in Boston* with you, everything could be engineered from there, financially, it has been done before: as for ourselves, it would save our lives: as for myself, personally it would be the perfect reconciliation, either to a happy death, or to a new life: for I never felt more like working in spite of all this misery, and never more sure of myself: this would be, in reality, a great circle.

But to get back to Margie. We cannot be married for a year so we shall have to steer close to the wind during that time. I do want, for her sake, to stay out of the army long enough to marry her, and if I stayed in the States that would give me time to do God knows how much work, and who knows, the bloody war might end; I've volunteered in both England and Canada and been refused both places and I can't do more than that. If England still wants me, I think it only logical that I should see you before I go. But to avoid the pos-

* Bernice Baumgarten, Aiken's literary agent.
† Robert Linscott, then of Houghton Mifflin, now deceased.

sibility of the deportation angle, would it be too much of a trespass upon your compassion for me to suggest that if I can lay my hands on a few hundred bucks I, as it were, *send* Margie, who can cross the border whereas I at present cannot, on first to you as a sort of ambassador of the whole situation, while you meantime work like hell on the old man. If I can then come on afterwards, everything will be marvellous; but if I tragically cannot, I could by that time possibly have amassed enough money to get sufficiently far east in Canada to be not more than a night's journey from Margie—I am presuming of course that you could find somewhere for Margie to stay meanwhile—and Mary and yourself, and from that point of vantage, being once *there* and *near,* one might start arguing with the old man all over again. If this isn't too much of a presumption on Mary and yourself. You can point out, if you like, by the way, quite bluntly that you feel definitely from my letter that now it has turned impossible to join the army in Canada, that if I am thwarted in my desire to see you and finish my work in the States, the results will be immediate and tragic.

Of course eventually I shall probably have to join up and fight for the forces of reason but at the moment I am more concerned with preserving my own, which I consider no less valuable and certainly as remarkable as Hitler's. Meantime we want to be together as long as possible, and grab what little happiness we can, and be together until we can be married before I go. This will probably be impossible in Canada because conscription will come before the year is out, but do not suggest to the old folks that I consider it also impossible in America because of my nationality, thereby implying that I might wish to change a blue passport for a brown one.

Upon reading this over I fear you will come to the conclusion that I have already lost my mind but despite cheerfulness always breaking in you can see that we really are in a desperate situation. If my suggestion does not seem to you to be practicable can you think of anything else to do; for God's sake whatever you do do it quick before we sink for the last time.

Well, now for the work angle. I have written Whit Burnett to send you a book of poems called *The Lighthouse Invites the Storm;* have written Ann Watkins to send *In Ballast* to Bernice; have written to Los Angeles for *Under the Volcano* and the play, and am sending you, by the beginning of next week, the copy of a thing called *The Last Address,* the original of which I am sending to Bernice. As this is, among other things, about a man's hysterical identification with

Melville, I think it might interest Harry Murry, and would be grateful if you would pass it on, if you think so too.

Now, Conrad, old fellow, please help. So deeply do I feel that yours is the only star we can guide our bark on now, that I sense that my heart has made provision for so turning to you in the end by its first journey, years ago, to Boston and the Cape. You can save two good lives, I think, and lives worth saving, and lives you will be glad to have saved. Now, thank you from the bottom of my heart for the suggestions you have already made: my very best love to Mary, I have seen some of her Spanish pictures, "Man with the Concertina," etc., lately, reproduced, which are marvellous, and do send me news of you both and news too of the voyage that never ends. Margie sends love.

Malcolm

P.S. Is the new novel *Reading a Book?*

P.P.S. Since finishing this letter last night things have become suddenly even worse and if something doesn't happen pretty damn quick the situation will become like the postulated end of Kafka's *The Castle*, in which he was too worn out to write. There is an icy rain which hasn't stopped for days, we have both caught colds, and Margie has a cough. —— had told us that we must get out of here on Tuesday, which is the day he collects money for my board, and if that happens we will actually be penniless, in a strange and, believe me, damned hostile and ugly country with no place to go and no friends. The situation is too complex to explain just why this is so. When you write perhaps you'd better address me at the Hotel Georgia, where I shall *not* be staying but where I shall make arrangements to receive mail, and perhaps better send another letter here, just in case. Another idea: an appeal to Davenport, whose address I don't know, might help. We had an understanding about this. Or what about an advance on a novel on this situation by both of us, or all of us, to be called *Night Journey Across the Sea?* Or can you say that something has turned up for me, that you must see me somehow, and get funds from the old man that way: or could you get him somehow to finance an expedition here, since it is so serious: I mean it, Conrad, it is damned serious: and for once I am not to blame for it myself. The room is damp, muscles contract with rheumatiz, noses run, we cough like sheep, I fear Margie may become really ill. So as you see, as well as snow there is fog.

[25]

To Mrs. John Stuart Bonner

595 W. 19th Ave.
Vancouver, B.C., Canada
April 16, 1940

My dear Mrs. Bonner:

A line to thank you for the very interesting cuttings! Since receiving them, however, Denmark and Norway have been invaded, even now some other crisis is brewing, so that since many of the political speculations in the cuttings are now fact, I will not discuss them.

As for those which deal with enlarging the frontiers of the mind, with immortality—these are subjects which have always interested me. I have always believed that that which impedes the motion of thought is false and that we probably do not use in daily life more than a fraction of our true capabilities. Have you read any of Dunne? *An Experiment With Time* is a rewarding book if you have not. And Ouspensky. *A New Model of the Universe,* which aims, among other things, to base eternal recurrence upon scientific fact, is a terrifically exciting book, even if you do not agree with it. Also his *Tertium Organum.* (He generally appears on the library cards under "U," i.e., Uspensky.)

And a neglected but exciting American writer, whose specialty is the analysis of peculiar coincidences for which there exists no scientific explanation, is Charles Fort, particularly for the three books, *Lo!,* *The Book of the Damned,* and *Wild Talents.* I look upon the day I first hit upon *Lo!* in a public library as a red-letter day in my life. I know of no writer who has made the inexplicable seem more dramatic than Charles Fort.

I try to learn about astronomy from Margie and I am getting along slowly. But the little I have absorbed so far has very much enriched my work.

As for the mysterious heads from Tabasco—yes, here is something else which fascinates and torments me. I have before me as I write a folder of the Compañía Mexicana de Aviación which informs me that it is possible to fly from Mexico City to Yucatán and back for 331 pesos and 8 centavos. With the peso at five for a dollar this makes it only about $60. I sit here with this folder peering, as it were, with a telescope, at Mayan ruins, at wonderful names such as Chichen Itzá, Tekax, Izamal, Sayi, and when I walk about I walk on the white hot plough shares of lost opportunities, for when I was in Mexico I did not, for some obscure reason, visit Itzá, Tekax and so on. (I did, however, live in Oaxaca for a time, among the ruins of Monte Alban and Mitlá, which you find mentioned in Donnelly's book on Atlantis. My friends the Oaxaquenian students would occasionally promote private excavation parties, which they called "scratching the land." One day while "scratching the land" we came across a man, petrified in lava. How old he was I don't know but he certainly was not an ancient image or idol. When we tried to pick him up his head fell off. The rest had become so inextricably a part of the rock that we had to leave it. I shall never forget going back to Oaxaca at sunset, the natives triumphantly carrying the head before us. I told this to Jack and he wouldn't believe me, and now, I must admit, I scarcely believe it myself.)

Margie and I are just finishing a long novel of mine about Mexico; 1/10 of a million words we have written since January. Put like that, it sounds a lot.

After this we are going to revise one of Margie's detective stories, *Dark Rendezvous,* which I feel is excellent and certainly saleable, if, I think, directed to the right quarter.

Margie is well and happy.

Thank you again for sending me the cuttings which I always look forward to.

Yours sincerely,
Malcolm

To James Stern*

595 W. 19th Ave.
Vancouver, B.C., Canada
May 7, 1940

Dear Jimmy:

Jeeze, it was certainly good to hear from you and to think you've been in this hemisphere a year without my knowing it! I really caracoled on receiving your letter and am truly glad you made a happy marriage. You are one of the very best short-story writers we have so I know you will never stop writing so long as you have a pen. I sympathize with you about novel writing, though. There is no, as it

---

* Irish writer and translator.

were, satisfactory design-governing posture for a true short-story writer, and I can understand how, difficult to please as to form, you kick at the amorphousness of the thing. So the short-story writer (like Chekhov) wanders around graveyards thinking it is no go. It is probably not that you can't write a good novel but that no novel suggests to you that you want to go and do likewise. Nevertheless it seems to me that a writer like you would produce the best kind of novel, that is the shortish one perfect in itself, and without being full of inventories (like Joyce) or poems (like Faulkner) or conjunctions (like Hemingway), or quotations from quotations from other novels (like me, 7 years ago). It is possible to compose a satisfactory work of art by the simple process of writing a series of good short stories, complete in themselves, with the same characters, interrelated, correlated, good if held up to the light, watertight if held upside down, but full of effects and dissonances that are impossible in a short story, but nevertheless having its purity of form, a purity that can only be achieved by the born short-story writer. Well, all that is as may be. (And I don't mean the kind of novel, written by not quite true poets, such as *The Hospital*, by Kenneth Fearing, or *The Seven Who Fled* by Prokosch, in which the preoccupation with form vitiates the substance, that is by a writer whose inability to find a satisfactory form for his poems drives him to find an outlet for it in a novel. No. The thing that I mean can only be done by a good short-story writer, who is generally the better kind of poet, the one who only does not write poetry because life does not frame itself kindly for him in iambic pentametres and to whom disjunct experimental forms are abhorrent; such a man probably will end up anyhow by being a poet, in the manner of the later Yeats, but meantime, my thesis is that he is capable of writing the best kind of novel, something that is bald and winnowed, like Sibelius, and that makes an odd but splendid din, like Bix Beiderbecke. But that is all by the way and my God what brackish bilge is this on a cold posthumous Monday anyhow!)

Yeah, I know David Reeves. I found him sitting on my doorstep the day I was married and he seemed to know his way around my apartment better than I did. Nice fellow though; good on the flute too. Also experienced: had been a Volga boatman and had hopped on one foot from Sofia to Jerusalem, to die at the foot of the weeping cross. That sort of thing. His brother, poet J.M., loathed me at Cambridge for three years. I remember Peggy Lippe, Brock—where is Brock?—*et al.*, with varying nostalgias. Poor Rollo in Gibraltar—well, God somehow bless them. As for me, my life since last seeing you has been a sort of mixture of Manon Lescaut and *Crime and Punishment*. I was thrown, for a time, in Mexico, as a spy, into durance vile, by some fascistas in Oaxaca (by mistake; they were after another man. How it arose was: he was a friend of mine, very sober and a communist, and they could not believe, because he was sober, that he was an agitator and therefore thought he must be me, who was not sober, but, nevertheless, not an agitator, not a communist). I subsequently found it difficult to explain why I had absolutely had to be drawing a map of the Sierra Madre in tequila on the bar counter (sole reason was, I liked the shape of them). Jan had left me some months before, so I had no alibi. On Christmas Day they let out all the prisoners except me. Myself, I had the Oaxaquenian third degree for turkey. Hissed they (as *Time* would say), "You say you a wrider but we read all your wridings and dey don't make sense. You no wrider, you an espider and we shoota de espiders in Mejico." But it was an improving experience. For instance I learned the true derivation of the word *stool pigeon*. A stool pigeon is one who sits at stool all day in prison and inveigles political prisoners into conversation, then conveys messages about them. If he's lucky, he gets a bit of buggery thrown in on the side. So simple, but to think that I might have lived my life without knowing to what heights humanity could rise. They tried to castrate me too, one fine night, unsuccessfully, I regret (sometimes) to report. It ended up with a sort of Toulouse-Lautrec scene, myself, gaolers and all, simply walking, roaring with mescal, out into the night. They are looking for me yet.

We are living the most God-awful existence here, compared with which my dungeon in Mexico (compared with which in turn I may say the Château d'If's are simply sunny rooms in a cottage by the sea) is a mere picnic. Some people in the Oxford Group have been made trustees of my money after my numerous mishaps in one part of the globe and another, and they don't let me have any of it for myself. Margie is not supposed to be here at all, so if I could sell a few things it might well save our lives. At any rate, we have been working like hell; Margie has turned out very much to be the right gal, and being both partially screwy, of course, we should be sunk without each other. To make matters worse, what driblets of money there are threaten to be cut off. I already had some contact with Baumgarten through Conrad Aiken but she found what I had too cerebral and unsaleable. But the work I have been doing and am continuing to do is different. So, Jimmy, the odd honeyed word, the diplomatic smile on your part, to some George Davis* here, some editor of *Esquire* there, might be our salvation, which, with a more or less objective look at the novel about to be finished, would be worthwhile.

If we got enough dough we would plan to go east—Toronto, Montreal. I would dearly love to go to New York in the fall, before which I cannot apply, but I have not much hope. If we went east, near New York but in Canada, would there be any chance of your dropping up to Canada to see us? If we are independent by that time, our house is thine. It is, incidentally, extremely cheap living in Canada, but I daresay your obligations as a prospective citizen would keep you in the States anyhow. Only, this may be the last summer I shall have, for perhaps next summer I shall have to be sufficiently proficient in arson and murder to take part in the "Crusade" against the dicktasters. A dim outlook. One waits to see curiously what Mussolini (whom Haile Selassie once called "My Enema the Douche") will do. As for the pomes: *Esquire does* publish pomes, sort of pomes we might be expected to write, sort of pomes I sent you, *wiv picshurs too!* So maybe you could still charm them???? I'd be immensely beholden to you if you would put in the odd word.

Love *zu haus* and to your better half.

Malcolm

P.S. What do I look like? Somewhat less foul. I seem to be getting younger: probably second childhood. Where is McAlmon if at all? Is he the last man at the Dome? He was a kind sort of man. I should be glad to hear of it if somebody has anything good to say about me: so would you, if you lived in a freezing bison-smelling attic in Vancouver not knowing when there will be a knock on the door, with blackmailers, duns and Englishmen who think God an Englishman eight feet high upon your pen. (Not Cape† though, I fear, who recently refused me an advance; no good words from him.) By the way is East 68th half in Park Avenue, half in Yorkville, near the Metropolitan? It seems to me I once lived there or thereabouts so it may well be that you will observe my little doppelgänger poltergeist soul hoisting a drink in a bar in them parts.

P.P.S. Have just at the moment received the endearing news from England that the Government won't let *any* funds out at the moment.

* Editor of *Harper's Bazaar.*
† Jonathan Cape.

Yes sir, all this right at this moment by cable. *So,* would you, for God's sake, please send those poems off immediately to *Esquire,* because they are the kind of poems they print (wiv picshurs as I said before). Since we are obviously right down the spout in a country where we have no status and no right to get a job, let alone go on relief, you will agree with me that the time has come for action. The poems may not seem to represent action but the $50-odd they would pay would keep us for a month and moreover they might become interested in other work which would net us enough for several months. I have a *very Esquireish* story called *June 30, 1934,* that I could get ready in about a week. Could you tell me the name of the editor—is it Arnold Gringrich or who—and I would send it direct to him if you would do me the favour of just paving the way a little meantime with some guff about O'Brien or something. The story is about their length, no great shakes, but is *Esquireish,* as I say, and potentially O'Brienish, and wouldn't let you down. So please rally round, my dear old egg, will you? We are faced with the buttons off the chairs in the station waiting room for our next meal. We progress from Manon Lescaut to *Crime and Punishment* to—possibly, shall we say?—"Two years as a scab lavatory attendant in Saskatchewan."

Cheers,
Malcolm

To Harold Matson*

1236 W. 11th Ave.
Vancouver, B.C., Canada
July 27, 1940

Dear Hal:

I read in *Life* this week that the knowledge a man is to be hanged concentrates the mind mightily.

What with the sunset of the Western World, of the Boyg, conscription imminent here, and a reprieve, in spite of volunteering, from enlistment which has been prolonged God knows why until now, and may go on long enough to complete more work, such a concentration has been operating here.

Some seven or eight months ago I wrote you about a former novel

* Lowry's literary agent.

of mine, *In Ballast to the White Sea*, which Ann Watkins had. Then my motive was to raise some money through a source which seemed hopeful. It did not work, but I have managed to get the work I hoped to do done just the same without the money or with a modicum from elsewhere.

Having completed some important part of it, my feeling was to see where my loyalty and obligation lay in case it should succeed.

It very definitely lay, in my conscience, with Whit Burnett and yourself (I am in a bit of an obliquity about Ann Watkins, not because I still owe her that $20), but whether or not what I might have accomplished was in the nature of an Indian gift to either of you I wasn't so sure.

Anyhow, I have written a book that I really feel might be important, *Under the Volcano*, and the honestest thing I could think to do with it was to send it to Whit and ask him to let you, if you wished or would (for I am somewhat of a prodigal son) arrange the details of it; that is, either in case he took it or really considered, if he didn't, that it stood a good chance elsewhere and would not be so much waste drain on a petty cash department as in the past. I have not yet heard from Whit about this and naturally do not like to chatter about it to him while he has it. I would be, of course, tickled to death if he would publish it: but I am beginning to feel perhaps that I have overestimated it, that he won't take it, or that, if he personally likes it, others in the firm do not. I am a bit hangdog about all this at such a time, but there it is. If it does not hit for him, Robert Linscott of Houghton Mifflin, Boston, has, through Conrad Aiken, professed an enthusiastic desire to see it, which might be borne—if it be not unethical—in mind. Anyhow, in the position I am placed, I do not want it tossed to and fro across the border, so, as time closes in again, I am asking you if you would do me the favour on Whit's advice, when it comes, of taking charge and having a friendly look into it. It is "original" if you fear for past Websterian, not to say Miltonian, minor lacks of ethics on my part, nor is it drunkenly translated with a handpump out of the original Latvian. It is as much my own as I know of.

Under the Volcano might, I feel, be a *really* good book: might be, I threaten it. Some parts of it the war has undone. There are a few abstractions and meaninglessnesses which a state of peace would have written out of the thing, and which even now, a friendly eye would freeze out, and its worth be enhanced.

So much for that: there are others to follow, if given time: but that is a start, or a restart. It is for you to judge or to say no.

Meantime I have a quite different kettle of fish a'boiling. I am expecting (as well as to be hanged) to be married again, as soon as may be, which one has been hoping is not too late. My collaborator in this venture, one Margerie Bonner, has just completed a "mystery novel" by name *The Last Twist of the Knife*. She is here in Canada under the same compulsions as I. If I seem too much of a Jonah altogether from any point of view I would be immensely beholden to you if you would read this book and calculate its chances and act for them, if you think they are good. I can promise, as I cannot for myself at present, many from this same pen.

The book, hers, has a swiftly moving, excellently told, dramatic and logically worked-out story: it is not full of the same kind of permutations and combinations as mine: and I believe there is a ready market for this and what might follow it up. It has the commercial virtues (I believe), and it is intelligently and sensitively written. And it is a good narrative.

Anyhow, may I send the book along, and quite apart from what you may decide to do about me, or should I say my other me (either, in this case being to some extent the other's neither), may I ask you to consider it? I would deem that a favour: and I do not think you would regret it. Her potentialities are steadier and more easily to be gauged than mine. We ourselves are a firm with a divided nature but a shared purpose. The success of one prolongs the other's life, all other things being (as they sadly are not) equal.

Yours faithfully,
Malcolm Lowry

P.S. Re Linscott, of Houghton Mifflin. I am more or less committed through Aiken to give him the first refusal of the *Volcano* if it fails with Whit. I mention this to you because it might be that Whit has already given you the book and has not, to save my feelings, wanted to say anything about it to me until some verdict has been reached between you as to its salesability. It may very well be that you will not want to handle it at all because of the fact that my work was already out of your hands. But in this regard I made no commitments elsewhere. At the time I last wrote you I was desperately in need of money and Conrad Aiken had suggested that perhaps his agent, Bernice Baumgarten, might give me a price on the whole bolus, as it were, through Aiken, as at that time I thought I would be called up any minute. It was a very vague idea which politely came to naught: Conrad Aiken now has most of my work. If the *Volcano* is taken, there are at least three books, already written, to follow that up. My motive, however, in writing you now is not primarily financial or a business one at all. I felt I had written a good book which justified the trust you and Whit had put in me. If Whit takes it I want you to have the commission on it and handle my work, which has now been brought to practical fruition, in future. If not, and I seem still to have potentialities, I would have the satisfaction of knowing that I had acknowledged as well as I could my great feelings of obligation to you both. I had meant this to be a sort of surprise—pleasant, I hoped—to you, coming through Whit. The uncertainty of events, and the near completion of Miss Bonner's book, impels me to write to you now. If you feel it unorthodox to handle my work, I would at least like Miss Bonner to have as good an agent as yourself. Anyhow, please let me know what you feel and whether you will read at least, which of course commits you to nothing, her book. In that case it would arrive in about two weeks.

PART II: *1941–1945*

To Harold Matson

Dollarton P.O.
Dollarton, B.C., Canada
January 6, 1941

Dear Hal Matson:

I am sure that you will feel the same sense of relief at receiving this letter as we do at having finally made up our minds to write it. But first of all let us say this, unequivocally and sincerely: we appreciate the difficulties involved and we are deeply grateful for all your trouble on our behalf and the fact that we have not succeeded is certainly not your fault. Perhaps it is partly due to our geographical distance and the difficulty of communication, partly to the almost prohibitive anxiety of the times, partly to just plain bad luck, and partly, let us be humble, to our own lack of proper material. Anyhow, it seems that we have become merely a liability to you and not the asset we hoped to be and therefore we feel that it is unfair to you to have us any further on your conscience.

On the other hand, we are not proposing to quit: far from it, we propose to redouble our efforts. Malcolm was determined, and still is, God willing and if time allows, to complete the work which he started and which represents so many years' thought and effort. He has nearly finished his new version of *In Ballast* (which he sent in synopsis to the Houghton Mifflin Fellowship Contest and which was eliminated, and we didn't want to write this letter until it was settled) and he is at present working hard on a completely new and, we are sure, better version of the *Volcano*. We realized ourselves, upon rereading it some time ago, that it was unfair not only to you but to him to try and market it in the version which was sent to you. At that time he wrote you, asking you to withdraw it, you will remember, and a new version has been growing in the interim which will eliminate most of its obvious defects, clarify and strengthen the narrative, etc. In thinking the book was so good when we sent it to you, perhaps we confused a spiritual victory with an aesthetic one, since it is impossible to convey to you the difficulties under which it was completed—which is, of course, no substitute for actual merit. But we know that within its matrix there *is* a novel which is not only truly good but saleable, and we only feel a relief and a sort of gratitude that by some fluke it was not sold in its present form. As for *In Ballast*, stripped of its former obscurity and lengthiness, it too has emerged, we feel, into its proper form and in the next few months we shall have something solid to go on.

As for me, well of course my work is in an entirely different category and all I can say is that while I am very naturally disappointed, I am not discouraged and I intend to keep on trying until something clicks, since I feel that mine is perhaps more merely a matter of luck—and of better writing on my part too, which will come I am sure with more work, maybe on the sort of trial and error method. Anyhow, I am struggling with the skeleton of a new one and I know that once I got started I could produce two books a year.

But all this determination and optimism on our part does not change the present situation for you: which appears to be practically a dead end. So we feel that the only fair thing to do is to release you from any further effort on our behalf, so just bundle all our stuff up and ship it back to us collect. We'll probably send it out ourselves from here and if we should sell anything we'd be delighted if you'd handle the business for us.

We hope you will understand how we feel, as we have tried to understand how *you* must feel by now; we believe that you will understand that we are deeply appreciative of our debt to you and are only trying to do what seems best. So once more let us thank you for all you've done and assure you of our sincere friendship and gratitude and wish you a full measure of whatever happiness and prosperity there can be in these anxious times.

Faithfully,
Margerie Bonner
Malcolm Lowry

P.S. Malcolm says don't waste money sending the *Volcano,* he has a copy here so just chuck it in the furnace. Specifically, just send my two books and Malcolm's *The Last Address*; I think that's all.

To Harold Matson*

Dollarton P.O.
Dollarton, B.C., Canada
March 4, 1941

Dear Hal:

I'm sorry I've only given you further disappointments with *Under the Volcano*, so far, and it may be that the adverse conditions under which the book was finally written influenced me to think it was an artistic triumph when it was only a sort of moral one.

I think on rereading that Martha Foley's judgement is maybe a just one in part; there *is* too much preoccupation with time, and the pattern does not emerge properly.

So I am rewriting it. I think it foolish to embark on an absolutely new project at this time. And, in order to show you the sort of thing I am doing, I am sending you part of it as a short story, which I feel you can sell, where you could not sell *June 30, 1934,* for instance, or even the book itself. I have cut and cut and cut and of the story as I send it to you I am extremely proud and would very much like to know what you think about it as soon as it is convenient for you.

I had three magazines in mind: *Harper's Bazaar, Esquire,* and *Decision.* I may be quite wrong. Anyhow, I leave it to you what to do with it, but please tell me what you decide because I do not think the feeling is wish fulfillment this time that I have rung the bell. What I had in mind was: that publication of the "story" would be a good start, and would help the novel with the publishers. I do not know if *Decision* is any good: I heard it was influential, and perhaps you would tell me about this. If you send it to *Harper's Bazaar* (ed. George Davis) perhaps you could mention James Stern's name, who has highly praised my short stories and who is a frequent contributor. He said I could suggest this, but maybe it wouldn't do any good. Might it be worth while, for the sake of getting it in print quickly, to try *Decision* first, which sounds like a likely bet to me? And if you send it to *Esquire,* perhaps send it to Arnold Gingrich, whom I know slightly, through Jimmie Stern and by correspondence— well, use your own judgement.

I am under the impression that you do not handle poetry, Hal, isn't that right? Unable to help myself now in this respect—and that fact that I have not been a poet hitherto having been the psychologi-

* See Appendix 1.

cal cause of most of my troubles, and yours with me—I have been writing a lot of poetry, and sending it here and there, without any success yet. If I am wrong about your handling poetry tell me. Would it be too much to ask you to send me the address of *Decision,* which I can't get here, so that I could send them some poetry? If I get a cheque for any of my poems I will send it straight to you without cashing it for I cannot otherwise send money out of the country; mean amount though it would doubtless be, it would be a symbol.

Oh, and Hal—do you have the hapless and ambulatory *In Ballast to the White Sea* and *The Lighthouse Invites the Storm:* I thought I would put these in shape. You will see the ruthless cutting in the excerpt from the *Volcano* I send you and that is how I would treat them.

Now—re Margerie Bonner. She is now finishing a new and better murder, tentatively called *Cloudburst in Deep Cove.* I am helping on this and the plan is to have the final copy done by the end of the month (sooner, she says), let it simmer for a fortnight, and during this fortnight to revise the earlier one, *The Last Twist of the Knife,* bearing Virginia Stong's suggestions in mind, then send you both together.

Is this O.K. with you? We feel that the second one would implement the promise of the first. Please tell me about these things as soon as you may; I am absolutely determined you are not going to have had all this trouble for nothing and that one day your trust will be repaid.

Yours sincerely,
Malcolm

To Harold Matson

Dollarton P.O.
Dollarton, B.C., Canada
June 25, 1942

Dear Hal:

Flecker's Magic indeed! Permit me if I rather more than vicariously triumph too. You make us a happy shack, and shapes like justifications begin to float down the river. As for those beneath, it looks as though some of them have been brought ashore and found saleable timber and were only masquerading as derelicts. Let me add my deep gratitude to Margie's! But as she will tell you something of how the news affects her, a vague word of myself.

I have been down these last months with a somewhat rare and comic affliction known as "the Bends." During treatment for this it was discovered that I had had a streptococcic glandular infection for about a dozen years. This looks like unpleasing news but I see it good because, since treatment for this, eagles and mountains have dropped away from my mind. I am now nearly better. Doctors here didn't understand how I lived at all, though. That the toxicity thus, indisputably often at its maximum during your great and strained patience with me, might, if it would explain death, explain indeed some too apparent oddnesses and unratified irreliabilities on my part in the past, as well as the almost total fog in the *Volcano* as was, we have the doctor's word. (As it might to Whit.) I seem to see your face, around corners, looking at me less rebukingly now, since we held on.

But I shan't trouble you again until I have reduced the risk of being a strain on the petty cash department to a minimum. I promise you this: something really *good is* on the wing *this* time, *sans* self-deceptions, from this side. You will probably hear oftener from the more promising other, since, as I point out to Margie, *now* her work begins.

All thanks again and best wishes.

Malcolm

To Mrs. John Stuart Bonner

Tuesday
[1942]

Dear Mrs. Bonner,

I have read "Awaiting Palomar" with great pleasure and my feeling about it could lead me into a disquisition on how all the arts in general overlap, only I want to be concise and relatively prompt for Margie's reply.

I realize you wrote it hurriedly, but that was quite as it should be for our, or my, suggestion was made with the aim perhaps of finding out what form was choosing you, rather than vice versa, which, speaking from experience, I think is the major problem to cope with when you are possessed with an unstaunchable impulse to create order out of chaos.

That order was, recently with us, a pier: and I assert that that pier is a poem too: for argument's sake, let us assume that everything which is good and has order and inner cohesion is a sort of poem; definitely, and for the moment let's not go too far afield. I think that all first-rate short stories are first rate because they are essentially "poems," they are bound together by an integrity which is essentially poetic. *But* this does not mean that "poetic" prose, *i.e.*, "flowery," has anything to do with poetry: it has less to do perhaps with it than prosaic poetry has to do with poetry: let me not quibble however. Roughly speaking, stark, bald and simple prose has more in common with poetry perhaps than elaborate and overweighted verse. So you might try your "Ghost Star" as a short story and send it to us, though write it, if you like, as a poem (and it still would *be* a poem) in stanzas: let the rhyme, etc., go hang for the time being.

A poem (or such a short story) is, I think, an entity apart from its author: but it may have to find out what it is from people apart from its author and be helped by various people to exist.

As an example of what I mean by a poem that is a short story, here is one of Rabindranath Tagore's: it is a poem, though it belongs to no fixed form and is more like a question merely. You might experiment along this line as a sort of design-governing posture (that's a good phrase) for the "Ghost Star."

Day After Day

Day after day, O lord of my life, shall I stand before thee face to face? With folded hands, O lord of all worlds, shall I stand before thee face to face?

Under thy great sky in solitude and silence, with humble heart shall I stand before thee face to face?

In this laborious world of thine, tumultuous with toil and with struggle, among hurrying crowds shall I stand before thee face to face?

And when my work shall be done in this world, O King of kings, alone and speechless shall I stand before thee face to face?

Back to "Awaiting Palomar," of course it has, as you say, enough— and indeed to spare—good material to encourage us to see what we can do with it; it has an ennobling theme indeed: on the other hand opinions differ, different artists might treat it different ways,

what we might do with it would not be what you could do with
it: so it is to be hoped what one may have said will serve to encourage *you* further to work on it, which I think ought to give you
more satisfaction than were we to say, which one might easily, "By
Jove, that's marvellous material, that, we must use that and buy
that motor boat we've had our eye on with the proceeds"—though,
alas, the proceeds from poetry, even of the highest calibre, tend to
provide a somewhat leaky potential boat: we would, of course, give
you the proceeds: but poetry must never be approached from a financial angle to begin with *or* one will certainly never make any money
out of it. To get back to "Palomar." I personally prefer the idea of
calling it simply "The Milky Way." I would simplify, where possible; notice how in this example the discipline of poetry has clarified
and rendered the prose excellent "poetry"—if you strip it down a
little further—quite without rhyme. Viz. The beginning of an excellent story in the purest, the most excellent, the most ancient tradition of all, that of the fable, but in this case a modern fable, which
could also be a poem.

The Milky Way

In the beginning, when man first lifted his eyes to the heavens, he
saw a silver band of light trailing across the distances of space.
He wondered at its beauty and pondered on its light.
Since then, the ancients of every race, of every climate, have left to us
the legends and myths of this marvel of the skies.

Do you see? I think avoid, in this prose or poetry, or both, in
this "order," "poetical" words and clichés such as *clime*, etc. (Never
mind your synonyms—you don't need 'em: the humble simple vocables are best). But this was intended—this and Tagore—as a pointer,
for a way to do the "Ghost."
    I thought perhaps that, while touching on the Eye of Palomar if
you like, you should not use it as the whole basis for your climax:
though we do not of course know what the new telescope will dis-
close, it can hardly be anything more miraculous than the miracle
of our own existence. Thus while you might have a sound cause for
asking "Will it do all this, the Eye of Palomar?" the answer to "Can
it do *less?*" is definitely yes, it can—even while you can acknowledge
all the genius and wonder of the thing. But whatever the real power
of the real 200-inch telescope, you weaken the poetical power of your
poetical telescope by attributing at once too much and too little

power to it, and too much of an irrelevant kind of power, by making it into a kind of cure-all and Santa Claus as well.

So that it would seem to me a better idea if, while you bring in the Palomar telescope *as the resolution of the Galileo theme*, as it were, and of the *wisdom of mankind*, you close your poem as you have begun it, more on the theme of the Milky Way itself. I most heartily approve of your theme. As Emerson says: "Something is wanting to science until it has *been humanized*. The table of logarithms is one thing, and its vital play in botany, music, optics, and architecture, another. There are advancements to numbers, anatomy, architecture, astronomy, little suspected at first, when, by union with intellect and will, they ascend into the life, and reappear in conversation, character, and politics.

"But this comes later. We speak now only of our acquaintance with them in their own sphere, and the way in which they seem to fascinate and draw to them some genius who occupies himself with one thing all his life long. The possibility of interpretation lies in the identity of the observer with the observed. Each *material* thing has its *celestial* side; has its translation, through humanity, into the spiritual and necessary sphere, where it plays a part as indestructible as any other."

To go back to the more technical side of verse: you might try a few sonnets just for practice. The form is this: 14 lines, 5 beats—generally ten syllables—to a line, and the rhyme scheme is abba-abba-cde-cde or ab-ab-cd-cd-ef-ef-gg. For instance:

a The thing to know is how to write a verse
b Whether or not you like it, whether or not
b The Goshdarned thing will put you on the spot
a And Petrarch will not save you from the curse

And so on for ten lines more. The iambic pentametre (above) is the real metric base of English poetry, also of blank verse: though I have tried to show how poetry and prose are, at their best, though in a literal sense opposites, somewhat mixed up.

Well, I hope this has been some help and you might have another go at it along these lines. And we are awaiting the "Ghost Star" with interest.

Much love
from
Malcolm

To Harold Matson

Dollarton P.O.
Dollarton, B.C., Canada
June 6, 1945

My dear Hal:

Several days ago I dispatched, after taking some thought, the MSS of the new *Under the Volcano* to you: it may take some time to reach you, therefore I am writing this letter now in the hope it may arrive more or less coincident with it.

I took thought—and also the extraordinary liberty, for which I hope you will forgive me, of sending it at all—because of the trouble and patience you have had with it in its former state: my idea had been, after all that (to say nothing of the expense you must have undergone on its behalf), to send it round myself in its revised version, and if anyone took it, then to ask you the favour of acting for it and me again, if it seemed worth your while.

I felt, however, that it ought to be in your hands and so sent it, feeling that this time there was perhaps a fairly substantial chance it might click with somebody without so much trouble, and also, whether this be so or not, because I very much wanted your opinion and value that.

The book was to have been the first part of a trilogy: the third part is a dead loss, utterly consumed (save for a tattered circle of three or four burned pages, all of which more or less concern fire, for some reason) in a holocaust that took our house a year ago tomorrow, which had to be the 7th; but doubtless this can be rewritten in time and the second is still happily extant; I feel that I have about ten such books in me, if and when I can get around to writing them. As it stands, the book required a short preface, and some notes, and if it seems worth it, these will follow in due course. Of course, it may not be any good at all: five years ago I deceived myself into thinking I had pulled it off, as of course I had not done: however, I feel now it may be a pretty good job and myself justified in sending it to you, since my impression is that the majority of its faults in the older version have been done away with, at least, as well as some of the objections which various publishers raised as to its publication.

The Lost Weekend was a considerable blow to me and I do not know how far the success of that book would militate against the success of this: I suppose there will be people who will say it is noth-

ing but a pale reflection of that excellent study, for the fact that
nearly all the alcoholic part was written before I had ever heard of
that book can weigh but little with the reader; having read, finally, the
horrible thing I did my very utmost not to be influenced by it and
even hoiked out what I thought to be a quite fine passage because on
reconsideration it seemed to possess something of the other book's
rhythm; on my side I can say that *Under the Volcano* begins, so to
speak, where the other leaves off, and after all the former is about lots
of other things as well. Even more damaging to me was the impact of
The Lost Weekend upon the second part of the trilogy which is based
upon the novella I had called *The Last Address*. However, in the
final analysis I am up to something quite different and all this will
probably turn out not to matter, when I have got over my unworthy
professional jealousy on the score. (*The Lost Weekend* is not to be
confused with *The Last Week End,* by my friend John Sommerfield,
author of *Volunteer in Spain,* written ten years ago and I believe
published by Wishart in London, in which no less a figure than poor
old ex-Malcolm plays a part not wholly unlike that of the hapless
Birnam in *The Lost Weekend.* However.)

As for Margie, while delighted with her new contract, etc., she has
so far failed to receive the corrected proofs of the second part of *The
Shapes That Creep* from X, as per his promise; whether she is right or
wrong, for her part in not sending back the uncorrected proofs of the
second part (*i.e.,* corrected only by her), I don't know any better than
she; but doubtless some light will dawn again soon from the inscru-
table Scribner's, which will make it all more clear. She has just got
over a bad session in hospital with blood poisoning, contracted while
rebuilding our house, from a rusty nail in the foot. She is now getting
on well again, however, as is the new house which we are building
literally ourselves—someone agonizingly built *over* our old bedroom,
in spite of our stakes left there on the site, but we have transcended all
this and are making a very fine place indeed, which will be even better
than the old one.

A great friend of mine who was at college with me—a well-known
radioman in Canada, ex-editor of *Experiment,* etc., and ex-assistant
director with Lubitsch in Hollywood—has written (which is more to
the point) a very interesting and moving novel centred in pre-war
Italy entitled *Teresina Maria:* I told him he could not do better than
send it to you and I hope he has done so and if so that it will meet
with your approval. Whit published some of his early work: he is also
an excellent poet and has lots of things boiling, including two other

novels and many short stories. I think he would be a very good venture if he could get re-started in the literary field, which he was away from to some extent while concerned in radio, movies, etc., not to say the English blitz. His name is Gerald Noxon—very familiar here, as I say, on the air.

I was very touched indeed by your kind remembrance of me, which was relayed to me by Margie, and this is indeed sincerely reciprocated. I thank you also for the suggestion concerning the extraordinary experiments that were being carried out by your acquaintance in tapping the memory and indeed had I not had on my mind at that time so much that I wanted to forget I should have come immediately to New York and availed myself of the offices of your friend; perhaps at some later date it would not be too late to attempt something of the sort but at that period I was not sufficiently in balance, I think. Meantime both Margie and I are continuing to work hard. I thank you for everything you have done for her, and again, for me, though I have not yet rung the bell.*

I enclose a short note from Duell, Sloan & Pearce that may or may not be of some use now.

With very kindest regards, believe me
Sincerely yours,
Malcolm

To Conrad Aiken

[*Dollarton, Fall, 1945*]

Dear old Conrad:

Thanks for yours and have been meaning to write a really fat informative and diverting letter—in fact made all the notes for same, but I want to get this letter off now so it will be in time to wish you bon voyage, therefore I must make a sacrifice of the other for the time being. Yes, the phoenix clapped its wings all right all right, in fact gave such a bloody great resounding clap that the poor bird nearly broke its neck and had to be immolated all over again. As you know we went east after the fire. The grave preceded us however. The interminable golden bittersweet awful beautiful Eastern Autumn (which I'd never before experienced) restored Margie, whose childhood was in Michigan, to *some* extent, but me it almost slew. It had a worse effect

* See Appendix 2.

upon me in fact than on Henry Adams, though the Noxons'* Niagara-on-the-Lake is something to see: really beautiful. I was in shocking bad form and worse company so all in all, though I was very disappointed not to see you—albeit I *heard* you—it was perhaps just as well that I didn't. How the Noxons bore with me—if they really did—I don't know. Actually the business of the fire seemed to drive us both slightly cuckoo. Its traumatic effect alone was shattering. We had to live through the bloody fire all over again every night. I would wake to find Margie screaming or she would wake to find me yelling and gnashing my teeth. Apart from these diversions (fortunately the Noxons were sound sleepers but when we moved to a house of our own it grew much worse), fire itself seemed to follow us around in a fashion nothing short of diabolical. Betty had painted a picture of a neighbor's house in Oakville that Margie and I had thought of renting for the winter because it vaguely resembled our old home, and one day when everyone was out I sat in the attic studying this picture which I liked very much. My concentration on the picture was somewhat marred by the fact that in my imagination the house kept bursting into flames and sure enough, about a week later, that's precisely what the house did, they couldn't get the fire engines through the woods, nothing of the kind had happened for fifty years in that rural route, and there was a terrific to-do, through all of which Margie and I, for once, calmly slept. Then when we went down to Niagara-on-the-Lake the house next door to ours, one night while we were over at the Noxons, went up in a blaze. We heard the shouts and bells and saw the awful sun (I don't know why so much Emily Dickinson today) and of course thought it was *our* house and ran over in a panic, so much so that Margie was not even convinced it was *not* our house, by the time we had got there, and took all our manuscripts out into the street. And to cap everything when we returned here, it turned out that the house where someone had been good enough to let us store our bedding and some few things we had left after *our* fire, had in our absence itself burned down, totally demolished, and our bedding and stuff with it, the house mysteriously bursting into flame for no reason at all apparently one calm mild evening when the owners weren't even there. Margie and I had invented a horror story, a murderer, a black magician, one of whose specialities was the starting of fires by means of incomprehensible talismans. This fictitious gent's name was Pell and the MSS concerning him I had happened to rescue from our fire. S'welp me bob if the owners of this house don't turn out to be

* Gerald Noxon and his wife Betty.

Pell too, though there had been no connection at all originally. And so forth; altogether about fifty other odd senseless sad terrifying and curiously related things that make me sometimes think (taking it all in all) that maybe I am the chap chosen of God or the devil to elucidate the Law of Series. Unfortunately it would seem to involve one in such rotten bad art: or need it not? At all events, I have been reading Kant's *Critique of Pure Reason* to see if that would help.

When we arrived back here too it was to find that someone, strangers and vultures, had disregarded our burned stakes and notices and built smack on half our old site, blocking our southerly view, a great tall ugly creation to be full in the summer of rackety rickety children and hysterical fat women who meantime had pulled down the flags we left —perhaps too dramatically—flying on our poor old ruin, thrown dead mice down our well, and shat—even on the walls—all over our toilet. This of course is a crime, according to the local folkways, the mores, or whatever, though we had no legal toehold in the matter, pioneer's and squatter's rights having been abolished: our few fishermen friends— with ourselves the only permanent inhabitants—arrived back too late from Alaska to prevent it, and our local Manx boat-builder only got in- sulted and nearly beaten up when he tried to put a stop to it. They had no excuse; knew we were coming back. We could have knocked their house down ourselves and had the support of even most of the summer community, but like a fool or not I decided to be Christlike about it with the result that we had them in our hair all summer while we were building on what space was left for us, our new neighbours even calling us greedy because we made the most of that, until one day the owner came over and asked why we wouldn't speak to them more often and accused me of putting a curse on them and on their house, that they couldn't be happy there, that the youngest child had almost drowned the day before, and so on, and that they'd had one mis- fortune after another, ever since they'd built there, to which I replied that while we forgave them, all right, they had never had the charity to perceive that there was anything to forgive, moreover if you built on top of a guy's soul, you couldn't be sure what would happen, and if something you didn't like did happen, it was no use coming round complaining to us and looking as if they'd swallowed Paddy Murphy's goat and the horns were sticking out of their arse. All round, quite an ethical problem.

To be frank, it is ourselves who have had most of a share in this misfortune. Margie ran a nail through her foot the first day we got the lumber in—cellulitis set in, then blood poisoning, shortage of doctors, and finally hospital, and probings, and a horrible awful anxious time that was. Meanwhile she received the first part of her proof for her novel but we are still waiting for the promised proofreader's copy of the second part, Scribners having held her first novel now for over four years (it is getting into the fifth year) without publishing it, and although they signed a contract for a second novel with a time limit set for publication date at this fall, it is already this fall and still Margie hasn't had so much as a smell of the proofs of this second novel, which was supposed to be at the printers last Christmas, so it looks as though a breach of contract looms, with what small comfort that is for the poor author. I then proceeded to cut off the end of my thumb while doing some ripsawing with an ordinary saw, which set us back with the building and for the last two months I have been in bed practically unable to move with a toxaemia caused by an osteomyelitis due to a tooth that became abscessed and had to be removed. There is a shortage of dentists—they will not take new patients, even if you are hopping with agony as I was, and on V.J. Day too, with the drugstores all shut. But on the other hand there is apparently also a surplus of dentists: they are threatening to open offices on the street because of the housing shortage. But I myself have not been able to find a trace of these dentists. Meantime there has been an average of two murders a week here, most of them by or of children: a pet slayer likewise is at large who has disembowelled thirteen goats, several sailors' monkeys, twelve pet rabbits, and is doubtless also somewise responsible for the apparition of half a cocker spaniel in a lane near West Vancouver. Just the same we have built our house and paradise has been regained. I forgot to say that no sooner had paradise been regained than we received the notice that a new law had gone through and that all our lovely forest was to be torn down and ourselves with it within a year and turned into "autocamps of the better class." This placed our new house —which by the way has the distinction of being the last example of such pioneer activity on the Vancouver waterfront property—under a sentence of death that was finally too much for our sense of humours and my temperature went up within a quarter of an hour to 103. A sad story, you say, almost as poignant as the "Triumph of the Egg." Not a bit of it. Reprieve has come. There will be no autocamps of the better class, and no neighbours either, of the worse class. We may live here for three years at least, as we are doing, without molestation or paying any rent at all and then buy the land too, that is the part we want and we are being given first choice—for a reasonable price. Thus does your old Malc, if still a conservative Christian Anarchist at heart, at last join the ranks of the petty bourgeoisie. I feel somewhat like a Prometheus who became interested in real estate and decided to buy up his Caucasian ravine.

At the moment we are living in the house without inside walls, it's pouring with rain, and it doesn't leak. What triumph. Herewith our handiwork—also the pier we built ourselves, all that was left of our old house—it used to come out of our front door: the vultures wedged themselves in just beyond, hoping to use our pier too, not to say our well.

My novel—the *Volcano*—seems to have gone smack into the void, no intelligent comments so far or encouragement. I think it is really good, though *The Lost Weekend* may have deprived it of some of its impact—alack, prosaic justice?—if not confused with *The Last Week End* by John Sommerfield, in which it actually is old Malc who goes all too recognizably down the drain, and pretty feebly too. I was planning to send you the *Volcano* in some trepidation but with some pride too, but I don't like to saddle you with the only copy in my possession and I don't at present see how I can get back the only available other one before you sail. So please take the will for the deed for the time being. I'll learn 'em eventually, as Mr. Wolfe once said, I feel.

The only difference in my present status since I wrote the above is that while we are still living in the house without inside walls the roof is leaking in six different places. But now your letter about the *Collected Poems* has arrived and I hasten to make some reply in time, though please forgive me if what I say seems hastily digested. In brief, these are the ideas which immediately occur to me and I hope they are not merely confusing. I think the idea of reversing the chronological order is very good, in fact as good as can be—though I think perhaps "The Soldier" might profit by being dislocated out of the new order and being placed, if not actually among the symphonies, somewhere near them in the second volume. What I mean is if the poem does not belong to the symphonies, "The Soldier" does to the notion of the Divine Pilgrim. Houston Peterson or somebody once put the possibly erroneous idea in my head that you had once thought of including "Tetélestai" also under the Divine Pilgrim heading, and even if this is erroneous and "Tetélestai" not a symphony this is worth thinking of if you haven't already rejected it. As for the early poems I would certainly put in everything that can possibly be of use to the fellow-poet and student of your work—"Discordants with Youth that's now so bravely spending" and as many of the actual "Cats and Rats" turns and movies as you have space for. They latterly certainly stay with me as unique and powerful work, whatever you may think of them. I would also take the opportunity of exhuming from undeserved limbo such pieces as "Red petals in the dust under a tree," "Asphalt," "Tossing our tortured hands to no Escape" (though not very early, 1925 model? but very fine) and even the "Succubus you kissed" lampoon you wrote agin the Imagists which has a historical interest, and giving the dates of all these.

I don't know about a selection from "Earth Triumphant," but I would be inclined to make a short one—possibly you are right to disown it, but I myself cannot forget the "unaccustomed wetness in my trousers" with which I read it at your Uncle Potter's. The only other departure that comes to me would be to start the whole collected poems with "The Morning Song of Senlin" and end them with "The Coming Forth by Day of Osiris Jones." I must say I like this notion per se exceedingly, if it would not play too much hob with your reversed chronology. Whatever you do, I am very glad a *Collected Poems* is coming out and very best luck with them.

If, by the way, you have any old *Harper's Bazaars, Vice Versas, Southern Reviews* or what not you are thinking of throwing away— no old *Dials*, alack?—we would be immensely beholden if you would wrap a paper around them and shoot them in this direction C.O.D. or something, for we are absolutely stuck here for such reading matter, all intelligent American magazines having been unprocurable for donkey's years: on the other hand it occurs to me it is probably a poor time to ask, what with you packing and all: so if it's too much trouble, just forget it.

Well, bon voyage, old fellow and our very best love to you both and best wishes for Mary's success and our very best again to her and you and also to Jeakes.*

Malc

* Jeakes House, Conrad Aiken's home in Rye, Sussex.

To Mrs. E. B. Woolfan*

Cuernavaca, Mexico
[November, 1945]

My very dear sister Priscilla:
   I have temporarily written myself out of news—waiving the formal, this note comes from the heart, with real love and gratitude. Were I to attempt to say all that I feel for the way you opened your home and your hearts to me it would take another novel as long as the *Volcano*. But I know that being *muy simpático* you will take a likewise *simpático* attitude to my inarticulacy and will understand. I had long looked forward to meeting you but it rarely if ever happens that the reality exceeds the anticipation as it did with you. I was proud, grateful and charmed, all at once. There are many things here that would interest and amuse you and also give you the creeps—things wonderful, things horrible, things wonderful-horrible—especially some of the new houses. What do you think of our living in M. Laruelle's house, and all by accident, the only one we could get—chevron-shaped windows and all: it gives us an odd feeling of living *inside* a book, a kind of intra-dimensional life. We walked out of the house the other night into a full eclipse of the moon—there was the moon, looking incredibly near and spherical, and apparently coming nearer: we thought it was some terrestrial visitor and that we had gone completely cuckoo. Give Mother our best love and tell her we are writing her together today. Adiós. God bless.

Your brother,
Malcolm

To Mrs. John Stuart Bonner

Cuernavaca, Mexico
[November, 1945]

My very dearest Mother:
   I was so proud and so delighted to meet you, and traces of your kindness, thoughtfulness and sensitivity were so much everywhere in the house, even to the books at one's bedside, that I was very chagrined to think how inadequately I must have expressed my appreciation:

* Margerie Lowry's sister.

but it was wonderful having the privilege at last of seeing you and talking to you and I enormously enjoyed my visit.

We had a very fine trip here and I have described this in part to Priscilla and Bert, who will doubtless relay it to you. The night before last Margie saw Achernar and Canopus for the first time; and how thrilling that was! (I should have said just Achernar in Eridanus for the first time, for of course you can see Canopus sometimes in Los Angeles.) Last night we ran into something that would have interested you. We went to see an old friend of mine, previously having observed the full moon rise over the volcano Ixtaccihuatl, then came out into the street to find a lunar eclipse in progress which became total as we walked back toward our pension. At each gap between the walls, through a vista of trees, we had a strangely beautiful glimpse of the increasing eclipse until finally, round a turn, it was total, and the moon turned a rusty brown. After dinner we had to pay some more visits in total darkness but when we finally got home and we climbed to our balcony the moon was out of her eclipse, and the stars were shining. They were winking like jewels out of white fleecy clouds and high up the brilliant normal full moon was sliding down a wide sapphire night sky into a kind of white ocean of fleece. We both thought of you and wished you were here to share it all.

A Mexican was singing away to himself at the other end of our verandah, and we wondered if he were not singing half from relief that the world had not come to an end after all and the moon was with us as usual! (I must admit to being pretty relieved myself that the world had relinquished its shadow because for some reason I had never seen previously even a partial eclipse of the moon and so had been feeling definitely uneasy all evening.)

Well, Mother, this is just a little note to tell you that we are thinking of you often and also to say how enormously I appreciate how much trouble and work Priscilla and you went to to make me feel at home and happy with you, which I certainly was!

Now *hasta la vista,* and God bless you—till the next time.

Your affectionate son,
Malcolm

PART III: *1946*

To Jonathan Cape

24 Calle de Humboldt
Cuernavaca, Morelos
Mexico
[January 2, 1946]

Dear Mr. Cape:

Thank you very much indeed for yours of the 29th November,* which did not reach me, however, until New Year's Eve, and moreover reached me here, in Cuernavaca, where, completely by chance, I happen to be living in the very tower which was the original of the house of M. Laruelle, which I had only seen previously from the outside, and that ten years ago, but which is the very place where as it happens the Consul in the *Volcano* also had a little complication with some delayed correspondence.

Passing over my feelings, which you can readily imagine, of involved triumph, I will, lest these should crystallize into a complete agraphia, get down immediately to the business in hand.

My first feeling is that the reader, a copy of whose report you sent me, could not have been (to judge from your first letter to me) as sympathetic as the reader to whom you first gave it.

On the other hand, while I distinctly agree with much this second reader very intelligently says, and while in his place I might have said much the same by way of criticism, he puts me somewhat at a loss to reply definitely to your questions re revisions, for reasons which I shall try to set forth, and which I am sure both you and he would agree are valid, at least for the author.

It is true that the novel gets off to a slow start, and while he is right to regard this as a fault (and while in general this may be certainly a fault in any novel) I think it possible for various human reasons that

* See Appendix 3.

its gravity might have weighed upon him more heavily than it would weigh upon the reader per se, certain provisions for him having first been made. If the book anyhow were already in print and its pages not wearing the dumb pleading disparate and desperate look of the unpublished manuscript, I feel a reader's interest would tend to be very much more engaged at the outset just as, were the book already, say, an established classic, a reader's feelings would be most different: albeit he might say *God, this is tough going,* he would plod gamely on through the dark morass—indeed he might feel ashamed not to— because of the reports which had already reached his ears of the rewarding vistas further on.

Using the word *reader* in the more general sense, I suggest that whether or not the *Volcano* as it is seems tedious at the beginning depends somewhat upon that reader's state of mind and how prepared he is to grapple with the form of the book and the author's true intention. Since, while he may be prepared and equipped to do both, he cannot *know* the nature of either of these things at the start, I suggest that a little subtle but solid elucidation in a preface or a blurb might negate very largely or modify the reaction you fear—that it was your first reaction, and might well have been mine in your place, I am asking you for the moment to be generous enough to consider beside the point—if he were *conditioned,* I say, ever so slightly towards the acceptance of that slow beginning as inevitable, supposing I convince you it is—slow, but perhaps not necessarily so tedious after all—the results might be surprising. If you say, well, a good wine needs no bush, all I can reply is: well, I am not talking of good wine but mescal, and quite apart from the bush, once inside the cantina, mescal needs salt and lemon to get it down, and perhaps you would not drink it at all if it were not in such an enticing bottle. If that seems beside the point too, then let me ask who would have felt encouraged to venture into the drought of *The Waste Land* without some anterior knowledge and anticipation of its poetic cases?

Some of the difficulties of approach having been cleared away therefore, I feel the first chapter for example, such as it stands, is necessary since it sets, even without the reader's knowledge, the mood and tone of the book as well as the slow melancholy tragic rhythm of Mexico itself—its sadness—and above all establishes the *terrain:* if anything here finally looks to everyone just too feeble for words I would be only too delighted to cut it, but how can you be sure that by any really serious cutting here, especially any that radically alters the form, you are not undermining the foundations of the book, the basic structure, without which your reader might not have read it at all?

I venture to suggest finally that the book is a good deal thicker, deeper, better, and a great deal more carefully planned and executed than he suspects, and that if your reader is not at fault in not spotting some of its deeper meanings or in dismissing them as pretentious or irrelevant or uninteresting where they erupt onto the surface of the book, that is at least partly because of what may be a virtue and not a fault on my side, namely that the top level of the book, for all its *longeurs,* has been by and large so compellingly designed that the reader does not want to take time off to stop and plunge beneath the surface. If this is in fact true, of how many books can you say it? And how many books of which you can say it can you say also that you were not, somewhere along the line the first time you read it, bored because you wanted to "get on." I do not want to make childish comparisons, but to go to the obvious classics what about *The Idiot? The Possessed?* What about the beginning of *Moby Dick?* To say nothing of *Wuthering Heights.* E. M. Forster, I think, says somewhere that it is more of a feat to get by with the end, and in the *Volcano* at least I claim I have done this; but without the beginning, or rather the first chapter, which as it were answers it, echoes back to it over the bridge of the intervening chapters, the end—and without it the book—would lose much of its meaning.

Since I am pleading for a rereading of *Under the Volcano* in the light of certain aspects of it which may not perhaps have struck you at all, with a view to any possible alterations, and not making a defense of its every word, I had better say that for my part I feel that the main defect of *Under the Volcano,* from which the others spring, comes from something irremediable. It is that the author's equipment, such as it is, is subjective rather than objective, a better equipment, in short, for a certain kind of poet than a novelist. On the other hand I claim that just as a tailor will try to conceal the deformities of his client so I have tried, aware of this defect, to conceal in the *Volcano* as well as possible the deformities of my own mind, taking heart from the fact that since the conception of the whole thing was essentially poetical, perhaps these deformities don't matter so very much after all, even when they show! But poems often have to be read several times before their full meaning will reveal itself, explode in the mind, and it is precisely this poetical conception of the *whole* that I suggest has been, if understandably, missed. But to be more specific: your reader's main objections to the book are:

1. The long initial tedium, which I have discussed in part but will take up again later.

2. The weakness of the character drawing. This is a valid criticism. But I have not exactly attempted to draw characters in the normal sense—though s'welp me bob it's only Aristotle who thought character counted least. But here, as I shall say somewhere else, there just isn't *room:* the characters will have to wait for another book, though I did go to incredible trouble to make my major characters seem adequate on the most *superficial* plane on which this book can be read, and I believe in some eyes the character drawing will appear the reverse of weak. (What about female readers?) The truth is that the character drawing is not only weak but virtually nonexistent, save with certain minor characters, the four main characters being intended, in one of the book's meanings, to be aspects of the same man, or of the human spirit, and two of them, Hugh and the Consul, more obviously are. I suggest that here and there what may look like unsuccessful attempts at character drawing may only be the concrete bases to the creature's lives without which again the book could not be read at all. But weak or no there is nothing I can do to improve it without reconceiving or rewriting the book, unless it is to take something out—but then, as I say, one might be thereby only removing a prop which, while it perhaps looked vexing to you in passing, was actually holding something important up.

3. "The author has spread himself too much. The book is *much too long* and over elaborate for its content, and could have been much more effective if only half or two thirds its present length. The author has overreached himself and is given to eccentric word-spinning and too much stream-of-consciousness stuff." This may well be so, but I think the author may be forgiven if he asks for a fuller appraisal of that content—I say it all again—in terms of the author's intention as a whole and chapter by chapter before he can reach any agreement with anyone as to what precisely renders it over-elaborate and should therefore be cut to render that whole more effective. If the reader has not got hold of the content at first go, how can he decide then what makes it much too long, especially since his reactions may turn out to be quite different on a second reading? And not only authors perhaps but readers can overreach themselves, by reading too fast however carefully they think they are going—and what tedious book is this one has to read so fast? I believe there is such a thing as wandering attention that is the fault neither of reader nor writer: though more of this later. As for the eccentric word-spinning, I honestly don't think

there is much that is not in some way thematic. As for the "stream-of-consciousness stuff," many techniques have been employed, and while I did try to cut mere "stuff" to a minimum, I suspect that your reader would finally agree, if confronted with the same problems, that most of it could be done in no other way: a lot of the so-called "stuff" I feel to be justified simply on poetical or dramatic grounds: and I think you would be surprised to find how much of what at first sight seems unnecessary even in this "stuff" is simply disguised, honest-to-God exposition, the author trying to proceed on Henry James' dictum that what is not vivid is not represented, what is not represented is not art.

To return to the criticisms on the first and second page of your reader's report:

1. "Flashbacks of the character's past lives and past and present thoughts and emotions . . . (are) often tedious and unconvincing." These flashbacks are necessary however, I feel: where they are really tedious or unconvincing, I should be glad to cut of course, but I feel it only fair to the book that this should be done only after what I shall say later (and have already said) has been taken into account. That which may seem inorganic in itself might prove right in terms of the whole churrigueresque structure I conceived and which I hope may begin soon to loom out of the fog for you like Borda's horrible-beautiful cathedral in Taxco.

2. "Mexican local colour heaped on in shovelfuls . . . is very well done and gives one an astonishing sense of the place and the atmosphere." Thank you very much, but if you will excuse my saying so I did not heap the local colour, whatever that is, on in shovelfuls. I am delighted he likes it but take issue because what he says implies carelessness. I hope to convince you that, just as I said in my first letter, all that is there is there for a reason. And what about the use of Nature, of which he says nothing?

3. "The mescal-inspired phantasmagoria, or heebie-jeebies, to which Geoffrey has succumbed . . . is impressive but I think too long, wayward and elaborate. On account of (3) the book inevitably recalls . . . *The Lost Weekend.*" I will take this in combination with your reader's last and welcome remarks re the book's virtues, and the last sentence of the report in which he says: "Everything should be concentrated on the drunk's inability to rise to the occasion of Yvonne's return, on his delirious consciousness (which is very well done) and on the local colour, which is excellent throughout." I do not want to quibble, but I do seem to detect something like a contradiction here. Here is

my mescal-inspired phantasmagoria, which is impressive but already too long, wayward and elaborate—to say nothing of too much eccentric word-spinning and stream-of-consciousness stuff—and yet on the other hand, I am invited to concentrate still *more* upon it, since all this can be after all nothing but the delirious consciousness (which is very well done)—and I would like very much to know how I can concentrate still more upon a delirious consciousness without making it still more long-wayward-elaborate, and since that is the way of delirious consciousnesses, without investing it with still more stream-of-consciousness stuff: moreover here too is my local colour, and although this is already "heaped on in shovelfuls" (if excellent throughout) I am invited to concentrate still more upon it and this without calling in the aid of some yet large long-handled scoop-like implement used to lift and throw earth, coal, grain and so forth: nor do I see either how I can very well concentrate very much more than I have on the drunk's inability to rise to the occasion of Yvonne's return without incurring the risk of being accused of heaping on the mescal-inspired phantasmagoria with—at least!—a snow plough. Having let me have my fun, I must say that I admit the critical probity in your reader's last remarks but that it would be impossible to act on his suggestions without writing another book, possibly a better one, but still, another. I respect what he says, for what he seems to be saying is (like Yeats, when he cut nearly all the famous but irrelevant lines out of the *Ballad of Reading Gaol* and thereby, unfortunately for my thesis, much improved it): a work of art should have but one subject. Perhaps it will be seen that the *Volcano*, after all, *has* but one subject. This brings me to the unhappy (for me) subject of the *Lost Weekend*. Mr. Jackson likewise obeys your reader's aesthetic and does to my mind an excellent job within the limits he set himself. Your reader could not know, of course, that it should have been the other way round— that it was *The Lost Weekend* that should have inevitably recalled the *Volcano;* whether this matters or not in the long run, it happens to have a very desiccating effect on me. I began the *Volcano* in 1936, the same year having written, in New York, a novelette of about 100 pages about an alcoholic entitled *The Last Address,* which takes place mostly in the same hospital ward where Don Birnam spends an interesting afternoon. This—it was too short I thought to publish separately or I would have sent it to you for it was and is, I believe, remarkably good—was accepted and paid for by *Story Magazine,* who were publishing novelettes at that time, but was never published because they had meantime changed their policy back to shorter things again. It was however, in spite of Zola, accepted as more or less pioneer work in that field, and nine years and two months ago when I was here in this same town in Mexico I conceived the *Volcano* and I decided really to go to town on the poetical possibilities of that subject. I had written a 40,000-word version by 1937 that Arthur Calder-Marshall liked, but it was not thorough or honest enough. In 1939 I volunteered to come to England but was told to remain in Canada, and in 1940, while waiting to be called up, I rewrote the entire book in six months, but it was no damn good, a failure, except for the drunk passages about the Consul, but even some of them did not seem to me good enough. I also rewrote *The Last Address* in 1940–41 and rechristened it *Lunar Caustic,* and conceived the idea of a trilogy entitled *The Voyage That Never Ends* for your firm (nothing less than a trilogy would do) with the *Volcano* as the first, infernal part, a much amplified *Lunar Caustic* as the second, purgatorial part, and an enormous novel I was also working on called *In Ballast to the White Sea* (which I lost when my house burned down as I believe I wrote you) as the paradisal third part, the whole to concern the battering the human spirit takes (doubtless because it is overreaching itself) in its ascent towards its true purpose. At the end of 1941 I laid aside *In Ballast*—of which there were 1000 pages of eccentric word-spinning by this time—and decided to take this mescal-inspired phantasmagoria the *Volcano* by the throat and really do something about it, it having become a spiritual thing by this time. I also told my wife that I would probably cut my throat if during this period of the world's drunkenness someone else had the same sober idea. I worked for two more years, eight hours a day, and had just ascetically completed all the drunken parts to my satisfaction and there were but three other chapters to rewrite when one day round about New Year's '44, I picked up an American review of *The Lost Weekend*. At first I thought it must be *The Last Week End*, by my old pal John (*Volunteer in Spain*) Sommerfield, a very strange book in which figured in some decline no less a person than myself, and I am still wondering what John thinks about this: but doubtless the old boy ascribes it to the capitalist system. *The Lost Weekend* did not appear in Canada till about April '44, and after reading the book it became extremely hard for the time being to go on writing and having faith in mine. I could still congratulate myself upon having *In Ballast* up my sleeve however, but only a month or so later that went completely west with my house. My wife saved the MSS of the *Volcano,* God knows how, while I was doing something about the forest, and the book was finished over a year ago in Niagara-on-the-Lake, Ontario. We returned to British Columbia to rebuild our house and since we had some serious setbacks and accidents in doing so it took some time to get the typescript in order. Meantime, however, this *Lost Weekend* business on top of everything else had somewhat got me down. The only way I can look upon it is as a form of punishment. My own worst fault in the past has been precisely lack of integrity, and that is particularly hard to face in one's own work. Youth plus booze plus hysterical identifications plus vanity plus self-deception plus no work plus more booze. But now, when this ex-pseudo author climbs down from his cross in his little Oberammergau where he has been hibernating all these years to offer something really original and terrific to atone for his sins, it turns out that somebody from Brooklyn has just done the same thing better. Or has he not? And how many times has this author not been told that *that* theme of all themes couldn't sell, that nothing was duller than dipsomania! Anyway Papa Henry James would certainly have agreed that all this was a turn of the screw. But I think it not unreasonable to suppose either that he might have added that, for that matter, the *Volcano* was, so to say, a couple of turns of the screw on *The Lost Weekend* anyway. At all events I've tried to give you some of the reasons why I can't turn the *Volcano* into simply a kind of *quid pro quo* of the thing, which is what your reader's suggestions would tend to make it, or, if that's unfair to your reader, what I would then tend to make it. These reasons may be briefly crystallized. 1. Your reader wants me to do what I wanted to do myself (and still sometimes regret not having done) but did not do because 2. *Under the Volcano,* such as it is, is better. After this long digression, to return to the last page of your reader's report: I agree:

A. It is worth my while—and I am anxious—to make the book as effective as possible. But I think it only fair to the book that the lengths which have been gone to already to make it effective as possible *in its own terms* should be appreciated by someone who sees the whole.

B. Cuts should possibly be made in some of the passages indicated, but with the same reservations.

I disagree that:

A. Hugh's past is of little interest

B. or relevance

for reasons I shall set forth. One, which may seem odd, is: There is not a single part of this book I have not submitted to Flaubert's acid test of reading aloud or having read aloud, frequently to the kind of people one would expect to loathe it, and nearly always to people who were not afraid of speaking their minds. Chapter VI, which concerns Hugh's past life, always convulsed people with laughter, so much so that often the reader could not go on. Apart from anything else, then, and there is much else—what about its humour? This does not take care of its relevance, which I shall point out: but to refer back to something I said before, I submit that the real reason why your reader found this chapter of no interest or relevance was perhaps that I had built better than I knew in the previous chapter, and he wanted to skip and get on to the Consul again. Actually this chapter is the heart of the book and if cuts are to be made in it they should be made on the advice of someone who, having seen what the author is driving at, has at least an inspiration equivalent to that of the author who created it.

I had wanted to give in the following pages a kind of synopsis of the *Volcano* chapter by chapter, but since my spare copy of the MSS has not reached me from Canada I will simply suggest as well as I can some of its deeper meanings, and something of the form and intention that was in the author's mind, and that which he feels should be taken into account, should alterations be necessary. The twelve chapters should be considered as twelve blocks, to each of which I have devoted over a period of years a great deal of labour, and I hope to convince you that whatever cuts may be made there must still be twelve chapters. Each chapter is a unity in itself and all are related and interrelated. Twelve is a universal unit. To say nothing of the 12 labours of Hercules, there are 12 hours in a day, and the book is concerned with a single day as well as, though very incidentally, with time: there are 12 months in a year, and the novel is enclosed by a year; while the deeply buried layer of the novel or poem that attaches itself to myth, does so to the Jewish Cabbala where the number 12 is of the highest symbolic importance. The Cabbala is used for poetical purposes because it represents man's spiritual aspiration. The Tree of Life, which is its emblem, is a kind of complicated ladder with Kether, or Light, at the top and an extremely unpleasant abyss some way above the middle. The Consul's spiritual domain in this regard is probably the Qliphoth, the world of shells and demons, represented by the Tree of Life upside down—all this is not important at all to the understanding of the book; I just mention it in passing to hint that, as Henry James says, "There are depths." But also, because I have to have my 12: it is as if I hear

a clock slowly striking midnight for Faust; as I think of the slow
progression of the chapters, I feel it destined to have 12 chapters
and nothing more nor less will satisfy me. For the rest, the book is
written on numerous planes with provision made, it was my fond
hope, for almost every kind of reader, my approach with all humility
being opposite, I felt, to that of Mr. Joyce, *i.e.*, a simplyfying, as far
as possible, of what originally suggested itself in far more baffling,
complex and esoteric terms, rather than the other way round. The
novel can be read simply as a story which you can skip if you want.
It can be read as a story you will get more out of if you don't
skip. It can be regarded as a kind of symphony, or in another way
as a kind of opera—or even a horse opera. It is hot music, a poem,
a song, a tragedy, a comedy, a farce, and so forth. It is superficial, profound, entertaining and boring, according to taste. It is a prophecy, a
political warning, a cryptogram, a preposterous movie, and a writing
on the wall. It can even be regarded as a sort of machine: it works
too, believe me, as I have found out. In case you think I mean it
to be everything but a novel I better say that after all it is intended
to be and, though I say so myself, a deeply serious one too. But it
is also I claim a work of art somewhat different from the one you
suspected it was, and more successful too, even though according to
its own lights.

This novel then is concerned principally, in Edmund Wilson's
words (speaking of Gogol), with the forces in man which cause him
to be terrified of himself. It is also concerned with the guilt of man,
with his remorse, with his ceaseless struggling toward the light under
the weight of the past, and with his doom. The allegory is that of
the Garden of Eden, the Garden representing the world, from which
we ourselves run perhaps slightly more danger of being ejected than
when I wrote the book. The drunkenness of the Consul is used on
one plane to symbolize the universal drunkenness of mankind during
the war, or during the period immediately preceding it, which is almost the same thing, and what profundity and final meaning there
is in his fate should be seen also in its universal relationship to the
ultimate fate of mankind.

Since it is Chapter I that I believe to be chiefly responsible for
your reader's charge of tedium, and since, as I've said, I believe that
a reader needs only a little flying start for this apparent tedium to
be turned into an increasing suspense from the outset, I will devote
more space to this first chapter than to any other, unless it is the
sixth, saying also in passing that I believe it will become clear on a

second reading that nearly all the material in I is necessary, and if
one should try to eliminate this chapter entirely, or chop up all the
material in it and stuff it in here and there into the book in wedges
and blocks—I even tried it once—it would not only take a very
long time but the results would be nowhere near as effective, while
it would moreover buckle the very form of the book, which is to be
considered like that of a wheel, with 12 spokes, the motion of which
is something like that, conceivably, of time itself.

Under the Volcano

(*Note:* the book opens in the Casino de la Selva. Selva means wood
and this strikes the opening chord of the *Inferno*—remember, the
book was planned and still is a kind of Inferno, with Purgatorio
and Paradiso to follow, the tragic protagonist in each, like Tchitchikov
in *Dead Souls,* becoming slightly better—in the middle of our life . . .
in a dark wood, etc., this chord being struck again in VI, the middle
and heart of the book where Hugh, in the middle of his life, recalls
at the beginning of that chapter Dante's words: the chord is struck
again remotely toward the end of VII where the Consul enters a
gloomy cantina called El Bosque, which also means the wood (both
of these places being by the way real, one here, the other in Oaxaca),
while the chord is resolved in XI, in the chapter concerning Yvonne's
death, where the wood becomes real, and dark.)

I

The scene is Mexico, the meeting place, according to some, of
mankind itself, pyre of Bierce and springboard of Hart Crane, the
age-old arena of racial and political conflicts of every nature, and
where a colorful native people of genius have a religion that we can
roughly describe as one of death, so that it is a good place, at least
as good as Lancashire or Yorkshire, to set our drama of a man's
struggle between the powers of darkness and light. Its geographical
remoteness from us, as well as the closeness of its problems to our
own, will assist the tragedy each in its own way. We can see it as
the world itself, or the Garden of Eden, or both at once. Or we can
see it as a kind of timeless symbol of the world on which we can
place the Garden of Eden, the Tower of Babel and indeed anything
else we please. It is paradisal: it is unquestionably infernal. It is, in
fact, Mexico, the place of the pulques and chinches, and it is im-

portant to remember that when the story opens it is November 1939, not November 1938, the Day of the Dead, and precisely one year after the Consul has gone down the barranca, the ravine, the abyss that man finds himself looking into now (to quote the Archbishop of York) the worse one in the Cabbala, the still unmentionably worse one in the Qliphoth, or simply down the drain, according to taste.

I have spoken already of one reason why I consider this chapter necessary more or less as it is, for the terrain, the mood, the sadness of Mexico, etc., but before I go on to mention any more I must say I fail to see what is wrong with this opening, as Dr. Vigil and M. Laruelle, on the latter's last day in the country, discuss the Consul. After their parting the ensuing exposition is perhaps hard to follow and you can say that it is a melodramatic fault that by concealing the true nature of the death of Yvonne and the Consul I have created suspense by false means: myself, I believe the concealment is organic, but even were it not, the criterion by which most critics condemn such devices seems to me to be that of pure reporting, and against the kind of novel they admire I am in rebellion, both revolutionary and reactionary at once. You can say too that it is a gamey and outworn trick to begin at the end of the book: it certainly is: I like it in this case and there is moreover a deep motive for it, as I have partially explained, and as I think you will see shortly. During Laruelle's walk we have to give some account of who he is; this is done as clearly as possible and if it could be achieved in a shorter or more masterly fashion I would be only too willing to take advice: a second reading however will show you what thematic problems we are also solving on the way—not to say what hams, that have to be there, are being hung in the window. Meanwhile the story is unfolding as the Mexican evening deepens into night: the reader is told of the love of M. Laruelle for Yvonne, the chord of tragic love is struck in the farewell visit at sunset to the Palace of Maximilian, where Hugh and Yvonne are to stand (or have stood) in the noonday in Chapter IV and while M. Laruelle leans over the fateful ravine we have, in his memory, the Taskerson episode. (Taskerson crops up again in V, in VII the Consul sings the Taskerson song to himself, and even in XII he is still trying to walk with the Taskerson "erect manly carriage.") The Taskerson episode in this Chapter I —damned by implication by your reader—may be unsound if considered seriously in the light of a psychological etiology for the Consul's drinking or downfall, but I have a sincere and not unjustified conviction that it is very funny in itself, and justified in itself musi-

cally and artistically at this point as relief, as also for another reason: is it not precisely in this particular passage that your reader
may have acquired the necessary *sympathy* with Geoffrey Firmin that
enabled him to read past Chapter II and into III without being
beset by the tedium there instead—and hence to become much more
interested as he went on? Your reader has omitted the possibility of
the poor author's having any wit anywhere. If you do not believe
this Taskerson incident is funny, try reading it aloud. I think that
wit might seem slightly larger on a second reading: also the drunken
man on horseback, who now appears to interrupt M. Laruelle's rev-
erie, by hurtling on up the Calle Nicaragua, might have a larger
significance: and still more on a third reading. This drunken horseman is by implication the first appearance of the Consul himself
as a symbol of mankind. Here also, as if tangentially (even if your
reader saw it as but another shovelful of local colour) is also struck
the chord of Yvonne's death in XI; true, this horse is not riderless
as yet, but it may well be soon: here man and the force he will release are for the moment fused. (Since by the way there is no suggestion in your reader's report that he has read the rather important
Chapter XI, in which there is incidentally some of the action he
misses, I had better say at this point that Yvonne is finally killed by
a panic-stricken horse in XI that the Consul drunkenly releases in
a thunderstorm in XII (the 2 chapters overlapping in time at this
juncture) in the erroneous, fuddled yet almost praiseworthy belief
he is doing somebody a good turn. M. Laruelle now, avoiding the
house where I am writing this letter (which is one thing that must
certainly be cut if I am not to spend my patrimony sending it airmail), goes gloomily toward the local movie. In the cinema and the
bar, people are taking refuge from the storm as in the world they
are creeping into bomb shelters, and the lights have gone out as they
have gone out in the world. The movie playing is *Las Manos de
Orlac,* the same film that had been playing exactly a year before
when the Consul was killed, but the man with the bloody hands in
the poster, via the German origin on the picture, symbolizes the
guilt of mankind, which relates him also to M. Laruelle and the
Consul again, while he is also more particularly a foreshadowing of
the thief who takes the money from the dying man by the roadside
in Chapter VIII, and whose hands are also covered with blood. Inside
the cinema cantina we hear more of the Consul from the cinema
manager, Bustamente, much of which again may engage our sympathy
for the Consul and our interest in him. It should not be forgotten

that it is the Day of the Dead and that on that day in Mexico the dead are supposed to commune with the living. Life however is omnipresent: but meantime there have been both political (the German film star Maria Landrock) and historical (Cortez and Moctezuma) notes being sounded in the background; and while the story itself is being unfolded, the themes and counterthemes of the book are being stated. Finally Bustamente comes back with the book of Elizabethan plays M. Laruelle has left there eighteen months before, and the theme of Faust is struck. Laruelle had been planning to make a modern movie of Faust but for a moment the Consul himself seems like his Faust, who had sold his soul to the devil. We now hear more of the Consul, his gallant war record, and of a war crime he has possibly committed against some German submarine officers—whether he is really as much to blame as he tells himself, he is, in a sense, paid back in coin for it at the end of the book and you may say that here the Consul is merely being established in the Grecian manner as a fellow of some stature, so that his fall may be tragic: it could be cut, I suppose, even though this is exactly as I see the Consul—but do we not look at him with more interest thereafter? We also hear that the Consul has been suspected of being an English spy, or "espider," and though he suffers dreadfully from the mania of persecution, and you feel sometimes, quite objectively, that he is indeed being followed throughout the book, it is as if the Consul himself is not aware of this and is afraid of something quite different: for lack of an object therefore it was the writer's reasonable hope that this first sense of being followed might settle on the reader and haunt him instead. At the moment however Bustamente's sympathy for him should arouse *our* sympathy. This sympathy I feel should be very considerably increased by the Consul's letter which Laruelle reads, and which was never posted, and this letter I believe important: his tortured cry is not answered until in the last chapter, XII, when, in the Farolito, the Consul finds Yvonne's letters he has lost and never really read until this time just before his death. M. Laruelle burns the Consul's letter, the act of which is poetically balanced by the flight of vultures ("like burnt papers floating from a fire") at the end of III, and also by the burning of the Consul's MSS in Yvonne's dying dream in XI: the storm is over: and—

Outside in the dark tempestuous night backwards revolved the luminous wheel.

This wheel is of course the Ferris wheel in the square, but it is, if you like, also many other things: it is Buddha's wheel of the law (see VII), it is eternity, it is the instrument of eternal recurrence, the eternal return, and it is the form of the book; or superficially it can be seen simply in an obvious movie sense as the wheel of time whirling backwards until we have reached the year before and Chapter II and in this sense, if we like, we can look at the rest of the book through Laruelle's eyes, as if it were his creation.

(*Note:* In the Cabbala, the misuse of magical powers is compared to drunkenness or the misuse of wine,· and termed, if I remember rightly, in Hebrew *sōd,* which gives us our parallel. There is a kind of attribute of the word *sōd* also which implies garden or a neglected garden, I seem to recall too, for the Cabbala is sometimes considered as the garden itself, with the Tree of Life, which is related of course to that Tree the forbidden fruit of which gave one the knowledge of good and evil, and ourselves the legend of Adam and Eve, planted within it. Be these things as they may—and they are certainly at the root of most of our knowledge, the wisdom of our religious thought, and most of our inborn superstitions as to the origin of man—William James if not Freud would certainly agree with me when I say that the agonies of the drunkard find their most accurate poetic analogue in the agonies of the mystic who has abused his powers. The Consul here of course has the whole thing wonderfully and drunkenly mixed up: mescal in Mexico is a hell of a drink but it is still a drink you can get at any cantina, more readily I dare say than Scotch these days at the dear old Horseshoe. But mescal is also a drug, taken in the form of buttons, and the transcending of its effects is one of the well-known ordeals that occultists have to go through. It would appear that the Consul has fuddledly come to confuse the two, and he is perhaps not far wrong.)

Final note on Chapter I: If this chapter is to be cut, can it not be done then with such wisdom as to make the chapter and the book itself better? I feel the chapter makes a wonderful entity and must be cut, if at all, by someone who at least sees its potentialities in terms of the whole book. I myself don't see much wrong with it. Against the charge of appalling pretentiousness, which is the most obvious one to be made by anyone who has read this letter, I feel I go clear; because these other meanings and danks and darks are not stressed at all: it is only if the reader himself, prompted by instinct or curiosity, cares to invoke them that they will raise their demonic heads from the abyss, or peer at him from above. But even if he is not prompted by anything, new meanings will certainly reveal themselves if he reads this book again. I hope you will be good enough not to remind me that the same might be said of *Orphan Annie* or *Jemima Puddleduck.*

II

You are now back on exactly the same day the year before—the Day of the Dead 1938—and the story of Yvonne's and the Consul's last day begins at seven o'clock in the morning on her arrival. I do not see any difficulties here. The mysterious contrapuntal dialogue in the Bella Vista bar you hear is supplied by Weber, you will later see if you watch and listen carefully, the smuggler who flew Hugh down to Mexico, and who is mixed up with the local thugs—as your reader calls them—and Sinarchistas in the Farolito in Parián who finally shoot the Consul. The chord of *no se puede vivir sin amar,* the writing in gold leaf outside M. Laruelle's house (where I am writing this letter, with my back to the degenerate machicolation, and even if you do not believe in my wheels—the wheel shows up in this chapter in the flywheel in the printer's shop—and so on, you must admit this is funny, as also that it is quite funny that the same movie happens to be playing in town as was playing here nine years ago, not *Las Manos de Orlac* as it happens but *La Tragedia de Mayerling*), is struck ironically by the bartender with his "absolutamente necesario," the recurring notices for the boxing match symbolize the conflict between Yvonne and the Consul. The chapter is a sort of bridge, it was written with extreme care; it too is absolutamente necesario, I think you would agree yourself on a second reading: it is an entity, a unity in itself, as are all the other chapters; it is, I claim, dramatic, amusing, and within its limits I think is entirely successful. I don't see any opportunity for cuts either.

III

I think will improve on a second reading and still more on a third. But since I believe your reader was impressed by it I will pass over it quickly. Word-spinning flashback while the Consul is lying down flat on his face in the Calle Nicaragua is really very careful exposition. This chapter was first written in 1940 and completed in 1942 long before Jackson went Lostweekending. Cuts should be made with great sympathy ("compliments of the Venezuelan Government" bit might go for instance) by someone—or by the author in conjunction with someone—who is prepared for the book to sink slowly at a not distant date into the action of the mind, and who is not necessarily put off by this. The scene between the Consul and Yvonne where he is impotent is balanced by scene between Consul and María in the last chapter: meanings of the Consul's impotence are practically inexhaustible. The dead man with hat over head the Consul sees in the garden is man by the wayside in Chapter VIII. This can happen in really super D.T.s. Paracelsus will bear me out.

IV

Necessary, I feel, much as it is, especially in view of my last sentence re III about the action of the mind. In this there is another kind of action. There is movement and swiftness, it is a contrast, it supplies a needed *ozone*. It gives a needed, also, sympathy and understanding of Mexico and her problems and people from a material viewpoint. If the very beginning seems slightly ridiculous you can read it as satire, but on a second reading I think the whole will improve vastly. We have now the countermovement of the Battle of the Ebro being lost, while no one does anything about it, which is a kind of correlative of the scene by the roadside in VIII, the victim of which here first makes his appearance outside the cantina La Sepultura, with his horse tethered near, that will kill Yvonne. Man's political aspirations, as opposed to his spiritual, come into view, and Hugh's sense of guilt balances the Consul's. If part of it must be cut, let it be done with a view to the whole—and with genius at least, I feel like saying—and let it not be cut so that it bleeds. Almost everything in it is relevant even down to the horses, the dogs, the river, and the small talk about the local movie. And what is not, as I say, supplies a needed ozone. For myself I think this ride through the Mexican morning sunlight is one of the best things in the book, and if Hugh strikes you as himself slightly preposterous, there is importance to the theme in the passage *re* his passionate desire for *goodness* at the close.

V

Is a contrast in the reverse direction, the opening words having an ironic bearing on the last words of IV. The book is now fast sinking into the action of the mind, and away from normal action, and yet I believe that by now your reader was really interested, *too* interested in fact here in the Consul to be able to cope with VI. Here at all events the most important theme of the book appears: "Le gusta este jardín?" on the sign. The Consul slightly mistranslates this sign, but "You like this garden? Why is it yours? We evict those who destroy!" will have to stand (while we will point out elsewhere that the real translation can be in a certain sense even more more horrifying). The garden is the Garden of Eden, which he even discusses with Mr. Quincey. It is the world too. It also has all the cabbalistic attributes of "garden." (Though all this is buried far down in the book, so that if you don't want to bother about it, you needn't. I wish that Hugh I'Anson Fausset, however, one of your own writers, one whose writings I very much admire and some of whose writings have had a very formative influence on my own life, could read the *Volcano*.) On the surface I am going to town here on the subject of the drunkard and I hope do well and amusingly. Parián again is death. Word-spinning phantasmagoria somewhere toward end of first part is necessary. It should be clear that the Consul has a blackout and that the second part in the bathroom is concerned with what he remembers half deliriously of the missing hour. Most of what he remembers is again disguised exposition and drama which carries on the story to the question: shall they go to Guanajuato (life) or Tomalín, which of course involves Parián (death). For the rest the Consul at one point identifies himself with the infant Horus, about which or whom the less said the better; some mystics believe him responsible for this last war, but I need another language I guess to explain what I mean. Perhaps Mr. Fausset would explain, but at all events you don't have to think about it because the passage is only short, and reads like quite good lunacy. The rest I think is perfectly good clean D.T.s such as your reader would approve of. This was first written in 1937. Final revision was made in March 1943. This too is an entity in itself. Possible objection could be to the technique of the second part but I believe it is a subtle way to do a difficult thing. Cuts might be made here, I guess, but they would have to be inspired at least as much as the chapter was.

VI

Here we come to the heart of the book which, instead of going into high delirious gear of the Consul, returns instead, surprisingly although inevitably if you reflect, to the uneasy, but healthy, systole-diastole of Hugh. In the middle of our life . . . and the theme of the Inferno is stated again, then follows the enormously long *straight* passage. This passage is the one your reader claims has little or no interest or relevance and I maintain he skipped because of a virtue on my side, namely he was more interested in the Consul himself. But here the guilt theme, and the theme of man's guilt, takes on a new shade of meaning. Hugh may be a bit of a fool but he none the less typifies the sort of person who may make or break our future: in fact he is the future in a certain sense. He is Everyman tightened up a screw, for he is just beyond being mediocre. And he is the youth of Everyman. Moreover his frustrations with his music, with the sea, in his desire to be good and decent, his self-deceptions, triumphs, defeats and dishonesties (and once more I point out that a much needed ozone blows into the book here with the sea air) his troubles with his guitar, are everyone's frustrations, triumphs, defeats, dishonesties and troubles with their *quid pro quo* of a guitar. And his desire to be a composer or musician is everyone's innate desire to be a poet of life in some way, while his desire to be accepted at sea is everyone's desire, conscious or unconscious, to be a part—even if it doesn't exist—of the brotherhood of man. He is revealed as a frustrated fellow whose frustrations might just as well have made him a drunk too, just like the Consul. (Who was frustrated as a poet—as who is not?—this indeed is another thing that binds us all together, but for whose drunkenness no satisfactory etiology is ever given unless it is in VII. "But the cold world shall not know.") Hugh feels he has betrayed himself by betraying his brother and also betrayed the brotherhood of man by having been at one time an anti-Semite. But when, in the middle of the chapter, which is also the middle of the book, his thoughts are interrupted by Geoffrey's call of "Help" you can receive, I claim, upon rereading, a *frisson* of a quite different calibre to that received when reading such pieces as "William Wilson" or other stories about doppelgängers. Hugh and the Consul are the same person, but within a book which obeys not the laws of other books, but those it creates as it goes along. I have reason to believe that much of this long straight passage is extremely funny anyway and will cause people to laugh aloud. We now proceed into the still greater nonsense and at the same time far more desperate seriousness of the shaving scene. Hugh shaves the corpse—but I cannot be persuaded that nonetheless much of this is not very hilarious indeed. We are then introduced to Geoffrey's room, with his picture of his old ship the *Samaritan* (and the theme is struck remotely again of the man by the wayside in VIII) upon which ship it has been mentioned before in I, etc., that he either has committed or imagines he has, but was certainly made in part responsible for, a crime against a number of German submarine officers—valid at least as any crime we may have committed in the past against Germany in general, that ugsome child of Europe whose evil and destructive energy is so much responsible for all our progress. At the same time he shows Hugh his alchemistic books, and we are for a moment, if in a pseudo-farcical situation, standing before the evidence of what is no less than the magical basis of the world. You do not believe the world has a magical basis, especially while the Battle of the Ebro is going on, or worse, bombs are dropping in Bedford Square? Well, perhaps I don't either. But the point is that Hitler *did*. And Hitler was another pseudo black magician out of the same drawer as Amfortas in the *Parsifal* he so much admired, and who has had the same inevitable fate. And if you don't believe that a British general actually told me that the real reason why Hitler destroyed the Polish Jews was to prevent their cabbalistic knowledge being used against him you can let me have my point on poetical grounds, I repeat, since it is made at a very sunken level of the book and is not very important here anyway. Saturn lives at 63, and Bahomet lives next door, however, and don't say I didn't tell you!

The rest of the chapter, and all this is probably too long, takes Hugh and the Consul and Yvonne, meeting Laruelle on the way (I hope dramatically) up to the house where I am now writing you this letter: the point about the postcard the Consul receives (from the same tiny bearded postman who delivered your delayed letter to me on New Year's Eve) is that it was posted about a year before in 1937 not long after she left, or was sent away by the Consul (following her affair with Laruelle but probably so that the Consul could drink in peace), and that its tone would seem to suggest that her going away was only a final thing in the Consul's mind, that really they loved each other all the time, had just had a lover's quarrel, and in spite of M. Laruelle, the whole thing was absolutely unnecessary. The chapter closes with a dying fall, like the end of some guitar piece of Ed Lang's, or conceivably Hugh's (and in this respect the brackets earlier might represent the "breaks")—oddly but rightly, I felt, the path theme of Dante, however, reappearing and fading with the vanishing road.

I believe on rereading this chapter it will seem to have much more relevance than before and its humor will appear as more considerable. On the other hand this is undoubtedly the juiciest area for your surgeon's knife. The middle part of the shaving scene was written in 1937, as was the very end, that much comprising the whole chapter then. The new version was done in 1943 but I had not quite finally revised it in 1944 when my house burned down. The final revisions I made later in 1944 comprised the first work I had been able to do since the fire, in which several pages of this chapter and notes for cuts were lost, and it well may be the job is shaky or forced here and there. This is the first point in the book where I can be persuaded to share your reader's objections, I think, to any extent. Some of it may be in a kind of bad taste. On the other hand I feel it deserves a careful rereading—I say again and again in the light of the form and intention I have indicated, bearing in mind that the journalistic style of the first part is intended to represent Hugh himself. In brief, I could stand even slashing cuts were your surgeon to say, "This would be more effective if such and such were done," and I saw he was taking everything into account. If a major operation by a sympathetic surgeon will save the patient's life, O.K., but, even though I do live in Mexico, I'm damned if I'm going to help him cut out his heart. (And then, when he's dead, "just flop it back in again anyhow," as the nurse said to me having just attended the post mortem.)

VII

Here we come to seven, the fateful, the magic, the lucky good-bad number and the scene in the tower, where I write this letter. By a coincidence I moved to the tower on January 7—I was living in another apartment in the same house, but downstairs, when I got your letter. My house burned down on June 7; when I returned to the burned site someone had branded, for some reason, the number 7 on a burned tree; why was I not a philosopher? Philosophy has been dying since the days of Duns Scotus, though it continues underground, if quacking slightly. Boehme would support me when I speak of the passion for order even in the smallest things that exist in the universe: 7 too is the number on the horse that will kill Yvonne and 7 the hour when the Consul will die—I believe the intention of this chapter to be quite clear and that it is one your reader approves of and I think too it is probably one of the best in the book. It was first written in 1936, rewritten in 1937, 1940, 1941, 1943, and finally 1944. Parallels with *The Lost Weekend* I think are most in evidence in this chapter. One long one that does not appear and which was written long before the L.W.E. I hoiked out with a heavy heart, but imbued with the spirit of competition, then added something else to my telephone scene to outdo him. I was particularly annoyed because my telephone scene in III and this one before I revised it, as I have said, were written long before Jackson's book appeared. Another parallel toward the end when he had his drink before him he doesn't pick it up will have to stand: it was written in 1937 anyway. I allowed myself also in the conversation in the middle with Laruelle a little of the Consul's professional contempt for the belief that the D.T.'s is the end of everything and I think if you ever publish the book you might do me justice by saying that this begins where Jackson leaves off. If there must be cuts here again I say they should be made by someone who appreciates this chapter as an entity right down to the bit about Samaritana mia and with reference to the whole book. There were the usual thicknesses and obliquities, stray cards from the tarot pack, and odd political and mystical chords and dissonances being sounded here and there in this chapter but I won't go into them: but there is also, above all, the continued attention to the *story*. The horseman, first seen in IV and who is to be the man by the roadside, is seen again going up the hill, and whose horse, with the number 7 on it, will kill Yvonne. This chapter constitutes almost the Consul's last chance and if the book has been read carefully I feel you should have a fine sense of doom by this time. *Es inevitable la muerte del Papa* is quite possibly just an anachronism, but I feel it must stand for I hold this a fine ending.

(Notes re local colour heaped on in shovelfuls: this chapter is a good example and every damn thing in it is organic. The madman futilely and endlessly throwing a bicycle tire in front of him, the man stuck half way up the slippery pole—these are projections of the Consul and of the futility of his life, and at the same time are *right*, are *true*, are what one sees here. Life is a forest of symbols, as Baudelaire said, but I won't be told you can't see the wood for the trees here!)

VIII

Here the book, so to speak, goes into reverse—or, more strictly speaking, it begins to go downhill, though not, by any means, I hope, in the sense of deteriorating! Downhill (the first word), toward the abyss. I think it one of the better chapters; though it needs reading carefully, I feel the reader will be well rewarded. Man dying by the roadside with his horse branded No. 7 near is, of course, the chap who'd been sitting outside the pulquería in IV, had appeared singing in VII when the Consul identified himself with him. He is, obviously, mankind himself, mankind dying—then, in the Battle of the Ebro, or now, in Europe, while we do nothing, or if we would, have put ourselves in a position where we *can* do nothing, but talk, while he goes on dying—in another sense he is the Consul too. I claim the chapter proceeds well on its own account while these meanings are revealed without being too much labored. I think the meaning is obvious, intentionally so, almost, in a sense, like a cartoon, and on one plane as oversimplified as journalism, intentionally too, for it is through Hugh's eyes. The story on the top plane is being carried on normally however, and while the local political significance would be clear to anyone who knows Mexico, the wider political and religious significance must be self-evident to anyone. It was the first chapter written in the book; the incident by the roadside, based on a personal experience, was the germ of the book. I feel that some wag not too unlike your reader might tell me at this point that I would do better to reduce the book back to this original germ so that we could all have it printed in O'Brien's *Best Short Stories of 1946*, with luck, instead of as a novel, and against this resourceful notion I can only cite the example of Beethoven, who also was somewhat inclined to overspread himself I seem to think, even though most of his themes are actually so simple they could be played by just rolling an orange down the black keys. The chapter is more apropos now than then, in 1936: then there were no deputies—though I invented them in 1941: now there are; in fact one is living in an apartment downstairs. I don't think it can be cut: but if it must be, it should be done with the same reservations I have made elsewhere. As for the *xopilotes,* the vultures, I should add that they are more than merely cartoon birds: they are real in these parts, in fact one is looking at me as I write, none too pleasantly either: they fly through the whole book and in XI become as it were archetypal, Promethean fowl. Once considered by ornithologists the first of birds, all I can say is that they are more than likely to be the last.

IX

This chapter was originally written in 1937 but then it was through Hugh's eyes. Then it was rewritten as through the Consul's eyes. And now—as it must be for the sake of balance, if you reflect—it is through Yvonne's eyes. Possibly it could have been seen just as well through the bull's eyes, but it reads very well aloud and I think is among other things a successful and colorful entity in itself and musically speaking ought to be an exceedingly good contrast to VIII and X. Readers might disagree about flashbacks here—some think it good, others suspecting a belated attempt to draw character and at that a meretricious one—though I feel many of your *feminine* readers might approve. The flashbacks are not here though either for their own sake, or particularly for the sake of character, which as I said was my last consideration as it was Aristotle's—since there isn't *room*, for one thing. (It was, I think, one of your own writers, and a magnificent one, Sean O'Faolain, who put this heretical notion even further into my headpiece about the comparative unimportance of character anyway. Since he is a wonderful character drawer himself, his words bore weight with me. Were not Hamlet and Laertes, he says, at the final moment, almost the same person? The novel then, he went on to argue, should reform itself by drawing upon its ancient Aeschylean and tragic heritage. There are a thousand writers who can draw adequate characters till all is blue for one who can tell you anything new about hell fire. And I am telling you something new about hell-fire. I see the pitfalls—it can be an easy way out of hard work, an invitation to eccentric word-spinning, and labored phantasmagorias, and subjective inferior masterpieces that on closer investigation turn out not even to be bona fide documents but like my own *Ultramarine*, to be apparently translated with a windmill out of the unoriginal Latvian, but just the same in our Elizabethan days we used to have at least passionate poetic writing about things that will always mean something and not just silly ass style and semicolon technique: and in this sense I am trying to remedy a deficiency, to strike a blow, to fire a shot for you as it were, roughly in the direction, say, of another Renaissance: it will probably go straight through my brain but that is another matter. Possibly too the Renaissance is already in full swing but if so I have heard nothing of this in Canada.) No, the real point of this chapter is Hope, with a capital H, for this note must be struck in order to stress the later downfall. Though even the capacity of the intelligent reader for suspending his disbelief is enormous I didn't intend that this feeling of hope should be experienced by the reader in quite the ordinary way, though he can if he wants to. I intended somehow the feeling of hope per se to transcend even one's interest in the characters. Since these characters are in one way "Things," as that French philosopher of the absurd fellow has it, or even if you believe in them you know perfectly well that they are ditched anyhow, this hope should be, rather, a transcendent, a universal hope. The novel meanwhile is, as it were, teetering between past and future—between despair (the past) and hope—hence these flashbacks (some of them could doubtless be cut slightly but I don't think I could do it). Shall the Consul, once more, go forward and be reborn, as if previously to Guanajuato—is there a chance that he may be, at any rate on the top level?—or shall he sink back into degeneracy and Parián and extinction. He is one aspect of Everyman (just as Yvonne is so to speak the eternal woman, as in *Parsifal*, Kundry, whoever she was, angel and destroyer both). The other aspect of Everyman is of course Hugh who all this time is somewhat preposterously subduing the bull: in short, though with intentional absurdity—the whole book for that matter can be seen as a kind of gruesome and serious absurdity, just like the world in fact—he conquers the animal forces of nature which the Consul later lets loose. The threads of the various themes of the book begin to be drawn together. The close of the chapter, with the Indian carrying his father, is a restatement and universalizing of the theme of humanity struggling on under the eternal tragic weight of the past. But it is also Freudian (man eternally carrying the psychological burden of his father), Sophoclean, Oedipean, what have you, which relates the Indian to the Consul again.

If cuts are made those things and the fact that it is a unity in itself, as usual, should be taken into account. It was finally completed as it stands in 1944.

X

This was first written in '36–'37 and rewritten at various periods up to 1943. This final version was written after my fire, in the summer and fall of 1944, and I dare say this is another obvious candidate for your surgeon's knife. Nothing I wrote after the fire save most of XI has quite the integrity of what I wrote before it but though this chapter seems absolutely interminable, indeed intolerable, when read aloud, I submit it to be a considerable inspiration and one of the best of the lot. The opening train theme is related to Freudian death dreams and also to "A corpse will be transported by express" of the beginning of II and I can't see that it is not extremely thrilling in its gruesome fashion. Passage that follows re the "Virgin for those who have nobody with" ties up with opening pages of Chapter I and were written previously, as was the humorous menu section. I can see valid objections though to the great length of some of the Tlaxcala stuff from the folder: but I was absolutely unable to resist it. I cut and cut as it was, I even sacrificed two good points, namely that Tlaxcala is probably the only capital in the world where black magic is still a working proposition, and that it is also the easiest place in the world to get a divorce in, and then could cut no more: I thought it too good, while the constant repetition of churrigueresque "of an over-loaded style" seemed to be a suggestion that the book was satirizing itself. This Tlaxcala folder part has a quite different effect when read with the eyes, as it will be (I hope)—then you can of course get it much more swiftly; and I had originally thought it would possibly go quicker still if some experiment were made with the typesetting such as the occasional use of black letter for the headings juxtaposed with anything from cursive down to diamond type for the rest and back again according to the reader's interest or the Consul's state of delirium: some simplification of this suggestion might be extremely effective but I do not see how it can be very popular with you and is perhaps a little much anyway. At all events I believe there are strange evocations and explosions here that have merit in themselves even if you are not closely following what is happening, much as, even if you can't make out what Harpo is saying, the sound of the words themselves may be funny. Revelations such as that Pulquería, which is a kind of Mexican pub, is also the name of Raskolnikov's mother should doubtless not be taken too seriously, but the whole Tlaxcala business *does* have an underlying deep seriousness. Tlaxcala, of course, just like Parián, is death: but the Tlaxcalans were Mexico's traitors—here the Consul is giving way to the forces within him that are betraying himself, that indeed have now finally betrayed him, and the general plan of the whole phantasmagoric thing seems to me to be right. Dialogue here brings in the theme of war, which is of course related to the Consul's self-destruction. This chapter was finally completed about a year before atom bombs, etc. But if it does so happen that man is now in danger of finding himself in the evil position of the black magician of old who discovered suddenly that all the elements of the universe were against him, the old Consul might be given credit for pointing out as much in a crazy passage where he even names the elements uranium plutonium, and so forth; undoubtedly it is of no interest as prophecy any more, but I can't say it dates! This little bit is, of course, thematic, if you reflect. At the end of this chapter the volcanoes, which have been getting closer throughout, are used as a symbol of approaching war. In spite of its apparent chaos this chapter has been written very carefully and with attention to every word. It, too, is an entity in itself, and if it must be cut I ask that the cutter see it also as an entity and in its place in the book. Though I suggest it is dramatically extremely powerful, regarded in a certain light, I am more disposed to have this chapter and chapter VI cut than any other, if cuts there must be, and if in the case of this chapter it is merely rendered more dramatic and more powerful.

XI

This was the last chapter I wrote and [it] was completed in late 1944, though I had had its conception in mind for a long time. My object was to pull out here all the stops of Nature, to go to town, as it were, on the natural elemental beauty of the world and the stars, and through the latter to relate the book, as it was related through the wheel at the end of Chapter I, to eternity. Here the wheel appears in another guise, the wheel of the motion of the stars and constellations themselves through the universe. And here again appears the dark wood of Dante, this time as a real wood and not just a cantina or the name of one. Here again too appears the theme of the Day of the Dead, the scene in the cemetery balancing the scene of the mourners at the opening of the book, but this time it has tremendously more human emphasis. The chapter again acts as a double contrast to the lesser horrors of X and the worse ones of XII. On the surface Hugh and Yvonne are simply searching for the Consul, but such a search would have added meaning to anyone who knows anything of the Eleusinian mysteries, and the same esoteric idea of this kind of search also appears in Shakespeare's *Tempest*. Here however all the meanings of the book have to be blended somehow in an unpretentious and organic manner in the interest of the tale itself and this was no mean task, especially as Yvonne had to be killed by a horse in a thunder-storm, and Hugh left holding a guitar in a dark wood, singing drunken songs of revolutionary Spain. Could Thomas Hardy do as much? I suspect your reader, who doesn't even mention the very important fact of Yvonne's death, of not reading this chapter at all—and I take this again as a compliment that he was too interested in what happened to the Consul to do more than glance at it. Be that as it may, I feel passionately that the chapter comes off, partly because I came to believe so absolutely in it. Actually someone being killed by a horse in a thunderstorm is nothing like so unusual an occurrence as you might suppose in these parts, where the paths in the forests are narrow and horses when they do get frightened become more wildly panic-stricken than did the ancestors of their riders who thought the horses Cortez sent against them were supernatural beings. I feel that this chapter like all the rest calls for a sympathetic rereading. It is quite short and I don't think can be cut at all and is *absolutely necessary.* Yvonne's dying visions hark back to her first thoughts at the beginning of Chapter II and also to Chapter IX, but the very end of the chapter has practically stepped outside the bounds of the book altogether. Yvonne imagines herself gathered up and swept up to the stars: a not dissimilar idea appears at the end of one of Julian Green's books, but my notion came obviously from *Faust,* where Marguerite is hauled up to heaven on pulleys, while the devil hauls Faust down to hell. Here Yvonne imagines herself voyaging straight up through the stars to the Pleiades, while the Consul is, simultaneously and incidentally, being cast straight down the abyss. The horse of course is the evil force that the Consul has released. But by this time you know the humbler aspect of this horse. It is no less than the horse you last heard of in X and that first appeared in IV, likewise riderless, during Hugh and Yvonne's ride, outside the pulquería La Sepultura.

(*Note:* Is it too much to say that all these chords, struck and resolved, while no reader can possibly apprehend them on first or even fourth reading, consciously, nevertheless vastly contribute *unconsciously* to·the final weight of the book?)

XII

This chapter was first written at the beginning of 1937 and I think is definitely the best of the lot. I have scarcely changed it since 1940—though I made some slight additions and subtractions in 1942 and substituted the passage "How alike are the groans of love to the groans of the dying," etc., in 1944, for another one not so good. I do think it deserves more than rereading carefully and that it is not only not fair to say it merely recalls *The Lost Weekend* but ridiculous. In any event, I believe, it goes even on the superficial plane a good deal further than that in terms of human agony, and, as his book does, it can widen, I think, one's knowledge of hell. In fact the feeling you are supposed to get from this chapter is an almost Biblical one. Hasn't the guy had enough suffering? Surely we've reached the end now. But no. Apparently it's only just starting. All the strands of the book, political, esoteric, tragic, comical, religious, and what not are here gathered together and in the Farolito in Parián we are standing amid the confusion of tongues of Biblical prophecy. Parián, as I have said, has represented death all along, but this, I would like the reader to feel, is far worse than that. This chapter is the easterly tower, Chapter I being the westerly, at each end of my churrigueresque Mexican cathedral, and all the gargoyles of the latter are repeated with interest in this. While the doleful bells of one echo the doleful bells of the other, just as the hopeless letters of Yvonne the Consul finally finds here answer the hopeless letter of the Consul M. Laruelle reads precisely a year later in Chapter I. Possibly you did not find much to criticize in this chapter but I believe it will immeasurably improve when the whole is taken into account. The slightly ridiculous horse that the Consul releases and which kills Yvonne is of course the destructive force we have heard of before, some fifteen times, I am afraid, in this letter and suggested first in I, and which his own final absorption by the powers of evil releases. There was a half-humorous foreshadowing of his action in VII, in terms of a quotation from Goethe, when Laruelle and he were passed by the horse and its rider, who waved at them and rode off singing. There still remain passages of humor in this chapter and they are necessary because after all we are expected to believe and not believe and then again to believe: the humor is a kind of bridge between the naturalistic and the transcendental and then back to the naturalistic again, though that humour I feel always remains true to the special reality created by the chapter itself. I am so inordinately proud of this chapter that you will be surprised when I say that I think it possible that it too can be cut here and there, though the deadly flat tempo of the beginning seems to me essential and important. I don't think the chapter's final effect should be depressing: I feel you should most definitely get your katharsis, while there is even a hint of redemption for the poor old Consul at the end, who realizes that he is after all part of humanity: and indeed, as I have said before, what profundity and final meaning there is in his fate should be seen also in its universal relationship to the ultimate fate of mankind.

> You like this garden?
> Why is it yours?
> We evict those who destroy!

Reading all this over I am struck among other things such as that writers can always grow fancy and learned about their books and say almost anything at all, as Sherwood Anderson once said in another context, by how much stress is laid on the esoteric element. This does not of course matter two hoots in a hollow if the whole thing is not good art, and to make it such was the whole of my labour. The esoteric business was only a deep-laid anchor anyway but I think I may be forgiven for bringing it in evidence since your reader never saw that the book had any such significance at all. That is right too; I don't care whether the reader does or doesn't see it, but the meaning is there just the same and I might have stressed another element of the book just as well. For they are all involved with each other and their fusion is the book. I believe it more than comes off, on the whole, and because of this belief I am asking you for this re-evaluation of it as it was conceived and upon its own terms. Though I would be grievously disappointed were you not to publish it I can scarcely do otherwise than this, believing as I do that the things that stand in the way of its appreciation are largely superficial. On the other hand I am extremely sensible of the honor you do me by considering it and I do not wish to be vain or stubborn about cuts, even large ones, where a more piercing and maturer eye than mine can see the advantage to the *whole,* the wound being drawn together. I can hope only that I have made some case for a further look at the thing being worth while. Whether it sells or not seems to me either way a risk. But there is something about the destiny of the creation of the book that seems to tell me it just might go *on* selling a very long time. Whether this is the same kind of delusion, at best, that beset another of your authors, Herman Melville, when he wrote such berserk pieces as *Pierre* remains to be seen, but certain it is in that case that no major alterations could have altered its destiny, prevented its plates from being burned, or its author from becoming a customs inspector. I was reading somewhere of that internal basic use of time which makes or breaks a motion picture, and which is the work of the director or cutter. It depends on the speed at which one scene moves and on the amount of footage devoted to another: and it depends also on what sequences are placed between others, because the way movies are made allows you to shift whole sequences about. I believe that the reader whose report you sent me was at least impressed to the extent that he read the book creatively, but too much so, as if he were already a director and cutter combined of some *potential* work, without stopping to ask himself how far it had already been directed and cut, and what internal basic use of time, and so on, was making him as interested as he was.

But what, I repeat, of the reaction of your first reader? There is a certain disparity in tone between your letters of October 15 (received in Canada Nov. 2) and that of 29th Nov. (received here in Mexico Dec. 31) i.e., in your first one you do not mention any criticisms but simply say that your reader was greatly impressed and that it was a long time since you had begun to read a book with such hope and expectation as in reading *Under the Volcano* and seizing, perhaps too hastily, on this, I can deduce only that your first reader was tremendously more sympathetic towards it??? You also said, "I will send you a cable when I have finished reading it so it is possible you may get a cable before receiving this letter." Of course I now see why you found this extremely difficult or impossible but at that time I waited and waited in vain for that cable as you can only wait in winter in the Canadian Wilderness, unless it is in Reckmondwike, Yorks. When therefore I received your letter of 29th Nov. here on New Year's Eve, with your second reader's report, it produced, together with the sense of triumph, one of those barranca-like drops in spirits peculiar to authors and it is to this I must attribute the time I've taken to reply. Talk about turning the accomplishment of many years into an hour glass—but I never heard of it being turned into a mescal glass before, and a small one at that! However after puzzling my brains, I decided that however your own feelings might lean x-ward or y-ward of the crystallization of reaction, you were putting me, as you had every right to do, on the spot. In short, you were saying: "If this book is any damn good as it is he'll explain why!" I was being invited, I thought, if necessary, to do battle. So here is the battle. For taking such a long time about it I sincerely apologize but it has been a difficult letter to write.

I have now received your second letter with a copy of the report and I thank you for this. On your twenty-fifth anniversary I heartily congratulate you. It seems to me that among other things your firm has done more international good than any other. For myself, my first school prize was *The Hairy Ape*, ourselves being allowed to choose our own prizes when they were books, so with your volume of O'Neill's plays containing *The Hairy Ape*, complete with Latin inscription inside, I was therefore presented by the Headmaster on Prize Day. Those O'Neill volumes with the labels, I guess, sent me to sea and everywhere else, but also for the Melville volumes, the O'Brien books, Hugh I'Anson Fausset, and among lesser known things the strange Leo Steni novels, and Calder-Marshall's *About Levy*, for these and hundreds of other things besides I am eternally grateful. When I was looking in '28 or '29 for some work in England by the American Conrad Aiken sure enough I found *Costumes by Eros* published by your firm and this led to a lasting and valuable friendship. (I believe him indisputably one of the world's nine or ten greatest living writers and I mention in passing that ⅔ of his stuff has never had a fair hearing in England and is probably just lying around somewhere. I believe him to be living now at his old English home again at Jeakes House, Rye, Sussex.) All this by the way.

I have spoken of thinking of the book as like some Mexican churrigueresque cathedral: but that is probably just confusing, the more especially since I have been quoting Aristotle at you, and the book has in its odd way a severe classical pattern—you can even see the German submarine officers taking revenge on the Consul in the form of the *sinarquistas* and semi-fascist *brutos* at the end, as I said before. No—please put all that down to the local tropic fever which just recently has been sending my temperature up too far. No. The book should be seen as essentially *trochal,* I repeat, the form of it as a wheel so that, when you get to the end, if you have read carefully, you should want to turn back to the beginning again, where it is not impossible, too, that your eye might alight once more upon Sophocles' *Wonders are many, and none is more wonderful than man*—just to cheer you up. For the book was so designed, counterdesigned and interwelded that it could be read an indefinite number of times and still not have yielded all its meanings or its drama or its poetry: and it is upon this fact that I base my hope in it, and in that hope that, with all its faults, and now with all the redundancies of my letter, I have offered it to you.

Yours very sincerely,
Malcolm Lowry

To Dr. E. B. Woolfan

Cuernavaca, Mexico
[April, 1946]

Dear old Bert:

Margie, I see, is her old ebullient self. What she means by fanfare I don't know. Though I'm sure the darling thinks she knows. What it probably will amount to is a few bad cocktails and some publicity the book and I could do well without. The truth is the terms Reynal and

Hitchcock* have offered in New York were super excellent but today they have suddenly capitulated and the terms have become more so. They too, like Cape, will let me have my every holy word and won't tamper with a line. They also suggest I come to New York at publication time instead of right now. For myself, I have forgotten already completely what the book is about, the double success on the same day being like receiving an atom bomb between Rolando's fissure and the Island of Reil. I don't even walk today which is Good Friday, and though I am quite harmless and cheery you can imagine where I think I am. Since the book will probably kill my English mother stone dead if she ever reads it (which she undoubtedly won't, just like my American brother), I am going to ask you if you will be so good as to send the following cables (a) to my mother (b) to my eldest brother, to whom owing to some genteel limey priority I ought to break the news first. Will reimburse of course, as for others, when get to Los Angeles. All thanks again to my sister Priscilla for her faith in that book and to my American mother for hers and also say I will answer her marvellous and beautiful letter to me when I have dealt with this and to her all love. I hope I can stay with you—or near—when we come to L.A. I am a burden I know, but I could live in the garage or even with Ichabod in his cage, preferably if he is on the bourbon. We would gnatter harmlessly to each other.

Best love,
Malcolm

Evelyn Lowry, Inglewood, Caldy, Cheshire, England. Delay writing due most excellent news regards work dearest love writing. Malcolm Lowry

Stuart Lowry, Corvalley, Upton, Cheshire, England. Book accepted England America simultaneously forgive silence heretofore thanks Donald degree writing love Malcolm Lowry

P.S. These can go what I think they call Night Letter Cable or some such which allows 20 words including address and signature. Thank you again for your trouble.

* American publisher of *Under the Volcano*.

To Mrs. John Stuart Bonner
Dr. and Mrs. E. B. Woolfan

Dollarton, B.C., Canada
June 7, 1946

Dear Mother, Priscilla and Bert:

Just a line to thank you enormously for all your kindness and hospitality toward me.

I know that you went to no end of trouble on my account to make me happy, comfortable and at home, which I was, and though in return my contribution was precisely naught, that did not mean I did not deeply appreciate everything in my sloth-like manner: nor can I think of you all without a deeply heart-warming feeling.

Thank you very much indeed, Bert, for the typewriter. I think it a much better typewriter than Margie's and no, please do not give the shoes you gave me away to anyone else. Instead allow my spirit to walk about the house in them, which has the added advantage that the spirit in question will not fill every nook and cranny with cigarette smoke.

Our house is still here but civilization, so called, is closing in upon us a little too much for our liking: there is another Englishman here who lives up a tree and perhaps he has the right idea, or at any rate a cunning perception of man's place in relation to the world.

I think we might buy an island: live half each year on it and work, and travel the other half.

I daresay you saw in the papers, or *Time* (issue May 13), and were trying kindly to conceal from me, the fact that Curtice Hitchcock* dropped dead of a coronary thrombosis. Apart from all my other feelings I did not know how far this was going to affect matters since he was the one originally mainly interested in the *Volcano:* my agent has assured me that all the editors are equally enthusiastic, but it was an eerie coincidence, remembering the *Volcano's* theme (only against death does man cry out in vain) and eerie too to find his signature on my contract awaiting us here, suggesting that it must have been about the last thing he did.

In San Francisco we saw, hard by the Matson Line sheds, two freighters moored: one named *Cape Friendship,* the other *Hitchcock Victory,* and one may be pardoned if this too gave one something of a start.

* Member of publishing firm, Reynal & Hitchcock.

Well, we are happy here except that I am distressed to think that our preoccupation with my work is interfering with Margie's but I guess it will all come even in the end.

I cannot believe that our manuscripts will not arrive from Mexico eventually, so do not worry about that on our account. Please give our kindest regards to Edna and her husband. And with fondest love to you all,

Malcolm

To A. Ronald Button*

Dollarton, B.C., Canada
June 15, 1946

The following is a statement of what happened to my wife and me in Mexico and wherever possible is verified by dates, names and places.

I am an Englishman, resident in Canada. My wife is American. We left Canada on November 28, 1945, and flew to Los Angeles via United Air Lines, for the purpose of visiting my wife's mother, Mrs. J. S. Bonner, and her sister and brother-in-law, Dr. and Mrs. E. B. Woolfan of 1643 Queens Road, Hollywood, California. From there we proposed to go on to Mexico to spend the winter for purposes of travel and health. At the Mexican consulate in Los Angeles, after making application and waiting the required 24 hours, I obtained a visa on my English passport and we were both given Tourist Cards. These would expire June 10, but we were at that time planning to return to Canada not later than the end of April. I was carrying two passports, my old one, which would expire the end of December but on which I had received my American visa from the American Consulate in Vancouver, B.C., Canada which was good for one year, and my new one, procured from the British Consulate in Los Angeles, on which I was given the Mexican visa. We also carried my birth certificate, my wife's birth certificate proving her American citizenship, our marriage license, and letters from our bank in Vancouver. At the Mexican Consulate in Los Angeles I produced both my passports and pointed out to them that I had been in Mexico from November 1936 to July 1938. I was not at all sure that I, being English, did not require to

* A California attorney.

go through even further formalities: but I was assured that all regulations had been complied with and that all was satisfactory.

After visiting my wife's family we departed by American Airlines and arrived in Mexico City on approximately December 12, 1945. A few days later we left for Cuernavaca, Morelos, where we rented an apartment at 24 Calle de Humboldt, the proprietor of which is Señora María Luisa Blanco de Arriola. We lived in this apartment in Cuernavaca with the exception of a few trips to Oaxaca, Puebla, Tlaxcala, etc.

Certain explanations are necessary at this point. I had written a novel set in Mexico called *Under the Volcano* and had received a virtual acceptance of it (later verified) by my publishers, Jonathan Cape, London. A subsidiary reason for voting for the trip was that it would be a possible opportunity to correct, if necessary, some of the idiomatic Spanish and possibly make a few notes for a preface to the book of a friendly nature to Mexico. Not that the book should be construed as unfriendly: to the contrary. On the other hand I felt it might be misunderstood in Mexico, since many shades of opinion are reflected in it, which is not surprising since that country is used as an analogue of the world itself. But there is no political resolution, other, that is to say, than a democratic one: in fact no resolution at all unless it is, perhaps, a moral. On our Tourist Cards we gave our occupations as writers (escritores) but we entered as tourists and remained as tourists with no intention of "working" in Mexico, or taking any money from Mexico for any work done while there, and in fact we did no work while there with the exception of a few notes.

On Friday the 8th of March, after several happy months, we left Cuernavaca for another brief trip, stopping in Taxco and Iguala, and arrived in Acapulco on Sunday the 10th of March, 1946. We stayed at the Hotel Quinta Eugenia at Caleta Beach. On the following Thursday, March 14, two men from the Office of Migración came to the hotel and asked to see our papers. It should be pointed out that Acapulco is a port of entry and as a consequence all names of tourists are sent into this office as a matter of course. My wife had packed our bags while I was attending to reservations, etc., and since we only intended to be away a week at most and she was afraid of theft (we had had many things stolen) she unfortunately left our papers in the apartment in Cuernavaca. Needless to say I knew by experience how important it is to have one's papers with one when travelling in a foreign country. But a new policy of sympathetic attitude toward tourists that pertained in the state of Morelos (superficially at least) did not incline one to take a serious view of our omission. We had never been once asked for our papers since checking in at the airport in Mexico City. I believe it is not, by the way, illegal not to have your papers with you so long as you have them at your place of residence. We therefore explained to the men from the Migración where our papers were and asked them what the trouble was. They announced that we would have to remain in Acapulco, at that hotel, until they checked on our Tourist Cards with Mexico City and said they would send a wire that day regarding this. They also told me that they had an unpaid fine against me to the amount of 50 pesos* for having overstayed my leave in 1938 and further, because they had pursued this fine until 1943, apparently not aware I had left the country in July 1938, that they had in their files a letter saying that I was not allowed to enter Mexico without permission of the Chief of Migración. This latter injunction I knew nothing about whatsoever. As to the 50-peso fine for having overstayed my leave, I must now make a further statement regarding that.

In November of 1936 I had originally entered Mexico through Acapulco, arriving by boat, and had returned to Acapulco again in the early spring of 1938. Since I had then a "rentista's" status I had had already further extensions on my original visa or card or whatever but at this time I required a further extension and had been wrongly advised, so far as I can recall, that I could get it there in Acapulco, since that had been my original port of entry; and I was also planning to leave from here by the Panama Pacific line. I applied for this extension and was then told, after many delays, that it was necessary to go to Mexico City to procure it. Very possibly there were other factors that I have forgotten: I have a vague recollection that [the Panama Pacific] suddenly stopped running their ships at a time when I could have left Mexico within the period then allotted me. Either that or my money was delayed in arriving through the American Express in New York. At all events I went to Mexico City, in company with the then Chief of Migración in Acapulco, whose fare I paid to and probably from Mexico City, and also his hotel room at the Biltmore Hotel, and various expenses. I had by now overstayed my leave by, I think, not more than a few days. I cannot, however, swear to this. In Mexico City I went with this Chief of Migración, a man by the name of Guyou (I cannot recall the exact spelling) to the main office of Migración on Bucarelli St. and was given, to the best of my knowledge,

* At the time, about $10.00.

a further extension of six months. At any rate I certainly left Mexico well within the new time given me with no further difficulty that I can remember over my papers at any point, though I had other difficulties, chiefly personal. My first wife had returned to America in December 1937 and I had been, and still was, to some extent, very ill, the consequence of dysentery, malaria and rheumatic fever. Also there had been, as I said, some confusion about my income arriving, due to my changes of address or other misunderstanding, and as a result I had become somewhat in debt. My parents having become anxious about my health put a lawyer at my disposal and my income was paid through him, and before I left Mexico any and all debts were paid in full. I am certain that if any fine was imposed it was also paid at that time—indeed it *must* have been or I should certainly not have been allowed to leave. I left Mexico in July 1938 and was admitted to America at Nogales. I was not aware, I repeat, of any unpaid fine nor of any such letter from the Chief of Migración. Utterly oblivious that there might be anything held against me I applied for my visa and Tourist Card to enter Mexico in 1946 in good faith, and was given them by the Mexican Consulate in Los Angeles as stated.

To return to Acapulco and my statement of what happened there in March 1946: my wife, who was still not in the best of health, and I, went every day into the office of Migración and waited some hours but no word from Mexico City was forthcoming. Meantime I was racking my brains to discover if anything else could possibly have caused this injunction against me and I remembered this: in 1937 my first wife and I had put up a bond as "rentistas." This had been mainly arranged through her and a friend and when she left in 1937 she took the papers concerning this bond with her. So far as I know I was still within the time limit of this bond when in Acapulco in 1938 and do not believe I could have got an extension if the bond had run out. But late in 1939, or early in 1940, when I was in Canada, I received word through my father's lawyer that the man who had underwritten this bond had been intimidated by the authorities for a whole year on the false grounds that I had not left the country at all. To straighten up this matter I immediately went to the acting Mexican Consul here in Vancouver, produced proof that I had indeed left in July 1938 and this proof was forwarded to the necessary authorities so that they would cease intimidating this man, whose name I cannot now recall. I am certain also that if any compensation was due him it was paid, via funds at my disposal in America, since I believe it was then impossible to send funds out of this country.

Anxious to discover the precise truth with a view to remedying matters I now asked the Sub-Chief of Migración in Acapulco to show my wife and me what was against me in his file and he was generous enough to do this. He only gave us a short while to look and the Spanish was too complicated to take in at a glance. I ascertained however that there was nothing about any bond whatsoever and that the file was mainly concerned with the government's unsuccessful attempt to recover this 50-peso fine. Guyou however was mentioned, as was my trip to Mexico City with him. I could not help noting that the excuse he had given for my not having paid the fine, which of course I *had* paid, was that I was too *ebriadad* to do business with.

I ascertained two facts of importance however from this file. First that the edict forbidding me to reenter the country without special permission was filed about two months after I had left it, in September 1938, which explained why there was nothing about the bond. For they could scarcely forbid me to reenter the country without having prior knowledge of my having left it, and if they possessed this knowledge, what right had they to persecute the underwriter of my bond for a year on the grounds that I was still in Mexico? The second fact was that my date of entry into Mexico was wrongly given as September 1936. Actually it was November 1936: apparently an innocent mistake, this could nevertheless make it appear I had overstayed my leave that much longer, for here were two months extra credited to me when I had never been in the country at all. I have gone into all this as fully as possible because this was the only time I was ever allowed a glimpse of what purported to be held against me. When the British Consulate inquired, they were never informed but were merely told somewhat vaguely that "there had been some trouble." Later, when my wife and I were in Mexico City with an interpreter and witness we made every effort, as will be seen, to discover the reason for the treatment we received, but by this time they had emphatically denied that they had anything against me at all.

I now observed something else. The Sub-Chief of Migración showed me the telegram he had sent to Mexico City explaining that we did not have our Tourist Cards with us, etc., and asking for instructions. In this telegram he had given the name of my *first* wife as being here with me in Acapulco, although we had repeatedly explained the situation to him. My wife had given him her name, stated that she was *not* with me in Mexico in 1938, had never been in Mexico at all before, and that she was, as a matter of fact, in Los Angeles in 1938 and completely unaware of my existence. He replied that he had looked in my old file and found out what my wife's name was and we needn't try to tell him it was something else. In the end I believe we convinced him of the truth. He was himself going to Mexico City the following day and he stated that he would go himself and correct this error. I do not know whether this mistake on the part of the Sub-Chief of Migración in Acapulco was ever cleared up or not, despite repeated efforts, for later on, in Mexico City, if not Sr. Corunna, someone in his office still seemed under the impression that my present wife was indeed my first wife who had entered under a false name for some obscure purpose of her own, and for all I know nothing ever really convinced them to the contrary.

On Wednesday, March 20, 1946, a man from the Oficina Federal de Hacienda came to our hotel. He refused to come into our room but stood on the porch, having called the manager and several of the employees of the hotel also, he threatened us, using abusive terms in a loud voice, demanding instant payment of the same 50-peso fine. It was very difficult to understand him as he became quite incoherent in the end, but we finally persuaded him to meet us that afternoon at 4 o'clock in the office of the Department of Turista, where there would be a man who would interpret and act as witness for us. We therefore met at this office, where a man who is second in command at the office, Sr. Obregon, interpreted for us and said that unless the fine was paid at once I would be taken to jail. It must be repeated that our papers and money were in Cuernavaca; we had only taken a limited amount with us for the trip and had already paid for telegrams, long distance telephone calls, et al to Mexico City in an effort to expedite the matter; our hotel bill was running on in Acapulco and our rent was now due in Cuernavaca, and all this we had explained fully without the slightest sympathy toward our plight being forthcoming. They merely said they would doubtless hear from Mexico City tomorrow, or "Mexico City is very slow." The man from the Hacienda said finally that he would give me until Saturday morning to pay the fine and would take my watch (or something else) as security. Sr. Obregon, who was most kind throughout, therefore said that if such procedure was necessary he would himself keep the watch as security and this he did. The Chief of the Department of Turista had meantime telephoned the Department of Migración and was, at our request, inquiring about a long distance call purported to have been put through at our expense that day to Mexico City regarding our case. He reported that they had been told in Mexico City that they had no knowledge of the case at all and knew nothing about me whatsoever, but that still they would not release us. I protested that since there was absolutely nothing against my wife it was wrong to hold her and she went on to add that she should be allowed to go to Cuernavaca and get our papers and money, and that if she was not allowed to go she or I would call the American Consul long distance to Mexico City and apply for aid. This was relayed by phone and the Chief of Turista told us that the Chief of Migración had now said that my wife would be allowed to go to Cuernavaca but that she must leave at once and be back by Saturday. It was impossible at such short notice to get reservations and she was forced to leave on a second-class bus to make a night trip alone across Mexico. I will not go into the obvious dangers of such a trip. She arrived in Cuernavaca at 5 A.M., got our papers and money and proceeded to Mexico City where she appealed to the British Consulate. She went to the British Consulate since I am, as stated, an Englishman and it was I and the 50-peso fine, etc., against me that was, or seemed to be, the trouble. Moreover as a British subject herself by marriage she was entitled to his protection. She was unable to see the Consul General but presented our case to Mr. Percival Hughes, the Vice Consul. He looked through our papers carefully, said that they were in perfect order, was most sympathetic, made notes of the numbers of our Tourist Cards, my passport, all dates concerning the matter, etc. etc. She told him of the fine and all that she knew concerning the reason for it and he said that if she would stay over night in Mexico City he would go with her the following morning to the Department of Migración and straighten the whole matter out. The following morning, Friday, March 22, he informed her that the Consul General had ordered her to return to Acapulco and pay the fine there. He said that they would go, however, to the Migración office that morning and see that we were released at once. She returned to Acapulco by bus and on Saturday morning we went, together with a Mr. W. Hudson, who acted as interpreter and witness, to the Oficina Federal de Hacienda. There we paid the fine. We saw the man who had come to our hotel to demand payment and the Chief of Hacienda. We asked for the return of my watch and said that we objected to the manner in which this man had acted at our hotel as being totally unnecessary and embarrassing. He then denied threatening me with jail or having taken the watch. We asked that Sr. Obregon be sent for which was done. He arrived, very graciously returned my watch, and entirely corroborated our statement as to threats, etc. The Chief of Hacienda then informed us that their man had no right to make threats or to take the watch, that all he was empowered to do was quietly to present me with a bill. He further ordered an apology, said that the Constitution of Mexico had been breached by this action and that we could make a complaint if we wished and that we had two witnesses. This we declined to do out of a reciprocal courtesy to the courtesy which was being shown us at this point by the Office of Hacienda. Mr. Hudson, who had also been with us on one occasion to the Oficina of Migración and had seen my file there, said that this was a mistake made in their own office and not my fault. The Chief of Hacienda, who was very courteous throughout this interview, agreed, while Sr. Obregon expressed himself as dubious whether a fine of 50 pesos could be pursued for as long as 8 years anyway and sportingly promised to try and get it back for us if he could.

We then took the receipt for the fine, our papers, and went with Mr. Hudson to the Office of Migración, showed our papers and the receipt and asked if we were now free to leave. They said we could not leave until they heard from Mexico City. The British Vice Consul had promised to wire us at once if anything was wrong at his end: he did not wire us. He had also instructed us, if we were not immediately released upon my wife's return from Mexico City, to wire him. We did so and received no reply.

They kept us at Acapulco, where we were forced to come every day to the Office of Migración, down into the town of Acapulco where the heat is extreme, and wait for hours, frequently in an empty office.

Meanwhile however the Sub-Chief of Migración had returned from Mexico City and when we saw him delivered himself as follows: that in Mexico City they had, unfortunately, disclaimed any knowledge of receiving his wire, which might account for some of the delay. He said, however, that they had now found my file there, in which was a record of another fine, this time for 100 pesos, which had been paid. He also said that there was a photograph of me there with a beard. This was true, I had grown one for fun in 1937, and it was on the duplicate of my card or whatever as a "rentista." When I asked him if we could go now, he said that he had asked the Secretary of Migración there if he would not let us go and the Secretary had said, "No, don't do that." When I asked him if there was anything further on the file, real or imaginary, which could account for this treatment he said, "I don't know." But he implied that the beard was a bad thing in itself, so bad indeed that my wife, in spite of her papers being in perfect order, in spite of there being nothing whatever against her, and her being an American citizen, could not now go either. So we remained in Acapulco.

[98]

A statement of this kind is not the place to describe the feelings with which we received the news that Mexico City had disclaimed all knowledge of receiving the wire. But we naturally wondered if it had not been sent very much later than stated, while we were kept waiting in the interim; just as we wondered if the phone call to Mexico City by the Department of Migración had ever been put through at all.

So we waited in Acapulco.

About 10 days after my wife's return from Mexico City we received a letter from the British Consul General, Mr. Rogers, saying that the Mexican authorities had decided to deport me and asking if my papers were in order to return to America, although my wife had shown these papers at the British Consulate to the Vice Consul, Mr. Hughes, who had written all this down, as before stated. We telephoned the Consulate long distance and spoke with Mr. Hughes who could give absolutely no reason for this action by the Mexican authorities and said they did not know why it was being done. He said he would talk to them further and wire me. This he did not do and I called him again some days later. He then said that I was not to be deported but might be asked to leave the country, but again could not say why as they had given him no reason. Finally, on Thursday, April 4th, the Office of Migración in Acapulco, who themselves disclaimed all knowledge of this deportation order, said they had themselves decided we had been there too long and that they would give us a letter on the following day which would allow us to go, but made it obligatory that we appear at the office of Migración in Mexico City on Monday, April 8th. The following day, 22 days after they first came to the hotel, they gave us this letter permitting us to leave.

We went to our apartment in Cuernavaca (where I promptly received the almost insane news that the book set there in Mexico, for which I was proposing to write a friendly preface, had been accepted simultaneously in both England and America) and on Monday morning went to Mexico City with an interpreter, Sr. Eduardo Ford, owner and proprietor of the restaurant "Bahia," 12 Jardín Morelos, Cuernavaca, Mexico. We were kept waiting in the office until it was too late to accomplish anything, and were told to return in a few days.

It should be said that it is about fifty miles from Cuernavaca to Mexico City but this gives no idea of the character of the trip. Though it only takes two or two and a half hours it is necessary to climb to an altitude of over 10,000 feet and one frequently arrives deafened. The climate likewise is completely different: one leaves Cuernavaca in tropical heat and you are likely at this time of year to run into a snow storm in the mountains: beautiful in itself, such a journey, endlessly repeated under such conditions becomes a nightmare, especially since it is difficult to make reservations either by car or bus, both are prone to break down on the way, and from all this my wife's health especially began to suffer. Despite this we managed to keep every appointment during the following four weeks punctually, yet we never waited less than three hours and usually four or five hours. We are far from wealthy people; had budgeted our vacation very carefully, and we were put to what was for us near fatal expense to make these frequent trips for ourselves and often an interpreter. For though we may specify only what happened during certain visits, it should be borne in mind that there were many more visits when despite promises nothing happened at all and we were kept waiting in a vacuum: we calculated that we travelled well over a thousand miles during those four weeks simply between Cuernavaca and Mexico City and probably it was more like twelve hundred.

To resume: we returned on Friday, April 12, and were informed that our case had been sent to the Office of Inspection. We waited there the usual hours, finally saw an inspector whose name I do not know but who was in charge of our case and whom I shall have reason to refer to many times more, simply as the inspector. He took all our papers (including the receipt for the fine which was incidentally never returned to us) and our identification and consulted with the Chief of the Office of Inspección, one Sr. Corunna. The fine had been paid and our papers were in order. But the inspector now noted that on our Tourist Cards we had given our occupation as writers. He then said that as writers we should not have been allowed to enter Mexico at all as tourists and should have had a working permit or some other form of passport and asked if we would like immigration papers. Both ourselves and our interpreter were astounded at this statement. Our interpreter remarked that there were thousands of writers, singers, and painters busily painting pictures all over Mexico, and inquired if all of them had entered the country on immigration or working papers, and if it was against the law for any artists to come to Mexico for a vacation. The inspector was himself somewhat taken aback but recovering himself stated that while it was true that they did not have immigration or working papers that actually they should have. Since we ourselves personally knew three artists who, on Tourist Cards only, were painting in Mexico and one of whom had been giving lessons to Mexicans and taking money for these lessons, besides writers who had certainly been writing articles for magazines published in Mexico, such as *Modern Mexico,* etc., and none of these people had been molested by the Government in any way, we were somewhat puzzled. We protested against what appeared to us to be discrimination, saying that if this were so it was not our fault but that of the Mexican Consulate in Los Angeles, but to no avail. I said that we were not working in Mexico, had taken no money in Mexico for any work done in Mexico nor had any intention of doing so; that we had, being writers, naturally taken some notes, mostly in the form of simply a day-to-day journal, or of the "jot it down" variety, possibly to be transformed later into a short story or some travel articles my wife had thought of writing after our return to Canada, and so on. Whether or not I said anything about having taken notes for my proposed preface I don't remember. The inspector admitted that the taking of such notes could hardly be called "working" in Mexico. Nevertheless, he insisted that we *were* working, and demanded that we put up a bond of 500 pesos apiece and promise not to do any *more* work while we were in Mexico. We insisted that we had not done any work per se. He said that the bond would be necessary however and gave us until Monday morning to produce the cash or the bond. This struck me as just possibly poetic justice in my case but our interpreter, Sr. Ford, was highly indignant and said that the inspector had just remarked to him that actually, of course, this was more or less extra-official, and further that the inspector said that if I had given the Chief of Migración in Acapulco 50 pesos to put in his pocket that the whole thing would have been settled there and that the head office would never have heard of it. And this I was to hear repeated many times: that the defection was the original defection of my failing to pay the "mordida." The British Vice Consul himself said this to me openly later on in this same office and further advised me that it would be as well to offer the inspector 100 pesos or so, and in fact it was impossible to sit in that office as long as we did without witnessing with one's own eyes the truth of this.

But somewhere, during the foregoing conversation, we did something in all innocence that doubtless complicated matters still further. In the belief that the inspector doubted that we were who and what we said we were, or perhaps because by this time we were beginning to doubt our own identity, I showed him a copy of my wife's novel, (*The Shapes That Creep*, Scribner's, published January 14 of this year) my contract from Jonathan Cape of London, and also the telegram from Reynal and Hitchcock of New York re the acceptance of my book. The book had been finished in 1944 in Canada.

However, on this day, April 12, the inspector said to our interpreter, Sr. Ford, that if we put up this bond or the same amount of cash by Monday morning that our papers would be returned and that we would be free to stay in Mexico without any further molestation until the expiration of our Tourist Cards which would be on June 10th.

It is, of course, necessary to obtain someone with property to underwrite such a bond and this was difficult to do on such short notice because I knew no one in Mexico City who could do this and furthermore the following week was Holy Week and on Monday all bonding companies would be closed. However, our witness and interpreter, Sr. Ford, was highly indignant at the procedure and offered (in spite of the fact that he was fully informed by myself of my previous error—if error it was—over just such a matter) to underwrite the bond himself, giving as security his own restaurant in Cuernavaca. He managed to obtain this bond for us and on the following Monday morning we presented it and asked for our papers. We were taken in to see the Chief of the department, Sr. Corunna, who was very insulting to my wife, ordered her out of his office, and refused to give us our papers. We had said that we wished to leave Mexico as soon as possible and Corunna, whose technique is to shout, demanded the date of our leaving. I explained that we wished to fly as I did not feel the long train trip was good for my wife, and since Mexico was the port of exit when flying we could not possibly obtain our ticket without our papers. He then asked for the approximate date of our leaving and I told him as soon as we could possibly get reservations on the return of our papers. Calming down slightly he then told us to return again, as nearly as I can recall, about a week later when we would be given our papers, which were now in order. He assured us finally that all was well, that there was nothing to be concerned about, that it was a matter of no importance.

It may well be asked at this point why I did not appeal to the British Consulate again for help, or my wife did not go to her American Consul, although she is, as I have said, by virtue of marriage to myself also a British subject and equally has a right to apply to the British Consulate. She did not go to the American Consul because it was my status that had precipitated the situation and she had only been drawn into it on that account and the American Consul could do nothing for me, and therefore nothing, we thought, would be achieved by this action. I did not appeal again to the British Consulate, save on one more occasion, because by this time I had lost faith in their ability, or willingness, to assist me. And finally, because we were continually assured, by everyone in the Office of Inspection, despite the mental cruelty of this treatment, and right up to the very last moment, that our papers were in order, that they had absolutely nothing against us, and that there was nothing at all to worry about, and the various delays were simply a matter of governmental red tape and slowness.

The day previous to our next appointment with Sr. Corunna, we had Sr. Ford telephone him long distance from Cuernavaca. Sr. Ford talked with Corunna, who assured him that our papers were there, perfectly in order, and that we could now come and get them any time we wished. Therefore on or about April 23 we went to Mexico City to get our papers, intending immediately upon receipt of them to make application for airplane reservations. Meantime I had wired my bank in Canada to send money to the Banco Nacional de Mexico in Cuernavaca. By this time we were running short of cash, because of all these extra expenses, but it was impossible to obtain either the money from the bank or the money from my agent at the telegraph office, as I was without any identification whatsoever, the Government having it all, so I was therefore also unable to buy tickets to leave the country, although I had several hundred dollars between the bank and the telegraph office. Sr. Corunna once more refused to give us our papers, which, however, he repeated, were now in perfect order, and there was absolutely nothing for us to worry about. At that point Mr. Hughes, the British Vice Consul, happened to come into the office on some other business and, since he was there, I did appeal to him again to try and get me some part of my papers, some identification I could present in order to get my money, since the telegraph office would send the money back to New York if I did not claim it within a day or two more. Mr. Hughes then spoke to Sr. Corunna on our behalf and Corunna assured him that everything was all right, that the only reason we were not given our papers that day was because they had once more been sent back to the Office of Migración where they were on the desk of a man who was not in his office that particular day. He said that if we would return on Friday he would have the papers for us and that there was no further question or delay. We therefore made a definite appointment for Friday morning at 11:30 A.M., at which Mr. Hughes also volunteered to be present. Mr. Hughes further stated to us on that morning that it was he himself who had procured our release from Acapulco on the morning of Friday, April 9th, from the Office of Migración in Mexico City and had seen the telegram which had been sent. It seemed rather odd to us that it had been on Thursday, April 8th, that the Office of Migración in Acapulco had said that they themselves were letting us go, but we made no great issue of this. Mr. Hughes further said that a week after they had first ordered my wife to return to Acapulco (on the promise that he or the Consul General would go that morning to the Migración) they had sent the office boy over who returned with the report that I was to be deported. This trouble shooter, it will be shown, at least told part of the truth.

On Friday, April 26th, therefore, we returned once more to Mexico City to keep our appointment with Mr. Hughes and Sr. Corunna. When we arrived, on time, after a journey of more than usual difficulty during which our transportation twice broke down and which had required four cars to get us there, Mr. Hughes was not there and my wife telephoned him while I sought an opportunity to speak again to Sr. Corunna. Mr. Hughes explained to my wife that he had been too busy at the Consulate to keep his appointment with Sr. Corunna [but he had called Corunna and had learned] that our papers were still on the desk in the department of Migración, and that the man who had them was once more not in his office, or rather was there, but had simply made up his mind not to do any more work that day. Mr. Hughes had reiterated our plight, the necessity for identification, etc., but Sr. Corunna had replied that he was unable to give us anything. My wife appealed to Mr. Hughes to make some further effort to help us, or to find out what, if anything, was wrong, but he replied that he could do no more for us at all.

I then spoke to Sr. Corunna myself and was told to return the following morning. We returned once more to Mexico City the following morning and again I spoke with Sr. Corunna. After some long discussion during which he repeatedly shouted at me as usual in an insulting manner—I kept my wife out of the conversations so far as possible because of his savagely hysterical method of conducting them— he went, in the end, to the Office of Migración and procured my old, cancelled passport for me. He further told me to come once more to Mexico City on the following Tuesday, April 30th, when the man who had our papers would be there without fail and they would then definitely be returned to us. However he once more demanded when we intended to leave, and I once more explained that we could not make reservations without these papers or buy tickets until I could get my money.

We returned to Cuernavaca and I received the money from the telegraph office that Saturday afternoon, just in time, as they were about to return it to New York. On Monday morning I went to the bank and received the money I had wired for to my Canadian bank.

On Tuesday morning we went once more to Mexico City and to the Office of Inspection. The inspector then informed us that it was necessary for us to come with him and have some photographs taken for our immigration papers. I think at this point my wife said, very understandably, that she didn't want immigration papers but only wanted to leave Mexico, and if I did not say it myself it was only because I was engaged in keeping the temper which I knew it was their prime object for me to lose. I asked to be allowed to speak to Sr. Corunna, saying that he had promised to give us back our papers without fail that morning. This was refused. I then inquired why they suddenly had decided to change our papers and my wife asked to be allowed to go to the Department of Turista to obtain an interpreter who would explain more fully, since the inspector was difficult to understand, our Spanish not fluent, when he became excited. This was also refused and we were taken across the street where photographs were made under the assurance that these photographs were for immigration papers. In them I look a criminal and my wife (the inspector rudely snatched off her hat at the moment they were taking the photograph and her hair was disarranged) like a madwoman. Anyone seeing these photographs would wonder not that we were to be deported but that such people could be at large at all, which I take it is the impression such pictures are designed to give. On the other hand, the strain was beginning to tell. Meantime we had been told that these photographs would be ready at 2 o'clock and that we must wait in the Office of Inspection until that hour. We were refused permission to go to lunch, or even to go out for a cup of coffee—though I explained that as usual we had had to leave Cuernavaca very early in the morning and my wife was fatigued—or, in fact, to leave the office for any reason whatsoever, being assured, continually, however, that Sr. Corunna would see me in a moment and that everything was quite in order. At 2 o'clock my wife went and got the photographs, which the inspector regarded as being uproariously ridiculous and laughed loudly and long. At 2:30 the inspector suddenly informed us, after Sr. Corunna had left and the office was just closing for the day, that it would be necessary for us to be at this office again on the morning of May 2 (May 1 being a holiday) at 12 noon, with all our luggage.

We protested that we could not understand the reason for this. We wished to remain in Cuernavaca, where we had paid the rent of our apartment, until leaving Mexico and did not wish to go to the further expense of living in Mexico City at an hotel. Also we did not understand why, after being assured, and the Consul likewise assured, that all our papers were in order, that there was nothing whatsoever against us, after we had put up the bond, etc. etc., why, we repeated, we were thus abruptly commanded to bring our luggage to Mexico City. The inspector became very angry and seized my arm, said that if I did not understand I should come with him at once to jail. He further abused us for not living in Mexico City. When I explained hopelessly that we loved Cuernavaca and wished to make the most of living there until our departure, he demanded to know the name of the hotel we were living at in Mexico City. He further said that if we were not in the office on May 2, at 12 noon, with our luggage, he could come to Cuernavaca and put us under arrest. The office was then closed, everyone had gone, there was nothing we could do that day. Once more therefore we returned to Cuernavaca. That evening we saw Sr. Ford, who informed us that the bonding company, Central de Fianzas, S.A. Motolinia 20, Mexico City, had telephoned him long distance that afternoon to say that the Government had cashed in our bond, and required him, Sr. Ford, to immediately make good the 1000 pesos or be jailed and his business confiscated. They had obviously cashed in this bond while keeping us waiting in the office insisting to us meanwhile that everything was quite all right. The following morning, May 1, Sr. Ford received a telegram from the bonding company verifying the fact that the Government had cashed the bond the previous day. We have this telegram in our possession and I now quote it: *Hoy hizo efectivas secretarias Gobernación fianzas esponsos Lowry. Suplicamosle remitirnos inmediatamente un mil pesos importe garantías objeto no perjudicar interés. Central de Fianzas, S.A.* We therefore paid Sr. Ford the 1000 pesos and we have his receipt for the money.

On the following morning, Thursday May 2, we left Cuernavaca with our luggage in company with Sr. Ford, who was going to the bonding company to pay them the 1000 pesos, and went to Mexico City. We arrived 2 hours ahead of time in the hope of finding out what the difficulty was and making some last effort to present our case to the authorities in its proper light. Also another Mexican citizen, sympathetic with our case and a man of some influence, had offered to meet us there at 10 A.M. and act as interpreter and witness for us. We waited for him until 10:45 but he did not arrive. We then went into the Department of Turista, where we had left our luggage for the time being, and saw Sr. Buelna, the chief of that department. The time was short, as we had to appear in the Office of Inspección with the luggage at 12 noon, but we explained our case and asked for help. At first he stated that he was unable to do anything at all since it was not in his department. However there were in his office at the time some American tourists who could not help hearing and in the end he kindly telephoned to someone in the office of the Sub-Secretario of the Interior and arranged for us to see the Sub-Secretario, Dr. Pérez-Martínez, in a few minutes, when he would be finished with his conference with the Secretario. Dr. Martínez would, he said, at least give us a hearing. We went to the office of the Sub-Secretario, our names were sent in, we said the matter was urgent in the extreme, and waited over three quarters of an hour. By now it was nearly 12 o'clock and the inspector came into the office and ordered us down to the Office of Inspección. We explained that we were waiting to put our case before the Sub-Secretario, since we had been informed that he was the final authority in such matters. The inspector again ordered us to come at once to the other office, but still hoping for a hearing on our case we waited.

My wife, while I remained there still in hopes of obtaining a hearing at the last moment, then went back to see Sr. Buelna to ask at least that we be given an interpreter and witness. Sr. Buelna at first replied that this was impossible, but in the end was kind enough to provide us with one. In company with this witness we went to the Office of Inspección. Here we waited, and asked to see Sr. Corunna. We were informed that Sr. Corunna had his orders from the Sub-Secretario regarding ourselves and that it would be impossible for us to see him. We tried once more to find out why we were being treated in this extraordinary manner and at this the inspector became very angry and said that we had "said bad things about Mexico." This we denied—it could be called true only in the sense that we were objecting to this treatment now—stating as we had many times before that we loved Mexico and her people, which was so and still, despite this experience, is so, and that we still wished to discover what was wrong, still wished a fair hearing, as we felt sure that there must be some final misunderstanding worse than all the others regarding our case. We were then told that we must accompany the inspector to 113 Bucarelli, where we would be given our papers and allowed to go. Since we knew that this was (as it were) a jail and not a government office we protested. We asked for the British Consul. My wife asked for the American Consul. This was denied. We were told again that we were merely going to this 113 Bucarelli to get our papers, and were taken, under our protests, to this place. Once inside, we were forced to sign our names in a register. We once more protested and demanded to see our Consuls, asking what their intentions were regarding ourselves, if they meant to deport us, and if so, why? The inspector denied emphatically that we were to be deported. We then asked the interpreter, who was visibly wilting, to please telephone our Consul immediately, and he replied that he would inform Sr. Buelna of the situation.

My wife and I were then taken into a small barred room where there were already two other men in bed and no lavatory facilities for my wife, there being only one inordinately filthy lavatory for all four of us, which had no door and opened directly off the room where we were kept. We were informed that we were being held incommunicado, and locked in. The Chief of this place, however, was extremely courteous and was distressed by the lack of privacy for my wife. He also sent out for some food for us, at our expense naturally, saying that we could not possibly eat the prison food. This was true: there was no prison food. Or if so they were not going to provide us with any free. Everyone here was kind and sympathetic, and the Chief finally opened up another sort of room for us beyond the first one and brought us his own blanket, which, he explained, was clean. It should be mentioned however that our luggage had meantime been brought to this place and deposited in an outer room. Later we discovered that our wardrobe trunk had been broken open and half of my wife's clothes were missing and also our camera. This theft can only have taken place at the Turista office or at 113 Bucarelli as there was no other opportunity. We had had nothing to eat all day and our food did not arrive until afternoon, simultaneously with the inspector. He gave us only five minutes to eat and then ordered us into a taxi in which we were taken to the railroad station and immediately put aboard the train. All further protestations or demands to see our Consuls were futile. Escape was impossible: the inspector was armed.

Our train was a day coach with no berths and my wife and I were forced to sit up all that night and to stay within sight of the inspector every minute. We both inquired of him several times the reason for this treatment. We asked if we were being deported and he replied definitely, no. He stated that his orders were to take us to Nuevo Laredo and there to give us our papers and allow us to cross the border to America alone and unmolested. We asked him why the bond had been cashed and he insisted that it had not been cashed. We then showed him the telegram proving that it had been cashed and he then said he had no knowledge of it at all. He, of course, had the tickets. He sat where he could watch our every movement, but apart from the sense of shame and embarrassment it caused, he did not actively molest or persecute us and indeed allowed us to eat our meals in the dining car by ourselves. The stewards, conductor and train men were however left in no doubt as to our status and we were by and large made to feel like criminals.

When the train arrived in Nuevo Laredo it was after midnight of the second night: there was a severe thunderstorm and all the lights in the train had gone out. We then asked him for our papers, which he had promised, and with that he began throwing our luggage out of the window of the train and as the train began to pull out (it was a very brief stop) ordered us to get out, and in fact my wife, who had got off on the wrong side of the train had to cross back through the train while it was moving, narrowly escaping a serious accident.

We then proceeded in a taxi, with our luggage, to the Mexican Immigration office, situated directly at the edge of the bridge across the Rio Grande River. There we waited again, watching the lights of Laredo on the American side of the bridge, while the inspector conferred with a clerk whom he had ordered to write something on a typewriter. It was now about 2 o'clock in the morning. Presently this document which the clerk had been typing was presented to my wife to sign. When she read it she discovered it was a deportation order, stating that she admitted she was being deported for having broken the immigration laws of Mexico. Since they had all denied that we were being deported, and had never at any time given any reasons for this action, unless it was the inspector's remark that we had said "bad things about Mexico," and we had never at any time been given a fair hearing, and it was absolutely untrue in her case that she had broken any immigration laws whatsoever, and moreover I understand that you have to be given 24 hours notice in writing of any such impending deportation, my wife refused to sign. The clerk became very distressed and begged her to sign, implying grave danger if she did not. I told her not to sign and stated that I had no intention of signing any such order either. The inspector became violently angry and incredibly insulting and since he had a gun and she was being threatened in no uncertain terms I finally told her to sign: there was no choice and in order to avoid being separated from her I then likewise signed, but we both stated that we completely repudiated the charge and that we were signing the document under pressure. They then told my wife that since she was an American she was free to go, and could walk across the bridge, but the American Immigration office now being closed for the night I could not go until it opened in the morning. She refused to go without me and they then, curiously enough, urged her to go. I did not, by that time, trust their good will in the matter—if all this why not *ley fuga?*—and though I had at first told her to go I now felt it would be safer for her to remain with me. The inspector then left, having given orders that we were both to be held in the office until the following morning. The clerk however, once the inspector had left, took pity on my wife, who was utterly exhausted and in a condition of nervous shock, and arranged for us to go to an hotel, under guard, for a short time so that we might at least have a bath and a brief rest. At 5:30 A.M. another man from the Immigration Office came to the hotel and took us back to the office.

Once more we waited in the Immigration Office. We had been informed the night before that the American Immigration opened at
7 A.M. and that at that time we would be allowed to go. Therefore,
shortly after 7, we asked if we could now leave and cross into America.
We were informed that it would be necessary for us to see the Chief
of this Immigration Office and that he would be in between eight and
nine o'clock. At nine o'clock the second in command of the office arrived and we presented our case to him as well as we could. We assured him that we were positive there had been some serious mistake,
that we had been told over and over again that our papers were in
order, that we had done nothing to provoke this peculiar treatment,
that we had signed the paper the previous night under strong protest,
and so on. He was courteous, but said we would have to wait for the
Chief. Again we waited; a little later, while I was speaking to someone
else in the office, my wife again spoke to the second in command. He
informed her that the inspector had left instructions that we were to
be held there until he returned for us that morning. What disposition
was then to be made of us we were never quite informed, but it was
intimated that my wife was to be taken across the border by the
inspector and deported to America, since she had refused to leave
without me the previous night. What they proposed to do with me I
cannot make any sworn statement about, but the implications were not
pleasant. We now once more briefly placed our case before this Sub-
Chief, who took a most charitable and Christian attitude toward the
whole thing. He very kindly allowed us to go and have a cup of
coffee, saying he would speak to the Chief about us when he came in.
These were moments of suspense. When we returned the Sub-Chief
had spoken to the Chief and told us that we would be allowed to leave
at once, as we had requested, before the onset of the inspector, who
was of course by now long overdue, it being after 10 A.M. I believe that
we had convinced this Sub-Chief at least of our integrity, for he now
returned our papers to us and made every effort to help us get away
as quickly as possible. He procured a taxi for us, we were rushed
through the Mexican customs without their even opening our luggage
(while the Sub-Chief, as it were, stood guard outside, watching for the
inspector) and we swiftly crossed the bridge into America.

Our joy and relief at entering the United States were boundless.

While I was waiting in the Office of Immigration in Laredo, Texas,
as being a British subject my papers had to be inspected of course and
my readmission card filled out, we saw the inspector, who had apparently followed us right across the border, pass by in a towering
temper, and that, I am glad to report, was the last we saw of this man.

What he did or said I have no way of knowing. My papers being in order I was admitted that morning, Saturday the 4th of May, into the United States.

From Laredo we proceeded to Los Angeles, via Braniff, Continental and American Airlines, where we paid a visit to my wife's family and thence back here to our home in Canada. Immediately upon arriving in Los Angeles we consulted an attorney who advised us to prepare this statement and have it notarized.

To sum up our case my formulation of it would be something like the following:

That against my wife there was nothing whatsoever, that she had contravened no immigration regulations whatsoever, and that she was simply being made to suffer for being my wife. That against myself, setting aside such contributory factors as the 50-peso fine, there was against me fundamentally only the fact that I had entered a country that I was not permitted to enter without special permission of the Secretary of Gobernación, my defense for such action being that I was unaware that any such injunction existed against me, and my proof that I was unaware of this injunction being in their own files, where it was stated that they had pursued an alleged unpaid fine against me until the year 1943 without being able to locate my address. If, since the injunction in question was placed in the files against me in September 1938, two months after I had left the country, they had made any communication at that early date re such an injunction to any second party such as a lawyer acting for my father in Mexico and Los Angeles who might know my address, I had to the very best of my knowledge and belief not been notified of this fact, and the proof that no such communication could have been made without double-dealing somewhere lay in the fact that the only further communication I ever received re my former visit to Mexico was in 1939 or 1940 when I heard something which was incompatible with any edict forbidding me to return: the authorities claimed to believe I was still in the country. As before stated I then went to the acting Mexican Consul here in Vancouver and established the fact that I had left in July 1938. Furthermore, the Mexican Consulate in Los Angeles granted me my visa and Tourist Card although I told them I had been in Mexico before and waited 24 hours as previously stated. And finally, if Sr. Corunna did not believe that I had acted in all good faith, why did he profess and reiterate for one month that all was well and my papers were in order and that we could depart unmolested? Why did they tell us the photographs were simply being made for immigration papers, or insist until the last minute, at 2 o'clock in the morning at the border, that we would be given our papers back and allowed to leave? Why was it made impossible for us to obtain any basis for some proper accounting of what was being done with our 1000-peso bond, by giving us such short notice to leave our apartment in Cuernavaca, and by withholding Consular protection from us at the last moment by holding us incommunicado in 113 Bucarelli? Why, after having told the British Consulate I should be asked to leave the country, did they then require us to put up a bond, giving their solemn promise that if we did so we would be free to stay until the expiration of our Tourist Cards in June? Why, above all, if they sincerely wanted to get rid of us, didn't they simply let us go?

During the entire period of over 7 weeks we made every effort to cooperate with these authorities in every way, to find out precisely what the difficulty was with a view, if possible, of straightening the matter out. But I was never told the precise reason for this injunction being issued in the first place, or allowed to present my case to anyone in authority who would listen to me. So far as the Gobernación was concerned, we were never given a fair hearing. In fact we were never given a hearing of any sort by them. Whatever their motives in my case for this protracted persecution of the nationals of two friendly countries there seems no excuse nor warrant: and for my wife, an innocent American citizen, what was done to her amounts to a crime.

I swear that this statement is to the best of my knowledge and belief absolutely true.

Very truly yours,
Malcolm Lowry

To Albert Erskine*

Dollarton, B.C., Canada
June 22, 1946

Dear Mr. Erskine:

Thank you very much indeed for your letter and your more than heartening words and I am replying as quickly as I can.

My carbon copy of *Under the Volcano* was left behind in Mexico itself, to be sent on (together with many notes, and a draft of another novel) but it hasn't arrived yet, after 7 weeks, so I have only a working copy with different page numbers from yours to go by. Of course I can

* Lowry's editor at Reynal & Hitchcock.

locate myself by simply a word or two and I think I've done all right here where you've mentioned a specific sentence.

I've brought up a few more points in addition to yours while I'm at it and since I'm in a hurry to get this off airmail please forgive me for putting them in here instead of in the notes.

Can La Despedida be used to mean The Parting in the sense that I've used it for the name of the picture of the split rock in Chapter II? If not it should be simple to find the right word. I meant to verify all such points in Mexico but it turned out I didn't have time to do them all. Los Manos de Orlac should of course be *Las* Manos de Orlac throughout. There are liable to be a few other such mistakes in Spanish, typographical errors or whatnot where the Spanish is used conventionally and meant to be correct. Cervantes' remark in Chapter X (¾ way through) for instance, where they are discussing lighting 3 cigarettes with one match and which begins: *La superstición dice . . .* should perhaps be checked. On the barrels at Señora Gregorio's (end of VII) mansanillo should be manzanilla, rumpopo, rumpope. (I met her a month or two ago by the way, still doing fine. I said "Goodbye." She said "The same to you." The character named Juan Cerillo in IV—also Dr. Vigil—had been, alas, murdered, after too much mescal.) I may have spelt some of the perfectamentes and excelentísimos wrong too, in spite of all care in I and V. The picture of the demons and drunks I call Los Borracheros in VII (at the beginning in Laruelle's house) I could swear *was* called Los Borracheros in fact: but I have not been able to verify the existence of such a word at all so maybe we'll have to think of something else.

I'm very flattered you ask about *Ultramarine.* I have a copy but I think the book, which set out to be good, is an inexcusable mess of which I've been very ashamed for 13 years. The first and only real version was lost by Chatto and Windus* and I rewrote it in two months from notes salvaged from a waste paper basket and a few published bits. I wouldn't like to send you my copy without first having crossed out about half of it. That would leave about 125 pages of good, original work, however, and I've always wanted to rewrite it. But it is essentially a short novel. There are no short cuts for getting it except from me, I hope: it is, thank God, out of print.

I wrote another short novel called *Lunar Caustic* in 1936 (rewritten in 1940) which has never seen the light. *Under the Volcano* was originally planned as the inferno part of a Dantesque trilogy to be called *The Voyage That Never Ends. Lunar Caustic* was the purgatorial part, but was to be much expanded. I lost all the notes for its

* The publishing firm.

expansion in a fire, but though rather unmotivated, it's probably better as it stands, though it might need a month or two's work on it. The Paradiso part was called *In Ballast to the White Sea,* was a good deal longer than the *Volcano* and was completely destroyed in the fire here which took our house and all our books. We rebuilt the house.

I've got masses of poems left (one of which was published by *The Atlantic Monthly)*—enough to make two volumes I'd thought of calling *The Lighthouse Invites the Storm* and *Wild Bleeding Hearts.* But otherwise I'm more or less in the position of having to start again.

I'm absolutely so delighted you are publishing the *Volcano* you will forgive me rambling on.

Answers to your notes follow.

Yours sincerely and most gratefully,

Malcolm Lowry

P.S. By the way, two other books called "Volcano" (just like that) have to go and get themselves published within the last year—one about Paracutín, the other a mystery by Hugh somebody, published in the *American Magazine.* Does that make any difference? I'd loathe to change the title after so long. The Day of the Dead is my only alternative but it's not half so good. And besides it's bad luck, like changing the name of a ship.

To Albert Erskine

Dollarton, B.C., Canada
June 30, 1946

Dear Mr. Erskine:

I have now got back my carbon copy of the *Volcano* with the same page numbers as yourself and I am going through it with a fine tooth comb with an eye on your notes again and I will whizz my results to you airmail chapter by chapter, or sometimes two to three chapters at a time, as they are finished anyhow, and with a view to saving you as much trouble as possible. If I get long winded or ask irrelevant questions which cannot be answered please pay no attention, time being of the essence, I will not stop to revise, and by formulating certain questions I may be answering them for myself as I go along, and in this category is probably the question about "Le Gusta esta Jardín," etc., though of course I shall always be glad of your advice and when I remain in doubt, your final word.

1946

Not in this category is the following question. I had at one time thought of appending a list of notes to the book, which would help to elucidate such matters in the deeper layers as that the garden can be seen not only as the world, or the Garden of Eden, but legitimately as the Cabbala itself, and that the abuse of wine (*sōd*) is identified in the Cabbala with the abuse of magical powers, and so forth, à la Childe Harolde. It was also my intention to acknowledge in these notes any borrowings, echoes, design-governing postures, and so on, as used to be in the custom with poets, and might well be the custom with novelists. Of these there are remarkably few, and they became less and less as I carved and hacked away at the book down to its final form, so that of the design-governing postures, for instance, there remain virtually none. A few echoes still survive, however, nearly all deliberate. The question is whether they are still worth while acknowledging in notes at the end, as a matter of interest if for nothing else, if I have time for that, or whether, failing that, they should be altered, which would be a grief, and probably unnecessary. Since the book was written with enormous care and meticulousness, and its integrity is not in doubt from my point of view, you must put this down to a slight neurosis of mine on this particular subject, due doubtless to an Elizabethan unscrupulousness in my evil youth in other works mercifully forgotten save by the author's mediæval conscience.

These echoes are mostly all in the first chapter, and here only one seems worth bothering about (page 16) where I am uncertain of my reference. I will cite them in order however: P. 3 the single phrase "bangs and cries" (of the fiesta)—though nothing else in the passage— is lifted from a rather stupid story by J. C. Squire, chiefly about duck shooting, though also in relation to a fair, but for all that I cannot improve on those words and won't alter them either, unless I have to. P. 11 the words "personal battle" occur somewhere in D. H. Lawrence's letters where he is discussing the first World War and saying something to the effect that it was the "personal battle" that should be carried into the soul of every man in England, a similar thought, but I hate to put it in inverted commas and my wife says Lawrence did not originate it. P. 16 there is another echo of Lawrence's letters, I think, in the passage beginning "And now M. Laruelle could feel their burden pressing on him from outside . . ." and this I would be extremely obliged if you would look up for me, if you have the *Letters* to hand, because I cannot do it myself: I can't get the book here. It is a nuisance if I am right too, for the sentence took a long while to write: the echo would seem to inhere in the phrase "with their secret mines of silver," and not elsewhere: this could thus only be from one of Lawrence's letters when he was living at the Hotel Francia, Oaxaca, circa 1924 (as I myself did in 1938 and 1946), at the time he was excoriating Murry, so it should be easy to check—what I wish to know is whether the similarity requires any slight alteration or further attention on my part, or whether it is justified as it is: I know he speaks of the Oaxaquenian hills "standing round, inhuman," and of the hidden (or secret) silver mines, and of course I was thinking of the same hills and the same mines, in spite of the fact that I had transferred them to Quauhnahuac—alack, having written this, which I cannot well cross out, my wife now says that the passage I mean re the "secret mines of silver"—if it indeed is phrased at all like that— is not to be found when Lawrence was writing from or of Oaxaca, but from some desolate place further north in Mexico, like Chihuahua or Sonora—*The Woman Who Rode Away* country, in short—but in the *Letters* at a date not far off from the one I've mentioned. P. 19 "There was always the abyss" a similar thought occurs in Julian Green's *Personal Record*—God knows where it is and it is almost too banal to mention, but it was in my mind that M. Laruelle might have read that book, and I had originally tried to get in "As Julian Green had suggested," or something, but found it too difficult to compound with Quauhnahuac. P. 46 "unbandaging of great giants"—there is a not dissimilar image in Virginia Woolf's *To the Lighthouse* for noises at night in a deserted house, but I had not read that book when I wrote this passage. P. 47 "jonquil" in relation to dawn is unfortunately one of Faulkner's favorite adjectives too, in that connection. It is of course just right here and I have done my damndest to get away from it elsewhere though I have needed it badly in both VII and XII, neither violet nor lilac nor anything else having precisely what I wanted. There are very few such things left in any of the other chapters that I can think of at the moment, save the repeated "Compañero" in VIII and XII, which was vaguely suggested by something in *The Rainbow Fields* by Ralph Bates, though there are plenty of obscure points, which combined with such as the above, would make for an interesting page or two of notes. I never read a novel with notes at the end before but I don't see why it should not be done. I've certainly read plenty that need them. The objections here are (a) time (b) that they may interfere with the purity of the general format. But I would like your advice on the subject.

My sincerest apologies if I am putting you to undue trouble over this but we live under tough conditions here and my wish is only to be as helpful as possible in the briefest possible time.

With kindest regards,
Malcolm Lowry

P.S. By the way, are you going to send the proofs all at once, or in batches? It matters not but I am excited to know.

To Albert Erskine

[July, 1946]

Dear Albert Erskine:

I have received the first batch of manuscript up to and including Chapter VI, but not yet the second half of the manuscript, and not yet the duplicate proofs. However we have been working night and day and have nearly finished corrections so when the rest of the stuff arrives I shall get it back to you sine mora. On the other hand today is Friday, my own deadline for getting it all to you by Wednesday, and the duplicate proofs have still not arrived: para consecuencia unless I should send it by V-2 rocket or by space ship I don't see how you will get it by that day. It's true they may be waiting for me up at the post office now but it'll still take me at least a day to transfer everything from one proof to another so that even at best I won't be able to get it off tomorrow: and the P.O. is shut Sunday. I hope this will not throw us back; they have suddenly become slow here about airmail and books, and things even get hung up at the border or the customs.

Meantime I have run into an infatuation with sound of own words department (incredibly, indescribably) and infatuation with other people's words department: unusual (E. A. Poe) supplication (Nordahl Grieg) seething (Conrad Aiken).

I hope I won't be too trying. At least I haven't wired you (yet) to put the whole thing in the first person at the last moment. Nor yet put in an S.O.S. for Napier's *Peninsular War* or Cicero's *Epistles* without which it could not be corrected at all. You have done an absolutely marvellous job on the proofs, the typography et al., and I feel so moved by this, as well as by your understanding of the book, which is better than my own, that I feel the words all ought to be better somehow to live up to it.

Hasta la vista,
Malcolm L.

To Albert Erskine

Dollarton, B.C., Canada
August 17, 1946

Dear Mr. Erskine:

Just a note to inform you I'm still extant and to say how much I enjoyed our correspondence and appreciated the trouble you have gone to and were going to on my behalf.

I hope I got you the corrections in time.

The reason I haven't written in further reply is that I became suddenly seized with an indescribable loathing at the mere sight of my prose, at the mere sight of anything I write, in fact, even a cheque (perhaps particularly a cheque).

I acquired a baby seal and same swam out to sea: doubtless a good thing. Our cat went up a tree and we got that down. My wife has recently had a detective story published, minus the last chapter: since the explanation of the murders is in there, this must be something unique in literary history. Only we don't know, since we can't get the book. In fact, we didn't even get the proofs. It is raining. My uncle is in the garden with his good strong stout stick. I hope all is well.

Yours very sincerely,
Malcolm Lowry

To Maxwell Perkins*

Dollarton
British Columbia, Canada
September 15, 1946

Dear Mr. Perkins:

I wish to call your attention to a crashing and cynical injustice perpetrated by your firm. Knowing of you as a man of integrity, I

* Chief editor at Scribner's, and editor of Scott Fitzgerald, Ernest Hemingway, and Thomas Wolfe.

should be extremely obliged if you will bear with me and not immediately refer this to what you conceive to be the proper department, a quite futile procedure in this case, as I hope you will shortly be convinced.

As for myself, I am a writer, my publishers are Reynal and Hitchcock, New York, and Jonathan Cape, London, and my name Malcolm Lowry (not to be confused with Malcolm Cowley, who once wrote an article about you and Scribner's in which he mentioned that you rather missed the old type of villain in business, or words to that effect). The injustice in question however, concerns one of your own authors, Margerie Bonner, and myself only in that she is my wife. I am writing this letter for her since she is, at the moment, sick and unable to cope with it herself. She has had two books published by your firm this year, both mystery novels: *The Shapes That Creep*, which received good reviews and which, according to a recent statement of royalties due her, has had a good sale, and *The Last Twist of the Knife*.

The Shapes That Creep was submitted to your firm precisely half a decade ago, was kept for nine months, and in June of 1942 was accepted. The contract was signed, publication for fall of that year was indicated (although there was no time clause in the contract), and she was told she would receive the galley proofs shortly.

I should mention here that at that time the person handling, so to say, my wife's work for Scribner's was (I say "was" advisedly because it quite patently is not now being "handled" by anyone that I know of) a Mr. X, and no doubt he also had his difficulties during these years and I feel certain he is an excellent, likeable and capable fellow. This would seem to be less the point than precisely what this excellent, likeable and capable fellow achieved or failed to achieve in relation to my wife's work. Here, then, are the facts.

The Shapes That Creep was, first of all, according to Mr. X, coming out, as stated, in the fall of 1942—this being relayed through her agent for she had no direct word from Mr. X at this time. Over a period of six months, from, say, August 1942 to January 1943, my wife was promised, periodically, that she would have the proofs in "about a fortnight." We live in the wilderness of British Columbia where a letter is somewhat of an event (that of course is not your fault), and this was to be her first published novel. Every day she would go up to meet the post, and every day be disappointed and this went on for another six months when she was informed through her agent that the book had been postponed again till the winter of

1943: once more she began to expect the proofs, once more the daily ordeal of the post and once more, every day, the disappointment.

You have doubtless experienced such disappointments yourself, every writer has to take them: but please wait a moment, for I believe what follows to be almost unique in the annals of publishing. This kind of thing: proofs the next fortnight, postponement, no word at all for months, the daily crucifixion of the post, and so on, began again in 1944 and went on right through 1944.

At this point, to be perfectly fair to your firm, there were, of course, any number of good reasons that could be brought forward for these postponements: the war, paper shortages, etc. etc. Many well-known writers were having their books postponed, as we well knew. By March of 1944 my wife asked her agent if possibly she herself should write your firm in an attempt to ascertain what the status of her novel was, feeling that some sort of contact might be established that would give her some encouragement. Her agent replied that anything was worth trying: that he himself—even at this comparatively early date in the long history of her difficulties with Scribner's—had never had such an experience with a reputable firm like yourselves and did not know what more to do. He gave her X's name and she immediately wrote him. There was no reply. She wrote again, sending the letter registered mail: no reply. She telegraphed: no reply. All this complete lack of any contact with one's publisher was not exactly stimulating or helpful to a young American author just starting out, but I should say here that she had not been idle in the meantime. She had completely rewritten and revised her first book, the recently published *Last Twist of the Knife,* and had written a serious novel, *Horse in the Sky.* She had also nearly completed another mystery novel entitled *The Moon Saw Him Murdered,* when (again through no fault of yours) our house burned down.

This was bad, but chiefly, as it happened, for me. She lost no work except her spare copies of *The Last Twist of the Knife,* the only one being with her agent in New York, awaiting publication of *The Shapes That Creep* before being submitted to your firm. However, after we lost our home, we went east where we stayed, near Toronto, with the news commentator, Gerald Noxon.

By this time my wife was almost reconciled to the postponements; the paper shortage was certainly a real thing and it was more the cynical manner with which the whole thing seemed to be conducted, or not conducted, that made it intolerable, especially in the light of those articles about yourself in *The New Yorker* by Malcolm Cowley, in which Scribner's appeared to be sitting very pretty indeed and were a firm by which any author would be tickled pink to be published.

Besides, Noxon and I read my wife passages from Kafka's *The Castle* and also extracts from Joyce's correspondence with Grant Richards, to help her to take "the long view." She had, however, quite given up hope of ever seeing her work in print, and her agent having also been thinking the blackest thoughts was just on the point of demanding the return of her manuscript from Scribner's when on my advice my wife herself went, in July 1944, to New York.

Here she encountered the business-like, erudite and amiable Mr. X who assured her—astoundingly!—that Scribner's would be very sorry to lose her, that *The Shapes That Creep* had already gone to press, was scheduled for October publication of that year, and that the galleys would be along in "about a fortnight." He further inquired if she had any other books to follow up *The Shapes That Creep* and my wife had her agent send him the copy (the only copy extant because of our fire: X was informed of this fact) of *The Last Twist of the Knife.* Indeed, the only disappointing news she brought back was that Mr. X would not consider reading her serious novel because it had been found that it didn't pay for a writer to have "two careers," i.e., a serious and a mystery one. Since my wife had not yet begun to have one career, and *The Shapes That Creep* was already becoming somewhat out of date to her mind, Noxon and I graduated her from Kafka's *Castle* to his *The Trial,* in hopes that she might, in case of accident, take a longer view still.

For now once more began the waiting for the proofs which were, definitely this time, X said, to arrive "in a fortnight." September, October, November and December came and went, with no proofs, but meanwhile X notified her that Scribner's had accepted *The Last Twist of the Knife.* After a month or six weeks—this is mentioned not because it normally would be a long time but simply because it involved another broken promise—the contract arrived and an advance was paid of $350, only this time there was a time limit in the contract: *The Last Twist of the Knife* was to be published not later than Fall, 1945. X said that Scribner's wished her to make certain alterations and additions, to which she agreed, and stated that he *had mailed* the MSS to her for these corrections, together with his notes, and she should receive it within a day or two. Now she had two things to watch the post for; neither arrived. Time went by, and she became more and more anxious about the MSS, since it was the only one. We were attempting to trace it through the post, when, finally, various long distance phone calls and telegrams elicited the news from X that the MSS had *not,* after all, been mailed, but had been "mislaid." Also it developed that Scribner's had changed their minds regarding the additions and alterations they had requested her to make. I quote from a telegram of X's dated January 12, 1945, in my possession: "Have recalled *Last Twist* and sent to press you can make minor corrections in galley sheet due any day now scheduling for fall publication—X."

In February, 1945, we returned to British Columbia to rebuild our burned house and the situation was now this: *The Shapes That Creep* was scheduled for Spring publication and the proofs were due "within a fortnight." *The Last Twist of the Knife* was scheduled for Fall publication and the proofs of that also would be along "any day now," so as to give her time for these (now) minor corrections your firm wished her to make. This was naturally of equal importance to her since she also wished her book to be as good as she could possibly make it.

In April of that year, 1945, an astounding thing happened. The proofs of *The Shapes* actually *did* turn up. That is, the *proof-read* proofs of the first half: with these proofs came a letter from X stating that the similarly *proof-read* proofs of the second half would be turning up "within a fortnight," and X had also promised to read these proofs himself before they were dispatched to her, as he had kindly done in the first half. Sure enough, a second batch of proofs arrived, but not proof-read, so that the situation was not clear: my wife for her part made her corrections on the proof-read galleys of the first part and returned them promptly, but she didn't want to correct the second batch because according to X's advice she would then be correcting the wrong proofs and would have to do the work all over again. She wrote X asking what he desired her to do regarding these un-proof-read galleys of the second half: there was no reply, and she never received the promised proof-read galleys, in spite of writing again and again, or any further word regarding them. She has not, in fact, from that day to this, ever had one more line or word from him or any member of your firm. So that, when *The Shapes* finally was published, it was without her corrections on the last half and not merely this, but with many corrections she did make on the first half completely ignored. It should also be mentioned that in addition to the letters she wrote in regard to *The Shapes* she wrote continually and anxiously about *The Last Twist,* which, you perhaps remember, was reported to have gone to press in January 1945. But she has never had one more word regarding *The Last Twist* either, from your firm. However, in October of last year, 1945, my wife, with the actual intention of being sporting, wrote her agent asking him to intimate to X that he was taking you into breach of contract, in case the terms of the contract had been forgotten. Hal Matson, who is her agent and also mine, was away on holiday, but his secretary, on receiving my wife's letter, answered at once, reporting that she had telephoned Mr. X in regard to *The Last Twist of the Knife* and that he stated that he had written, or was writing, my wife and that the galley proofs were in the mail, or would be shortly. Needless to say neither letter nor proofs or any further explanation were forthcoming.

In December of last year, having given up all hopes for both books, we took a trip to California and hence to Mexico—by which time you had already broken your contract for *The Last Twist of the Knife*. When we reached Los Angeles we discovered, via the booksellers journals, that *The Shapes* had actually been twice announced for publication: in June 1945 and October 1945, postponed again, and now was announced a third time, while *The Last Twist of the Knife* had also been announced, without a date given.

No replies being forthcoming to any letters, as usual, and her agent being in as great a state of bewilderment as she, she arrived in Mexico equally concerned about both books. True, they seemed a little *nearer* to coming out, but there was a really agonizing question (to the author) in regard to *The Last Twist*—why had she never received the proofs? Perhaps the MSS had actually been lost and never found. And then, perhaps she still might receive the promised proofs—and the proof-read proofs of the last half of *The Shapes That Creep*.

In order to give no chance for any of these Utopian proofs to miscarry, my wife wrote X in January 1946, registered mail, giving our address in Mexico. This letter was couched in extremely stinging terms: every other human approach having failed, she thought perhaps this might bring some result. As regards *The Last Twist* she said that if she did not hear from Scribner's soon she would put the whole business, as she had, and still has, a perfect right to do, in the hands of a lawyer, reluctant as she was to become involved in this sort of thing. But even this brought no reply.

Then, sometime in February, quite by accident, I came across a copy of *The Shapes That Creep* in the American Book Store in Mexico City and bought it for her.

So there it was at last, published. She had not, of course, received her promised author's copies (she still has not received them) but as a consequence of its publication she wrote again to Scribner's, rescinding her previous letter, reminding them, once more, of her address, and asking if some new start could not be made, upon an honourable and decent basis, even complimenting them upon the good taste shown in the general format, etc., and trying also once more, since everything cannot be done through one's agent, to establish a friendly relationship with her publisher. She also asked, for the umpteenth time, for some news of *The Last Twist of the Knife* and about the proofs of this book.

There was, God help you, no reply.

On returning to Canada in May of this year she wrote again, this time to our agent, about *The Last Twist of the Knife,* the proofs of which she was still somehow expecting to arrive. The only reply he could give was that he had "no reason to believe that any new methods would change the habits of certain people at Scribner's."

Then, at the beginning of August, my wife received a fan letter, forwarded her from Scribner's, which reads as follows: "I have just finished reading, and enjoying, your mystery story *The Last Twist of the Knife,* and I am writing to protest its abrupt ending. The book ends with Turgeon confessing to the two killings, and we are left with no explanation of his motive in murdering Paul, even if we accept the supposition that Delight was blackmailing Turgeon. I have read a number of books lately in which several pages were missing, and am wondering if this happened in *The Last Twist of the Knife* as I can't feel that the story is complete. We, readers, cheerfully accepted books with poor print, many typographical errors, and the subject matter spoiled by sheets missing, during the war—but we *are* complaining that it continues as of this date. If you really finished your story with Turgeon's confession I apologize to the publishers but if they *left out* the final pages I shall not forgive them for ruining a good story."

This letter was her first knowledge of the book's publication, and suggests, as you see, that this book, of which she has never—I have to repeat myself—seen the proofs, and still to this day has not seen as a book, has been published without its last chapter. Subsequent reviews, received through her clipping service (. . . "Motive and solution are just too nebulous for this mystery fan" ". . . the solution, which is sudden and without adequate explanation" ". . . so incredibly badly ended that it seems as though it could never possibly have come from the author of the delightful *Shapes That Creep"*) substantiate this and testify to the weakness of the ending, and the detection. We are unable to obtain a copy of this book here in Canada so far, but my wife wrote to someone in Los Angeles, who bought and read the book and sent her a report on it which leaves no possible doubt in our minds: the book has been published without its last chapter. On top

of everything else, this puts my wife very unfairly into the position
of having committed, from the mystery writer's point of view, an
unforgiveable crime, a crime which she did not commit, for though
I don't think the book as a whole was so good as *The Shapes*, it was
excellently complete and the detection, per se, was actually better than
that in *The Shapes*. But the omission of the last chapter, with its all-
important tying up of motives and clues and the rest, has done her, she
feels, considerable damage as a writer of mystery stories, for as the
book stands, we are told, there is absolutely no reason given for the
murders at all.

I can testify to the fact that when this book was sent to our agent
the last chapter was there, intact and complete, and my wife can
testify to the fact that when she was in New York she saw this copy in
the office of her agent, just before it was sent to Mr. X, and looked it
through to be sure it was the correct version, since, you will remember,
she had rewritten this book, and that it was complete at that time.

It is possible that somebody at Scribner's might have lost this last
chapter and your firm would not be responsible for it, or it might
have been mislaid in some other way for which your firm still would
not be responsible, but in this case somebody at Scribner's must have
known that it was lost and my wife should have been given a chance to
write that part again. And if the book had gone to press, as X stated in
his wire of January 12, 1945, how could he be unaware, as a mystery
expert, that it lacked a last chapter? If my wife had ever been sent the
proofs she would of course have seen at once that it was lacking, and
perhaps—who knows?—that is why she never *was* sent the proofs. I
am so disgusted when I think of this that I scarcely have the heart to
recapitulate all the unnecessary lies, the carelessnesses, the complete
protracted cynical disregard for human feelings and common forthrightness that has permeated Scribner's dealings with my wife's work
and which makes this last incident a more than last straw. The whole
thing strikes me as shameful and unspeakable, and at the same time
so utterly senseless—what is your motive? And if the thing is motive-
less, as it would appear, how can you continue to employ such irresponsible people and maintain your reputation, or indeed any reputation at all?

Writers often tend to be high-strung creatures and my wife is no
exception: she has been so continually tormented and worried by this
damned thing for so many years now that this last discouragement has
actually affected her health. From one standpoint, looked at with a
bleak abstracted relative eye, it all may not seem so much, yet it is

impossible to convey in a letter such as this the anguish and strain, for a *writer,* of such an experience.

It is true we shall probably be going east again this winter, as Reynal and Hitchcock have invited me to be in New York at publication time of my novel; perhaps this time Noxon and I will entertain my wife with selections from *Crime and Punishment. . . .* It may be that such ordeals and disappointments may come to have in time a positive value to one who is essentially a serious artist. That does not make Scribner's blame—or X's—any the less. After all, mystery story writers also have souls and possibly even destinies.

Personally, I do not believe that all this should be taken lying down. In fact I'm sure it should not. For whatever your legal position in the matter, your ethical position deserves your attention. So, I respectfully ask you, what, in her position, would you do?

I am sending this letter by registered mail to be sure that you, or someone at Scribner's, will receive it.

Yours very truly,
Malcolm Lowry

To Maxwell Perkins

Dollarton, B.C., Canada
September 20, 1946

Dear Mr. Perkins:

Thank you very much indeed for your prompt and kindly wire.* Simply as a signal from the beyond I may say its therapeutic value was prodigious, for I think you can understand how one can come to doubt, over such a long period, not only one's achievement but one's very existence.

Re your request for my wife to furnish a last chapter for *The Last Twist of the Knife:* we assume from this that the chapter in question has been, in some way, mislaid or cannot be found at present. She'd been considering the possibility that whoever edited that suitably named book had simply put it out without this chapter for some reason of his own, and that it would still be in your files with the MSS. However she certainly could rewrite the last chapter soon if only she had a copy of the book itself. I think I mentioned that she hadn't yet even seen it (or the proofs) and all we had to go on were a "fan"

---

* See Appendix 4.

letter, some reviews, and a report from Los Angeles, to establish that it doesn't *have* an ending, though there seems no doubt this is so. We have tried to get a copy here in Vancouver several times without success (you should know that it is considered definitely low-minded to try and buy any kind of a book in Canada, even from a bookseller: "Have you a copy of *The Last Twist of the Knife?*" "No, all last week's copies of *Life* are sold out") and since she wrote it so long ago, she can hardly pick up the threads now without something to start from—and I think I mentioned that the MSS your firm had was her only one due to our fire.

Thank you again for your courtesy in replying so promptly; we shall be awaiting your letter with the greatest interest and, on my wife's part, renewed hope that at last all this may be resolved in a friendly and civilized manner.

Yours very sincerely,
Malcolm Lowry

To Maxwell Perkins

Dollarton, B.C., Canada
September 30, 1946

Dear Mr. Perkins:

I am much beholden to you for your understanding letter and also for your second telegram and all of this of course goes for Mrs. Lowry too.

My statement re Canadian bookstores here was no exaggeration: we had had *The Last Twist* on order here for some time but there was no telling whether the order ever went through, though they said yes.

Considering the number of crossed purposes, telephones off the hook, and inexplicable confusions in this episode—for example, we arrived back in Canada from Mexico in May, we were in touch with Hal Matson, so I don't see why she didn't get her author's copies—I was beginning to think that the explanation if any might more fairly lie in a metaphysical direction; and my inclination toward such an explanation—in part at least—was strengthened rather than otherwise when upon opening your kindly-meant special delivery parcel—the brave man does it with a knife!—we discovered that while the jacket of my wife's book was all right, in fact excellent, and what was within was all right too, it wasn't Margerie Bonner's *The Last Twist*, but Marion Strobel's *Kiss and Kill!*

I am afraid, though it verges upon unsportsmanship, if not sadism, that I have been unable to resist telling you this, but perhaps the curse is taken off by the information that as a result of this innocent error we were unable to stop laughing for twenty minutes.

The other volume was O.K., and was indeed *The Last Twist of the Knife* for which many thanks; or rather was, sure enough, merely The Knife without the Last Twist, and somewhat bloodstained as to proof-reading at that—however, my wife has now read it, certain old notes for the last chapter have been found, and though the job seemed at first something like putting a linoleum on an engine room floor, I think I can safely say you'll have the copy for the last chapter within the week.

My wife has been somewhat under the weather recently, as I think I said, but is considerably better, and will write you herself when she sends off the copy.

Yes, it has been a pleasure hearing from you too, this in strong distinction from the always uniquely horrible experience of being in the right, only less horrible indeed an experience than being in the wrong, unless it's more so.

Well, I must stop, for I'm off to the movies to see Murnau's *Last Laugh*—true, it's taken rather a long time to get here—to be closely followed next week by *The Fall of The House of Usher*—perhaps I shall take Kant's *Critique of Pure Reason* with me to read on the bus.

With kind regards from us both,

Yours sincerely,
Malcolm Lowry

To Albert Erskine

[Dollarton, November, 1946]

Dear Albert Erskine:

My God, how does one survive it, if indeed one does survive it? Why are there not stained glass windows in memory of all the authors, and all the publishers too. Oh God, St. Erskine. Oh Christ, St. Lowry. Last night I was haunted by an individual, not a hollow man, much worse than that, but a man who had been absolutely crushed flat by a book, flat as one of those pressed canterbury bells that one's mother sends one from England now and then; and this man, believe it or not, was me.

Meantime my wife, having happily recovered otherwise in health, is troubled at night by commas wiggling around her ankles like tadpoles, but that bite and even *sting* her: by colons that swell up like cannonballs: and ghosts of galleys that try to wrap themselves around her in the manner of a winding sheet. (The day after tomorrow we're going to see *The Pirates of Penzance*.)

The day after tomorrow we are not going to see *The Pirates of Penzance*. At least I don't think so. (For that read, now, tomorrow.) The reason is the galley-proofs—duplicate. Yesterday I sent a wire re their non-arrival: today I got your wire (wrongly relayed over the phone) and also a notice from the Canadian National Railway Express (in spite of your having sent it Air Express) dated November 4th. And in spite of your having sent it Special Delivery. Snag is neatly expressed in remark on red label on package which as far as I can read it says:

Canadian National Express
IN BOND
From Tomb To Maul
Deliver to Collector of Customs and Excise
Vancouver

Important Notice—Agent at Destination must not Deliver This Shipment unless he has evidence that clearance through customs has been arranged. When released by customs officer the agent at customs port should affix a "Cleared Customs" sticker (Form 5246).

All this in spite of Air Express Prepaid Waybill numbers and God knows what trouble you went to: I'd have warned you if I'd remembered that nothing but straight airmail or post goes straight through but I'd forgotten we were a foreign country: at all events I've got it, which is the main thing, after a nightmarish day in Vancouver chasing from office to office and giving them hell to no avail: it is now 7 o'clock Wednesday night November 6th—your parcel is dated October 31—today is the day you should have had it back; tomorrow, November 7, the day you mentioned it should go to the printers. So I better see how fast I can work—and how.

Well, here goes: occasionally an asterisk on proofs will refer you to a letter—and what is apposite there you will find, in the following pages, somewhere among the other remarks pertinent to the particular chapter.

In haste,
Malcolm Lowry

N.B. *Extra Note* Re dedication, somewhere:
To Margerie, my wife.

To Jonathan Cape

[*Dollarton, November, 1946*]

Dear Mr. Cape:

Absolutely up to the eyes in proofs—will you do me an enormous favor in the interests of God, literature, and one of your writers; I speak of the late-lamented Mr. Melville.

A year or so ago my wife and I were hitting the high places in radio—we even got written up in *Time* as having achieved some of the best in radio. To cut a long story short, we did finally a serious radio dramatization of *Moby Dick,* of a character to completely revolutionize radio.

While most people in the C.B.C. agreed it was the most magnificent script they'd ever had, they achieved a change of heart at the last moment, said the public wouldn't stand for it, would we change it, and we said no.

We also gave up radio, this being indeed a job worse than driving geese to water, even at its highest, or at any rate you can't mix it with serious writing too strenuously.

However, now we read that Branes is doing a serious dramatization of *Moby Dick* and I will bet my bottom dollar that the idea came via us through the radio grape-vine.

That is not the point so much as that no one else *could* do *Moby Dick* as we have done it—it is too damned hard and too many problems to be solved—if we were to shoot our script to him *quam celerime,* in the certain knowledge that when he sees *our* script he'll have to haul whatever else he was cooking out of production, if he's got that far.

But even, at worst, our script cannot fail to be a help: it's consummate of its kind.

Since I don't know the address of the B.B.C. would you kindly send this thither by space rocket and a bevy of messengers, or at least by the next post, this being the favour, though I must say I would have taken the liberty of asking you to forward it anyhow, since it will have far more authority as arriving from Melville's publisher, or as if from H.M. himself, whose ghost we like to think we can hear saying, "Save me."

You only haven't got my wife's book because she hasn't got it yet from the agent.

You will have my proofs soon.

[130]

We are wallowing in success, feeling in fact like starving men whose eyes are being stuffed with potatoes.

I had a letter from Innes Rose* who had returned from the wars, I am relieved to hear; should you encounter him would you tell him I will write him as soon as I can.

Happy Hallowe'en, Happy Xmas and also Happy New Year.

Ever sincerely yours,
Malcolm Lowry

P.S. I find myself making some of the cuts intimated by your reader, in spite of all the hubbub I made.

To Albert Erskine

[*New Orleans, December, 1946*]

Dear Erskine:

(In dear old Ultima Thule that is a rather stern form of address, so that whenever I am addressed as Lowry, courteous though it be, I always quail slightly, feeling that it is immediately going to be followed by a formal invitation to be thrashed within an inch of one's life by the Headmaster, or by some such remark as: "For Christ sake, didn't I tell you ten minutes ago to go down to that Chief Engineer and fetch up a bucket of steam!" But my wife tells me that in these States its implications—as of course I knew, nor are they obviously here—are not so. Please enjoy a quiet laugh here at my expense. I have just spent a wonderful afternoon with my wife, wandering round old New Orleans, visiting the pirate La Fitte's dens, observing certain relics of tortures, and also apprehending a delicate panorama of certain red coats—of course not limeys—lying flat on their faces, slaughtered, in what looked to me—though could it be?—a hail storm. You'd polished them off anyway. I was also so fascinated by the history of the river-boat *Robert E. Lee* in the museum I had to be dragged away by main force, not however, before having learned the following:

EXTRA!

Lee arrived at St. Louis at 11:20. Time out from New Orleans, 3 days 18 hours, and 19 minutes. *Natchez* not in sight. *Natchez* old time— 3 days 21 hours and 58 minutes.

* British literary agent.

EXTRA!) Please notice I closed the bracket.

In haste.

Reactions re cover, etc.—and far more than cover. Before I go on to that, re the book, the "everything in it," as you have presented it, is a marvellous creative job.

Re the cover—I like everything about it; here is, verbatim, my wife's and a very knowledgeable friend of hers reaction—as accurately as I can get it down, on the spot.

"Really a work of genius, if you stare at it long enough, you're down through into the Ultimate Pit of blackness, not only is it the vortex, but the SHAKY vortex,—(note comma and dash) not only from the point of view of salesmanship; right, from the point of view of the book—sinister quality, quality of horror, and yet great dignity."

That is what they say, and I agree.

Re Jimmy Stern—he is an old pal, the best and most amusing of fellows, as also of writers—but he really hated all but one poem of all my past work; quite deservedly too: I felt, if any one would give the *Volcano* the brush-off, though it hurt him, it would be Jimmy. Have you read *The Heartless Land?* I am tickled pink he liked the *Volcano*.

Re the parcel you have so generously sent me, containing the other book, I don't know what to say; a thousand thanks—but if it shouldn't arrive tomorrow, I may indeed, should it prove impossible to cope with the Haitian postal arrangements, have to do as you suggest. God bless and a Merry Christmas all over again to you and Mrs. Erskine from us both.

Malcolm Lowry

P.S. Although we are now leaving, like the *Pequod*, on Christmas Eve.

To Albert Erskine

[New Orleans, December, 1946]

Dear Mr. Erskine:

We went over the page proofs in the back room of a brawling New Orleans bar hard by the post office, drinking very good beer out of fine copper tankards, but today when we went back they threw us out.

"This is a bar, not an office."

Apparently you can gamble, play confidence games, and even murder in these joints, and you can listen to the thrice God-awful hillbilly music that seems to have put a stop here to jazz—of which I am both a passionate admirer and an ancient aficionado, and of which this is the home—but a fellow can't look at his proofs.

"We don't know what kind of a thing it is you're doing, and the boys are asking questions."

I spoke to an old guy who'd once played with Venuti and he said: "Boy I like to play like you say, but nobody asks for it anymore, and what the hell can I do with a guitarist like I got." So I'm feeling pretty hurt this morning—but apart from that New Orleans is superlatively wonderful; moreover I've got to do something about that Spanish moss before I die.

Well, I've got your list and I've checked the names of the people I know. I'm a bit dubious about my list however: I've no way of knowing how interested some of them would be, friends or no, and I'm not sure if Conrad Aiken, for example, is in England or America. The Jane Aiken I mentioned is an editorial researcher on *Time* and is Aiken's daughter, whom I knew as a child. I'd like a review copy to go to Conrad A. though. I'm not very clear about those to whom review copies might be sent with any profit; but these I have marked anyway with a tick and a star; those whom I merely *know* simply with a tick. But there's one name I missed and should put in; that is Michael Redgrave, the actor, an old and good college friend of mine who is at present in America making a movie, I believe, for Fritz Lang. So far as I know his address is Diana Productions, Universal City, Calif., and I certainly would like if possible a review copy to be sent to him.

For the rest; thank you again for everything. Re coming to New York I feel I ought to have explained before to you that I very much wanted to do this when I was originally asked by your firm through my agent if I could—that was way back in April and my plans were at that time to proceed straight from Mexico to New York; but then I was informed by my agent that you didn't want me to do this, and that it might be better for me to come at publication time. Between May and October it would have been very difficult for me to come anyway but I would have made it if I had been informed by my agent of any change of plans—for my part I would have preferred being in New York during the period of editing; feeling that that was when I could have been the most help. But the final word I had from my agent was that Mr. Hitchcock had decided that my trip was unnecessary until perhaps publication time, and there the matter still rests.

Since I want to get this back to you by return mail and am in fact finishing it in the P.O. itself—loitering in this building prohibited—I'll keep anything further for another letter. Hope my telegram was comprehensible.

> Very best wishes,
> Malcolm Lowry

To Albert Erskine

New Orleans
December 26, 1946

Just like the old days of my grandpappy—the crew got so *perfectamente borracho* they couldn't (and finally wouldn't) take the ship out (I don't blame them, I think it will sink at the dock before we get aboard, which ought to be 5 minutes ago)—argal, we spent a wonderful Xmas Eve and day reading and *eating* your wonderful edition of Daumier, though will have to send it back c/o you. All thanks to you and Mr. Taylor. God bless you.

> Lowry

PART IV: *1947*

PART IV 1942

To Albert Erskine

Hotel Olaffson
Port-au-Prince, Haiti
January 25, 1947

Dear A.E.—

Thank you and thank you again. And again I thank you. Sincerely, and not in the Cyranoesque sense.

Weird things here: toy cemeteries and doves with ruby eyes. And an American editor with a cricket cap, carrying *Moby Dick* in his pocket, whose house has just burned down and who is an expert, to boot, on James Shirley, the only other ex-poet, beside myself, which my college of St. Catharine's, she who was broken on the wheel, ever succeeded in not producing.

Strange and ever terrible, mystifying and wonderful things here. M. Marcelin (*Canapé-Vert*) and myself and wives drinking Coca-Cola and Christ knows what or into where. He, Marcelin, Philippe Thoby-Marcelin, is a marvellous fellow. He also is an exquisite poet. And he has written a miraculous book of children's stories. Rinehart, I think, won't take them. His poems are not translated. Half of them were lent to the Mexican Ambassador and never returned. That, at least, I can understand. His last book was horrendously mistranslated. And he can't speak a damn word of English and though he writes beautiful French for some reason speaks mostly Creole. Shouldn't you or some-one write him a letter, in French? Is that an unethical suggestion? Or New Directions? Or will you think? I want like hell to help and it is moreover also because one *should*. I believe sincerely in this exchange of ideas between chaps of different countries. Valery Larbaud—he showed me the letter—thinks he is one of the greatest poets France (sic) ever produced and though he is a Haitian without a cent who lives on a mountain I bloody well agree. We disappear into those mountains on Friday. Voodoo? It is real. In one flash Rinehart,

Scribner's, and Reynal and Hitchcock will be deprived of their greatest authors. I hope I do not mean that. It is what used to be called a joke. Perhaps I only meant that I would revenge myself on that bloody Jackson by depriving Rinehart of one of theirs. Not to be taken seriously.

Words follow to be taken more seriously. They even have to do with business. Is my old and revered and loyal Norse forefather, Harold Matson, alive? Or has he turned into perhaps, a troll, or even a black magician, too, like what they say I am here, and hence just disappeared, back to Grimanger? For it seems there have been other confusions too, which in fairness to myself, should be straightened out, as they used to say of the Consul. Thou hast misprised me when thou speakest of me as if asking for another advance. When Mr. Hitchcock first accepted the *Volcano* it was with the proviso that I would come to N.Y. at once and do some editing with him. He offered (in addition to the generous advance of $1500) to pay $500 toward expenses for my trip, $250 paid for directly by the firm and the other $250 to come out of my later royalties. I agreed to this and wired Matson that I would come. Then it seems Mr. Hitchcock read the *Volcano* again over the week end and decided he did not want to make any changes or edit it with me. So then Mr. Hitchcock said that he wanted me to come to New York at publication time and that the $500 mentioned ($250 to come out of my later royalties as before, $250 given me for expenses—whatever *they* are) would apply if I would come at that time. As I wrote you before, I myself wanted to come to N.Y. during the period of editing but I acceded to his wishes in the matter and finally agreed to come to N.Y. at publication time. I can assume only that my ancient and revered forefather who has been bloody patient with me for about 200 years with no remuneration for himself has never explained this to you, and I'm sorry, but I wanted to make it clear to you that I was not asking for any *further* advance but merely inquiring, quite innocently (hic!) about a proposition made to me which I understood was still valid.

That's about all.

Save various notes for another book, such as:

toy tin house with peaked roof

a house like a child's toy made of lace paper

beaming flamboyant trees, made of ferns, "leaning"

flamboyant trees *leaving* flamboyant trees, "trees that will never be written."

cure hangover with Enos Fruit Salts

D.T.s ditto—Paracelsus?

The strange American whose house had just burned down while Marcelin and I were talking about fire and who played cricket. Would you like to wear my cricket cap? Sings "Men of Harlech" in morning, stamping.

the dark man that follows us behind graves.

an invisible voice whispering from behind a wall: "Gimme five cents please." It is a boy up a trumpet tree.

healthy and swimming at midday, normal, wondering how soon the crisis was going to hit again: servants chuckling: "Fou" "Bonveur"

A thunderous cat
being constructive
being conclusive

love,
Malcolm Lowry

P.S. Please try and help Philippe Thoby-Marcelin—he is a great and truly good man.

To Albert Erskine

Nowhere
[Haiti, February, 1947]

Dear Albert Erskine:

Yes, you were absolutely right about the preface and Jackson and etc. and I wrote Cape telling him to deracinate it.

I think I may have written you a somewhat peculiar letter—my last one: it seems I was going down with a fever, with a cough, and so forth; my doctor being the author of an interesting book entitled *La Crise de Possession dans le Vaudeau* (at which you might like to take a look) he let me out of bed rather earlier than he should have to see a ceremony the Marcelins had discovered for us was taking place and to which they were taking us: the result is we have been up for two terrific days and nights witnessing that which the doctor, who did not accompany us, had never himself witnessed, nor, I daresay, anyone else extant.

But the final result is I feel rather better, if still a bit groggy from injections, and the voodoo: the voodoo priest, perhaps recognizing a kindred spirit, has promised to initiate me by fire if and when

I return—do you think that is really a good idea? (Just the same I really would like to be a voodoo priest.)

I think I wrote about Philippe Thoby-Marcelin and brother in an unethical manner.

Hullo, hullo—at this moment (naturally!) I receive your letter. But how can you have failed to—but I see perhaps your—anyhow we are great friends of the Marcelins by now—I meant Philippe-Thoby was the poet, per se, of the brothers, and a first-rate one in my estimation and more too.

Anyhow I will speak to him this afternoon, when we are seeing him (if I think it proper).

My hospital was called the Notre Dame in a place known as Canapé-Vert.

My God I am mixed up: but I shall become practical later.

The favourable reviews of the *Volcano* frightened the hell out of me*—I have scarcely even been able to look at them, but I do thank you again sincerely for all you have done.

No, I certainly was not trying to dun another advance out of you— what a godawful thought even to sit in the ether for five minutes— or isn't it? It doesn't sound even honest even though it's true.

Outside my window in the hospital was a leaning forest of small green nameless trees crowned by one very little sweet tree, blowing. . . .

We leave tomorrow by air for Miami, thence by bus—I should certainly think—

> Best wishes,
> Malcolm Lowry

To Frank Taylor†

> *Harrison Hot Springs Hotel*
> [*Spring, 1947*]

Dear Frank:

I feel like a louse not having written before but assure you that what with one thing and another and my putting it off because I wanted to write you a *good* letter (a symptom of narcissism) and also

---

* See Appendix 5.
† Formerly an editor at Reynal & Hitchcock who collaborated with Erskine in bringing out *Under the Volcano*.

because I was waiting for news of *you* both; and so on; but I hope you will take the will for the deed. In case the above address does not exactly speak for itself, for Harrison Hot Springs suggests to me a super name for some sort of jazz outfit, or some kind of Canadian Capers—a native dance—ditto for some sort of jazz number, or some kind of diabolical mattress, I should add it actually is a spa, and diabolical at that, for people subsist here on a diet of sulphur, potash, repainted golfballs and occasionally a cold omelette, but what Margie and I came here for was to do some hiking, take a rest from our leaking rooftree, and write some letters, and also to mount the good strong white horse of our uncle standing with our nephew in the garden. We were very sorry not to see you again before we departed but I know you must have been on what someone once called the "horns of a Domelia" about the Chicago project, and I'm likewise very sorry indeed that this hasn't worked out as you would have wished; I hear you may be at Random House. I wish you and Albert all luck, certainly as I just wrote to Albert, it is lucky for Random House, but I will not say more before I hear more: for myself I feel highly excommunicado, and much the glowering stepson in my now spiritually tenuous nexus with Reynal Teamwork, Inc. *Bisweilen* I continue to receive good and generous reviews on the *Volcano* from the U.S. but have been more or less panned here, especially in Vancouver and Toronto, by people who have not read the book at all and have made no attempt to. Set against this have come absolutely shatteringly favorable ones from San Francisco, Chicago, Dallas, and a wonderful one from Providence—D.C. de J.— spells David Cornel de Jong? I am working on *La Mordida*. Perhaps Albert told you Margie's serious novel *Horse in the Sky* has been taken by Scribner's. There is plenty more good news from this end too. Thanks an inarticulate million for all you have done and your marvellous generosity to Margie and myself in New York. With all best love from us to both you and Nan,

God bless,
Malcolm

To Fletcher Markle*

[*Dollarton, May, 1947*]

Dear Fletcher (and Gerald,† if extant??)

For Pete's sake. . . . It wasn't that I was bothering about the records, or the cuttings, or Dilworth, though very many thanks for the wire.

It was just merely that I hadn't heard *anything*, not the broadcast, nor yet whether you personally and Gerald were pleased with it, nor whether you thought it came off, nor whether it actually did come off, nor absolutely bloody nothing and meantime we have been here quietly piddling in our pants with suspense.

Every day I have been expecting a letter from Gerald—but no letter. Of course I realize the pressure of the work: then after the event?

Conceive of yourself in Siberia with a play coming off in Moscow which is a great ambition of yours: and no word but after six months of anxiously waiting for every post you receive word, relayed through a commissar from the producer that always supposing that certain auxiliary circumstances are equal and that dog teams are not requisitioned for something else you may be permitted in a month or two to see part of the envelope on which at one time had reposed part of the script. This I admit is an exaggeration but all I wanted was, as it were, a single word or phrase like: O.K., Hot Diggety, or even We are not amused.

I was anxious for your sakes too for I would have been unhappy to think the first thing you did didn't come off and I would have felt rather responsible.

But the silence now makes me think it didn't come off: but then of course perhaps it did.

I realize you are very busy and probably have not time to consider such involved feelings as this or perhaps you rightly felt that you have already considered them enough.

Gerald, you blighter, donde es that allerverdampfter carta?

At all events, all the very best of luck to you in Babylon there from Utima Thule.

Blessings,
Malcolm

* Originator of "Studio One," he produced *Under the Volcano* as his first play, April 29, 1947.
† Gerald Noxon dramatized the novel for "Studio One."

1947

To Jacques Barzun*

Dollarton, B.C., Canada
May 6, 1947

Dear Mr. Barzun:

You've written, to my mind, such a horribly unfair criticism of my book, *Under the Volcano,* that I feel I may be forgiven for shooting back.

Granted that it has been overpraised to the extent where an un-favorable review seems almost welcome, and granted that your review may end by doing me good, it rankles as an even harsher criticism, if just, could never do; and I feel that this is not only unsporting but weakens your whole general argument; people simply won't listen to your very necessary truths if you do this kind of thing once too often.

Ah ha, I can hear you saying, well I can tear the heart out of this pretty damned easily, I can smell its derivations from a mile away, in fact I need only open the book at random to find just what I want, just the right food for my article: I do not feel you have made the slightest critical effort to grapple with its form or its intention. What you have actually succeeded in doing is to injure a fellow who feels himself to be a kindred spirit.

I do not think there was any need, either, to be so insulting about it. You are intitled to "fulsome and fictitious" and you can say if you wish (though it is not specifically true and there is certainly no ir-refutable evidence of the former) that I am "on the side of good behavior and eager to disgust you with tropical vice." But when you say "He shows this by a long regurgitation of the materials found in *Ulysses* or *The Sun Also Rises"* are you not overstepping the mark in an effort to be scornful? For while few modern writers, myself in-cluded, can have altogether escaped the influence, direct or indirect, of Joyce and Hemingway, the "materials" in the sense you convey are not to be found in either of these books. "And while imitating the tricks of Joyce, Dos Passos and Sterne, he gives us the heart and mind of Sir Philip Gibbs." What tricks, precisely, do you mean? A young writer will naturally try to benefit and make use of what he has read, as a result of which, especially in technique, what Van Gogh I think calls "design-governing postures" are from time to time inevitable. But where I found another writer in the machinery—the writer you

* Critic and educator.

are reading at the moment, Richards has pointed out, is nearly always the villain—I always did my utmost to sweat him out. Shards and shreds of course sometimes remain; they do in your style too. But so far as I know I have imitated none of the tricks of the writers you mention, one of whom at least once testified to my originality. As a matter of fact—and to my shame—I have never read *Ulysses* through, of Dos Passos I have read only *Three Soldiers,* and of Sterne I have never been able to read more than one page of *Tristram Shandy.* (This of course does not rule out direct influence, but what about what I've invented myself?) I liked *The Sun Also Rises* when I read it 12 years ago but I have never read it since nor do I think I've ever been particularly influenced by it. Where the *Volcano* is influenced, its influences are, for the most part, other, and for the most part also I genuinely believe, absorbed. Where they are not you can put it down to immaturity; I began the book back in 1936 when I was 27 and doubtless, in spite of many rewritings, it carries a certain stamp of that fact. As for Sir Philip Gibbs are you not just being gratuitously cruel? Perhaps if you would really read the book you would see that quite a lot of it is intended to be—and in fact is—funny, as it were a satire upon myself. Nor, I venture to say, do I think that, upon a second serious reading, you would find it dull.

After Sir Philip Gibbs I can almost forgive you for juxtaposing at random two not very good passages from Chapters III and IX as though they were contiguous, as an example of bad reporting. But even if those passages are not so hot, what of the justice of this kind of criticism? I'd like to know what you'd do with the wretched student who loaded his dice like that for you.

The end, I suppose, is intended to crush one completely. "Mr. Lowry has other moments, borrowed from other styles in fashion, Henry James, Thomas Wolfe, the thought-streamers, the surrealists. His novel can be recommended only as an anthology held together by earnestness."

Whatever your larger motive—which I incidentally believe to be extremely sound—do you not seem to have heard this passage or something like it before? I certainly do. I seem to recognize the voice, slightly disguised, that greeted Mr. Wolfe himself, not to say Mr. Faulkner, Mr. Melville and Mr. James—an immortal voice indeed that once addressed Keats in the same terms that it informed Mr. Whitman that he knew less about poetry than a hog about mathematics.

But be that as it may. It is the "styles in fashion" that hurts. Having lived in the wilderness for nearly a decade, unable to buy even any intelligent American magazines (they were all banned here, in case you didn't know, until quite recently) and completely out of touch, I have had no way of knowing what styles were in fashion and what out, and didn't much care. Henry James' notebooks I certainly have tried to take to heart, and as for the thought-streamers (if you're interested in sources) William would doubtless be pleased. And I'm glad at least it was earnestness that held the anthology together. Nonetheless I shall laugh—and I hope you with me—should in ten years or so the Voice again be heard decrying some serious contemporary effort on the grounds that its author is simply regurgitating the materials to be found in Lowry. I shall laugh, but I shall on principle sympathize with the author, even if it is true.

Be this as it may. Any other kind of duello being inconvenient at this distance, I had begun this letter with the intention of being, if possible, as intolerably rude as yourself. I even bought an April *Harper's* to provide myself with material and sure enough I found it springing up at me, just as to you, from my work, your ammunition: for did I not immediately find you lambasting Señor Steinbeck in vaguely similar terms, although at much greater length, accusing him of almost everything except stealing his bus from me—you of course didn't know I had one, it is in Chapter VIII (a crime I may say of which he is innocent and vice versa) and speaking of his anti-artistic emotion of self-pity, by which I take it you do not of course mean your *own* anti-artistic emotion of self-pity by any chance?

There is an interesting passage here too:

In the makers of the tradition, that is to say in Balzac, Dickens, Zola, Hardy, Dostoevsky, down to Sinclair Lewis and Dos Passos, there is an affirmation pressing behind every grimness, an anger or enthusiasm of despair which endows mud with life and makes it glow like rubies. The energy of mind makes even a surfeit of facts bearable, while plot enmeshes the characters so completely that the reader is compelled to believe in a fated existence, at the very moment when he knows that he is only the sport of the writer's will.

Good: but why, at that rate, are you so ready to jump upon the affirmation pressing behind the grimness in the *Volcano?* So ready to jump upon it indeed as soon as you saw it (because it was in capital letters doubtless) that you quite missed the anger or the enthusiasm of despair that it was following? Did you not trample the one to death without even taking the trouble to see if the other was there at all, without taking *any* trouble, in short, except to exhume Sir Philip Gibbs from his dull grave in order to have a cheap sneer at my expense? And if so, why? I could tell you, but this is as far as my rudeness will take me.

For one thing, I have just got another batch of reviews, all of them good, and all of them more irritating than yours. For another, the book is to be translated into French: the very tough editors, I am relieved to say, think more highly of it than you, which is something. And for another I just have news from England that one of my best friends—Anna Wickham, the poet, if you're interested—has just hanged herself in London.

> God has raised his whip of Hell
> That you be no longer weak
> That out of anguish, you may speak
> That out of anguish, you may speak well.

She once wrote. My wife, by a coincidence having bought me a week ago, in Canada, the only edition of her poems (praised by D. H. Lawrence—and why didn't you drag *him* in?) that can have been sold in 20 years, bought them for me indeed two days before Anna died. So life is too short or something.

And the grammar of this letter is bad. And it will remain so. So, doubtless, are the semantics. And the syntax. And everything else.

With the general tenor of your criticism in *Harper's* I am enormously, as I hinted, in accord. That for instance political books should be read with the historian's scepticism, and with the historian's willingness to see the drama of both sides, that we suffer from intellectual indigestion, philosophic bankruptcy, and adulterated "brews" of one kind or another—be they behavioristic or what-not, that we are being done down by half thoughts, regurgitated unthoughts found in so and so—how true: I might remind you, though, that there are sometimes deeper sources and not everything comes up your own service elevator.

I think I said that the *Volcano* had been over praised and also praised for qualities it probably doesn't possess and I think that one of the things I wanted to say was that that seemed no good reason for you to tear it to pieces for faults it doesn't possess either.

I wish, sincerely, that you would read it again, and this time, because you don't have to write about it, look instead for what may be good in it. It sings, I believe, considerably—the whole thing—in the mind, if you can stand the partial bankruptcy in character drawing and what actually *is* fictitious about it, the sentences like Schopenhauer's roast geese stuffed with apples.

But on the side of good conduct no. I myself savagely reviewed it for a preface for the English edition—though they would have none of it—thus—never mind the "thus" but ending: All applications for use by temperance societies should be accompanied by a case of Scotch addressed to the author. Now put it back in the three-penny shelf where you found it.

Moreover I had even toyed at one time rather lovingly with the notion of having Hugh and Yvonne killed off while too sober and the Consul returning cheerfully and drunkenly to his duties to mescal and the British Crown under a miraculously transformed and benign Poppergetsthebotl.

You might also remember that so far as the latter was concerned I was doing what I fondly believed (in spite of *L'Assommoir*) to be a pioneer work. *The Lost Weekend* et al did not come along until, as always happens, it was virtually finished, and at that for the fifth time. Moreover it will both horrify and relieve you to learn that it was only the third of a book, if complete in itself, most of the rest having been destroyed by fire.

And if you want sources—what about the Cabbala? The Cabbala is only in the sub-basement of the book but you would discover therein that the Cabbala itself is identified with the "garden" and the abuse of wine with the abuse of magical powers, and hence with the destruction of the garden, and hence with the world. This myth may have somewhat confined me: for though one might sympathize with Mephistopheles, Faust is a different matter. But perhaps I cite this only to show you how much more loathsome the book might have been to you had I put this on the top plane. I very much believe in what positive merits the book has, however. (I don't know if Sir Philip Gibbs ever thought about the Cabbala, I have a gruesome suspicion that that is precisely the sort of thing he may have thought about.)

At all events I am now writing another book, you will be uninterested to learn, dealing roughly speaking with the peculiar punishment meted out to people who lack the sense of humour to write books like *Under the Volcano*. So far, I am pretty convinced that nothing like it has been written, but you can be sure that just as I am finishing it—

Sans blague. One wishes to learn, one wishes to learn, to be a better writer, to think better, and one wishes to learn, period. In spite of some kind of so-called higher education (Cambridge, Eng.) I have just arrived at that state where I realized I know nothing at all. A cargo ship, to paraphrase Melville, was my real Yale and Harvard too. Doubtless I have absorbed many of the wrong things. But instinct leads the good artist (which I feel myself to be, though I say it myself) to what he wants. So if, instead of ending this letter "may Christ send you sorrow and a serious illness," I were to end it by saying instead that I would be tremendously grateful if one day you would throw your gown out of the window and address some remarks in this direction* upon the reading of history, and even in regard to the question of writing and the world in general, I hope you won't take it amiss. You won't do it, but never mind.

With best wishes, yours sincerely,

Malcolm Lowry

P.S. Anthology held together by earnestness—brrrrrr!

To James Stern

Dollarton, B.C., Canada

[June, 1947]

God bless you old bird for your letter, and good luck—this a plea for more *Chesterfieldian* advice.

P.S. We are both trying to read your new book at once (title not right in my mind, *The Secret Damage? The Hidden Damage?* be not offended, I could not remember the title of the *Volcano* the other day— but I know your book's *purport*).

P.P.S. I have been reading Jim Agee's and Evan's book *Let Us Now Praise Famous Men,* too, you see: surely one of the most important in all American literature, and one of the finest and most beautiful: and *useful*—I think I will begin my education on it—God damn it, he even tells me how I (we) built my (our) house in it. Give all love to him and his—and to Tanya, say loveletters blessings from us both. I hope you are well again and thank you for washing out my blood-stained singlet.

Malcolm

I know you will be delighted to hear Maxwell Perkins just accepted Margie's *Horse in the Sky!!*

* See Appendix 6.

[148]

To Albert Erskine

Dollarton, B.C., Canada
June 24, 1947

Dear old Albert:

Thank you immensely for your letter, which I think crossed with a pigeon of mine sent winging cryptically through the red forest of the post.

It was super thoughtful of you to send the list of books: the Modern Library always afflicts me with nameless and wonderful senses of early draughts and distillings: *McTeague* I think was the first book I ever read, the *Seven That Were Hanged* the second, both in Modern Library editions my brother, come back from Dallas, gave me. (The Bible didn't come till far later, hasn't yet come indeed, alas, perhaps.) Tell me the price—do we get a cut rate? (I don't think the Bible is in the Modern Library.) At all events I sometimes feel you should go back to the floppy edition of those days.

Of course you must know Bob Linscott—a wonderful fellow!

And how is the good Frank?

Margie has her proofs off to Scribner's and I have earache partly due to over swimming, partly due to the fact that my ear canals spiral in the wrong direction and don't even come out in the right place perhaps—so that a doc, aiming to treat same, nearly deafened me instead.

Yes, I was pretty good at golf once, I broke the boys under-15 record, and also later under-18, held for fifty-odd years by Johnny Ball (later open champ) in 1924: I did the first 8 at the Royal Liverpool (Hoylake) in 28 once in the annual boy's show there when I was 14½, broke down at the 9th a short hole took in six (still two under actual par so far) but came back in the last 9 in the late forties but still broke the record. But later I took to socketing* and even beer perhaps and dreadful nervous twitchings on the green. When I began to think I was really good I became lousy. But should you care to—er —look you will still find my record inscribed on the wall in the Royal Liverpool to this day: there is a very nice pub beyond the 17th green, on the other side of the road, called The Bull also. My record isn't quite fair altogether because Johnny had to use a gutta-percha ball in them days. But I beat H. H. Hilton's winning score too, who didn't,

---

* I.e., "shanking," or swinging an iron so that the face of it strikes the ball at the intersection of the shaft and the blade.

and several others who later became amateur or open champs. My record wasn't beaten until sometime in the 30's, balls and clubs were getting better or perhaps even the players: to me, the holes were getting longer and more complicated.

I have been working hard on *La Mordida,* and that is exactly like those holes: Only here I have both to plan the holes and play the game too. In order to make them easier one can make them shorter or whatever, then one overshoots the green, or cross winds and sheep, ghostly foursomes, arrive from nowhere. Perhaps one should take to tennis again—well, balls anyway. I don't see that this golfing style is very helpful either: perhaps one should write more like Edmund Wilson in *Hecate County,* a man who calls a spade a club. . . .

For the rest, a very stern crimp in my soul, your not being *there,* so to say; into what roughs, out-of-bounds and quagmires we shall get ere the book be finished, and stymies at the last green, one knows not, therefore spiritually inscribe our handicap, put it up to twenty-four, and wink some Drummond light from extramundane clubhouse at the end, else we are lost in the ultimate Hell Bunker.

In effect, apart from not liking the Chief of Gardens too much, the news is this: there is earache, and sundry other health worries on Margie's side, though I feel all will prove triumphantly negligible.

In addition we ran into one A. J. M. Smith, whom you mentioned: we played him the *Memphis Blues* on the guitar so hot he jumped right out of the window, into the sea however, where he floated for a time, and even came up eventually to ask for some poems for an anthology. A poor egg.

Margie has some 50 typed out but I have some more weeding out to do before I can send you any.

I have asked Farrar and Rinehart to send you a book by Antony Lespes entitled *La Terre et les Hommes.* They had already refused this book when I was in New York but had still failed to let him know to date.

It is in French, but it might be Random's meat. It ought to be someone's at all events.

Also—what about Marcelin's *Tailleur pour Bêtes?* Marcelin wants to add a story or two to it before they are published.

I have managed to find a field for his poems here at last and doubtless they will filter through back to America again, I doubt not into some kind of anthological deathlessness somewhere.

All best love to Peggy and Frank and Nan from us both—and of course to yourself.

God bless,
Malcolm

To Albert Erskine

Dollarton, B.C., Canada
August 13, 1947

Albertissimo!
Christ what a breeze! And again Christ what a breeze! And again, how may I thank you. Or how may I presume. What with Studs Mulligan and Buck Lonigan the élan of the captive bullfinch and the dying Antony howling for a drink being hauled up a clock tower in a coalbasket by Cleopatra with ropes—which I never knew, and why didn't Shakespeare use it—and did Dryden, who translated the Plutarch, use it in *All for Love*—I am all, as the saying is, of a doodah: yes I am all of a doodah. I am in a mammering and at a stay and upon the horns of a Domelia. I thank you. And once again we thank you. Though how thank you enough? We are building a special bookcase to accommodate the beautiful books and the house begins to look really like a home for the first time. You've no idea what a difference it makes and how it causes the Lowry's, not to say the Penates, face to shine.

For the rest, you are right, we have been a bit slack, a bit on the loafing side; though I've written the first of a first draft of *Dark Is the Grave* and have started on the second. I can't make the first chapter come out right, but when I do I'll send it along: in fact I'll try to send it along in installments, unless my multiple schizophrenia gets the better of me and I decide I ought really to revise *Ultramarine* and *Lunar Caustic* first. Then there are the poems. But we are at least back at a system of work again. And the beach—though we were earlier in the season invaded ("The King of the Squatters") by reporters—is, I dare say on account of this, pretty well deserted. We rise at six and beam at the molten sun and swim much as of yore, only even better, save that we have lost our po' guitar in the sea: returned by Laocoön, when somewhat plastered, to Neptune.

For the rest I have no news: my brother liberated the Channel Islands single-handed without a shot being fired, there being nobody there apparently to shoot, my mother sends me the *British Weekly* and the *Illustrated London*—or someone sends it for my mother, for they always have "Master Malcolm" pencilled upon them—and my nephew, a Lieutenant in the R.A.F., has put in a request that his bibulous uncle send him some unused Canadian stamps. Margie's book is coming out, we hope not printed backwards, and thank you very much indeed for the *Sewanee Review*—the most heartening and encouraging review of the *Volcano* I yet have read (albeit I made the slight mistake of reading the *Kenyon Review* immediately after it).

Lastly I have my usual impractical request to make re the Haitians, the San Domingans and the Doukhobors etc.

To be specific and serious, I have from our friend Philippe Thoby-Marcelin a letter informing me that the firm of Rinehart has turned down his latest book, written in collaboration with his brother, *The Finger of God*. Be it not forgotten before I go on that their novel *Canapé-Vert* won the Latin-American novel prize and that Mr. Edmund Wilson thought highly enough of that book to devote a long article to it, in fact he mentioned it the other day again—it is, indeed a highly significant book. (I doubt not, indeed, that it deserves to go in the Modern Library.) But be these things as they may, it is, for him, quite a confusing and pathetic letter, not the least for being written in French and asking for advice which I don't think I can ethically give him since, so far as I know, Ann Watkins is still his agent. But what seems to have happened is that he sent the book direct to Rinehart instead of to Ann Watkins and Rinehart wrote back to Marcelin—since they knew I'd referred some other work from them to you— asking if they should send it to yourself, whereupon Marcelin has written to me asking me should he instruct Rinehart to send it to you and if so would there be any chance you or Random House might be interested, to which I can only reply (a) How the hell do I know, (b) I can only ethically try to help with such work as Ann Watkins herself has not been able to place—(I've had some potential success, by the way, here, with the poems)—But all this takes so long and meanwhile the author goes on starving and gnattering upon his isle—I don't think he realizes that he's nearer to N.Y. than I am, however. With all this in mind do you think you can find out what's what? One thing at least is clear to me: here is an opportunity for someone to take over where Rinehart has just thrown away a first-rate artist. I am in a bit of an ambiguous position. I begin to think that I may, through good but impractical intentions, have damaged his position at Rinehart and Ann Watkins. But this would seem unimportant beside the fact that so far as I can see the Marcelins are now "loose" and it would seem an honourable venture for some publisher to pick them up. Marcelin is one of the very few first-rate geniuses I have ever met. So could you inquire from Ann Watkins what the situation is,—at least, even if you read not the French, you could cause Random House to get first refusal? Or cause even the Chief of Gardens—perish the thought—to gloze upon it? But if you don't wish, would you please get Ann Watkins on the job for him again? If they sent the thing to Rinehart direct, and now he's asking me for advice, and both these things over Ann Watkins' head, I think it can be fairly ascribed to lack of cash and lack of knowledge of the general procedure. But at any rate the *Finger of God* and *Tailleur pour Bêtes* would be a beginning, a chance for someone to take over and cash in where Rinehart have let go.

In any event—all our very best love to you and Peggy—also to Frank and Nan—thanks a million again.

> God bless,
> Malcolm

To James Stern

Dollarton, B.C., Canada,
September 17, 1947

Dear old Jim:

It was swell to hear from you, twice, from the auld sod and Paris both: you gave no address, and I hesitated to write care of American Express in the Rue Scribe (a good playwright by the way) and now I regret not having done just that. But we gathered you would be back by the 11th, and so I and we arise from contemplation of your gloomy and handsome mug upon the jacket on *The Hidden Damage*—quite indeed the gloomiest I have ever beheld albeit with that part used to be called: character, not to say soul, writ large upon it—to welcome you back.

For ourselves we are riding rather high. I have gone into a kind of Indian wrestler's training to commit a new opus: Margie's book coming out (did you get the copy she had Scribner's send you?) and we have done some short stories in collaboration, both doing good work: at least we are making the effort. One has even gone some distance toward—in your words—"purging oneself of one's filthy little fears." At least we have put a new roof on the house and rise before dawn.

It is superb here in the autumn—the only inhabitants, and the tide coming up so high you can dive out of the window into the sea.

Meantime it is queer in this paradisal atmosphere to read the *Studs Lonigan* trilogy—a monumental piece of self-deliberation if there ever was one, and about whose merits the critics seem to have somewhat misled a fellow, being a work, for all its monotony and ugsomeness, essentially of the best kind of artistic piety, calculated in every way to make a writer pull up his socks, supposing him to have any.

Meantime also we seem to have a spot of cash, for once, thanks to the good Albert, and subsequent sundry pieces of awesome luck, in fact quite a lot of cash, so this place being really a bit too tough in the winter I had thought to betake Margie and self where it is doubtless even tougher, in short to the place lately vacated by yourself, namely Paris. To which end I wonder if you could give the family any information (we propose to go by freighter, and if possible later shift for a while to Morocco, even look at Italy, before returning here) of this nature: what can you live on in Paris? How far does the franc go or does that matter? Can you live on $200? or does it cost $500? Hotel? Do you have to write for reservations? Is Sylvia Beach still there? Do they demand that you have any set sum of money? General advice. Places to eat, drink, starve; friends alive or dead—or messages to be delivered for yourself, and so forth. Can you get an extension in France on the three-month tourist visa procured here? Are tourists in general frowned upon? What not to do: Chesterfieldian council. We both have the status of landed Canadian immigrants so we do not come under the English ruling that forbids travel; Margie still has American citizenship. Since ironically I don't think I shall be able to go to England, that is I could, but it might take too long to get out again, how does the ruling against travel affect Englishmen from England travelling for business, etc? In short anything you can think of, or have time for. The *Volcano* is coming out fairly soon in France, also Norway, Sweden, Germany, Switzerland and Denmark, so I have a sort of raison d'être for being in Europe: but perhaps it would be a bad idea to mention it.

All our very best love to Tanya—as to Albert, Jim Agee, Kazin, Dawn Powell—not to say Djuna Barnes and the windblown Auden—drink a health at the Lafayette—I hope you had a good trip and the very heartiest congratulations on the swell *Hidden Damage* and I hope it is bringing in the pennies likewise—where and under what title do I look for the next? (Do not, either, reproach me for liking *The Force* so much—perhaps if you will examine it again you will see how uni-

1947

versal it is. The monotony—the dream—the town that was so much less than its glow—the disillusion, the savage almost creative act of intercourse; a sort of mating with the fissure between the dream and reality. That is a wonderful scene also at the dance, and it remains one of the finest short stories I know, though you have done better, and of course can.)

Hasta la vista,
Malcolm

To Philippe Thoby-Marcelin

Dollarton, B.C., Canada
September 30, 1947

Cher Phito—

The *Volcano*'s eruptions having presented me with a little cash and wishing to share some avec notre frère we hastened to the bank to discover one is permitted to send precisely $50 out of Canada at once—herewith—which may look a little large in gourdes and which, while scarcely enough to feed the canary, has an almost Bacchanalian aspect when considered in terms of "trois étoiles"—you will notice that the cheque has quite a number of étoiles stamped on it, 40 in fact, so that it must at least be a good "brand" of cheque. It is in Margie's name because my money is in her name at the bank, or rather we have a joint account, so that you may take it as coming with love to you from both of us, and apologies that it is so little; but please do drink our healths.

For a cognate reason, alas, we may not come to Haiti this year; England is bankrupt, the Canadian dollar is only nominally upon a par with the American, and without endless and complicated grief it is impossible for a Canadian to cross the border into America with more than $10 in his pocket, and in order to come to Haiti it is first necessary to cross America, unless one should go by boat.

Investigation in regard to the latter is responsible for my saying that we will not be spiritually, however, very far from you after all, for, all being well, we shall be sailing for France in about 7 weeks from Vancouver upon a French freighter. At first we thought that this freighter would be stopping at Port-au-Prince but now the chances of this seem, we are very sad to say, slim. I do, however, have some money in France owing to me that it seems impossible for my agent to get into the

[155]

Western Hemisphere and taking this into account with the fact that I should like Margie to see Paris and Europe while it still exists, and the possibility also that you yourself may still be going to Paris, it has seemed to me a wise decision.

Revue Fontaine Mensuelle is publishing the *Volcano* sometime before March and if you are not coming yourself please give us instructions as to whom you would like us to see for you in Paris and what else can be done, and I shall try and see that these instructions are carried out to the letter; in New York I was handicapped by the phone ringing about the *Volcano*, a terrible cough and the terrible weather, that nearly killed me.

Margie's novel comes out October 6 and we shall send you a copy.

I have had no word as yet from Erskine concerning your work or M. Lespes, (or mine) and there is as yet no further news from here: but when there is I shall let you know. Perhaps you will have heard yourself.

I wrote to Rose in London concerning you and I certainly hope that you will have good news soon.

Please give our best love to Emmanuel, your brothers Pierre and Emil, the Pressoirs, John the priest, and all our friends in Haiti whom we hope to see again soon in spite of all.

Margie sends you her best love as do I and *nous t'embrassons fraternellement.*

Sincerely,
Malc.

To Albert Erskine

Dollarton, B.C., Canada
October 29, 1947

My dear revered old Albert:

I write to you, with a scalloped sky outside and clouds like a down-swirl of shark's fin, or even the Great Dipper, Van Gogh proved true in gray and winter and against a remote ploughed hurricane, a ramshackle plane flying very slow, and against that, what's more, the mountains showing an obscene sort of serge blue, and an old gasoline can banging under the house, and other purple passages I won't bother you with (to say nothing either of the two ravens, making love on Fri-

day the 13th on the gigantic dead fir tree) and just now, a rainbow
going up like a rocket.

Well, at all events I am writing because there is news. I shall leave
the more pressing for the last, meantime I am writing what fairly can
be described as a good book—I'm not sure, of course, precisely, being
a kind of sidestreet to my own consciousness; however, the report of
what is going on from my own point of view would seem to be pretty
good, as an objective observer I would like to wander some miles to
queue up, as a subjective one I would say without any qualification
at all that it is *tremendo siniestro:* at all events, *pazienza*—you will receive it in driblets, I will have a time to go through before I finish and
some of what I send you may seem a little wild. We progress towards
equilibrium this time instead of in the opposite direction, and the result is considerably more exciting, if not even more horrible, more
"inspiring" is probably the word.

Re Margie: the poor girl really does have a problem. On top of
everything else, Perkins died, his promises therefore seem to have gone
vacant. The last thing (you know the rest) in Perkins's correspondence
with Margie is that the book would have a fair chance. Here is some
estimation of what fair chance her book has got, from the *Publisher's
Weekly:* "The drama of a maid-of-all-work in a rural Michigan family.
Thurles Dungarvon inherits a fortune and thereupon starts to indulge
her dreams of being a great lady and of owning a stable full of
horses." My God—a publisher might as well have said of *Wuthering
Heights,* "Boy loses girl on Yorkshire moors and is then free to indulge his dreams of making a fortune and becoming a first-class bugger"—though it would at least have given the book some snob appeal.
I myself think *Horse in the Sky* is a pure, beautiful and lucid thing
and an excellent work of art. Margie has not had one single review or
a word from anyone in New York. This is doubtless due to the confusion resulting at Scribner's from the death of Perkins, but what can
one *do* about it? I propose to write myself to some of the reviewers
and call their attention to *Horse in the Sky,* not in the manner of a
husband taking up the cudgels for his wife, but quite objectively, to
call their attention to a good book.

All love from us both,

Malcolm

To John Davenport

S.S. Brest
[November, 1947]

Dear old Davvy:

Am writing this rolling down the northern California coast, being followed by three black albatrosses, each an iron bird with sabre wings.* Evidently practicing to be a left wing three-quarter: yesterday we found a dead stormy petrel on the bows, with blue feet like a bat: occasionally a large black oil tanker glistens by, empty as the *Marie Celeste:* and there tend to be golden sunsets in a blue sky.

Apart from that I have no certain news, save that we are supposed to be coming to France, but evidently not so directly as one thought: we are stopping in Cristobal, and Curaçao; and evidently also going to Antwerp; we have the Chief Gunner's cabin, and so far as I know we should be in La Havre on or about Xmas Eve.

The *Brest* is a freighter of the "French Line"—but seems to have a different agent in each port; but no doubt you could find out by letter from the French Line itself in Le Havre more certainly than we when we *do* arrive.

The Foreign Control Board in Canada proved very tough—and it got far tougher just the last six weeks when we were negotiating with them—so we're a good deal shorter on the finances than we thought we'd be: however we'd decided to go, so we are going, and I guess we'll get by—but almost certainly not in England, so far as I know yet.

However we live in hopes of seeing you somehow, somewhere. I find the sea intimidates me somewhat, for the first time: too big.

TO ABANDON SHIP

Le Signal d'abandon est donné par 6 coups brefs suivis d'un coup long. A ce signal vous embarquerez dans le canot No 1 Tribord ou 2 Babord.

Selon la direction du vent
Your lifebelt is in this stateroom.
Put it on as you would an ordinary jacket.

All the best to you and your Marjorie from us both.

God bless,
Malcolm

* The journey taken by Mr. and Mrs. Lowry out of which came the novella "Through the Panama," originally published in *The Paris Review,* now included in the volume, *Hear Us O Lord From Heaven Thy Dwelling Place* (Lippincott, 1961).

1947

To John Davenport

Dear old Davvy:
  Silent on a peak in Bragmann's Bluff . . .
  Silent on a peak on Monkey Point . . .
  The only passenger besides Margie and myself, a gentleman of the name of Charon: doubtless you have made his acquaintance on another plane? Here he functions as Robert Charon, Consul of Norway. Papeete, Tahiti, Society Islands—has a rather guttural laugh, I think he is a Turk.
  Or death takes a holiday on a Liberty Ship.
  We have also had four albatrosses, one, caught, on board: another huddled on the foremast, its great beak, from the captain's bridge, gold moving in the light: when its beak was there it made a third light.
  The little caught albatross sat on the afterdeck, with its red feet, and blue enamel beak.
  Mr. Charon would not come to see the albatross but stood on deck peering with a wild surmise at something he perhaps took to be a ferry (through a pair of binoculars which, doubtless because they were mine, did not work).
  So far so good—except that I forgot the water: Chacun est *prié* d'economiser l'eau attendu que nous ne pouvons par nous en approvisionner avant Rotterdam. En cas ou le gaspillage serait trop grand, nous serions obligés de rationner l'eau.
  Le signal d'abandon est donné par 6 coups brefs suivis d'un coup long.
  Your lifeboat is in this stateroom.
  Put it on as you would an ordinary jacket.
  Your arms through the shoulder straps.
            (Why do you not turn up the collar of your coat?
                                  November 29th, 1929)*
  —I mean 1947. Do not be afraid. Monsieur Lowry, he is the ancient mariner, said the steward, to Mlle. Zaza, wife of Salvadorean new passenger, who has no overcoat at all.

* A line from an early poem of John Davenport's.

Bananas trees—you like? Many bananas trees.

In short we are having a very wonderful voyage—quite beyond experience indeed, that is, at least, mine: we shall be passing south of Hartland some time within the next 2½ weeks—the French government has fallen in the meantime, so perhaps we shall turn the ship around and go to Tahiti after Mr. Charon. Somewhat prudently perhaps, we are going to Rotterdam first: hope (sic) to be in Le Havre on Xmas Eve, I hope too to see you and your Marjorie waving at us from the dock, even if it is but a hope; since, so far as I can see, you cannot possibly be there we shall tokenly wave just the same—please write: S.S. *Brest,* the French Line, Les Consignaires Rennis, Boîte Postal, no. 865, Rotterdam, Hollande (thank you)—where the ship's strange dream it is to be on December 18th.

Wonderful skipper on this ship, engineers, seamen, cats, stewards, pinard.

God bless you both from us both,

Malcolm

Please congratulate Wynyard* for me, give both him and John Sommerfield† my love and thanks; I am suffering from a slight surfeit of flying fish at the moment which is hard on the prose.

Anyhow you can keep posted about the peculiar progress of the S.S. *Brest*—which rarely rolls more than 35° to tribord or babord—by keeping in touch with the office of the French Line in London.

Pity about the pinard.‡

* Wynyard Browne, the novelist and playwright.
† The novelist: also an ex-sailor.
‡ This refers to various stains on the letters.

PART V: *1948–1949*

To Harold Matson

c/o Mlle. Joan Black
La Cerisaie
Vernon, Eure, France
[March 12, 1948]

Dear old Hal:

I have advised an extremely promising young writer named Eda Lord who has been through every kind of blistering hell from here to Cathay to send a story of hers that I much admire to Whit, and asked Whit, if it hits with him, to send it to you; and I quite frankly advise you to handle her work.

(Remember *me*—never a dull moment for 14 years.) But there is lots of fine material from where this came from—she has never been published before save in German. She is American, and it would make a hell of a difference were a story published in her own language.

As for ourselves, we hit a cyclone, 4 ships were lost and nearly ourselves . . . I miss Greenwich, your snow, yourself, Tommy, your kids, and the Ping-pong. I'll never forget that day, though the photographs didn't come out.

Margie has some kind of cinch for a film contract lined up in Hollywood: you should have been informed before now, but—not a mumbling word: this re *Horse in the Sky*. (Note: I perceive *Volc* in Books of the Year in *Time,* by the by, *Horse* in B. of the Month news: *Volc* apparently to be Book of the Month in France too.)

I have, over your head, given Fontaine some kind of illegal and egocentric permission to go beyond the terms of their contract in so far as that concerns its time limit; the reason being I am working with them upon it myself and want to see that it is good. Christ knows what Czecho-Slovakia will do!

Thank you for your letters—when they arrive.

I have a cold. And please do not forget Eda Lord.

God bless,
Malcolm

To Albert Erskine

Hotel de la Plage
Cassis, B. du R., France
[Spring, 1948]

Albert the Good,
  Sorry I haven't written.
  Maybe I am a bit berausgeshimmer,
  I don't eat my food and in my bed I have geshitten,
  Anyhow I am living here.
  In a comparative state of mundial fear—
  Also give my love to my dear Twinbad the bailer
  I mean dear Frank Taylor.
  This is written on the night of April 18th
  Anyway or the other, there is no rhyme
  Unless you can think of one above.

Save love
Malcolm

P.S. We encountered a cyclone—four ships lost
  Somewhat tempest tossed.

To Albert Erskine

Hotel Belvedere e Tre Re
Marina Grande, Capri
[July, 1948]

Dear old Albert:
  Since we both feel we absolutely have to meet in Europe we are abiding the question of your itinery (spelling mine) here in Capri and until hearing from you. With this in mind would you immediately upon receipt of this send us a night letter to the above address which used to be Bellevue or even Bella Vista. The proprietor is an artist, Lithuanian, whose papa was a bosom pal of Dostoievsky's. Papa reported that Feodor was an awfully nice fellow but sicka in the head. The other day we climbed Vesuvius. She recently giva the biga shake.
  God bless you for everything. Love to you and Peggy.

Malc

To Albert Erskine

c/o Joan Black
La Cerisaie
Vernon, Eure, France
[Summer, 1948]

Dear old Albert—for some benighted reason your letter got a little bit delayed: & for some even more benighted reason I, first, could not understand it, secondly, lost it—i.e. the postcard—possibly to identify myself without any shadow of a doubt as a privileged citizen of the Belgian Congo (in a thunderstorm) .˙. since I was dependent upon the hieroglyphics therein—not to say the address in order to reply—I have not replied. It will be a permanent cause of sorrow to me if my defection in this respect has in turn been responsible for our inability to meet at this moment. Against all this, however, it was wonderful & miraculous to meet at all. And please give our very best love to Peggy. I have to confess, however, that in spite of this comparatively lucid burst of correspondence, that I am going steadily & even beautifully downhill: my memory misses beats at every moment, & my mornings are on all fours. Turning the whole business round in a nutshell I am only sober or merry in a whisky bottle, & since whisky is impossible to procure you can imagine how merry I am, & lucid, & by Christ I am lucid. And merry. But Jesus. The trouble is, apart from Self, that part (which) used to be called: consciousness. I have now reached a position where every night I write 5 novels in imagination, have total recall (whatever that means too) but am unable to write a word. I cannot explain in human terms the incredible effort it has cost me to write even this silly little note, in a Breughel garden with dogs & barrels & vin kegs & chickens & sunsets & morning glory with an approaching storm & a bottle of half wine.

And now the rain! Let it come, seated as I am on Breughel barrel by a dog's grave crowned with dead irises. The wind is rising too, both on the ocean & in the stomach. And I have been kind to in a way I do not deserve. I have to write pretty fast. And I shall send this to Brussels pronto. Please wire c/o Joan Black, La Cerisaie, Vernon, Eure, if we can meet each other again, leaving quite out of account whether I can do the same for myself. A night dove has started to hoot & says incessantly the word "dream, dream." A bright idea. I remember always your kindness and generosity. Love to you both.

Malcolm

To James Craige*

Mont-Saint-Michel
[October 20, 1948]

My very dear Jimmy:
Here the tide comes in at 60 miles an hour and 48 feet high—there are quicksands all around and the swimming is much better *home* in Dollarton. Please guard our beloved house and pier, use it as you will.
Dearest love from Margie and Malcolm

To Albert Erskine

Dollarton, B.C., Canada
January 25, 1949

Dear Albert:
—blindage, blind alley, blinder, blindfish, blind man's buff, blindstaggers, blindstory, blindworm, blinkard, bliss, blithsome, blisterbeetle, B. Litt., blizzard—thanks a million for the dictionary. Others were not so lucky as we getting through latter, I mean the blizzard, as you probably read. Am back at work and grateful to have left Paris well astern. Will write. Love to you both. God bless and thanks again.

Malcolm

To Mlle. Clarisse Francillon†

Dollarton, B.C., Canada
February 16, 1949

Dear Clarisse:
We nearly didn't arrive here, but just made it. An American plane just behind us in Iceland couldn't land there because of the blizzard, and tried to return across the Atlantic to Scotland, but crashed, killing everyone on board. We were held up in Labrador and ran into a hurricane and temperatures of 44 below zero (Fahrenheit) in crossing Canada. Here we are all but snowed in; our pier is a partial wreck,

---

* A Manx boat-builder, friend of the Lowrys who helped them build their house.
† Co-translator with Stephen Spriel of *Under the Volcano* and friend of the Lowrys.

although that is the only casualty. The house hadn't even leaked and is warm and cosy.

(Please tell Dr. Courvoisier that I have made a very strange general recovery and I will detail it more in another letter in case it can be of some use with another patient. In brief—who was it said "I haven't time to write you a short letter?"—the paregoric threw me almost instantly into a terrible fit of shakes so I used sonoryl exclusively, about 3 the first day, 4 the second day, though never, I think, more than 4. Delayed in London for 14 hours by storm I drank very heavily indeed: innumerable pints of beer, brandy, and rum that we had brought with us. The next morning I breakfasted well on coffee, bacon, potatoes, brandy and sonoryl and we took off again across the Atlantic. Crossing the Atlantic to Iceland I drank innumerable whiskies at the bar and innumerable brandies with more sonoryl, though without becoming drunk and on the plane I also ate with increasing appetite. Snowed in in Iceland for 3 days with the plane's supplies locked up on board, and ours diminishing, I subsisted on one bottle of beer and on sonoryl the second day. My appetite correspondingly faded but I slept enormously without dreams of any kind. Towards evening the second day the passengers rebelled against their dry condition and although it was against the law, somehow some liquor was smuggled out to us from the grounded planes and I had little more than a pint of whiskey—we had to share it out—and on the third day we were completely dry until we took off in the evening, when I drank six double whiskies on the plane. When we arrived in Labrador about three in the morning, my appetite revived and I ate a vast amount of roast turkey and vegetables, drank a quart of milk and much fruit juice. I then had 3 whiskies at the bar and more sonoryl at the airport. We took off for Montreal but had to return to Labrador due to engine trouble, where we went to bed about dawn and I slept prodigiously. Stranger than this, I took a cold shower and shaved with a steady hand in the morning and ate an enormous breakfast of fruit juice, bacon and eggs, bread and butter and milk. During the journey from Labrador to Montreal I did not drink at all nor need to, but mostly continued to sleep, though for the first and last time since I left France I had wild, but not too unpleasant, if certainly half-delirious, nightmares: for instance, I thought I was kicking the head off the person in front of me and even apologized for this, and that a kind of electric stream running along the floor connected me from time to time with someone up ahead whom I couldn't see. In Montreal we had a long wait during which we drank some cocktails, ate heartily of liver and bacon, potatoes and vegetables washed down with much milk. During the colossal flight right across Canada from Montreal to Vancouver liquor was disastrously forbidden on the plane but fortunately we had bought a bottle of excellent whiskey in Montreal of which, with Margerie, I drank about half right under the nose of the snooty stewardess. At Vancouver we went to a pub, drank beer, pouring the rest of the whiskey into it, ate enormously, bought two more bottles of whiskey and went home, where we had a party, after which I sent myself to sleep with sonoryl. The next morning, although it was freezing, I rose as if automatically, made the fire and the coffee, and breakfasted upon ham and eggs, sonoryl, and the remainder of the whiskey and set off to the store to get food. Both these actions, in fact all of the actions with the exception of the whiskey drinking and the sonoryl, would have seemed to me extremely difficult if not impossible under the circumstances; the stove had scarcely been lit for 15 months, the path through the forest nearly impassable with snow and ice. I could not believe in my own coordination. My intention was to get a bus at the store, go to town and purchase some more whiskey, which was perhaps a psychological turning point, for instead I returned as soon as possible without any liquor and did not drink for the rest of that day. The next day, Saturday, a week since I set off from Paris, I also rose at dawn and did the chores: Margerie purchased some gin, of which we drank a little, but the next day and the next I drank nothing at all. By this time I had run out of sonoryl and switched to allonal, a sleeping medicine prescribed for Margerie. I took one tablet at night, and sometimes one and a half during the day, but steadily decreasing the dose, till by the following Thursday I had no need for it. I rose each day at dawn, worked hard physically in weather that has grown steadily worse—it is the worst in Vancouver's history—snow, blizzards, ice, the city of Vancouver is practically paralyzed and even has a blackout since the electric power has nearly given out—I both ate and slept like a pig. For some reason I also found I had lost my taste for tobacco and practically stopped smoking cigarettes altogether—at most 4 a day instead of 60 or so. We sometimes have a bottle or two of beer, or a few cocktails of gin and fruit juice before dinner, but the craving, the absolute *necessity* for alcohol, has stopped in a way I cannot account for; in fact it had virtually ceased a week from leaving Paris. What is remarkable in this (and I am experienced) is the complete lack of suffering during this period. For the last year I had averaged at least 2½ litres to 3 litres of red wine a day, to say nothing of other drinks at bars and during my last 2 months in Paris this had increased to about 2 litres of rum per day. Even if it ended up by addling me completely I could not move or think without vast quantities of alcohol, without which, even for a few hours, it was an unimaginable torture. During this last period here in Canada I have waited in vain for the shakes, in vain for the D.T.'s, or even worse horrors. My passage into a new regime, my turning of the corner, as the doctor would put it, if conclusive was virtually painless, and the temptation, finally at a minimum. And I have not touched any sedatives for a fortnight. What the moral of all this is I don't know, or how such an experience, unique to me, can help anyone else. I jot down these notes at random. (a) The patient, fairly intelligent and if not absolutely hopeless or a *danger*, knows far better than is generally believed *what he is doing*. (b) Towards everyone who coerces him to stop, his attitude is by no means necessarily pathological: there is a point where the coercer, the exhorter, *does* become an enemy, for the sufferer knows that he will drink more, somehow, anyhow, as it were for revenge, and it is in this cycle of lonely behavior of sadness that the sufferer shows himself pathological; on the other hand in so far as he recognizes it, his behavior is perhaps by that much less pathological. On the other hand again, the victim, while not amenable to suggestion where it becomes a matter of stopping, can be and is extremely suggestible to example, i.e. an ex-drunkard who nonetheless offers him a drink instead of a lecture can be a friend in disguise, also. Such apparently heretical advice as "All right, instead of drinking less, why not drink far *more*, only something stronger, and purer and *harder*," might work, by contradiction, wonders. I still believe that bad French red wine was my nemesis, I began to improve slightly when I took to rum and gave up taking vitamins. What about a campaign for better liquor rather than against alcohol? The indiscriminate use of Vitamin B_1 Forte was another villainous factor (by itself and without the simultaneous use of other vitamins in the B family, etc.): this I think is pointed out in *L'Homme et l'Alcool*, although I don't think that it mentioned that one's system could become actually intoxicated, in the sense of *poisoned*, by B_1. Since the "shakes" in any or all of its manifestations is throughout the greatest immediate fear next to running dry, it would seem to me that one or other of the non-habit-forming barbiturates should be often used in preference to strychnine or chloral, both of which can cause it, are habit-forming, and scarcely less than a desire.

I suppose that, as things stood when I left, the *Volcano* will be out in France in about a week or so; or is it to be postponed until March? Naturally I shall be only too glad, I hope, to hear any news you can send me of it and I hope also it is not causing you too much trouble. Please give my best love to Gabriel, whom I hope is better, and hard at work, and also all my best to Mike. Please thank him for me for what he has done and I hope he is pleased with the translation, as are you. Could you find out from Simpson about his article in *Saturday Night* that was coming out in Canada and please give him my best regards. Tell him I'd like to know more about that translation by Gide and others of my first book—I wish it didn't exist, but still. If he would send me the magazine or magazines that have it I would take good care of them and return them: I have his address. If he has not yet finished the article for *Saturday Night* you might suggest that he use this quotation I promised to send you, from the *Encyclopedia Britannica* and which I have now corroborated. This runs as follows and is to be found in the Year Book of the *Encyclopedia Britannica* for 1948, page 49, under the heading American Literature. ". . . But the year produced no new voice as commanding as that of the Canadian, Malcolm Lowry, in *Under the Volcano,* to presage a major movement among younger writers of fiction."

Have you any news of Margerie's *Horse in the Sky?* Or of the *romans de policiers: The Shapes That Creep* and *The Last Twist of the Knife?*

Please remember me gratefully to the chaps on the Club Livres de France: I apologize for not being able to spell anybody's name save that of M. Hôpital, possibly because I have to go to hôpital myself in a month or so to have an operation on those veins; the discoloration is very much better but the veins, because they now reach above my knee, have to be tied off: a minor operation and I shall be right as rain. Meantime I am working on another book. With best love and thanks and love from us both,

Yours affectionately,
Malcolm

To Harold Matson

Dollarton, B.C., Canada
February 23, 1949

Dear Hal:

I think Margie has told you that we are back home; sorry we couldn't stop and see you in New York but it just wasn't possible. Nothing much to report in a short note.

Fontaine fell down rather on the French translation and to tell the truth I can't make out if Fontaine is still extant: they gave me the advance however, and thank you for your permission as regards this. In the interim the Club Livres de Français took the *Volcano* for their Book of the Month—I think for this month or next—in fact it should be out now, the translation being by both Fontaine and Book Club people (perhaps Fontaine has indeed *become* the Club Livres) with my and Margie's assistance. They gave me an extra 20,000 francs on this already spent in France, and owe me another 20,000 on publication date (which I doubt if they'll be able to send, conditions in France being as they are now). Having had to make up my mind in a hurry I okayed this without consulting you, though Fontaine should have written you. Not much cash in American terms; but the Club Livres de Français is an extremely influential outfit and I felt you would approve.

Is there any news of the other translations? They should all be out long before now. I just missed the Italian translator in Florence, name of Luigi Berti. Einaudi—the head of the firm—is son of Italy's president, but inhabits Turin which we didn't visit.

No other news save I am trying to work on another book: I have to go to hospital for a leg or legs' operation in a month or so—circulation trouble—fashionable at least, being the King's sickness, though fortunately not so bad—and probably will be up and around in a week or so after.

Horse in the Sky didn't get a chance (albeit it made a Book of the Month Club recommendation). I wrote angrily to every intelligent reviewer I could think of—replies mostly stated that they couldn't get hold of the book. It's hard to think of a more crushing saga than Margie's.

Apparently I have blossomed out as some sort of poet: see the *Book of Canadian Poetry*, edited by A. J. M. Smith, second edition, University of Chicago Press—which is more than I have—and also in the *Encyclopaedia Britannica* (Year Book for 1948, page 49)—also more than I have done—under the heading American Literature. ". . . But the year produced no new voice as commanding as that of the Canadian, Malcolm Lowry, in *Under the Volcano,* to presage a major movement among younger writers of fiction." I wrote Reynal about it, thinking it worth an advertisement or something, even if a bit late, and he wrote back at once saying he certainly thought it was and would work out something that would feature it.

We spent an extremely jovial Christmas and New Year with your brother Norman and wife: we drank champagne and whiskey and went to the Flea Market. Norman and Anna had been having a beer in a bistro with someone who started talking for no reason at all about the

Volcano and informed him we lived in the pub next door—which is how we encountered in the first place.

With all the very best from us both,
Malcolm

To Albert Erskine

Dollarton, B.C., Canada
March 5, 1949

Excellentissimo Albert:

Am very sorry I haven't written before. Have no excuse save that I wanted to write a long letter. Who was it said: I haven't time to write you a short letter? We have had the most ferocious winter in history here, and we've had a tough time mushing through the forest getting our wood. Our pier was the only casualty, we found when we got home, and we've been repairing it and taking photographs of its slow development. The pier is the most sentient object of my acquaintance and our attitude towards it seems somewhat to resemble that of the Trobriand Islanders toward similar lowrys and penates. It is capable of crying and singing and also of considerable anger and I have also fancied on occasion that it was talking to itself, doubtless composing a subaqueous barnacly sort of poem.

Thank you very much for *Intruder in the Dust* which we value both for the book itself and your kindness in sending it. However I don't think I like it very much, if you will excuse me. For one thing, with all its merits I keep thinking that it is only the first part of the second draft of a novel to be called *Intruder in the Dust*. Lucas of course is a masterly character but it seems to me that Faulkner is straining like hell to stuff his thought into some kind of liberal tradition and even if this is necessary to the book when conceived of in relation to his work as a whole I don't see why its expression should be technically so comparatively feeble. It seems to me careless too, the writing sometimes almost frightening in its badness. Not that it is difficult exactly, but that I find myself often sinking through a quicksand of what is not even bebop without even a body at the bottom of it. But if you say I am wrong I shall read it again from another angle.

Thanks awfully for your thought re the Signet Books, which on 3rd thinkings really does seem a good idea, especially if you could bring yourself to do the abridging as hinted. In which case, tentatively I would suggest a brutal cut in Chapter I, perhaps just keeping the beginning, middle and end (this sounds like a joke, but you see what I mean) or even just the beginning and end: no cuts in II. An abridgement of the exposition in III where the Consul is lying on the road? and other small cuts, I don't know: IV intact, though we might cut Juan Cerillo altogether: V intact, I think; VI—your unfavorite—a whopping great cut in Hugh's thoughts especially re Bolowski (?) and in shaving scene with Consul—but keeping demons and what is necessary: VII largely uncut I *think,* though some surgery might be managed: VIII probably uncut but if so whittled a bit to make more of a *conte*—this seems doubtful: IX and X—amputation in both these, in Yvonne's thoughts in former, and guide-book stuff in latter and perhaps other hard-for-me-to-part-with Lowrecapitulations: XI intact: XII some muddy Lowromancings could go, and an eye could be poked out here, an arm lopped off there (etc.).

(Then what we have taken out, we can always put back again in a preface and footnotes, etc.)

Not so by the way, the *Encyclopedia Britannica* Year Book 1948 page 49 under heading American Literature says the following: ". . . But the year produced no new voice as commanding as that of the Canadian, Malcolm Lowry, in *Under the Volcano,* to presage a major movement among the younger writers of fiction."

Did you by any chance see that, or even spirit it in? Someone mentioned it to me and I thought they were playing a joke on me. I thought I wouldn't write you till I had corroborated it, which I now have. I did however take some pleasure in writing Reynal about it, being sure that he would not have seen it and not so much minding if it did turn out to be a joke. (He wrote back by return post saying they would work out an advertisement using same and enclosing the same advertisement you sent, with comment "Books like *Under the Volcano* are very few and far between. I think Knopf is stretching his imagination a bit if he thinks he has its equal." Ha.)

Since you mention money re the Penguin-Signet thing, I suppose yes, one could always use that too. I have, like you, to go into hospital fairly soon with a leg—a more or less minor operation—our gracious King's trouble though on a smaller scale, I am thankful. I should be out soon. Apart from that I am very well, in fact neither of us have felt fuller of optimisms and beans, though my correspondence may sometimes sound like Mr. Micawber's. I am also working very hard on the new book; at the moment like a dark belittered woodshed I'm trying to find a way around in with a poor flashlight. But when I've got it in order a bit I'll send some along.

Margie sends heaps of love to yourself and Peggy and Frank Taylor and Nan. As do I.

Love,
Malcolm

P.S. Also please give all our very best to Jimmy Stern, should you see him, and say we are writing. We heard via France that he has been awarded an award which if so seems very fine and very much deserved and if so please relay our congratulations.

M & M

To Downie Kirk*

Dollarton
Monday
[Early March, 1949]

Caro Sr. Downie:

La ringrazio molto—I mean may I worry you to take a quarter of an hour off more or less *sine mora,* not to say *quam celerime,* and explain to me what the blazes the enclosed letter is all about, if anything, for unfortunately about the only Italian words I understand therein are Italo and Svevo.

What I seem to gather is that he is asking, or wants me to ask, someone for a longer time in which the translation of the *Volcano* may be finished by himself or some person or persons unknown, which does not seem to me so surprising when you reflect that the gent is acknowledging upon February 7 a letter apparently written by myself upon February 21 and that therefore he may be supposed to have his own ideas about time. (Still, it may be important—for instance, what if he insists that it can't be finished before February 1946?)

We are looking forward to seeing you out here again soon. With all best regards from us both to Marjorie and Dorothy and *in attesa d'una Sua cortese lèttera La* (I hope this is right, hombre) *ringrazio di tutto e cordialmente La saluta il.*

Suo,
Malcolm

* A teacher of languages in Vancouver and close friend of the Lowrys.

To Downie Kirk

[Spring, 1949]

Dear Downie:

A thousand thanks for the translation and the letter. I have been down with flu, and now Margerie has it, though she is now recovering —but I am taking care of her so have no time for more at the very moment, if I want to catch the post. We have run out of wood in the blizzard too. Meanwhile here is the Marcelin, in English that leaves much to be desired, in our opinion, though it is extremely funny in places. *Time* mag. to the contrary, it is not about Voodoo, chiefly, but witchcraft: there is a difference, perhaps not apparent to the layman. Still it is well worth reading. (Warning—it is incredibly obscene in places too so don't leave it on the piano.) Again a thousand thanks for so very kindly translating the German, will reply as soon as Margerie stops sneezing. Both our loves to yourself and Marjorie and Dorothy.

Malcolm

P.S. We very much look forward to seeing you at Easter.

P.P.S. Do not dream of a White Easter.

P.P.S. Thanks again for the German translation—but what a gloomy picture it paints of contemporary German culture. As if we had to re-build our literature with no memory save of Alley Oop and Superman and perhaps not even that. (Also thanks for the French reviews.)

To Dr. and Mrs. Earle Birney*

Dollarton
March 26, 1949

My good Birneys:

Margie tried to contact Esther several times by phone—number always engaged, or wires crossed, or a distant voice in Sydney, N.S.— or even N.S.W.—trying to sell an oil well to another distant voice in Asbestos, Qu. Meantime I've been in hospital, having an operation. Very interesting. It lasted two solid hours and I was able to watch most of it. It seems to have been successful—they put me in the maternity

* Canadian poet, novelist, and professor of English literature, and his wife.

wing, to the alarm of an expectant father palely standing in the lobby. I explained that I was just one of those new, larger, as it were atomic babies just recently on the market.

I'm just out of hospital but won't be quite in circulation (sic) again until the stitches are out. I'm struggling to the Beethoven concert tomorrow night, however, to see how I can stand up, or sit down.

Thank you for the very merry evening—I reread *Titus Andronicus* in hospital, after the operation—in fact while it was still going on, for the doctor had forgotten something on the operating table and had to pursue me, needle and claw bar in hand, to the ward itself. It isn't really such a bad play after all. That is, there seems to be nothing wrong with it, save the writing and sundry little details like that. Dover Wilson has just maintained that it is by Shakespeare and Peele. We went to see *Hamlet* and *Macbeth*, both really excellently done, all things considered, though they cut out nine tenths of Malcolm's marvellous pseudo-condemnation of himself in the scene between him and Macduff, Act IV Sc. III—one of the most effective and bawdy brain-waves of Shakespeare, I've always thought in that particular place, and which has always made me rejoice in the name of Malcolm (er—relatively speaking, of course). And they cut out too much of the witches—becoming also involved in a curious kind of error in the interests of plausibility. That is, having Banquo's ghost in Act III Sc. IV apparently the result of an attack of the horrors—which was certainly quite convincing, and better than having the man actually appear to the audience—in order to be true to the special reality created by *that* they felt bound to make the subsequent appearance of the witches in Act III Sc. V and Act IV Sc. I also seem like hallucination. They didn't cut out the actual apparition of the witches, like they did of Banquo before, but ran the two scenes together, at the same time truncating them, and to make matters more complicated, here at the end, Banquo actually did appear to the audience. This would have been all right, and in fact very good, had not the same witches appeared at the beginning of the play to both Banquo and Macbeth himself, who was presumably then cold sober. It is a rather pretty problem, for I've never seen a performance of *Macbeth* yet where Banquo's ghost didn't cause trouble, and though here they solved it in a very reasonable manner, it was only at the expense of somehow upsetting the necessary illusion in the subsequent scenes. All of which merely shows that Cocteau is right when he says that theatre must remain consistently right in terms of the special reality of the theatre. On the other hand they played *Hamlet* uncut I'm glad to say —or would be, for unfortunately we had to go out and catch the

Deep Cove bus. It was a very good performance, what I saw of it, except for Polonius who seemed to be trying to do an imitation of Frank Morgan, and I thought that Stanley Bligh was somewhat mean about it. *Hamlet* without Rosencranz and Gildenstern, the court intrigue and the approaching war, and above all Fortinbras at the end, is to me rather meaningless as a play, for which reason I disliked Olivier's version, save for parts of the acting. (I didn't like *Henry V* any too well either—they hammed up Fluellen and Macmorris too much, when this, I take it, is meant to be straight, realistic, if boisterous, dialogue, precisely the kind soldiers would use.)

Thank you very much for sending me your student reviews and also for the *Outposts*. The reviews are, as well as flattering, damned interesting to me, especially the one that laid the stress on the mystical and religious catabasis traced by the Consul. This pointed out something in my intention I didn't know myself but which is certainly there: more of this later. All this means a lot to one.

I received a letter telling me you had spoken most kindly of the *Volcano* on the radio and for this, Earle, I am very grateful. Thanks awfully. The chap, a neighbor and collateral relative of Jimmy's, a philologist and language master at Lord Byng's, named Downie Kirk (holy great cow, what prose is this?) is relaying to me what you said. Now I curse myself for not having a radio—I hadn't gathered you were giving the talks so soon. I have heard nothing but the most complimentary comments upon your broadcasts.

How goes the novel? What you read was exceedingly good, it's so rare that something actually makes one laugh aloud (Joyce's complaint re *Ulysses:* "They might at least have said it was damned funny") which yours certainly does, does still in fact. And it seems to have just the right combination of humour with underlying seriousness. You once asked me if I could think of any novels roughly in the same picturesque genre that might be suggestive. *Schweik* of course—though it doesn't wholly come off. I believe I mentioned *Carl and the 20th Century*. I don't remember the author. The only character is Carl— the rest are simply statistics. (There's much the same thing at the end of *Schweik* but in this case the whole book is like that.) One short chapter in this mode might be effective. And have you read Saul Bellow's *Dangling Man*? Perhaps this is too far from your intention, but you might find it worth reading. *Dead Souls*, again, may seem remote but if you haven't read it, there is some sense in my suggesting it. For one thing, in addition to being extraordinarily funny it is one of the most lyrical and nostalgic novels ever written. Or so it seems to me. The swing between farce and the purely lyrical might be of value technically. And the almost Moussorgsky-like sadness and longing he is able to distil simply by describing some crummy little hotel.

Well, I'll have to stop. Do please come down soon—the weather is splendidly wild: Götterdämmerung over Belcarra. All best love from us both to you both and to Bill and his noctambule.

Malcolm

Wywurk still sits greenly and untenanted here. Wish you would buy it, though don't know how much they charge. I saw some sinister people looking at it. How can I encourage you? Crazy neighbours, or no neighbours at all. Unparalleled view of mountain scenery and oil refineries. Plenty of cascara trees in back. D. H. Lawrence once lived in a house called Wywurk. In Australia however. He thought it should be called wyreworks.

To Albert Erskine

Dollarton
[May, 1949]

Dear old Albert:

Please forgive my long illness but I had an operation, etc. etc. It seemed all right, then I had a few complications etc.—now it is o.k., etc. Thanks awfully for the Melville. It was very kind of you. It seems to me Jay Leyda and yourselves have done a masterly job. Both "The Tartarus of Maids" (I'd read "The Paradies" for some reason) & "The Bell Tower" were new to me & both terrific, especially the former. I have a note or two, mostly ornithological. Page 64. The snow white angelic thing with one long, lance-like feather thrust out behind, the beauteous bird that whistles in clear silver-bugle-like notes (so far as the silver-bugle-like notes are concerned, there is, interestingly, an almost identical passage in Gogol's *Dead Souls*—Query, was *Dead Souls* ever translated in Melville's day, he was I think 10 years older, but had just died [1852] about the time Melville was writing the *Encantadas* and the renaissance of piracy was taking place in Chatham Island so the bird may have blown him the thought, through its bugle as it were)—the beauteous bird, anyhow, fitly styled the "Boatswain's Mate," as he says, *is a red-billed tropic bird,* and though Boatswain's Mate may be a good name for it, and even *a* name for it in sailor's parlance, I think he is confusing it with his man-of-war bird, the frigate bird, or the Boatswain's Bird—in Spanish, the *digarilla,* though I stand to be corrected. Moreover, while far be it from me to suggest that he *didn't* see penguins at the Encantadas, though they seem to me indubitably associated with less equatorial regions, I can't help (pp. 62–63) feeling he may have meant the murre, a bird which on land is almost identical with the penguin, though this is not, I think, generally known. Perhaps he got fed up watching them on land & didn't bother to see them swim. Or perhaps *some* penguins & *some* murres. Question: do I or do I not remember, in ancient researches at the N.Y. public library, coming across a volume, published in Melville's lifetime, called *The Apple Tree Table & Other Sketches?* Probably imagination. Likewise, didn't he sign the name Tarnmoor also to *Bartleby the Scrivener,* a story of *old* Wall Street? More imagination. Had silly letter from Cape, who has done *nothing.* See end of Temple Second (p. 165). I am awaiting news from France & Sweden at the moment. Could not place your quotation—perhaps Melville wrote it himself. Herman is writing poetry but keep it dark, you know how these things get around, etc. etc.

Malcolm is writing prose and will begin sending you some instalments in a month or 2. Please send me a letter, I feel a bit discouraged, though we are well, & our new house is beauteous. I had a good letter from Frank. You must miss each other. Best love to Peggy and yourself from us both,

Malcolm.

P.S. Good thing they didn't have postage stamps in the old days. What would the adherents of Charles I have said to one like this!

P.P.S. Or perhaps he meant, not *Bosun's* mate but *Totipal*mate Bird.

To Frank Taylor

Dollarton, B.C., Canada
July 1, 1949

My dear Frank:

Margerie is flying down to Nuestra Senora la Reina de Los Angeles de Porciuncula next Wednesday to visit—to visit *with,* I believe I should say—her family for a week, that is approximately July 6th–14th, and I was wondering if you could find time to tear yourself away from the divers responsibilities of the Ferris wheel long enough so that you may both have a chat again. At least she will be as disappointed as I, if you both cannot establish some contact, but on the other hand will understand as well as I, should it prove impossible, she having been in what I believe is termed the pixbiz herself. However I should be immensely beholden to you if in your Wizard of Oz-like eyrie you would set such hosts in motion as would enable her at least to reach you by phone, my experience being that you probably have to make this difficult out of self-defense, from people claiming not only to be Scott Fitzgerald, but doubtless representing Edward Fitzgerald too, and who insist that if you think you can get away with making a film of *Tender Is the Night* without taking an option also upon *Omar Khayyam*, you are very much mistaken. On the other side her address in Hollywood will be care of Dr. E. B. Woolfan, 1643 Queens Road, and her phone number is (we think) Gladstone 3830 or if not you'll find it in the phone book, he of the wolfish name being my quite admirable brother-in-law, who entertains himself mostly by listening to the chests of movie actresses and establishing whether they are good risks or not.

For the rest I want only to say how much I value and treasure the letter you wrote me about the *Volcano* and appreciate your having been its publisher. I am absorbed in the new book to the extent of sometimes fifteen hours a day, and boy, it has some theme, being no less than the identification of a creator with his creation—Pirandello in reverse, or, Six authors in search of his characters; or otherwise stated, Every Man his own Laocoön. Since the philosophic implications might prove fatal to myself, I have to preserve a certain detachment. I am going to surprise Albert, who probably thinks I am dead, drunk, or idling, or all three, with the beginning of it fairly soon, nor, should it prove really good and he eventually think it acceptable, am I going to let anyone else publish it, which loyalty is by proxy to yourself too. If it is no good on the first attempt, by which I mean, even now, the fourth, I shall have to write it again which would be a bore, for I shall never get a better idea if I wait till kingdom come. But between the idea and the execution falls the— yes, indeed it does.

For the rest, we have five snakes in our garden, of high intelligence, I am convinced, for they like to listen to me twangle the guitar. Their tastes are a bit gloomy, however, running to hymn tunes played in diminished sevenths. We have not yet made an arrangement of "Snake Hips" for them. I think they would consider it, having no brows to speak of, to be slightly low scale.

So may we all (as it were) meet again.

In any event, our best loves to Nan, the children and yourself,

God bless,
Malcolm

To Mrs. John Stuart Bonner

Dollarton
[1949]

My very dearest Mother:

Thank you for your many notes of affection and I am sorry I have not found time to write you again at length: but since here there is no time at all apparently, perhaps it is no great wonder if a fellow can't find it; and I am an atrocious correspondent anyway.

Re the situation regarding Russia, etc., in answer to your question, I have no very settled feelings though they might be crystallized something like this: she, being what she is, can behave in no other way, and we, being what we are, can behave in no other way either. I believe it is lack of knowledge of the intellectual and practical content of the Marxist philosophy that is responsible for most of our misunderstandings, and on her side, for her inhuman and abstract development of that philosophy, so far as her relations with other countries are concerned: where we have tried to compromise we have met with little but hypocritical and egoistic response but then abstractions brook of little compromise, and we have no plan: while they have.

So far as I am concerned I dislike this world intensely but still, like yourself, try to preserve one's feeling for the *earth,* the birds, and the universe.

With lots of love—and love to all,

Your son, affectionately,
Malcolm

To Downie Kirk

[Early October, 1949]

Dear Downie:

Thanks very much for your letter and for the invitation from Marjorie and yourself for October 7. We'd awfully much like to come but since correspondence between us at this short distance seems to take rather longer than it used to traverse the Roman Empire is it too much to leave it open? We are working hard on a movie treatment and whether we can come rather depends on how much work we have completed by then; at the moment it looks favourable, but we may run into a snag, and it seems rather important that we finish it *quam celerime*, if not indeed *sine mora*. At first I thought I couldn't come because I could scarcely bring my fracture board with me*; now it occurs to me I could sleep on the floor. *Is it too much to ask for a bit of floor?* (It would not—er—be the first time that I have done that.) I don't think it would put you to any more trouble.

I'm glad you're better now after your operation—the combination of a haemorrhoidectomy with a Catholic institution sounds sadistic enough, without the orderly, in all conscience. It sounds a dreadful experience. I'm touched at your reading the *Volcano* to your fellow-sufferers—if you want to make people feel really cheery you might find Maxim Gorky's *The Lower Depths* even more helpful.

I am worried about your Prof. Sedgewick's *Irony* book, which we can't find, though we've turned the house upside down looking for it—will you have another look? It's just possible that I returned it when *un poco borracho*, which is why I can't remember. Margerie remembers only returning the Graham Greene. I had the book by my bedside for some time when I was reading it; later I assumed it had been returned by her, but I can't remember that, nor can she. I certainly never lent it to anyone else, and as a rule we are extremely meticulous about books, so I feel badly about it. If it was actually a signed copy I shan't forgive myself if it has been lost. But where the devil can it be? The only explanation I can offer is that it has been pinched: though that doesn't sound likely. Somebody actually lifted a copy of the *Volcano* I had bought for someone, while I was in hospital, so it isn't entirely impossible. (Once in New York my apartment was broken into and a copy of Ouspensky's *New Model of the Universe* and a bottle of hair tonic was stolen: that was all: the matter had to be reported because of damage to the door—the strange theft was traced to a Negro, against whom I did not press charges, not wishing to start a race riot.) It is just conceivable that Birney, who lent me some other books, may have picked it up, thinking it was his, and I will ask him, though I don't think it likely he made the mistake. I definitely never took it out of the house. The most reasonable explanation, if it turns out finally that you absolutely don't have it, is, however, that it is still here, but that I put it away in some too safe place, something I have very occasionally done before. We shall look again carefully, therefore: and if neither you nor I find it I shall order you another one. That is scarcely adequately replacing it—especially, as I say, if it is signed—and all I can say is, I am most awfully sorry.

* Lowry had broken his back falling from his pier onto the rocks below.

I hope though it will have turned up somehow by Friday, if we can come. We look forward to seeing you both and talking, if we do. We saved a grebe. And the world progresses. . . . That is, seventy years ago, one would not have thought that today, in order to cross a street, one would have to be preceded by a 3-year-old child, as Valéry somewhere says.

All the best to your Marjorie and Dorothy from my Margerie and myself.

Love,
Malcolm

To Albert Erskine

Dollarton, B.C., Canada
November 7, 1949

My very dear Albert:

We were very disappointed not to see you and show you our house and some Rockies. But we will be happy if you had a good and constructive time. I have revised my opinion of *Intruder in the Dust* which does indeed fit into the great plan most impressively. Please tell Jay Leyda how much I enjoyed the Melville stories and his preface. I am working up another ornithological quarrel with Melville, who in his poetry refers to shearwaters as "haglets" and birds of ill omen. Haglets indeed—they are mystical and wonderful birds. And apart from the fact that one suspects him of thinking of jaegars. . . . And even then! Someone once let loose a ringed shearwater in Venice and in less than a week it had found its way home to a tiny island off the coast of Devon, where it was discovered vociferously talking to its family about the voyage. (Nobody knows whether it came right over the Alps or clear round via Gibraltar.)

We are working on a kind of enthusiastic deviation from usual work—will tell you when finished, otherwise am withheld by superstition. One reason for this was that the broken back produced another story so related to the one I was working on at the precise point where I was working on it that I had to revise my plans anyway—meantime this is an experience. Hope Peggy had a very good trip—we think of you both with affection and often. Any news of the haglet or even murre editions? By which Margie says you won't understand I mean Penguin.

The back is getting better, in fact is even better than before, so to speak. I just wrote something about a very remarkable book sent me by a friend of yours, Mr. Harry Ford, via Knopf; having sent it in I was pursued all night by a mixed metaphor wearing black boots, from which protruded a cockade, and moreover fully armed.

All love and God bless from us both to you both,

Malcolm

To Albert Erskine

Christmas, 1949

Dear Albert:

You will remark that these candles are not burning at both ends. Should you see Allan Tate you might tell him in reference to his recent admirable article on Poe that if the raven was nearly extinct in the forties of the last century it certainly is not extinct now. There are two kinds of raven—Corvus corax, and Corvus cryptoleucus. The former is nearly twice the size of a crow, but it flies like a hawk, flapping and soaring alternately, upon horizontal wings. It is found in most of the Western U.S.—on the whole replacing the crow in arid country or along rocky coasts. The latter is smaller and is found in the deserts of S.E. Arizona, South New Mexico, S.E. Colorado, S.W. Oklahoma, and west and south Texas. It has never been reported in Virginia. Neither raven has been heard to say *nevermore*. I myself have never heard it say anything stronger than *cheerio*. But more specifically the former raven says *c-r-r-ruck*: the latter *kraack*. We once observed two ravens mating upon a Friday the thirteenth, without any ill effects. The Indians here think that the raven is God. In any case it is the most anti-social bird in the world, with the exception of (a) the eagle (b) the albatross. This is all the news. We are working hard, having a good time and my back is better. We are both in very good health and hope you are. And we send our sincere love to Peggy and yourself,

from Malcolm and Margerie

PART VI: *1950*

PART VI: 1950.

To Mrs. E. B. Woolfan

Dollarton, B.C., Canada
[January, 1950]

My very dear Priscilla:
In addition to thanking you deeply for one third of the gorgeous McMalcolm which I have already worn with triumphant success and which lacked for nothing in everything that delights a Scotsman's heart unless it was the crowning Stone of Scone secreted in the breast pocket—also thank you very much indeed for the French review and please thank Preston* very sincerely for his courtesy and interest in translating it. But apart from liking it (as the reviewer says of the book) God what a gloomy ghoul it makes me sound! Especially when I think that my ambition was much as the famed Sullivan—to be a humorist. Won't even Preston think it a bit funny? Just a little bit, I hope, or I shall be hurt. (Though for that matter I see no reason why he should have to translate the book, as well as the review.) I am recently in receipt of some two dozen more French reviews—sent by the publishers—all of which, so far as I can gather (which is not very much), seem of a quite fantastic favourableness (though each one making me seem gloomier than the last), far more so than the New York ones, and the English ones, and the ½ one in the *Skjellerup Schnapps-tasters Annual*, and all of which are presently lost—just at the moment I had assembled them to send to you. I had also some months previously marked a very long very intelligent very enthusiastic resumé of Preston's work particularly in relation to *Unfaithfully Yours* that was sent to me by my mother and which appeared in the *Illustrated London News*. Particularly though it was an appreciation of *Unfaithfully Yours*—a film I missed when abroad unfortunately. I thought Preston probably had so many of such things that he didn't bother to look at them any longer: then I thought damn it, no—he writes his films too,

* Preston Sturges, film writer and director.

as well as directs them: perhaps having been glutted with praise upon the directorial swings he could—sentence impossible—escritorial roundabouts—what am I saying? But it is the New Year after all. I meant well but preserved the notice so faithfully that even as mine, I lost it—temporarily, I hope. I put things away (or if I don't Margie does).

Idea for a humorous situation.

Young man from parts unknown, with obscure ambitions to be a film director, who has spent last ten years writing a book about alcohol, anxious to impress his wife's family finds himself seated next to the cameraman of *The Lost Weekend*—which has come out meantime and is playing with enormous success at all the movie houses—while his own book is unpublished and shows every likelihood of remaining so—with a famous film director drinking a tankard of ginger ale at the head of the table—with his wife and his wife's family present, on an occasion that happens to be his 5th wedding annversary. A limited conversation begins between the cameraman and the Y.M.F.P.U., who having just had an operation for varicose veins, is drinking whiskey, doubtless with the object of improving them.

The cameraman (kindly): And you say you write too, young man?

Y.M.F.P.U.: Yes, sir. I try to.

The cameraman: What about?

Y.M.F.P.U.: Well, as a matter of fact, sir, alcohol.

The cameraman: H'm.

Well, God bless you all—we are a bit at sixes and sevens here, my mother having lately died as you know—and news delayed as it always is in Canada, etc. Thank you muchly again for the shirt, & Preston for translating the review. *Mad Wednesday* hasn't reached here yet, but we'll be right in to see it when it arrives—hope it goes well; of special interest to me because I saw a bit of it being made, and very excellent too.

> Best love
> from your brother,
> Malcolm

To Downie Kirk

Dear Downie:

This is a letter of thanks to you and Marjorie for a wonderful evening but also a letter of apology so it is addressed to you alone, since I do not feel even worthy of addressing your wife at the moment.

My Margerie has impressed me with my bad behavior but I can't very well write a letter of apology to her either and as for the behavior I can only hope that it does not seem so bad to you as it does to me.

I am also told I used bad language in front of your wife and Dorothy; this is utterly inexcusable of course—nor is it an excuse when I say that I would not have done so had I been aware of their presence. But I was not so aware and here you must believe me. I am deeply sorry.

That there are reasons for all this, such as that I must have had one too many phenobarbital (My faithful enemy Phenobarbas—treacherous to the last), or that I felt myself in some way frustrated—apparently a nearly total illusion—in my conversation with Les, that I was, or rather became—and in what a damned mean manner also—*borracho*, etc., are not proffered as excuses, but are merely set down in an unsuccessful attempt to make me feel better.

Thank you for coming downtown with us: but even here my selfishness had reached such a pitch that in fact I was trading on your generosity and disorienting yourself from your own orbit—a mixed metaphor appropriate to the nature of the potations of the guilty party.

That *jocular* sentence is ill-suited to my mood however, which is pretty grim. I would say it was totally grim—for I count it a failure in character if I of all people (because God knows my work should give me sufficient practice) can't keep my wretched Id in order for five minutes.

All I can say is that I hope your wife and you will forgive me. Though frankly I see no reason why you should. Nor why, should I say that I can at least see it won't happen again, I should even be given the opportunity.

For the rest our sincere thanks—I only hope I didn't cast too much of a shadow.

I would ask you though if you can—since it is the New Year—to put the whole thing out of your minds, hearts, and speech: expunge it as a wretched aberration for which I hope I can make amends.

Sincerely
Malcolm

To Mlle. Clarisse Francillon

Dollarton, B.C., Canada
March 1, 1950

Chère Clarisse:

First, we feel a million thanks are in order (for God's sake don't misread that as francs) though I think you deserve a million francs too.

On top of that I feel another million thanks are in order to you and Mike for the marvelous translation and, by canalization, to the Book Club for the marvelous-looking book.

My pleasure here extends from the format right down to the very printing because it emphasizes the fact that for all its length there is compression in the text: this is particularly felicitous in Chapter VI which one or two people thought slackened in English (one idea of which was to inject some of what Gide calls "ozone" into the book)— it may slacken slightly in the English, but it certainly doesn't look as though it does in French, giving one the feeling that it may have given that impression in English because the typography there tended to sprawl.

Re the translation itself, it seems to me *superb:* it feels superb. We do not live in French-speaking Canada so I can't as yet give you any other expert opinions, but nevertheless it *is* mysteriously possible for the author to be a sort of judge even without command of the language—if it is wrong, to him, something in the unity gives way visually and so far as I can tell, you and Mike have not only done your utmost but brilliantly succeeded in what must have been a horrendous task and, in all probability, it is often much better than the original: French and English far from complement each other verbally but when the meaning comes through in French as it seems triumphantly to do in your version, the very fact that you have not so much advantage of actual "ambiguity" in the words seems to make the meaning deeper and wider in range and certainly more beautiful in expression.

I would be very glad to know of some other opinions of the whole thing and I am very anxious to know if it is succeeding as you hoped—in fact I cannot wait to hear—and believe me, as much for your sake and sakes, if not more, than mine and it would be hard indeed to think of you two as feeling the work to have been in any sense in vain after the labor you have put into it, I hope you get all the credit that you deserve, and that I myself have not let you down.

Re the new conditions of the contract: my answer is of course, yes, so far as I am concerned, it seems to me more than generous: however, ethically speaking, I am obliged to refer it to Matson, which I have already done today, and I will let you know as soon as possible, that is, I shall get a reply air mail from him in a few days and will immediately forward it to you. I do not anticipate—in fact it is difficult for me to see how he has the right—to raise any difficulty. I am delighted about Correa—if *you* are, that is, and *I* should be: I am very sorry that your Fontaine will not bring it out, however—if there is any grief for you in regard to Fontaine, which you half suggest, I deeply sympathize, at the same time feel that you will swiftly drive out the grief with the nail of another triumph.

I am overjoyed that the *Volcan* should appear in *Combat*, however (among other things that delight me about this is that Julienne, who used to call me that Bad Egg and who takes *Combat*, will be able to read it before dinner, and I am writing her to say, Watch out, the Bad Egg is going to hatch in *Combat* shortly!). But it gives one surely a very good feeling to be published in *Combat*.

Re *Lunar Caustic*—again, so far as I am concerned, you have the go-ahead signal, but again it has to be referred to Matson, lest I make an ethical flaw with him, or you. So I will let you know about that at the same time. It is dubious that he has any control at all over this as a story, but I cannot be sure how I stand about a volume. I have had many ideas for re-writing that story and if you do it, I shall be glad to pass them on, though perhaps this will be unhelpful and it is better as it is. It was originally written when I was 26 years old—and has never been published in English, as I think I told you.

Thank you about Marcelin—and thank you a thousand times again about everything—I feel a bit uneasy about my preface still, but if it has made a "good impression," that will be O.K.

But as I say I cannot wait to hear whether the whole book has made "a good impression."

We were frozen in here during dreadful blizzards in the winter—my hand became frostbitten—I think I told you I broke my back, that has recovered however: nor has the devaluation of the pound helped:

somewhere along the line I must have made up my mind to be a Strong Man (like Mike). So, well, I have become a Strong Man.

Please give my kindest regards to Max-Pol* and thank him too for the excellent and kind postface though you can tell him that if I am the Consul I am also M. Laruelle at that rate, from Chapter II onwards if you look closely you could see that the whole book *could* be taken to be M. Laruelle's film—if so, it was my way of paying devout tribute to the French film, for it certainly was not an American one, nor yet English, and it would not have been Czech.

I wondered if you could somehow smuggle a copy, with my compliments, of your translation to Jean Cocteau, and tell him I have never forgotten his kindness in giving me a seat for *La Machine infernale* at the Champs Élysées in May, 1934: I went to see it on 2 successive days and I shall never forget the marvellous performance as long as I live— Whatever he personally may have thought of it. And so you see his infernal machine comes back to torment the Consul in Chapter VII. (My first French copy of *La Machine* was solemnly stolen in a pulquería in Mexico together with my dark glasses which I had left on the counter for a moment, by a bearded Mixtec Indian with two pistols who had been drinking in the corner. He rode off on his horse with it and I have often enjoyed the thought of the old boy reading it to his wife in the mountains, with my dark glasses and all, and a gourd of mescal, and wondering what he made of it—a story I feel that might please Cocteau himself.)

It did occur to me tangentially however that the *Volcan* through Mike's and your translation might create in him some wonderful inspiration for a play from it and I could not help timorously hoping it might fire his imagination: there is certainly some material there for him wherewithal to freeze the blood with deliriums, and at the same time mysteriously to ennoble one—as he inimitably can do.

Well, that's about all, save that the gent who gave me the inspiration for the cabbalistic significance of the *Volcano* died the day you sent me the translation—not without having received extreme unction however. A very good fellow—and we mourn his death. We attend his funeral tomorrow. To make matters worse, for his wife, somebody mysteriously shot his favorite old dog, his companion of some 15 years, on the same day! That has a reminiscent ring: but fortunately if he was a magician he was a white magician and the dog, one hopes, will lead him across the river to the other side—as ancient belief has it— and at all events not down the abyss: (it is a more mysterious and eerie coincidence than meets the eye however, for the theme of the

* Well-known French critic, editor, and author, Max-Pol Fouchet.

dog goes right through the *Volcano*). His last words to his wife were, "Do you know, I'm not really here, I'm beginning to function on a different plane already—it's quite an extraordinary experience, old girl—"

It will be difficult to avoid chuckling at tomorrow's Catholic ceremony, for all its apparent sadness, on remembering these words, for I have the feeling that in Catholic thought the planes are somewhat delimited, to say the least—and if, while they are wafting him to one, he is all the while sitting calmly upon another, while it won't make any difference, doubtless, the thought is irresistibly comic, which is perhaps as it should be: death may be a serious matter on both sides of the fence, but there is at least a good argument—one which was advanced by our friend himself—that all life is destined to have a happy ending, and we have not been deprived of the sense of tragedy purely out of aesthetic consideration by God.

Finally—the wooly bear garment, or tiger, saved our lives this winter and I wear one blue glove at this moment of writing upon my left hand that hasn't, by gosh, got quite warm yet, though it is spring now outside.

Thanking you again most sincerely and deeply for everything.

With the best of love from us both—

And deepest thanks and regards to Mike, whom I shall try and write in French if he will make allowance for the fact that I am working 15 hours per day—

Malcolm

To Downie Kirk

Dollarton
March 2, 1950

Dear old Downie:

Don't forgive me for not writing—do certainly though, the reason is I'm working 17 hours a day against time, and couldn't write, not even you—but will you please for my sake take your Greek cap off the hook, put on your gaff-topsail boots, your hood, assemble your bow of burning gold and taking a flying leap into your desk, what time the gramophone is playing the record about the antiquated old antique, repay my bad behavior by answering as soon as you conceivably can the following antiquated old antique and learned questions? What I want mainly are the names of two Greek ships, and one Greek town, in Greek capitals: the first ship ARISTOTLE, the second ship OEDIPUS TYRANNUS, the town ANTIPOLIS. The difference is that both of the names of the ships should be in modern Greek characters—capitals—the town in ancient Greek capitals—I don't think there is any difference, is there? But Aristotle in Greek ancient or modern would be Aristotelis, would it not? And Oedipus Tyrannus sounds like a Roman version and would not be Oedipus Tyrannus in Greek? Be that as it may, they both have to be translated visually in the work in question into ARISTOTLE and OEDIPUS TYRANNUS but I want them visually in Greek capital letters first for dramatic effect. Do you get the point? Don't bother to be too meticulous about getting it absolutely right either, but the thing is it comes at a dramatic and important point in the work as we are presenting it; it isn't a question of showing off knowledge I don't possess, but I don't want to make too naïve a mistake right off. Parce que γον δεαρ Downie, I don't know how to write these βλοοδη καπιταλς though I began Greek when I was acht (8) and forgot it when I was novum (9). But these νερδαγτερ capitals are of some importance in the work, as we hope to demonstrate with some delight to you when it is ὺν φαιτ α'κκογπλ. For the rest νεργιβ γ ιρ not to say uns.

Therefore so far there are 3 questions: how to write ARISTOTLE, OEDIPUS TYRANNUS and ANTIPOLIS in Greek capitals.

On the last question hinges another question which I will frame in a moment, then I have several more, and then, though I am not through, I will have to pretend that I am, because I have left these questions to the last moment on the off chance that you would show up at the inlet when the weather got better, but now we have not even time to go to the library to find an answer, supposing one could do so, which is extremely doubtful, and anyway I would rather ask you. In connection with Antipolis what I want is the wording of an hotel advertisement by a railroad in the Riviera, its ironic appeal is to Americans (in the work) so that I have to break it down in parts into *bad* English, but meantime it is better for me to know what it would be in *good* French. Here is my version of it, a mixture of bad French and bad English—I do not know yet how much bad English to use, this is irrelevant so long as I know what it would be in French, so I shall make the question clear immediately afterwards. (And by gosh I better had.)

Touriste Américain! Vous vous approchez maintenant de la ville ancienne d'ANTIBES. Original Greek name:
ANTIPOLIS (in Greek characters).

Originally Greek, founded by the Greek-Phoenicians, in the 3rd century, its latest walls were built by the great Vauban, and up till 1860 marked the Italo-French border.
HÔTEL DES ÉTRANGERS, ANTIBES, 5 km. Confort Moderne.
Patron: Charles Gausse (son délicieux couscous).
Beach Huts—vins—liqueurs—Bar
Everything for the American tourist at popular prices!

All I want to know here, therefore, apart from the all-important Antipolis in Greek capitals, is how to say in correct French: American Tourist! You are now approaching the ancient town of Antibes, etc.

I hope this is clear, but even if it isn't, the first moment it is not desperately trespassing on your time, I'd be awfully grateful if you'd have a shot at it, in fact it is very important to us if you would be so kind—and never mind if it isn't quite accurate, time is of the essence now, is the point, and though it can be corrected later, it would make a large difference in the presentation if at least I can make the Greek capitals look right.

There are 6 other questions, though of minor importance. How, roughly, should one translate "Daddy's Girl," as the name for a film, into French? (Fillette de Papa? Poule de Papa? but it musn't be too διρτη.) It should be ironic, if possible. It appears as an advertisement (much as *Las Manos de Orlac* does in the *Volcano*). And also, for two more advertisements, how would you translate into French as titles: (a) The Doctor's Dilemma (b) The Last Laugh.

And how would you say in French (never mind for the moment the apparent preposterousness of the question): Freud and Peary—famous astrological twins? Would it be gemeux astrologiques fameux —or what? This is for a scene in an astrologer's tent.

How do you say "Bon voyage," in German. (Or don't you?)

And finally, how do you say STOP! PAY TOLL! (the same sign that appears on the second narrows bridge) in French, German and Italian?

These last questions are subservient in importance to the others and if you can't figure them out right off, or don't have time, we'll be monumentally obliged if you'd give your attention to the Greek questions first—and if you have time, send in the others later.

Finally, I thought you'd be tickled to know, the *Volcano* has made a hit in France, where it is coming out three times in the next months: first in a classic series, then Correa, and it is also being serialized in the Paris daily newspaper *Combat*! They have decided that it is the writing on the wall, that your amigo is everything from the *Four Quartets* (which he has never read) to Joyce (whom he dislikes)—finally related him to the Jewish prophetic Zohar (of which he knows nothing—they have some other comments to make too, about Macbeth, but that is nothing to what someone is just going to say in Victoria, over the C.B.C., where they have decided that the Consul is really Moby Dick masquerading as the unconscious aspect of the Cadbosaurus in the Book of Jonah, or words to that effect.

I am going to present you with a copy of the French translation and we should have some fun out of it when you have glozed upon it.

For the rest, we have many of your books, kindly lent at your and Marjorie's good party never-to-be-forgotten. Of them I have read backwards and forwards the excellent *Concert Companion,* which has taught me a great deal about writing (I mean from the form of music, which was not why I borrowed it, however—but it also helped me to begin to understand music a bit better). Our friend Cecil Gray makes some rather good remarks therein—and I'm glad you liked his book—more of that later. Shean on Gandhi is interesting and important in substance as it could not help but be—but it doesn't seem quite as absorbing as his other books, though you may find it more so. Merton on monasteries contains some phenomenal coincidences and parallels of some interest philosophically which I would like to discuss next time we meet, when one wonders why did one borrow the book, but as a book I don't think you'll go for it much. On the other hand it is certainly interesting to know how Saint So-and-So was once Bill Louseweed listening to a juke box and it has a value of passionate sincerity and dedication which however is not the kind of sincerity or dedication (which he knows fairly well) that many people will read into it. Finally, of course, it should be considered on another plane altogether: it is of sufficient importance at this point in history, though he seems an unsympathetic character in many ways, even as a monk, that he has made clear to a few people, even though it must seem to those people an exceedingly questionable book—in the sense that it is a paradox in its own terms. How the hell can a writer go into a monastery and go on writing books and then pretend he's given up "everything," I ask you, isn't he a sort of Trappist monk to start with? That a monastery might, in essence, be the capital of the world at this juncture is a possibility which not even Nietzsche were he alive would care to question—or would he? Anyhow, it is a good idea—or is it?

I have some other funny and even dramatic things to say but will close now, merely intimating that it be understood how fine it will be to see you all again, asking your indulgence for my having suddenly persecuted you with so many questions, adding my hope that you will answer them too, and to that all our very best wishes to the three of you, also imagining that when Dorothy has not been playing the tune about the antiquated old antique on the gramophone, she will have been playing even better tunes of her own upon the more modern and sober—or at any rate upright—piano.

Again, kindest regards to the three of you from us both,

Malcolm

To Derek Pethick*

Dollarton, B.C.
March 6, 1950

Dear Mr. Pethick:

Thank you for your letter and I am flattered you are to speak about the *Volcano*. I am also delighted at your interest in it and by your remarks.

While you are not quite right about the *Volcano*, it is none the less an extraordinary piece of perspicuity on your part, for what you say would very largely be true of a book that does not now exist, and of which you cannot have known, the *Volcano* having been designed as the first part of a trilogy—and the third part which I refer to having been totally destroyed in a fire which consumed our house some years ago—we built another house on the ashes, however.

My wife says it would be more true to say that in the *Volcano* the Consul bore some relation to Moby Dick himself rather than Ahab. However it was not patterned after Moby Dick (the book) which I never studied till fairly recently (and it would seem not hard enough).

The identification, on my side, if any, was with Melville himself and his life. This was partly because I had sailed before the mast, partly because my grandfather had been a skipper of a windjammer who went down with his ship—Melville also had a son named Malcolm who simply disappeared—purely romantic reasons like that, but mostly because of his failure as a writer and his whole outlook generally. His failure for some reason absolutely fascinated me and it seems to me that from an early age I determined to emulate it, in every way possible—for which reason I have always been very fond of *Pierre* (even without having read it at all).

* In reference to a talk on *Under the Volcano* for the C.B.C.

But to get back to the key—if any—the *Volcano* has just come out in France, where they say the key is in the Zohar. This discovery is partly due to a misleading preface by myself, written while not quite sober, but there is something in it, so I'll give you a précis of what they say for what it's worth, if I can translate it. This is in a very learned postface by one Max-Pol Fouchet and now it seems I can't translate it but I'll try to give you the gist. Now it seems I can't even give you the gist so I'll have to try instead to answer some of the points you raise in terms of what I think he says, or has some significance in terms of what I think I say—(so far as I can see, while it doesn't make you wrong, it somehow or other gives the book more thickness than even you ascribe to it, or I thought it had).

To take the points in the wrong order: first, the zodiacal significance—in my intention it had none at all, least of all in relation to Melville—I am trying to be honest, so I refer things to my wife when in doubt—the quotation you mention from *Moby Dick*, Chapter 99, I am conscious of reading now as for the first time—it never occurred to me there was any such zodiacal significance in *Moby Dick*, for that matter—and the passage now affects me supernaturally if at all, as if it meant something literal for *me*, and it was I who had been tracing the round again.

Though there is some extra evidence, if you like, in Chapter VII when the Consul is in Laruelle's tower—the Consul remembers a make of golfball called the Zodiac Zone—a lot more evidence in XI (where the intention was astronomical however). The goat means tragedy (tragedy—goat song) but goat—*cabrón*—cuckold (the horns). The scorpion is an image of suicide (scorpions sting themselves to death, so they say—Dr. Johnson called this a lie, but there is in fact some scientific evidence for it) and was no more than that—or was it? for I now see the whole book takes place "in Scorpio"—the action of the book is in one day, exactly 12 hours, seven to seven; the first chapter takes place 12 months later on the same day, so it is also in Scorpio.

Now I'll have to begin at the beginning again. The truth is, I have never certainly fully grasped the fact that *Moby Dick* was a political parable, though I can grasp the fact that Ahab (in my grandfather's eyes anyhow) is on quite an important plane a criminal. I seem to remember that Starbuck and quite a few of the crew had the same idea too, but it seemed to me that his revengeful élan was shared to the extent that one could scarcely say the whole crew were enduring toil and danger simply to gratify his desire—what about the harpooners? Yes, what about them? I don't feel on very secure ground, but I have never thought of the book before in that way.

I can see that *The Confidence Man* is a political parable; and that "The Tartarus of Maids" is a sexual one. I see the applicability of the pursuit in *Moby Dick* today all right, but it never occurred to me that it was intended in that way then, unless in the sort of jocular manner that Melville's vast appetite reaches out all over the table and couldn't help stuffing something of the sort in. Now I have written the above it seems not only illiterate, but not what I mean at all, but I'll have to let it stand. But what you say would be in line with much of Melville's later thought.

The *Volcano* is, though, and you are quite right here, quite definitely on one plane of political parable—indeed it started off as such: Chapter VIII was written first, nearly 15 years ago—though I didn't mean it to suggest that the future belongs to those Mexican workers necessarily, or indeed to anybody at all, unless some true charity can mediate, and man's decency and dignity be reestablished. The police are the bloody police of the present, all right, but they are also "Interference"—interference with people's private lives—the stool-pigeon theme works both ways: one should intervene in the case of the man beside the road, Spain seemed a clear case for intervention, etc., or at least Hugh's intervention: it isn't quite as simple, to say the least, as this. And what about the Consul? How much good was it interfering in his case? Well, I meant to redeem the old bird in various guises throughout the trilogy, but fate put a stop to that—but I'll go on trying to tell you more about him in terms of the *Volcano* only, and the beginning of the letter. As a protagonist on one plane (says this French fellow, and I think he's right), he is a Faustian gent. The book somehow assumes—with some philosophic justice—that the ancestor of us all was perhaps a Magician.

The Consul has been a Cabbalist (this is where you get the Garden of Eden). Mystically speaking, the abuse of wine is connected with the abuse of mystical powers. Has the Consul perhaps been a black magician at one time? We don't know. What Max-Pol Fouchet doesn't say either is that a black magician is a man who has all the elements of the world (not to say universe) against him—this is what the Consul meant in Chapter X (written in 1942) enumerating the elements. In Chapter V (in the bathroom) you have a hint of similar dark forces in the background. The implication is that an analogy is drawn between Man today on this planet and a black magician. This, I feel, has to some extent come to have some basis in truth since writing this book.

(The Consul implies his war, as opposed to any Hugh might be involved in, is far more desperate, since it is against the very elements themselves and against nature. This is a war that is bound to be lost.) Oddly enough I put neptunium in but abandoned it for niobium (I thought it sounded sadder—it seems to me nobody, in my position at least, dreamed of atom bombs then—and yet you see, here one sat, just the same, dreaming up the swinish contraption without knowing it. I just took the elements out of the dictionary)—this is on page 304. As I say, this part was written in 1942—and by the time the atom bomb fell in 1945 the book had anyway been long on its way being rejected by publishers. I turned to this particular page just now and it gave me an eerie sort of feeling. The Consul has thus turned into a man that is all destruction—in fact he has almost ceased to be a man altogether, and his human feelings merely make matters more agonizing for him, but don't alter things in the least; he is thus in hell. Should you hold the Bergsonian idea that the sense of time is merely an inhibition to prevent everything happening at once—brooding upon which it is pretty difficult to avoid some notion of eternal recurrence—inevitable destruction is thus simply the teleological end to one series of possibilities; everything hopeful is equally possible; the horror would seem to exist in the possibility that this is no longer true on our plane and absolute catastrophe has fallen in line with our will upon so many planes that even the other possibilities are for us gradually ceasing to exist. This, I may say, is not very clear, as I have expressed it, so you better forget it. Anyhow, I don't believe it for a moment. Personally, I have a fairly cheery view of life, living as my wife and I do in the bush anyway. Nor was the book consciously intended to operate upon quite so many levels. One serious intention was to create a work of art—after a while it began to make a noise like music; when it made the wrong noise I altered it—when it seemed to make the right one finally, I kept it. Another intention was to write one really good book about a drunk—it was a blow to me when *The Lost Weekend* was published, just as I finished it. Another intention: I meant parts of it to be funny, though no one seems to have realized that.

FINALLY some odd and interesting things have happened in connection with the book itself (as they did with *Moby Dick*, by the way—while he was writing it, a whale sank a ship. Disaster struck the *Acushnet*—the original of the *Pequod*). After the war, at the end of 1945, I went back to Mexico again, taking my wife: absolutely by coincidence we found ourselves living in the original of M. Laruelle's tower, in Cuernavaca, now broken up into apartments. It was the only place we could find for rent.

I began the book back in 1936–38, when I was in Mexico. The news of the book's acceptance—both in England and America—arrived on the same day, in February 1946, from different firms in different countries, to this very tower in Mexico, and was brought by the same little postman who is a character in Chapter VI.

There are other, even stranger coincidences connected with it, some of them frightening, and not the least strange being in relation to your letter, which arrived on the same day as the French translation, but also on the same day as the funeral we were just about to attend of a very good fellow, a mystic—one would say if he was a magician he was a white one—who gave me much of the esoteric inspiration and material for the book. On the same day he died, coincidentally some brute shot his old dog (you will find the dog motif everywhere in the *Volcano*. Dog motif indeed—it makes me think it would make a good opera: now we hear the opening chords of the dog motif, by courtesy of Texaco Oil, etc.). . .

Finally thank you for your interest in the book—it is rather discouraging very often being a writer in Canada. Somebody put the *Volcano* in the *Encyclopedia Britannica Year Book* 1948–9, ranking it as the work of a Canadian over and above anything then current in American literature, but not one word did I ever hear of that here. In fact, apart from a few kind words by Birney and Dorothy Livesay,* all I have heard was from my royalty report, namely that the sales in Canada from the end of 1947–49 were precisely 2 copies. The *Sun* published only a few syndicated lines that called it a turgid novel of self-destruction, not for the discerning (or something) reader. This at least is Melvillean anyway; though it went very well in the States, and was even miraculously a best seller for a while: one month, believe it or not, it even sold more than *Forever Amber,* though it must be admitted *Amber* was getting a bit faded by then. In England it failed but quite honorably; in France they have put it in a classic series, yet another publisher is giving it wider distribution, and weirder still, it is being serialized in the daily newspaper *Combat.* As to the Swedish, Norwegian and Danish translations, I understand they are out, but I have not seen them. Nor, I imagine, has any Swede, Norwegian or Dane.

With best wishes,
Malcolm Lowry

* Canadian poet.

P.S. Hope this doesn't confuse you too much. I remain delighted by your interest—though I didn't want to leave you with the impression that the intention of the book was either completely despairing or that it contained any specific secular hope—finally I had meant to show in the trilogy that any revolution that did not appeal to the whole man, including the spiritual, would eventually abort—least of all is it a sermon against drink, that poor man's symphony, especially in B Minor, though why not D Major too, after all.

P.P.S. I hope you'll come and have a drink with us when you are in Vancouver.

To Frank Taylor

Dollarton, B.C., Canada
April 12, 1950

Dear Frank:

Here she goes. We don't know how to title it but perhaps that won't matter.

There was a sort of preface to it and is: and there are copious notes: the first turned into a sort of reply, from our bailiwick, to certain stimulating summations made at the movie conference reported in *Life* last June, particularly by Joseph Mankiewicz. It struck us, in brief, several months after reading his remarks, that writers who professed a love of the movie, but did little but criticise it, might best show their friendship by trying to write something good themselves of a practical nature: in order to show their good will, the obstacles should seem at the beginning all but insuperable, the rewards nil, and the project uninvited—all three you will agree met the bill here. When we say rewards we quickly qualify this by saying that this has nothing to do with our opinion of such a film's success, for there is a great deal, one feels, in the view advanced by Mr. Schary that the best films are the ones that make money, though this might be so for no obvious reason: considering this potentially, the point would seem to be not to close the gap merely between the aesthetic and the human or social values, or you get a documentary on the one hand, and by reaction the aesthetic at the mercy of the inhuman on the other: it would be to close the gap between them both in relation to eternal values: the best values are eternal values: they are also the most popular. But all values should attempt to maintain themselves at their highest level in terms of cinema. Then we would be getting somewhere. Something along these lines ran our argument in this letter just clumsily expressed, and this is not the place to go into it. There is much relevant in that foreword to how we went to work on the problems in *Tender Is the Night*,* however, but we hope the results may speak for themselves, without this foreword at present, which we haven't had time to finish. The same goes for the notes which will follow in due course. Here we intimated that Goethe had said there were thirty-seven different types of tragedy and we hoped (or feared) this might be the thirty-eighth. We went into anangke and perepeteia, directors for actors, fashions in automobiles, and these will follow in due course, no matter how useless. If not before you receive this, every time you see the remark *see notes* you will have to refer into a void, but please assume meanwhile that any doubts on the points the question raises as considered by us.

(To mention a very minor one—in one section we swiped a couple of lines of dialogue and two café names from the same author's *Babylon Revisited,* because it seemed to fit in, as in *Henry V* one saw something of *Henry IV;* however Shakespeare didn't try to sell *Henry IV* to Shirley Temple, let alone succeed in selling it to the *Saturday Evening Post,* so the possible hitch of copyright is not the same, but the importance to the film could not be less either, the idea we wanted being implicit anyway, and it only seeming important at the time, so you can count it out in advance, though for that matter no one would notice it, unless of course it doesn't matter.)

Finally this is sent to you in the earnest hope that it might in itself offer a challenge and help to start something or carry things along. Also it should be clear that it is intended as a practical basis for a film, though the grammar of the film has been scarcely used—scarcely words more complicated than cut, dissolve, or lap dissolve—and we don't always mean that of course, and any good or bad writing in it are either habit or incidental. The idea, however, was threefold, to try and give a vivid impression of a film actually in progress, a film that one had actually seen, and at the same time a film that, since it had not been made, left every scope for you or a director's imagination to work in. Since, perhaps understandably, there is no accepted form for this sort of thing we know of, we simply made one up. It is not meant *entirely* to be taken literally, not that it would be, but you might think we were naïve enough to think so. There are some tentatively suggested shots in the sanitarium sequence. And there are two sections, one in New York, and another at sea, that may be in

* See Appendix 7.

part unnegotiable, particularly, or as we have written it, the latter. Nonetheless, even if so, we felt strongly that a suggestion of the poetic and visual and aural *drang* in these two parts involved would relate the film enormously and add meaning to it: so they have been written in full. That is to say these two sections are not speculative in so far as they are completely realized and visualized and heard and play a part in the meaning of the whole adaption, and there is an excellent —indeed an unanswerable—artistic reason why something of the sort should be there at that point: but they may be assumed, where necessary, to be speculative, flexible, or inspirational, for the purposes of making the film. This of course goes for the whole thing in one way: but does not, in another, for we have, so to speak, *seen* the film, and you are supposed to be about to see it in a minute or two. But what you may see to cut, to put in, to improve, to take out, etc., etc., is equally part of the intention, while you are reading it. It may be too long, but we have proceeded on the basis that richness of material was surely better than poverty of the same, and incidentally we would like to think we had won some right to your feeling that we know where and how to cut if need be, for apart from anything else, we have left enough out for an opera by Puccini.

But we strongly feel its basic structure to be sound. Some of this you will find repeated in the preface, if it ever arrives. One thing occurs to me now we didn't put in strongly enough. Fashions, etc., but not merely fashions. The age is rather like this one: and what is in common, one felt, should be stressed, so that it should be the opposite of just another film about the jazz age to go spiralling down the drain. However with the correct use of jazz itself there is the possibility of subtly making the one too. It is even reasonable to suppose that this age is a form of recurrence of the other, not exact of course, but taking it in, as Time spirals on, which is what it demonstrably does, even if we are convinced it marches. Not to praise or blame in advance what you have not read, or the method used in writing it, we do feel constrained to qualify this from something in the preface, for we may have just given you the wrong impression. Not merely did we proceed on the basis that another film about the "jazz age" would not do but that another "psychological film" should be put in the wastepaper basket—it would make no money, it would not be "about anything," or not about anything worth while, would depress one to death, and last but not least be unfair to its author. Perhaps you might say that one has to start off by being unfair to the author by depriving his book of the incest motif, but there is much greatness in the book that is only implied in it—take away the incest and what do you have left?

The answer is everything: you have, for one thing, a great and unusual love story, on the other a sort of protagonist of the American soul, or of the soul of man himself, whose application to today is also patent. Do not let this blurb put you off—this is what should and can be done with it. Step right inside and see! Sex! Drama! Thrills! What should a doctor do? How should a doctor feel—with a human soul at stake! For, as we say, it is intended as a director's inspiration: or a producer's inspiration. In fact your inspiration. We hope it will fire your imagination. So perhaps we should term it: an adjustable blueprint for an inspiration for a great American film. To which we add further: for Frank Taylor.

With best love to you, Nan, and the children,

Malcolm & Margerie

P.S. I suppose we should add that this is now your property, to dispose of as you will, or not: at all events, by no stretch of the material imagination can it be conceived of as ours—so we say this, in case you felt anxious about spilling a Scotch upon it. We have a copy, but we show it to no one.

> We us excuse now that this work is doe
> How we never were yet at Citharon
> Nor on the monteine called Parnasoe
> Where the nine muses have their mansion.

P.P.S. This quotation arrived from my mother (Malcolm's) some time while we were writing this, in some *Illustrated London News*. I think it was marked, and was intended as a dig at me, for at all events there was a favourable review of the *Volcano* in another accompanying issue that was conspicuously not marked. It may look a bit phoney at first, but the more you look at it the more you look at it, that's sure! in fact we stuck it on the wall over the desk for some reason and in one way or another while working on the *Night,* have been looking at it ever since.

The only object worth achieving in this world is the ennoblement of man. It can never be more than a partial achievement, for man, like all terrestrial creatures, is imperfect and insufficient to himself. But he has in him the seeds of greatness, and whatever feeds, fosters and brings to maturity these vital seeds is, for short-lived man, beyond price. It is this alone which makes his checkered and tragic sojourn here worth while. And since man lives in communities, the test of a community's virtue is the capacity of its institutions and traditions to evoke the spiritual greatness of its members. A community which fails to do this is failing as a community and will in the long run perish, because it will come to consist of men and women who pass through life without ever becoming what they were intended to be: it will consist, in other words, of human failures. But a community which fires men with the desire to live nobly, to love, to create beauty and to suffer and endure for the sake of love and the creation of beauty, is a community worth preserving and dying for. Ancient Greece was such a community; so was the Judah of David and Isaiah. . . .*

To Christopher Isherwood†

Dollarton, B.C., Canada
June 20, 1950

Dear Christopher Isherwood:

It was a high spot indeed in our life when we read your letter speaking of our script in such generous terms. It would have been a high spot in mine anyway, the day I felt I had written something good enough to command praise from yourself. I've often felt like writing you in regard to your own work; I never thought I'd see the day you wrote me first. I do feel I have known you a very long time, however, through your work and through the eternal Marlowe who broods upon the cross currents of life's relationships.

For the script though, since you like it and where it comes off, my wife must take equal credit, she being the lady named Margerie Bonner who is a writer herself and the author of an extraordinarily good—and so far in destiny extraordinarily hapless—novel called *Horse in the Sky*. I hope enough really constructive commotions went into the making of the script that it will somehow come to a good fruition; one very sincere hope and motivation was that it would be a lucky thing for Frank. How it actually came into being strikes me as very curious indeed. One expects, and indeed welcomes, normal obstacles, but something so astonishing happened to the climate last winter we thought another ice age was upon us. This is supposed to be a fairly warm part of Canada; we built our house ourselves with lumber from an old sawmill, but didn't prepare for temperatures of fifteen below zero inside it, such as we had January and February. Nor

* Arthur Bryant, *Illustrated London News,* July 9, 1949.
† English author and playwright.

had anyone else prepared. Even so, we came off far better than people in the city, not having any modern conveniences to go awry. The city of Vancouver was cut off altogether for eight days from the outside world and we had stormy petrels flying beneath our windows. What they thought they were escaping from I don't like to imagine, but it was an exciting phenomenon I don't think has ever been recorded before in an inlet, in this latitude at least.

I find myself with so many things to say I am walking round in circles. What I would like to phrase properly, so that it doesn't sound too repulsive or impractical, is that should you ever find yourself in a mood where you feel like taking a rocket ship to nowhere, and have the time, we do wish you'd consider coming up in this direction and paying us a visit. It doesn't take so long by plane to Vancouver, and I think you'd find it interesting. We live in a shanty town, built on piles, in an inlet, with the forest behind, mainly deserted during the week save by a boat-builder, ourselves and a fisherman or two. At first all you see is a bay with shacks called Wy-Wurk and the like. But it is actually the remains of an old seaport of which we have often been the sole inhabitants. Dollar—hence Dollarton—was the ship-builder, but somebody took his ship building and his sawmill away from him and we're all that's left. Windjammers used to come here, and we've shouted to a Norwegian skipper of a passing freighter out of the window, below which there's enough water to float the *Mauretania*. At the week ends nowadays many of the shacks fill up so it is more fun during the week. We have a small boat and there are many islands where one may picnic. It is a wonderful place to swim if you like swimming and the forest is full of birds—we are just now (it is Midsummer's Eve) having spring and summer at once and the weather is marvellous. There is a fine view of the mountains: and also, for that matter, of an oil refinery. We could put you up on a sort of improvised contraption that we rescued from the sea but which is a great deal more comfortable than it looks. There are no conveniences but when the weather is fine as it is now there are no inconveniences either. We thought it might be a cheery place to discuss Tepotzlan and kindred subjects. The invitation, at all events, is very sincere from us both, but if it is too far, I hope, like Huysmans, you will at least think about it. We asked Frank too but I think he may have been put off by the bears. There are bears. But there are also deer. And ravens. Not to mention many rare wild plants such as the Blazing Star, Love Lies Bleeding, and even the contorted lousewort. And through what wild centuries roves back the contorted lousewort?

Anyhow, here we are, and you would always be more than welcome.

After this travelogue, again thank you very much indeed for your words. All the very best to you from us both.

Good luck!
Malcolm Lowry

P.S. I began to write this letter originally, returning the compliment (which I appreciate) in my own handwriting, such as it is—though I have no pen that works—taking advantage of this to write outside. But a cat spilt coconut oil on it. Then another cat spilt beer on it. Finally it blew into the sea. Retrieved thence it came somewhat to pieces and was, besides, a bit illegible. So I gave in, temporarily, to the machine age.

To Downie Kirk

Dollarton, B.C.
June 23, 1950

Dear Downie:

I have been meaning to write you for some time and had been hoping I would receive my promised copies of the French edition of the *Volcano* so I could send you one. However, I have so far received, in addition to the one you saw, only one paper-bound copy of the regular (not the book club) edition, and I wanted to give you a good cloth one of the first edition, the arrival of which I am still awaiting, so please bear with me a while longer. I also received an excellent review of the French version in the Paris edition of the *New York Herald Tribune* which says it is better than the original (though he hadn't read the original), however I am supposed to take that: and a caricature of the (English Canadian) author in a French paper that I trust is not only worse than the original but bears no resemblance to the original. I also have a copy of the Norwegian translation for you of which the only report we have so far is what it says on the cover—somewhat curtly—"En djevelsk roman." I am trusting that means devilish in the better sense, rather than hellish awful. We had the pleasure of meeting Marjorie one day when we were going to the movies, and she said you were a bit under the weather but I hope you are O.K. now. We were going to see the film of *The Hairy Ape* which I'd heard was good: it is *djevelsk* in the worst sense, however, though the suspense was subtly increased by the accident of the lights failing for one hour in the middle. People look very sinister and

[208]

strange standing about in the foyers of movies when the lights fail,|
and I made a note that I must use it in a book. Then I remembered
I had used it in *U.T. Volcano.*

Someone from outside came and cut down an enormous maple tree
(not far from the trail) you may have liked as well as we did, felling
it right across the path, with no thought for the birds who were
nesting in it, and all this to take one minute piece of wood out of it,
wherewith to make a fiddle. I thought of chalking on the stump:
"Would you like this to happen to you, you pig-dog? When you hear
your lousy fiddle it will make a noise like slaughtered birds." However
I decided that it would not be solving anything to discomfort the
inhabitants by adding my bit of grand guignol to what was already
djevelsk enough—and likewise, incidentally, the work of Scandinavians
—unless I could have done it in Scandinavian.

I meant to tell you before I had been reading the Spanish philosopher José Ortega y Gasset—I don't know how many books he has
written or works created, but *Toward a Philosophy of History, Inverte-
brate Spain, The Revolt of the Masses,* and *The Modern Theme* are
listed on the fly leaf, presumably because they are available in translation. I possess also a wonderful lecture of his on Goethe— first delivered
in 1932 in Germany, but reprinted in the *Partisan Review* at the end
of last year. It is the only article I have ever read that criticises Goethe
for his many-sidedness, his Leonardo da Vinci aspect. Ortega's thesis
is roughly that he should have stuck to maintaining himself as a poet
and not falsified his vocation by finding it necessary to be President
of the Weimar Republic, run a theatre, create theories of color, and
become a professional patriot and so on. This versatility is usually
considered a supervirtue so it is interesting to find someone who takes
the opposite view. The point seems to be that Goethe could have
acquired imaginative knowledge of these sort of things and used that
knowledge to support the substructure of his work—as Strindberg
practically became a historian in order to write his historical plays—
but in so far as he became their professional exponent, he was *not*
Goethe, and this might philosophically speaking be considered a dead
loss and a waste, and the world's dead loss, because "life itself is haste."
This is the sort of philosophy that seems to me particularly useful in
a public library when one is confronted with thousands of books that
one cannot possibly have time to read, so that one thinks: Ah, well, if
I only had more time, then what could I not read; how hopeless it
all is! For the fact is, on this view, even the thought becomes a waste
of time if life is a matter of stripping away inessentials from the
central core of one's being which is, in fact, one's vocation itself. This

makes life rather like fiction and in fact he says at one point in *Toward a Philosophy of History,* which I was reading:

Life in the zoological sense consists of such actions as are necessary for existence in nature. But man manages things so that the claims óf this life are reduced to a minimum. In the vacuum arising after he has left behind his animal life he devotes himself to a series of non-biological occupations which are not imposed by nature but invented by himself. This invented life—invented as a novel or a play is invented—man calls "human life," well-being. Human life transcends the reality of nature. It is not given to man as its fall is given to a stone or the stock of its organic acts—eating, flying, nesting —to a bird. He makes it himself, beginning by inventing it. Have we heard right? Is human life in its most human dimension a work of fiction? Is man a sort of novelist of himself who conceives the fanciful figure of a personage with its unreal occupations and then, for the sake of converting it into reality, does all the things he does—and becomes an engineer?

This probably recommends itself to me partly because if it is true, and man is a sort of novelist of himself, I can see something philosophically valuable in attempting to set down what actually happens in a novelist's mind when he conceives what he conceives to be the fanciful figure of a personage, etc., for this, the part that never gets written—with which is included the true impulses that made him a novelist or dramatist in the first place, and the modifications of life around him through his own eyes as those impulses were realized—would be the true drama (this would not be unlike Pirandello who—I quote from an article in the *Partisan Review*— "invents the convention of modern realism; instead of pretending that the stage is not the stage at all, but the familiar parlor, he pretends that the familiar parlor is not real as a photograph, but a stage containing many realities"—this is Shakespeare's speech come true. My feeling is that Pirandello may not have wholly appreciated how close to truth this view of human life might be, as a consequence of which the "realities" of "Six Characters of an Author," say, do not measure up to the profundity of the view, though I have not studied him sufficiently, and the accepted critical opinion upon Pirandello is apparently faulty) and I hope to finish something of this sort one day. But Ortega is not, here, at any rate, concerned with fiction: this is the thesis upon which he bases his value of history. Man is "what has happened to him." This is interesting too because it is a philosophy that starts with one's existence, ties in with Heidegger and

Kierkegaard, etc., and hence with Existentialism. This latter has become by now a music hall joke in France but there is none of the same despair in Ortega. One supposes that Sartre's Existentialism (so far as I can understand it, it is anything but new) is merely a sort of reach-me-down or second-hand philosophy, altered dramatically to fit the anguish of the French in the midst of [their] occupations, hurts, valours, resistances, duplicities and treacheries, and so give it some look of meaning—even so, it's refreshing to read a philosophy that gives value to the drama of life itself, of the dramatic value of your own life at the very moment you are reading. Who wants to read 3,000 pages that prove irrefutably that we don't exist? even if it is true? But I think what would be interesting to you in Ortega is his often philological approach to the unravelling of problems, and the great value he gives to philology itself. The word *snob* he tells me comes from *sine nobilitate,* and is a phrase that comes, incidentally, from Cambridge. The lists of students at Cambridge once apparently indicated beside a person's name his profession and rank. Beside the names of commoners there appeared the abbreviation: "s. nob:" *sine nobilitate:* whence the word "snob." That means that if you weren't the Duke of Bugnasty, like me for example, you were technically, at one time, a snob, which I certainly never knew before. In fact one thought it had come to mean the exact opposite—we tend to think that the Duke of Bugnasty would be, ex officio, a snob, or if he does not behave like one we would consider him remarkable. Ortega doesn't explain how the phrase itself came to be corrupted, but it turns out—through a footnote—to be all part of his general thesis and has nothing to do with the Duke of Bugnasty or otherwise, save that a Duke, or whatever, once had, in addition to rights, obligations. The real snob is the person who imagines he has only rights. What it comes down to is the business of vocation. To have found one's vocation, whatever it may be, is "to understand that one is alive for some specific and unexchangeable purpose."

The universal snobbism, [he says] so apparent, for example, in the worker of the present time, has blinded men to the fact that, if indeed all the given structure of continental life is to be transcended, the change must be brought about without a serious loss of its inner plurality. The snob, having been emptied of his own destiny and since it does not occur to him that he is alive for some specific and unexchangeable purpose, cannot understand that life offers particular callings and vocations. He is therefore hostile to liberalism, with the hostility of a deaf man for words. Liberty has always been understood in Europe as the freedom to be our real selves. It is not surprising that a man should want to be rid of it who knows that he has no real mission to fulfill.

This at first sight appeared to me, among other things, one of the most convincing arguments against communism I had ever read in such a short space: but in fact it is only a statement in defence of the old school of liberalism which it is so fashionable to denounce; and without the possibility of free discussion of revolutionary tenets, such as those contained in communism for that matter, and even the practical absorption of revolutionary tenets where they seem desirable, such a school could not exist. I suppose the thought is preëminently European, and based (as he says later) on Guizot's observation that in Europe no principle idea, group or class has ever triumphed in an absolute form (due to the progressive character and constant growth of the said liberalism). The thought a Marxist communist would instantly pounce upon—or ought instantly to pounce upon—as arising from Ortega's remarks, is that Russia is the only place where a really serious effort has been made on a large scale both to discover the particular vocation for which the individual is most psychologically adapted and also to clothe with some dignity and drama those vocations that otherwise are soul destroying (such as adjusting the same nut every day in a mass-producing plant). I think that is where the trouble lies, with (as usual) the machinery, or where at least the argument might begin. Mechanization—one pompously ventures—is the result of a creative technological faculty in man that has already begun to outwit itself. But the Russians—who never really had a capitalist system—do not seem to realize this, for the very people equipped to tell them this are forbidden to express themselves. For in Russia, in effect, the mechanic is exalted above everyone else. Deprived of a spiritual meaning to his life, deprived even of the luxury of cosmic despair, yet encouraged (which seems to be an advance on the Ford factory) to find some meaning in what he does himself, for he's not doing it any longer for his children, he finds and is encouraged to find that meaning in service to the State. This might solve that particular kind of robot-mechanic's problem very well, because he can feel, and probably it makes him feel unselfish and less like a robot, but unfortunately everybody else is expected to fall in line: a writer, for example, is supposed to be such a noble worker for the State, and so is the philologist (I notice by the way that the philologists in Russia have just got into a whole lot of hot water). Composers go the same way, the highest pay does not compensate the individual creative artist for lack of freedom of expression (we do not speak of individual freedom within the orchestra—one could have some fun too imagining Shostakovitch writing a decadent "bourgeois" trombone part for a "patriotic" piece) and Russia pays the price in the poorest art, the poorest music, the poorest literature in the world. Teachers must teach lies—all for the State. It seems so senseless when you look at it; for freedom of expression, as of religion, far from resulting in the destruction of communism, would probably win a multitude of adherents to it. True, freedom of expression would end by destroying the police state, and abolishing the stool pigeon, but surely the preservation of these commodities was not the goal of communism, or it would have found its adherents more exclusively among policemen and stool pigeons? And so one goes round the prickly pear, common sense finding one unfortunate solution to Russia's apparently insane behavior in the fact that she has been preparing to go to war for about the last 20 years and more, and so lives in a state of constant "war effort," with its attendant stringencies and "jelly-bellied flag-flapping": but I believe that, people's basic needs really being very simple, that there is more hope and life in Europe than meets the eye, and that its liberal tradition—which extends over here—will eventually save the day. That is a bit different from saying that democracy or Coca-Cola or British socialism will save the day but doubtless the vast majority of people everywhere mean the same thing within that part used to be call: soul. The rest is simply repetition of editorials. And since I set out to write this letter in order to palliate your colitis, if any, and not by speaking of purges, to give you Asiatic cholera, I had better say that I feel optimistic.

I want to thank you again deeply for so kindly translating those items for us: that work is now finished, and their correctitude must certainly have added to the effect which, so far, has been momentous in certain circles: but we are keeping our fingers crossed, so won't say more for the moment, out of a certain superstition.

We saw *A Streetcar Named Desire* and *Death of a Salesman*—of these, more later. We saw also *The Third Man,* and *Germany, Year Zero.* Both these are essentially poor films though for complicated reasons, I think, though both are probably well worth seeing.

We look forward very much to seeing Marjorie and yourself again soon, and we wish you a speedy recovery. Please give my regards to Dunc. And all the very best to you both and to Dorothy from us both.

Sincerely,
Malcolm

To Downie Kirk

[Dollarton]
Wednesday
October 18, 1950

Dear old Downie:

I got your letter a week ago with your very welcome and kind invitation and immediately made up a reply in my head—we were on the way to Crescent Beach for a day to look at birds—but when we got back we got rather anxious news I dare say you have read (re the beach); if not, forget I've told you and don't bother—see below. For I am somehow quite convinced it will blow over, and if it does not, we still have a few strong cards left to play, so we are not worrying now, though for a while we did not exactly feel like standing on our heads and in fact altogether there was Heavy Traffic on Canal Street emotionally: in addition to this I received the proofs of a Haitian novel (with a preface by Edmund Wilson) by a friend of ours —but so shockingly translated that we felt bound all but to retranslate the whole book for him in a week, no easy task without the original: hence the delay.

We would be delighted to come and will bring the records if it's not raining too hard: (the records are delighted they have been asked too).

With the bloody situation at your new school I deeply sympathize: you must indeed feel like Dante eating alien bread, and all I can say is that perhaps it is Ordeal E5 on the roll of ordeals and by the time you've solved the bitter problem you'll probably find that another more important problem has been solved automatically and triumphantly without making any effort.

Meantime I have been composing you a new grammar or system to entertain you which it is proposed can be used with effect while teaching the juvenile delinquent section in your temporary purgatorio.
Translate: Q. Where does the cousin of our aunt go in the morning?
        A. He goes to the bank.
        Q. Why does he go to the bank?
        A. He goes to get money from the bank.
        Q. How does he get money from the bank?
        A. He holds up the bank.
        Q. Where does the cousin of our aunt live now?
        A. The cousin of our aunt lives in Oakalla.

Translate: Shake my great coat!

          Q. What is in the great coat of our father?

          A. An eyedropper and a hypodermic syringe are in the great coat of our father. (This is for advanced students.)

          Q. Are there any watches in the great coat of our grand uncle?

          A. No. There are three clocks in the coat of our grand uncle.

Translate: (a) Send for a policeman who can be fixed.

          (b) We want a bootlegger.

Perhaps this is a little extreme, not to say bitter, but I hope you see the possibilities of the general drift. I think we passed your new school on the way to New Westminster and God it looked fine new shining and respectable and we hoped if it was yours you were happy there. But you never can tell what hells such appearances contain. Well, matters must look up if they can't look down. So we'll be along Saturday and we'll all cheer ourselves up.

Best love to yourself Marjorie and Dorothy from Margerie and myself.

                               Yours sincerely,
                               Malcolm

To Harold Matson

                           Dollarton, B.C., Canada
                               November 14, 1950

Dear Hal:

We just read the draft of our last letter to you and maybe it didn't seem clear because it wasn't very clear to us.

Therein was intended to be a request, if possible, for the $150 coming from the German translation. We had written this off against our debt to you (to which, sotto voce, if you have forgotten, you should add $7.50 for a United Nations article last June—this parenthesis being intended to make us sound more honest) but wondered if you could trust us with the owed money a little longer.

You may wonder why we're broke again after you've just pulled us out of the hole and the answer is we're not but we will be by the 1st of December if we haven't sold anything meantime. Prices have risen 270% here. Margie has been ill—a suspected brain tumor—a false alarm, thank God, but an expensive and harrowing one: she still has to have x-rays every few weeks.

Meantime we haven't heard anything from Hollywood of course or we would have immediately let you know. But this has been postponed by certain facts we aren't at liberty to confide at the moment. And we have a deep instinct that what we did was too good to be written off, Hollywood or no Hollywood. And fortunately I can say we've got half a dozen or more stories coming up, some at least of which must be saleable, and into all of which we have put, or are putting, our *all*. These are, in their probable order of arrival: "October Ferry to Gabriola," a story which you've had before, but which was no damned good. This we decided we couldn't collaborate on so I have completely rewritten it by myself and finally I'm extremely pleased with it and feel it will be as good as anything I've done, and saleable also. "Venus Is the Evening Star"—a story by Margie, and I think the best thing *she's* ever done. This is an extremely powerful story about Mexico, with an Anglo-German situation, and an extremely movie-wise one. "Present Estate of Pompeii," by me,—nearly finished, a story of our travels, and though I say it, excellent too. "Homage to a Liberty Ship," ditto. "Deep Henderson": about a dying hot musician who takes a bus and goes to Haiti, etc. "The Course": this is a story about the Hoylake golf course—scene of many of Bobby Jones' triumphs and incidentally, in the dim past, mine, and certainly has an interest for American readers, I feel. "A Heart-Warming Episode"—which describes the visit of an O'Neillish American dramatist to a puritanical English home. This expresses a sincere emotion all too rarely expressed—the cultural debt of England to America (er—not to speak of other debts just at the moment). Not so nearly finished are a story by Margie based on our travels in Italy, laid in the castle of Francesca da Rimini, and "Gin and Goldenrod," by me. "October Ferry" and "Venus" should be in the post in a week, hotly pursued by "Pompeii," And Many Others. The ending for one I just thought of this morning.

But naturally one can't expect them all to sell by Dec. 1. Against this—since I've been flawlessly wrong on the saleability of my work in the past (though I don't think I am this time) with the exception of the *Volcano*—I have planned a draft of *Lunar Caustic*, which was written as a long short story, as a novel. Albert said it was publishable as it stood, but even so, it can be improved: this would be part of the *whole* work at which I am dying to get down to.

Naturally we don't expect you to keep hauling us out of the abyss while you don't get any work from us: but this time *the work is there*. I mean it is before our eyes, beyond the potential stage, almost in the post.

I've tried to get out of the hole in other ways—such as journalism, writing an advertisement for a bank, etc. But it is a dead waste of time—for it takes time from doing the other work—moreover I haven't been successful at it, so far as I know, save for the United Nations thing, and even if so it benefits neither of us. I also have money in England (technically a lot of it) which I'm doing my damndest to get hold of, etc.

Finally we aim, in the next three years, to make not only ourselves but yourself a lot of money. It is my prophecy that this will be done.

Christ what an old story is this. Throw it in the fire. But we mean what we say nonetheless. Meantime we would be grateful if you would postpone the debt a little and send us the German thing, for unless something turns up from the last paragraph but one there is no immediate way to pay that either.

Best love to Tommy and the children from us both,

Malcolm

P.S. The new German contract, in German, signed by Klett, arrived today and I have signed it and posted it back. Thank you for it and thank your agent in Hamburg for me.

To Stuart Lowry*

Dollarton, B.C., Canada
—or perhaps I should spell it Dolorton
[Fall, 1950]

Dear old Stuart:

A towering sea is bearing down upon me. Gulls are balancing in the gale. A black cormorant is struggling low over the waves against the wind. All around me is a thunderous sound of breaking, smashing, trees pirouetting and dancing, as a full gale smashes through the forest. What is this? A seascape—or a suggestion for program music, as for Sibelius or Wagner. No: this is the view out of our living room window, while we are having our morning coffee. What I see is quite unbelievable, even for you, unless you have seen it—and where else would you see, but here, a house that is built in the

* Lowry's eldest brother.

sea and where the problems—and noises—are those that beset the mariner rather than the normal householder? It is wonderfully dramatic—too dramatic, even for me, for us, in some respects, for we now live under the shadow, at any moment, of losing it. This I've told you before. We only live here by grace of being pioneers, and Canada, alas, is forgetting that it is its pioneers who built this country and made it what it was: now it wants to be like everyone else and have autocamps instead of trees and Coca-Cola stands instead of human beings. In that way, for it has little culture at all, it could destroy its soul: that is its own business, no doubt—what we mind is that it threatens to destroy us in the process, an eventuality that it now becomes my duty to try and avoid. Have I mentioned that this is supposed to be a begging letter, even if addressed to one who can do naught, and is hamstrung even as I? One of those letters that you see, or may see one day, under a glass case in a museum—just as this house that we fear to be thrown out of someone may make money out of one day—for I am the only Canadian writer ever to be placed in the *Encyclopedia Britannica*—a sort of begging letter at least, though I don't know on what moral grounds I am presumed to be begging for what upon one plane of reasoning would certainly seem to have been once at least intended to be mine; begging being something I understand that even the tycoons of Canada may be driven to from their neighbouring country as an alternative to stealing, a practice I am inhibited from less on moral grounds than fear of the consequences and plain incompetence. However, I couldn't get myself in the proper mood of despair, even though, as a matter of fact, there is every reason for it. This proves that I am not really anything so wondrously effete (I am partly joking of course) and imitative as a latter-day Canadian, but simply an Englishman, i.e., a person who, upon overhearing himself pronounced dead, remarks: Bloody nonsense. With that we shall entitle this instead, "business letter," a euphemism that so far it seems singularly unentitled to. There is something wrong with my prose too this morning, but this I ask you to overlook. The foregoing however is my way of saying— even if I can't keep the cheerfulness out, that we stand in the shadow of eviction, and thus upon the brink of what is popularly known as disaster. The other people in the same position are mostly fishermen and may fish elsewhere; that is to say there are fish elsewhere. We however are fishermen of another sort in a place where there is plenty of fish but no place to sell it save very far away, by which time, if it has not indeed gone bad meanwhile, either it tastes so unique it is accorded a civic reception, or it realizes assets that, like the fish, are frozen. Of the more hopeful and constructive side of this later; all this, in my usual direct fashion, you may take to refer to the crucificial position of a writer in Canada, to which you may, though with less justice than you think if you can imagine for a moment that you are not Stuart but the late personality for whom you now stand *in loco* (loco in the nice sense) reply: Well, I didn't tell you to live there! From now on, however, I shall be strictly business-like. First I shall give you—an important item in the technique of such letters even when one understands perfectly well the utter fruitlessness of it—a list of my accomplishments, immediately followed of course by a similar list of catastrophes, during the last years, though on second thoughts I'll spare you some, and on third thoughts shall confine myself to the last year and a half.

(a) Have written and completed in collaboration with Margerie a detailed movie script—adopted from a novel you won't have heard of—upon which we worked, sometimes with the temperature below zero in the house, some fourteen hours a day—it was so cold at one point we couldn't take off our clothes for a fortnight—of which the report, from two of the greatest authorities on the cinema and a now famous Metro-Goldwyn-Mayer producer, was in brief that "it was obviously the greatest achievement in movies, what movies had been all adding up to, and that even to read, that it was comparable with the power of Theodore Dreiser and the titanic mental drama of Thomas Hardy's *The Dynasts.*" (I see no reason to be sparing of adjectives; they were not.) The producer is one of my ex-publishers of the *Volcano,* and you may in England see a minor film of his called *Mystery Street*—very well worth seeing.

(b) Succeeded in having the *Volcano* published in translation in Norway, Denmark, Sweden and France—in the first and last countries put into an edition with the classics of the world.

(c) Germany and Italy—now in preparation, which projects had formerly fallen through.

(d) Seen it hailed as the greatest masterpiece of the last ten years in the French translation in Paris. You could get the reviews yourself more easily than I could: but they have appeared everywhere, even in the famous *Figaro.* And there was a wonderful English appraisal of the translation in the *New York Herald Tribune* Paris edition. The publishers are Correa, and a special edition by the Club Livres de France. In fact it has had every honour showered on it there, and many French authors have received the Legion of Honour and been elected to the Academy for less.

(e) Been put in the *Encyclopedia Britannica*. (For how long? Are you comfortable there, Malcolm?)

Well I could go on with these, but I think it's time now for a few catastrophes, sometimes transcended catastrophes.

(a) Operation for a chronic condition of my legs. Successful and expensive.

(b) Continued anxiety—partly responsible for condition when you met me—of thinking one had T.B. Tests showed I have had T.B. at some time or other—when?—and am liable to it: but have it no longer. Have conquered anxiety neurosis on this score.

(c) Ditto and more important, that Margerie had cancer. She does not; but to that diagnosis I am grateful to her brother-in-law. Had she obeyed the dictum of doctors here she would have been treated as if she had so that she had the anguish of thinking she had.

(d) The pound is devaluated.

(e) Because of the success of the *Volcano* my editor, Albert Erskine, is invited to join the staff of Modern Library. You know who *they* are—you brought me up on them! But that leaves me still under contract to the publisher he has left. Erskine wants me to come over to Modern Library, which of course I want to do, but according to the terms of my contract I have to send my next novel to my old publisher and give him a chance to make me an offer first—and they are holding me to this as they are very anxious to keep me. On the other hand the advantages of going into the Modern Library, and keeping Erskine as my editor, far overweigh anything else. Incidentally my other editor became a producer at M.G.M. on the strength of my book. This is a complicated situation, which cannot fail to work to my eventual great advantage, but difficult to explain in a letter. But it is the opposite of an advantage now.

(f) Because of a dispute between the Harbour Board and the Provincial Government over our land, which we repeatedly tried to buy when we had money, we face eviction for the second time and it blows over.

(g) I break my back and have to wear a brace—the cost this time is not merely expensive, but calamitous. It was right after this (d) happened.

(h) I write to Alderson Smith: no reply. Am still waiting.

(i) I conquer broken back, the brace, but then am faced (sic) with my legs again. I conquer this by exercise and Margie's help. Also I literally owe my life to the way we live—from which we are once more to be evicted, only this time the threat seems much more positive.

(j) The pound falls further yet—or rather does so, in effect for us, because the Canadian dollar goes *up* to equilibrate the American, this it does on a free market and in a state of disequilibrium, fluctuating, in which it not only overtakes but threatens to go still higher than the American, with the result that my monthly income is now little more than $90—that has the purchasing power of little more than a fiver in the old days, and I am not exaggerating. Rent makes sympathetic and contradictory fluctuations of course, but you would be lucky merely to rent anywhere these days for $90 a month, without food—let alone live. I don't know if this aspect of the sheer hardship of the situation has struck you. What it comes down to is that to live on the income alone involves trying to live on somewhat less than the pay of Mary or Sarah, *without* everything being all found. This practically knocks us out entirely, robbing us also of the little margin of profit we had between the American exchange and the Canadian, and between that exchange now at the same rate and the exchange of the pound. Simultaneously prices came down a little, but no sooner have they done that than they go up still further, threatening yet worse inflation, though the pound, despite greater faith in it, remains the same.

(k) A notice of eviction that seems final, but with just a bare possibility of reprieve in it: but it scarcely seems possible it can last more than a few months.

(l) Margerie ill—with ourselves still in the dark as to what is really wrong with her: x-rays, brain tumor still suspected, treatment that must be continued, begins to put us into the category of the starving. Much may be done with oatmeal. I begin even to think of the saying, "Home is the place where, when they have to, they take you in." But where indeed is that, unless here? Her mother lives 2000 miles away in America, mine 10,000. And we have no friends in Canada save three fishermen in like case, a cat, five wild ducks, two seagulls, and, of course, a wolf.

(m) Naturally, one didn't expect to live on one's income, in the usual sense; though between books, that can become necessary, because if you live on an advance from your next book you're eating yourself, as the French say, literally, and if you get another job you won't write the book—which is one reason why so many writers quit being writers. But in my case the possibilities of work are or were three: teaching, radio, newspaper work. The first requires at least a year's negotiation and a complete rededication of one's life—and probably going to the Prairies, since the English are hated in B.C. The second pays starvation wages and moreover requires a car, while the third not only does that but would be senseless because what I do anyway to attempt to augment the income makes more money and comes into the category of free lancing. In short there is no possibility of a job where we live—short of turning sailor again or working in a sawmill—for taking one would mean abandoning the really practical hope we cling to in regard to our serious work, and also our house: and indeed at the moment we haven't got money even to *move* anywhere else. Even if I could get a labourer's job the cost of transportation would swallow the money we save by living in the house. And writing is a whole-time job or nothing, so it would mean quitting. Margie can't augment matters by getting a job herself because she's not well enough: besides, we do our work together. And for the same reason, however willing to turn my hand to anything, I couldn't leave her long enough in the wilderness by herself. In short it's better to stick to one's guns: only it seems that begging is a standard part of writing, or is about to become so. You may therefore count this as work, for it's my all too valuable time, not counting yours. It may interest you to know that there is a long broadcast tonight or tomorrow night on the subject of Malcolm Lowry, Canada's greatest most successful writer, which we can't listen to because our radio has run down and we can't afford to replenish the battery. The unkindest cut of all. Despite our love I have been warned that for Margie to live another winter under these conditions is very dangerous during the coldest part, so I had thought in all seriousness of applying for a job as tutor at the court of the King of Siam, which requires no courses, save in jazz music—and we may wind up there yet. While we are clinging to the poor house for all we are worth, we are still trying to make enough to live in the city over the nearly impossible months of December and January. (The climate has changed here during the last ten years and winters have been almost as cold as in the east, causing God knows what misery.)

Losing the house under these callous conditions—and they are totally callous and selfish—would be a blow considering all the others—having lost it by fire and rebuilt it ourselves—of such psychological importance that if we had our way we wouldn't live in Canada at all any more. Well, we don't expect our way. The object is to live at all. I have done more for Canadian literature than any living Canadian, and that is beside the point except when I say that despite

all this I have made a success of my life and had conditions been
equal would have made an assured income for life too—which I
may yet do, of course, through the Modern Library or the movie.
You could not expect more success of anybody than I have achieved,
and both of us have conquered other seemingly insuperable obstacles
too (you are not to judge from my health when you saw me—I myself have now never been fitter, exercise and swim every day, etc.) or
I wouldn't be writing like this. It is now evening, with a full roaring black gale outside, with the bottom out of the barometer, that
is not our barometer but someone's barometer.

Well, why go on. About the only thing we have left is a sense of
humour, and the feeling and hope now that what has been undi-
agnosable in Margie's condition is due to the manifold and obscure
results of a hysterectomy: which it may well be: but this in itself
is going to require prolonged treatment which at best merely means
expense we cannot afford. You get a wrong picture if you think we
are gloomy: but the actual situation is some ten times blacker than
I've painted it. So I won't paint it. I haven't liked to paint this
much. What it all adds up to is this: that while my prospects for the
future will eventually add up to an income for life (vide the Modern
Library and that you certainly can believe) we are at the moment
faced with a financial crisis—which is not caused by extravagance or
lack of forethought, by the way—even my trip to Europe will turn
out to have paid for itself, for without that, among other things, no
French translation, or rather none of any worth, would have come
out. This could happen to any businessman only we have no one
near enough to appeal to, and no way of floating a loan. It is an
acute crisis that should only be temporary, for apart from the new
novel and the projected film I have about ten short stories blocked
out for which I have an immediate market in New York, having
actually a request from 3 or 4 big magazines for my work (there is
no market at all in Canada, which is part of the tragedy) and I
simply cannot get the freedom and peace of mind to write them
properly—even though of course I am not ceasing to try.

And here we come to the age-old pay off to be found in the shrines
of every writer under a glass case in the museum—in short, if there
is any way, possible or impossible, for you to find any money for
me—bearing in mind that there certainly were provisions made for
crisis in Father's will—can you possibly look into this immediately for
I've put off writing till the last possible moment, hoping it would
not be necessary. However in your last letter, with very large foresight,

you did say: Hang on till October. Well, I've hung on. If there's nothing can be done, it has been in my mind, terrifying prospect though it is—though I do not consider it abject, and neither would she or you if I could make the circumstances plain—to write direct to the mater—would you advise me about this? But what else in fact am I to do, if all else fails? Damn it, I shall always remember she once gave me a three-penny bit. If of course—and the idea is naturally hypothetical—I did this she would refer it to you and about all I could ask you to do then is to ask her not to refer it to God, or perhaps, conversely, *to* refer it to God.

And all this, the consequence of ceaseless hard work and application. Well, I know you will do your best. Please forgive my writing. I hope the letter was amusing anyway. All my very best love to Margot whom I sincerely hope is in good health, and to Donnie, love and sincere welcome back from his ordeals and travels. In short God bless to you three from us both,

Malcolm

P.S. This letter is going to give me a nightmare tonight. So don't let it give you one. If you can't do anything, advice would be better than nothing, for at worst I can always get them to deport me back to England as a vagrant—something I think ought to be pointed out to the British Government who then might have to buy me a wig—on Father.

To Albert Erskine

Dollarton, B.C., Canada
[December, 1950]

Dear Albert:

Thanks awfully for the Faulkner, Albert, it's full of wonderful things—I had borrowed the book on the same day so Margie and I met face to face carrying the same book—and were later to be seen even reading the same book in bed—A Charles Addamsish cartoon—am concocting you a long letter. Best love to you and Peggy from

Malcolm

PART VII: *1951*

PART VII 195

To Albert Erskine

February 13, 1951

My dear Albert:

I hate to break a long silence in this way but can you somehow lend us $200 immediately? (I was always taught to begin a short story like this.)

Since the answer to this, the world being what it is at the moment, must be "no," your having said no and damned my importunity for asking, could you read what follows, see how it differs from such usual requests in terms of security, and see whether on the strength of that you can, even if you can't? We have nowhere else to turn, all possible avenues are explored or non-existent, and our condition having passed the stage of mere desperation, the plea itself turns moral. So far, not so good.

Here is the situation. We have been working hard—but without any material success, slowly using up our capital until for the last six months we've been obliged to live on our income, reduced, since the devaluation of the pound and the freeing of the Canadian dollar, to about $95 a month.

We've had latterly to waste the effort we would otherwise put into writing simply to keep alive but little by little we've begun to go under. Margie is sick and in almost constant pain: she has some sort of growth that is affecting her teeth, but it has been impossible to determine what kind, and now I can't even pay for the x-rays so she can't get any more. This is a callous and barbarous country in many ways. The store is on the point of stopping our further credit for food, and every day we face eviction from the house we built. Despite that $95 not Maxim Gorky himself could dream up any worse privations than we, and especially she, have had to suffer this winter, though I myself am physically O.K. But there is a point beyond which even William James' kind of voluntary poverty leads to despair. This is when it becomes involuntary. On the other hand we have been owed, for many months, $150 on the German translation of the *Volcano* which Hal will send the moment it comes through. The contract for this was signed last fall and on the daily expectation of this we have been living from day to day—though we have another expectation of a certain and legal nature I shall come to. But only yesterday we got the usual letter from Hal of rejection of our stories and postponement of the payment of the German advance (another one, signed for $750 fell through altogether).

Hal has been good enough to say that he'll send it through, despite the fact we already owe him $250 on the expectation of stories that either haven't sold or that we have been in too much misery or anxiety to write, so we could not ask him for more.

The other expectation is due to a grief. Last December 6th my mother died suddenly on her birthday, I had previously appealed to my eldest brother to do what he could, outlining our position and my anxiety about Margerie—Christ, even then!—because the Government had not been letting out all the money, it seemed, that I was legally entitled to even under the terms of their own stringencies. His reply, including the news of my mother's death, was that my financial position was very considerably improved and he as the chief executor of the estate was now in a position to help immediately. Other things being equal, I would now be quite rich in fact, but even as things stood my income would be sufficient to live on here. I understood him to say that under the circumstances he would be able to get some money through immediately before the will was probated, but instead silence closed down—a silence due, so far as I can see, to the fact that my family and solicitors are in the centre of the flu area in Liverpool where there have been a ghastly number of deaths, far more than they said in the paper. (Doubtless because of the coming Festival of Britain—do not let a little plague put you off, my dear American cousins, if you'll only supply the dollars, we've got in addition to wigs some nice gravestones all supplied by the Government.)

So this is something else we also have to tell the store keeper who is also unfortunately the post master. Nonetheless, however inhibited by Government or flu, something is bound to come through from this direction soon.

For the rest I have tried to write an advertisement for banks—and so on and so forth—all with complete unsuccess, and all in a vicious circle, as you see. Now we have'nt the peace of mind even to get the stories off. (We did that other long work also, of which we still can't speak; hope for that went up like a rocket the other week, one can't count on more than the Bergsonian ashes in one's face this week, though perhaps it'll be different next.)

Hal says that possibly he could get some kind of advance from Reynal-Brace on another novel—if I could give them a time limit—but I'm not going to do that because, if humanly possible, if you still want me, I want desperately to hang on to you as a publisher. This is an extraneous problem to the present one, or it would look like moral blackmail on my part—and I'd hoped and would like to discuss it separately, for it is all-important to me. The only thing I've said about the novel so far, you said, was smug, and I guess it was. But I have unsmugly worked out an unsmug project in my mind which, if of huge proportions, would more than live up to your expectations of me, if only I can find a chance to begin to execute it. Because of the accident of the fire coming so close to the acceptance of the *Volcano* and destroying so much work, I haven't been able to get it or recreate it in proper perspective until now: and what happened in Mexico at the time the *Volcano* was accepted is an important part too, that was hard to get into focus until now. Now, in addition to being an orphan, with you at another publisher's I feel excommunicated too.

Can you tell me as much of your plans as you feel I might know? I don't want to give you any feeling of responsibility, or imply a psychological dependence on my side, distressing to yourself, but if by some legerdemain I became transferred to Random House and then you decided to leave, I'd be in the same position as now. I don't think I can be blamed for wanting to grapple myself with hoops of steel to you as a publisher irrespective of the mutations of publishers and your own plans, etc. Well, I trust you will see the sincere thing I sincerely mean.

Re the projected novel, I will allow myself my one smugness in asserting that it should continue to pay you dividends long after I am dead (it includes the *Volcano*) or I feel it certainly could be of this calibre, with your sympathetic Eye hovering near, unless I know nothing of literature at all. (Margie was doing excellent work likewise until she had to stop temporarily.)

But to get back to the loan I asked you for. This would enable me to pay for the x-rays, and get some more, and put off the grocer with a reasonable expectation of the money from England having arrived before our next crisis falls due. Also it should enable us to get some more stories in the mail, and try and get my mind clear about the novel in terms of a presentation of it to yourself. I won't use the argument that I hope you'll be publishing some of these stories some day—though of course I hope this is true: some are sort of fragments of a novel.

I had originally intended to ask you for $150 on the basis that Hal would pay you back when the German money arrived, which it should any day. I think I've explained why I've no right to expect Hal to do that, even though he might stretch a point and do it. But in the absolute desperation of our situation it is very difficult to make clear that without some money one cannot work to pay it back. But this $150 from Hal to ourselves is promised as *absolutely certain,* and what we could do is, immediately we received it here, to pay it back to you. This would leave us $50 in your debt, which $50 together with our $95 would give us a little margin until the other English money got through. When that got through we could pay you back the $50. Thus we ought not to be in your debt more than two or three weeks on the $150, and may be no more than a month on the whole $200—shortly thereafter which Hal himself can be paid in kind. (We have half a dozen other stories coming up.)

But our whole problem is *time.* This agonizing business of Margie's won't wait, even if its outcome, as one hopes, proves simple. The storekeeper won't wait. Perhaps they won't even wait to evict us. Only England waits, while we brug around in ever wearier circles. And so I have written to you to ask you if you can help—according to the provisos above concerning repayment. I shall not be able to express our gratitude if you can.

All the best to Peggy and yourself from us both. God bless.

Malcolm

P.S. I send some French clippings—a new batch—there are about a hundred others, all very long, very intricate, and all of a vast enthusiasm. I was getting the more interesting ones translated for you and will send them on—all in all, the *Volcano's* had a better press, if possible, in Paris, than in New York—though the latter is no doubt partly due to the former. But I have yet to make a centime on all this. And its repercussions have, so far as I can see, been nil. The sales in Canada have been 2 copies and apart from some sold by the flying start you gave it in New York, my sole recognition here an unfavorable squib in the *Vancouver Sun.*

P.P.S. Margie wants these reviews back when you are through, and will you forgive me having written this letter?

To Albert Erskine

[February, 1951]

Friday, Saturday, Sunday.
On Friday afternoon posted second serial letter also containing immeasurable thanks for second $50 received easily and swiftly that morning.

This will—God's thanks to you—I believe enable us to slide back fairly easily from the appalling withdrawal to the good return next Sunday.

Sunday.
What has been chiefly appalling has been the strain on Margie in all this. Medically she needed and still needs a rest—particularly from this kind of strain—medically she needed and still needs attention, and it has largely had to go by the board: her courage and guts are phenomenal, however, and it seems to me it is peculiarly American and it must be the blood of her pioneer ancestors coming to the rescue: any other woman would have been "carted away"—as she puts it—long ago. In fact I myself have felt not far from being "carted away" once or twice.

Next Sunday will also be around the anniversary of your acceptance of the *Volcano* in Mexico in 1946, and of which period this ordeal seems like a repetition: it is also exactly the same period of the most critical part of *La Mordida*.

On Saturday afternoon when your telegram arrived announcing your letter, my relief and gratitude was so great I slept for 19 hours.

Meantime I am trying to write to Giroux though what I finally may have to say might be conditioned by your letter that will arrive tomorrow.

Re the poems—I decided that it was a form of unconscious moral blackmail or something to send them to yourself at this moment under these circumstances, expecting you to place them—as if it were just as easy as that—so I am figuring out another plan.

Most immediately—to try and pay back *quam celerime* re teeth—we have written that a payment sent us to the beetle-brained grocer-postmaster and sent back again as "addressee not known in Dollarton" for an old radio programme recently repeated in Toronto and of which Margie is largely the author, be sent to yourself, if the party to whom it was sent back can afford it.

But if this fails, I have other ideas. And besides that it occurs I first went to sea, as it were, 2 years before Carlsen and in those days we carried sails even on steamships, should all else fail. I hadn't thought about the sails but maybe I can find some sails.

Meantime—to change elements and metaphors—while fighting a blitzkrieg on one flank we are fighting a rearguard action on the other so that, should we have to endure defeat, that defeat be as little catastrophic as possible, but since we haven't quite worked out our plans here, I won't outline them.

From a letter I recently had—quite unsolicited—from Knopf I would certainly deduce that they wanted me, in default of Random House: but the decision I incline to at the moment, in the dreadful event that the latter despite your efforts reject me, would be to withdraw myself from circulation altogether, hang on somehow, and then offer the thing to yourself again a year from now, with the work further advanced (though sans advances).

This is what I would certainly do if I had only myself to think of, even though it is hard at the moment to see how the work could be so advanced, without one lucky break in the near future, though in three or four months the picture might be different.

But believe me, this is what I would want to do, if it were to seem at all morally feasible and what, in event of reverse, I am seriously considering doing.

Meantime—blithely to change metaphors once again—one feels slightly like a steeplejack who, far aloft, is not sure whether the rigging is slipping or the weathercock he has been sent to repair is not going to descend upon his skull with outstretched beak.

Both of us thank you profoundly for all your kindness.

With love,
Malcolm

1951

To Downie Kirk

[*February, 1951*]

Dear old Downie:

Thank you very much indeed for your letter. It made me feel a
whole lot better. And no sooner had we got your interesting book
home about the avalanche and the old villagers are digging themselves out than we read in the papers about a similar avalanche in
nearly the same place burying them again. Meantime we were digging ourselves out of *our* avalanche. And so it goes. I have received
this enclosed letter and can understand scarcely a word, not even if
it is bawling me out or not. But it obviously pertains to the German
translation (this is the one that will be dedicated to you) and it looks
as though I better answer it. What I seem vaguely to gather is that
it is from the translator himself who begins by being friendly, goes
on into the difficulties of the translation, and ends by asking some
questions about the obscenities on the menu in Chapter X. He also
asks me to elucidate something connected with Mexican land reforms
and a technical matter in the dialogue in Chapter II. Is this roughly
right or does he want to transpose a couple of chapters or something?
And how am I to answer about the obscenities if the translator is a
woman! I'd be enormously obliged if you'd tell me if the letter requires my immediate attention and if so, when you have time, give
me the drift of it. I'm going to reply in English because even if I
could reply in German I could scarcely elucidate a point in German
that depends upon mistakes being made in English by a Tlaxcaltecan
translating from a misprinted menu in Spanish and French. What a
wonderful word is Daseinsaussage! Is this a technical technico-archi-
techtonic term or may one order *Daseinsaussage,* from a menu too, *mit
zwei eier und Kartoffelnsalat und ein Stiefel Münchener?* Or is perhaps
Daseinsaussage his translation of my *boudin*—a sort of cousin to blut-
wurst? I know you will be pressed for time, so don't put yourself out, I
think you ought to charge me a fee for these questions I keep firing
at you. Still I feel the German translation is almost a family matter.
How goes the school? It seemed to me you had that situation finally
licked and I am very glad. Has Master Fury brought the jemmy of
my uncle? No. Master Fury is in the garden studying how to become
a Mercy. Yes, Rousseau had some children and the dog put them all
in an orphanage. Would you, when you have a moment, send back
the French reviews—don't bother at all about translating any part of

them now, I know you haven't time, but my sister-in-law wants to see them, and anyway I can let you have them back; if it comes to that I have some more, from the *existentialist press!* I'm tickled to death to be thought a master-existentialist: seems only the other day I was asking you what existentialism was. I see we have a repertory theatre: that is a bright sign. It is also a bright day and all in all one feels bright. I'm still hanging on to your *Tellers of Tales* unless you want it returned immediately. I'm trying to learn more economy of style. The *Avalanche* book is very good, though not in the way they say on the cover. *Sapphira* I have not had time to read yet. Say if you want these posted back. And don't forget the Daseinsaussage . . . sorry to trouble you. All the best love to Marjorie and Dorothy.

Mit freundlicher Begrüssung,
Malcolm von Lowry

To Downie Kirk

[April or May, 1951]

Mein lieber alter Freund Downie—

We were sad not to see you at Easter, and also that you have been under the weather, though delighted to get your letter, so here is something to amuse you, and I hope interestingly to divert you at the same time—not to say please you, I hope—everything from how to put the hex on your more troublesome pupils (though for God's sake don't use it like that for it might work) to some more *Daseinsaussage,* as well as a letter of gratitude in the same language, with which is incorporated needless to say my own too, hereby renewed.

Re the former it might interestingly be dipped into in relation to *The Pencil of God:* the work is by Marcelin's younger brother, himself an ethnologist (and, though it doesn't say so, a voodoo priest too, as is the illustrator, Hippolyte, or rather was, he having recently died, though not before having achieved an enormous reputation as a painter, a reputation that was as highly deserved in my opinion as it was inevitable perhaps in one who did not paint at all, more or less, unless possessed by John the Baptist), and I think it is endlessly fascinating, and moreover written in a French so translucent that even I can tell that it represents an achievement of *style too of a creative order.*

Though its style may be irrelevant to the terrifying abysses and potentialities of the human mind that it opens up! I would be delighted to see you and Limpus get together on it, since Milo, as I say, is a scientist too.

The pen seems to make too much impression on the paper so I carry on in pencil. I don't think the Marcelin is likely to be translated into English, though it is certainly an opportunity for someone. Of course I haven't yet been through it all—I couldn't resist sending it almost at once, since I thought it would be of great interest to you.

Needless to say, it is sent with a *pure* blessing upon it, as it were: this remark or precaution may seem peculiar in this material age, but the fact is that Milo would not have sent it to us in the first place, I believe, had we not been privileged to witness some of the mysteries in question, nor himself dared to write it, had he not been a high practitioner of the said mysteries themselves, thus being empowered to clothe them in the harmless and useful guise of inquiring science and comparative religion: so I am not giving away any secret I should not, nor are you in possession of a "magic" book that could wreak any damage (I once felt Margie and I were, as I told you, and so sent the book, that was another book of course, back)—if it makes you uncomfortable, send it back—all I can think of is, though this may seem absurd, I wouldn't let Dorothy see it; I have no idea of the power of some of the symbols should they be copied—it is merely in the good spirit of friendship to interest you. The most that can happen is that it might bring you some unexpected good luck, as happened to me once: though that is no harm: essentially Voodoo is a religion, to be regarded with reverence, since unquestionably it is the matter-transcending religion based upon the actual existence of the supernatural as a fact that is fundamental to man himself (I express myself very badly), compared with which most other religions are simply techniques to hide that fact, or confine the supernatural to relatively safe distances; it would seem that only the Negro race are powerful enough or holy enough to be able to handle it and even they of course often abuse it. Heaven knows what we would do with the same power. But that is not to say one should not regard with awe the great dignity and discipline that is behind it at its highest, nor its conception of God, nor the meaning that it gives to life—and all this on the part of a race we so often glibly think of as inferior, or comprising medicine men, or the powers of darkness and so on. *Heart of Darkness* indeed! Joseph Conrad should have been to Haiti. What he failed to understand was that the savages of the Congo had to some extent *subdued* the dark forces that are in nature by creating their religion in the first place, in order to subdue them; that that, in its way, was a civilizing, almost a pragmatic process. A white man comes along and is made a God and uses the same magic to keep and to gain power with these "unspeakable" rites, etc. But in my estimation it was the white man who had corrupted them with his own brand of unspeakableness. Anyhow that story—great though it is—is at least half based on a complete miscomprehension. (I'm not sure if my words make sense, and not sure I would know what to make of them were they played back to me on your magic recording machine.) It is clear that Comrade Joseph did not allow himself to be corrupted by any savages though: he stayed in Polish aloofness on board in company with some *a priori* ideas.

Anyway there you have a more than *Golden Bough* in one way, and return the books at your leisure; though Margie has barely looked at the volumes, neither one of us have time at present anyway to read them fully, whereas your mind will take in much more much more swiftly at what glances you may have opportunity for.

For the rest I enclose two letters from ten Holder*—one to yourself. I don't know what he says to you, save that the letter is a letter of thanks, but don't bother to translate it—unless there is some specific question that looks important that you might have time to translate—because he has sent me another questionnaire in English, I am well able to answer and I don't want to bother you. I have already taken up the matter of the dedication with Klett but did so again to make sure. I would have dedicated it to all 3 of you, also bringing in Dollarton, and our gratitude for lending us your house, and other more happy days, but for the identity of our wives' names, and the fact that an oblique question of consideration of space arose out of the feeling he might want to dedicate the translation per se as a translation from his end, to someone else. The dedication of Proust gets gummed up this way. So please all take the will for the deed—I hope it pleases you, but let me know if it doesn't and how I should alter it. (That this should not pass without its strange coincidence, the Karlheinz Schmidhus he mentions was one of my German teachers in Bonn, though not Godesberg (2 miles away), and if I learned little it was not his fault but mine, for usually being in the Rheinischer Hof; he was by far the nicest, the most brilliant, and the only genuinely kind teacher I had there, and we were great friends, despite my being such

---

* Translator of the first German edition of *Under the Volcano*.

a rotten pupil—and to cap it all, he has always reminded me very strongly of yourself.)

With best love from Margerie and myself to Marjorie, Dorothy and yourself and hoping to see you soon,

Malcolm

To Clenens ten Holder

[Dollarton, Summer, 1951]

Sehr geehrter Herr ten Holder:

Thank you very much for your most amusing letter, and also for writing to Downie Kirk, to whom I have sent on your letter, though he has not yet had time to reply to this.

I am exceedingly obliged to you in the matter of the dedication and I am certain that Downie will be delighted.

Re the Gothic headings, etc.—also I thank you, but of course I meant to say, only if you thought it a good idea yourself; but I am surmising that you do. I would very much like to hear your lecture at your Volkhochschule (what a wonderful word—does it mean Folk-happiness school?); also I sincerely appreciate the fact of your having discovered the *Volcano*. I hope you may preserve that feeling in regard to my work and that I may be worthy of it. The feeling of discovery, as well as having actually discovered something, especially in a foreign language, is a valid thing and hard enough to explain, and indeed is worth a novel in itself.

Enclosed you will find the answers to your questions, which are I hope adequate; they are at any rate fulsome, as a result of which I must unfortunately curtail this letter, in order to catch the airmail, though the letter cannot conclude without mention of what may be the extraordinary coincidence of your friend, Karlheinz Schmidhus, which, if so, would seem to entitle you to the discovery of myself on yet another plane.

There was indeed a teacher, when I was at Bonn-Koblenzerstrasse, in 1928, named Schmidhus, and one of whom I entertain the kindliest and most affectionate memories, for he was not only the most brilliant of the teachers there and the most well-liked—as brilliant a teacher as I was a dummkopf of a pupil—but he was a person of such great goodness and wisdom that I not only have never forgotten him but can describe him in absolute detail, even though this is 23 years ago, and my sojourn in Bonn only 8 weeks, and the reason for this no doubt is, that though as a child one sets forth expecting to meet people who are kind and patient in this life, it turns out to be extremely rare to meet a combination of that virtue in anyone of which patience is a component: he needed a lot of patience with me, as I had an almost abnormally slow mind, which caused me to suffer a great deal; however I can read German aloud today almost as well as a German—that was about the only class I took with Herr Schmidhus, who mostly dealt with advanced students, but then that was almost the only thing I learned at all in Bonn, outside the bar of the Hotel Rheinischer Hof. It was not for lack of many other excellent teachers, and to be able to pronounce German properly, even despite my other deficiencies, has been an enormous help and pleasure to me: for example, once having determined the meaning I can appreciate much German poetry, even extremely complex poetry, in fact I can appreciate some poetry without having determined the meaning. Rilke, strangely enough, I have sometimes been able really to understand in German, without being able to understand the English translation before me. It is true that this is confined to poetry: but with application and the time I could begin a study of German from there whereas another person, knowing far more to begin with, would get much less out of it.

Not the least strange part of this is that the Herr Schmidhus I knew—whether Karlheinz was his Christian name I don't know—was almost the exact double of the very Downie Kirk, likewise a teacher, you have just written to—in fact, to describe him, as I remember him, would be to describe Downie, that is, I put him about 4 or 5 years older than I was then, which was 18 or 19, so he would be about 23, that is, of somewhat above medium height, but with extraordinarily broad shoulders, and an extremely wide and intelligent forehead, he had, generally speaking, apart from being very pleasant-looking, an air of being much younger even than he was, an air of something boyish, full of life, and twinkle, against which, as if half disapproving of his own élan, he wore rather conservative, usually dark clothes. One thing I shall always remember; I pleased him because I showed a true appreciation even at that age, which the other English boys of course didn't, of the triumphs of the German theatre—even modern expressionist triumphs, and he was staggered that I even knew about "George" Kaiser, and what was more knew that he had written about thirty plays, and not just *Vom Morgens bis Mitternachts*, and set about righting (as you may right my rendering of *From Morn till Midnight*) my pronunciation immediately.

Gay-org Kaiser, Herr Lowry.

He didn't think as much of Gayorg as I did (I had just seen Claude Rains playing in *From Morn till Midnight* in England as I was later to have a minor hand in the production of the same at Cambridge, as also of Toller, whom I later came to know well, both in London and Mexico) but he was delighted just the same, as he was also delighted when I repeated to him that *Der Gross Gott Brown,* by Eugene O'Neill then playing at the Schauspielhaus in Köln—by far the most imaginative wonderful production I have ever seen of O'Neill, incidentally, far better than the play itself, which it had leant over backwards to extract the last juices of meaning out of, and where there weren't any, had provided some of its own—could not have been written surely without the influence of the said Gayorg. Herr Schmidhus promised to look into these deep matters, but perhaps was more pleased when I showed some knowledge of Wedekind; had this exchange occurred at the beginning of my short relationship, there might have been some reason for his extraordinary decency in always making allowance for my slowness and never embarrassing me, or holding me up as an example, but actually this occurred toward the end and it was perhaps the first indication he had that I was not a congenital idiot. I have therefore always held Herr Schmidhus in a place of unique esteem in my memory so if it should turn out by any miracle to be the same Herr Schmidhus—though if not, the coincidence of the name and the date and location becomes weirder still—please tell him so, with my love. Also I hope he can take a bit of pride in his old pupil because the influences that have formed the *Volcano* are in a profound degree and largely German, though it may be hard to see where they come from. (It was in Bonn I saw Murnau's *Sonnenaufgang;* 70 minutes of this wonderful movie—though it falls to pieces later, doubtless due to the exigencies of Hollywood—have influenced me almost as much as any book I ever read, even though I've never seen it since.)

It was through Herr Schmidhus too I acquired the love of Gothic printing that I hope not discommoded you in Chapter X.

For the rest, yes, we rebuilt our house, and were the carpenters and all.

We, too, endure some financial hardship here, even as you: there is no outlet for one's work in Canada, no magazines, and the U.S. is not interested, should the *mise en scène* be Canada and that *mise en scène* not contain a mounted policeman. It is difficult to make a living at 4000 miles distance, and it is hard to make a reply to the editor who says: Why don't you write another *Under the Volcano?* At least overnight. Moreover we have inflation.

We spent our money earned from the success of the *Volcano* in America—long ago. Old England sits like a broody hen on the most of the rest of our cash, expecting perhaps to hatch an iron virgin from it. We starve from time to time, but have a lot of fun just the same, and when we make some more cash, we shall come and see you in Württemberg.

I am very gratified about the Wibberli-Wobberli and your friend singing it on the guitar. I didn't compose it however. It was the traditional song of our family that all the Lowry brothers sang at a certain recurrent ordeal for new boys at school. It probably was a music hall song of the nineties, but I'm sure its copyright, if any, has long expired. I am not at all sure that the composer was not my eldest brother himself; anyway I'm convinced your friend will have got a better version of it on his guitar. I have composed some things, though, mostly jazz, also on a guitar. Indeed I was arrested in the street once in Bonn for playing and singing said guitar, in company with some of your countrymen and one of mine, on the occasion when we were celebrating the defeat of Essen *verein* at hockey, I having played inside left for Bonn *verein,* a refrain that went, every now and then, *Zwei–null!* We having defeated Essen 2–0. Also there was another song to the refrain: *Drei Segelmann.* . . . But the policeman didn't like it. Finally he decided he did like it but would fine us all a little bit just the same. Whereupon your countrymen swore gallantly they would go to gaol rather than we be fined. Whereupon we swore gallantly we would go to gaol rather than they be fined. Whereupon we all repaired to the Hotel Kaiserhof, and were fined just the same, though nobody, it seems to me mysteriously, paid.

And so, my dear Herr ten Holder, the very best of luck to you with the translation, and also to yourself, and to your wife, from myself and my wife—herself the author of an exceedingly good and wild novel, *Horse in the Sky,* in such a strange tradition, that of Emily Brontë's *Wuthering Heights,* a book otherwise without heir, I am sending it to you without her permission, feeling it would interest you.

And not forgetting the 2 rowdies, Peter and Johnnes. While as for the little Xicotancatzerl (by the way the original Aztec name was, as you probably knew, Xicotancatl, a Tlaxcaltecan hero) greetings from ours, whose seltsamer name does not reflect his benign character nor great gifts of singing, Citron-le-Taciturn.

> With kind regards,
> Malcolm Lowry

To Albert Erskine

Dollarton, B.C., Canada
June 5, 1951

Beloved old Albert:

After a fabulous lengthy grinding of machinery, such as once might have signified the final unbending of the Khedive in the matter of the hegemony of the Suez Canal, the liquidation of the Sikh of Sokotra, and the incorporation of the Maldive Islands into the British Commonwealth after the seduction of its cannibal Queen by a subaltern from Bridlington-on-Sea, the British Government has at last—after interminable and unfathomable investigations on every other plane too—condescended to permit me to receive £189:19:6½ on advance of what is left of what I take it is, nevertheless, mine, and will eventually arrive. This, I am to understand, is a concession, because technically speaking, my brother informs me, no money at all has still been released "on account of deaths" as the saying is, nor did this much release seem to have anything to do with the end of the fiscal year, as I had every reason to suppose from my brother, and as I told you.

But we are now as a consequence anyway in possession of some 560 extra bucks in addition to what I already have of my own, which is roughly $98 per month, according to the fluctuation of the pound. Thanks to what you so generously lent us yourself, which saved our lives, we were tided over our crisis, are out of debt here and are even in a position to pay you back today without precipitating another crisis should you need the money right off. So please tell us that *quam celerime.* I am dreadfully sorry (in fact I have been able only to send off one more) and despite promises we didn't hear from England so that we began to feel we were in the first chapter of *Bleak House* again.

On the other hand, though the mills of the gods grind exceedingly slow in England, they *do* grind, and now that one has some tangible proof that they are working I am almost certain to hear again soon.

The estate is being sold, and though the Government will take a disproportionate amount, my income cannot fail to be increased to some extent, nor can I fail to receive some fairly large—for us—addition to my capital. Moreover a law has just been passed I understand that does provide for the release of more money, for the present system has been proving mutually ruinous in respects that touch the Government's own bank balance, if any. (An ironic aspect of all this which I have quite forgotten until this moment is that even before I was of age I was in receipt of at least a couple of bequests from collateral relatives of whom I was mysteriously the favorite relation, every penny of which was invested by *force majeure* in my old man's firm that was later liquidated by Cripps. Or you might say I helped to liquidate it myself, for the only time I voted in England, when barely old enough, I voted Labour, out of what then seemed a sense of justice. But I did not vote for a *party,* simply for an independent individual with some belief in a coalition. My father was a Tory of Tories but he used to lunch every Thursday, I discovered, with a Scots socialist who was a financial expert and an authority on West Indian cotton, from whom I suspect him of having derived half his ideas on beating the market.)

This means in brief that though we can pay you back now—if it is not too inconvenient to you, we would feel safer in waiting a little longer until we see how we stand, both in respect to England, and when we have a little more work off. Since it seems I was too optimistic before, as regards the former, I would say before the summer is out; in regard to the latter I'll speak in a moment. We would not have hesitated to repay you instantly we received the £189:19:6½ (out of £200 originally sent—one felt like sending them back the 6½d as a tip, and asking what they thought they could do with the other eleven guineas that we couldn't, or even suggesting that had my brother had prior information he would have applied for £211:11:6½) were it not for the feeling haunting one in the truth brutally stated by Molière: ("Death is not always at the beck and call of heirs and while the grass grows, the cow starves.")

Even so we would not so have hesitated and would not hesitate now had you not so very thoughtfully intimated that you would prefer us to wait until we felt a bit safer. We are and we aren't. So please let us know for there is no reason on God's earth why we should make you suffer for trusting us: nor would you have to suffer for us on account of feeling that we were absolutely broke should we send it tomorrow.

[242]

Margie's health is steadily improving and our chief remaining anxiety is about the house, though this is only indirectly an economic problem: no amount of money perhaps can help us keep it, should they start to "develop" the land. On the other hand should we lose it our economic situation thus worsens overnight—to say nothing of any other aspects of it—and with this in mind it is wiser from our point of view to keep some money in, should this blow fall before England comes through or we have sold anything more. Scares of eviction come and go, and it is a situation of some universal significance I have always meant to develop in the novel; but it is a whole lot easier to write about than enduring, and while enduring for that matter as hard to write about as it is not to write about. The threat strangely enough now comes from America and not Canada, American interests having bought up all the neighboring property. But there is a chance they may prove more humane for that reason and let us stay or at least give us time to move which Canadians would not do.

So far as concerns work I have been fairly gravely inhibited by all these anxieties from accomplishing anything recently that is first rate or at the same time saleable, the more so since it has been as if the plot of the novel, which gets into all the short stories too, were catching up with me. But I am perfectly sure that the work when it is done will have a sounder quality for those particular things we have been or are going through and in short it seems to have done us a lot of good.

Margerie though, for her part, has had a real burst of creative genius and is just putting the final touches on a short novel called *The Castle of Malatesta*. This is such a really wonderful piece of work that partly for that reason, and partly because it seemed most practical, it having represented the piece of fiction in the family most nearly complete and I believe saleable, and it being absolutely necessary for us to get something in to Hal, that I have devoted five sixths of my time latterly to helping her get it finished, my help consisting in large part in getting out my own influence where maldigested and baleful and thus enabling her to give her own extremely original talent its head, and in acting as a sort of remote Fritz Lang, crosser of t's and p's, and supplier where necessary of strange noises-off. This—as often happens with me these days too—started as a short story, then became a novella, and has ended up as a rather longer than Jim Agee's really superb *Morning Watch* which we read with delight not long ago, so it should as a consequence be publishable as a volume. I don't know what Hal would want to do with it, or whether it has any transitional place in a magazine, but it should be finished this week and, having had a final version being typed as mopping-up operations were completed, should be off before the end of next. That means, allowing ten days for transit, that Hal should have it by about the 24th of June and I would extremely much like you to have a look at it. Though I have felt that unwittingly I've proved rather deleterious to Margie's destiny and freedom as a writer so far in one way and another, whether by advice influence opinion existence or sheer bulk I know not, I feel free to waive such considerations in regard to this and don't think I'm putting a wrong thought in the ether by stating objectively that it's quite one of the most remarkable short novels, certainly one of the most remarkable love stories, or stories of passion, ever written by an American woman. I have had various feelings of reluctance about asking you to read it because you might be personally embarrassed. If you hated it you wouldn't want to hurt me by saying so. And equally if you liked it you might feel we would be hurt if the circumstances were such that you couldn't put your opinion behind it. Having come after long cogitation to the conclusion that there is a good chance that, on the contrary, you would never forgive me, if because of these considerations I hadn't at least *tried* to have you read something that might for that matter easily become a classic, I hereby threw these considerations (what prose! Oh, Malcolm, what prose!) out of the window. I don't like to make any suggestions to Hal. Margie is afraid to say anything to you—naturally we can't be blamed for wanting both to be "ducks of distinction" (as she once amused you by saying) with the same publisher who would of course be yourself. That idea, never far from our minds, seems too marvellous to be true. But the fact is she has an enormous lot of guts, and enormous talent, and I am sure if she only had some encouragement would go a long way. At all events I hope it isn't too much to hope that you can find a way of getting a look at it—I would hope first look, my feeling being of course that I have spotted a winner for you. To sum up, the last thing we'd want to do is to put you on the spot or embarrass you because of the personal obliquities of the situation. She doesn't want anyone to publish it who doesn't feel some enthusiasm for it and belief in her—the Scribner situation was a nightmare—but enthusiasm can't be forced, and opinions differ. I know, even yours and mine (though I'm not sure I know where)—anyhow she doesn't want it to be published "owing to certain auxiliary circumstances." On the other hand if it is going to be published and going to be a success we don't want anybody else to have the credit except yourself, if it is the kind of thing you feel you can take credit for.

It's quite hard to disseverate her work and mine, at our serious best, that is, even though it is very different, in a larger sense: when we really get going like that, though we're two separate and very different writers, we're like one organism, and in that regard I owe her a terrific lot on the *Volcano*. So I more or less have to speak like this anyway. And it's even selfish in one way. If I can't keep her going, then she can't help me and then I fall to pieces. But to do me justice this is not the way I look at it. Her problem has been to keep herself going without me, or to know what she really wants of help for her own individual purposes, and in this she's triumphantly done just that.

As for me, I have a long short story more or less finished that is out of the Intermezzo part of the novel—this whole part will be called *Eridanus*. This part of the part is known as "The Forest Path to the Spring," and we aim to get it off when *Malatesta* is out of the way. There're a lot of other short things that have been held up and we should now get under way to Hal too; there is a kind of log jam in my work. "Forest Path" has some of the best things I've ever done in it, I hope you'll think. *Eridanus* is what I call Dollarton here: called such after the constellation—the River of Youth and the River of Death. Reading Dante the other day I came to the conclusion that the celestial scenery of pine trees and mountains inlet and sea here must be extremely like that in Ravenna, where he died and wrote and got the inspiration for the last part of the *Paradiso*. Then I discovered that Eridanus in mythology among other things *is* the River Po and where the Po emerges to the sea *is* Ravenna. It gave me quite a turn, though I'm sure I don't see why it should have.

But all this is not getting *The Voyage That Never Ends* written. It is not even getting blocked out for you. Even to do that in readable form would take me about four months without doing anything else, and perhaps it would be a good thing so to block it out?

I ought at least to park some of the material with you: it would be a lousy idea to lose another Paradiso completely—nothing in it at all for either of us. Perhaps you won't like the idea of *The Voyage* at first but I feel you will finally. But I ought to get down to it as soon as I can and think of nothing else for a long time if I'm ever to finish it—ideas seem to be escaping all the time, but perhaps it's merely "ripening" as Ryder puts it.

And other stories . . . damn them, but I better get a sheaf of them off first. But first, *Malatesta*.

I had a long and happy dream about *The Voyage* the other night— a dream of an interminable and fruitful discussion about *The Voyage* with yourself that unlike most discussions kept creating something beyond the discussion that took shape in some transcendental form continually, but while an actual "Voyage" of some kind was continuing: I kept waking up, but feeling so delighted I had to get back into the dream again—it was the most exceedingly happy and consistently cheerful dream I have ever had, as if the tyranny of prose, the ands, the buts, and the howevers did not exist, and all we had to do in order to write that book was to get on something and go somewhere, what class I don't know.

Well, I must sign off to catch the post (in a thunderstorm). Please tell us whether you need the cash right away or can await His Majesty's Paymaster's next convenience a little longer at not too much inconvenience to yourself.

God bless you from us both for sending it so swiftly and kindly and our best loves to both Peggy and yourself from us both,

Malcolm

To Philippe Thoby-Marcelin

[Summer, 1951]

KARAMBA, my very dear Phito,

Our best congratulations on *The Pencil* which I haven't time to discuss here, but will just content myself with saying that while it is not the best book *you* can do, nor was meant to be, it will very much surprise me if it does not become a classic, and this it fully deserves to do. I expect to see it reprinted many times and even students having to learn it in school (even if their parents object). Taking it as a whole the translation is very successful, I think: but there are quite a few errors of taste especially here and there in the wrongful or inconsistent use of American slang and one or two other points where one senses that a literal translation has not done you justice, or otherwise makes a slightly false impression: we are going to send you these suggested emendations at intervals of a few days—posting the first tomorrow (Friday) which will cover the first few chapters, which we are doing to save time, which may be of the essence for you.

In this way we shall indicate precisely where these suggested emendations should occur on the proofs which you will be able to check with your copy and consult about with a friend or adviser but without our sending you back the proofs themselves until afterwards, which we need here for this purpose.

Where possible we will try to avoid making suggestions that will mean resetting a paragraph but we earnestly counsel you to consider them in cooperation with someone else who knows English or your translator himself for we believe that these lapses, while not individually very bad, cumulatively might affect the reviews.

Please tell us *immediately* how much time you have, but in any case our first batch of notes will go off tomorrow.

Right at this moment we are facing eviction from our house, together with our neighbours the fishermen, please pray for us that this tragedy may be avoided, which it still just may: nonetheless, tragedy or no, you are going to get your notes on time and as stated, even if they begin moving our house away from under us while we are doing it. This is too long and complicated a story to go into here—but it is another story of sharks, believe me: we live on Government land which they will not let us buy, but meantime we are treated as without rights altogether, not even human ones, so that we have no legal toe-hold, unless I am clever enough to invent one. So please pray. It is worse for some of our neighbours than for us, who are still young and kicking after all.

God bless you and congratulations on your horrendous and witty Greek Grand Guignol comedy-tragedy again, and love from Margerie and myself,

ton frère,
Malcolm

To David Markson*

Dollarton, British Columbia
August 25, 1951

Dear David M.:

If I said all that your letter suggests to me it would lead us right smack into the primeval forces of creation and twenty years from now

* A student at Columbia University, writing a thesis on *Under the Volcano* for his master's degree.

I would still be engaged on the 15th volume of a Grundlage der Wissenshaft von Ausdruck and the letter would remain unwritten. So much for what you feared might be the "crudity with which you concocted your questions," concerning which let your mind be at rest; concerning yours of Aug. 9, let it be not only at rest but positively joyful—I am very glad indeed that you wrote it, as it goes without saying I was grateful to receive it, and as for the contents of *this* letter let your mind in advance be at rest too, though in motion—in fact just like the Tao—no psychic or psychological thunderstone is going to drop on your head, though it is to be hoped some manna (which possibly should be spelt mana) may fall, and though by virtue of the dignity of my years I may assume the right of speaking like a parent from time to time, it's not going to be as austere as all that: as a matter of fact this pseudo-copperplate handwriting and semi-colon technique will doubtless be gradually discarded as the letter proceeds—here it goes—as in Haiti, during what has begun as something resembling one's good old starched evening chapel days in England, with Madame, here's your pew, and the meek arrival of the Presbyter, and the congregation in their best clothes, are discarded the shining Sunday shoes of the Voodoo priest when, the drums having called down the gods from Olympus for the hundredth time, and himself possessed for the hundred and fiftieth, he hurls himself cheerfully into the flames: but first for the muted conversation in the vestry, and as the voluntary plays, my explanation—and my apologies for this—as to how the helpful daemon I promised to return to you got stranded in the chimney pot. . . . First I did write you and here is a précis of what I said.

I began by explaining about the forest fire situation, adding that although one did not have one very near yet you could breathe nothing else and even at a distance these things were enough to give you the horrors. So I would be brief, I said. Yes, Aiken's *Blue Voyage* was an enormous influence upon me, especially since (I made its acquaintance at the age of 18 in England having just returned from my first voyage to sea) not being able to find out anything about its author, I felt that Aiken was my own discovery. Of course the truth was Aiken was highly respected in a small circle in England, but I didn't find this out till much later, coming from a huntin' and shootin' family near Liverpool, who weren't interested in literary matters. Meantime I was not slow in taking up the dedicatory coincidence of C.M.L. either.* So much so that in no time at all I was practically of the opinion that the book was not only dedicated to me, but that I'd written it myself, and was thus, though an Englishman, extremely gratified, though I think privately I was damned annoyed, vicariously to receive the Pulitzer Prize a few years later. (Actually C.M.L. was Clarice Lorenz, Aiken's second wife.) I went on to add (in this letter drafted last June) that what I had to say in this regard would be of more use to you privately, as a novelist and as a writer, than in writing the thesis. It would lead me into a vast psychological field, not to say into the realm of the confidential and the intensely personal: and from the copy I have before me (as the saying is) it's not quite clear whether the subject is broken off at this point because I fear to appear to my discredit in that field if I am to be honest, or whether, in the attempt possibly to offset certain pitfalls that I imagine might confront *you* as a writer, I fear I may create some bran-new ones for you of my own. So at this point we get on to the Cabbala, to answer your question, and the subject is changed.

"Re the Cabbala," I wrote, "and the whole business of the occult, however right I may be about reducing my French preface to the level of some little doppelgängerelle's chatter, I feel bound to tell you as a fellow mortal of somewhat elder years who wishes to be useful, though not, so to say, to sway your mind, unless it be toward A Better Thing, that however much it may be intermediately important or even healthy for you to rationalize such matters, your rationalization is an illusion. As a matter of fact you could with some justice 'rationalize' the Cabbala itself (roughly speaking a system of thought that creates a magical world within this one that so far as I know has no pretense of being anything but an illusion—you may send it flying out of the window if you like, though perhaps it's not wise, it might come back by another one) but you can't rationalize or anything else the unknown depths of the human psyche—at least not in the way you mean. *You* have one, and its operations are to be found working within you too. (Of course you know this, and much more; still, while amassing the "much more," it's surprising what knowledge of one's own, indeed foreknowledge, one can overlook and which has been there all the time, as if waiting to be used. You'll just have to pardon the pomposity of all this.)

One of the clearest answers that comes immediately to mind in

* Clarence Malcolm Lowry signed his student writings at The Leys CML and sometimes CAMEL.

regard to all this is the sort of thing to be found in Jung's 20 year
old "Man in search of his soul," which I didn't read till the other
day, so forgive me if the suggestion seems infra-dig. More or less
popular and dry half-gobbledegookery though it is—and I dare say
psychologically superseded or out of date in places and what not—
you nonetheless might find it soundly full of the wisest kind of
speculation if you haven't happened to have read it. To revert, you
suggest Joyce would smile at it all. Not so. Joyce—whom I once
encountered smiling, however, in the Luxembourg Gardens—was on
the contrary an extremely superstitious (if that's the right word) man.
His only regret re Yeats' *The Vision*—which you should read too if
you haven't even if you can't make those cones work (I got so that I
could make just one cone work)—was that he did not use all that
tremendous stuff in a work of art. You may call it tripe. There's a
certain element of danger, maybe, in calling it anything else. Joyce
(who was looking for Aiken's "Coming Forth by Day of Osiris Jones"
when he died) even had a superstition, according to one of his
biographers, about the name Lowry, which occurs in his funeral
scene. No sooner had he given them these names, he delighted to
report, than one after the other these names acquired living, or
rather dead, counterparts, all of which had one thing in common, they
were found to have come to grotesque and tragic ends! I never
checked up to see if a stand-in called L. has already let me out but
whether or no it is enough to keep one fighting for a happy ending
till the day one dies against *that!* More seriously (if this is not serious)
you can readily see why, on purely psychological grounds, Joyce
might be a superstitious fellow. What goes up must come down, not
to say what happens when you throw nature out with a pitchfork. To
be superstitious is not indeed to be "mystical" but I let the point
rest for the moment.

Likewise I said I'd let Joseph Frank and Mark Schorer rest for the
moment, finding that chiefly interesting as having bearing on what
you do with the paper yourself: I noted, with a friendly salute and
as it were the purr of a fellow artisan, that if you have to write a
thesis, that you can't bear to write it in a form not suggested by the
substance, or at any rate not without form itself, thus showing, I
would say, the predominance of the artist in you over the critic: that
really means more than "Schorer's passing on and out," or should I say
"The Consul's passing out and on": my writing is not very clear at
this point, as one might say, gap in the manuscript, after this, and

as a matter of fact much more, not at all interesting; it goes on about *Las Manos de Orlac.*

Las Manos de Orlac—then—is a preposterous mad (and bad, though I pretend it was relatively good, which it perhaps was) movie of the German Ufa Wiene Caligari Fritz Lang Destiny Golden Age, with Conrad Veidt as Orlac: therein, Orlac was a great pianist who lost his hands in a railway accident, had the hands of a murderer grafted on by a "Mad Doctor," ever afterwards felt—no doubt because he'd played the Sleepwalker in *Caligari* too—impelled to commit murders; Hollywood made a remake in about 1936 of truly awe-inspiring badness, but with Peter Lorre imported from the Fritz Lang Ufa playing the doctor: the surgical sequences were in this version photographed by the Ufa genius Karl Freund so you get 5 minutes of that kind of Grand Guignol anyway, though the overall effect could not be worse: thematically speaking, though, the pelado in Chapter VIII—by extension the Consul, by extension M. Laruelle—gives the clue: the pelado's hands were covered with blood. So are man's.

Reception: This is a bit complicado; it was a considerable success—at least for me—even financial, in the U.S., though not as much as its presence as 5th on the best seller lists for some months would seem to indicate: it seemed to be most successful in Dallas, Texas, to my delight, and it once was cited in a best seller list as "one up" on *Forever Amber,* though to do *Forever Amber* justice *Forever Amber* had been going on rather longer, and we were both down at the bottom anyhow by that time: we waged quite a battle, though, for a while—I imagine about 15 or 16,000 copies altogether. Here in Canada it sold 2 copies—so far as I can gather—and was panned in the local paper. In England it was well received but did little better. In France it was greeted with enthusiasm and shoved into a Modern Classics series, as was the case in Norway; Sweden, Denmark, Italy and Germany have also made translations of it, though I have no idea of the outcome save in Denmark, where it flopped, and Germany, where it's coming out shortly, which of these last countries has taken the most serious attitude towards it. (I mean Western Germany, of course.) (Mark Schorer wrote two reviews of it—one extraordinarily sympathetic one in *Vogue* of all places—others demolished it, no less, and it also made the *Encyclopedia Britannica.*)

I then mention that it was Royal Welsh Fusiliering brother who'd insisted I be called Clarence after the gent of that name who was drowned in a butt of Malmsey wine, gave my regards to your friend Leonard Brown, intimating that if he was Firmin that was fine, for

I bring the Consul to life in a later book and make him do just the opposite, and all this without even joining Alcoholics Heironymus, though it must be said he changes his potation and even goes on a diet of Schopenhauer and vinegar for a while, and other remedies from Burton's *Anatomy of Melancholy,* even up to and including water which nearly makes him die of dysentery, and milk which gives him sinusitis, and tea which gives him an even worse attack of delowryum tremens; and then reverted to Aiken again, adding that I still thought he was a very great genius, and incidentally a much misunderstood one, but that it seemed to me that this touched on a subject so important for a writer launching away that I'd better write you a letter for your private ear on the subject (gap in MSS) for it yet remained to be explained how a boy of 18, more or less inexperienced save in one tough aspect of life, namely the sea (a fragmentary thing, but still I'd been a seaman—O'Neill sent me to sea, I guess—looked at it as such, not a passenger), could be drawn as by some irresistible teleological force toward an aspect of the mind or psyche of another much older, totally different in experience and nationality and outlook, and moreover, in *Blue Voyage* at least, with a philosophy and psychological *drang*—save where it touched beauty on the one hand, human misery on the other, expressed and linked through the phenomenal and magical usage of language—that he the boy, did not understand, and had he understood, would have found thoroughly inimical—for sheer lack of sunlight and air and mountains, if not blue water (you might call it pseudo-Freud and the philosophy of the "nothing but")—and then, as it were, stuck there, calmly disregarding among other things that Aiken himself, save in all but a few of his short stories which on the contrary are mostly a reversion of his prosaic and false and influenced side to almost nothing of lasting worth at all, as he would be the first to agree, say *Time* mag. what it may, had, with certain other exceptions, enormously and continuously developed in his poetry (but curiously I didn't know he was a poet at first) beyond that point into a metaphysical and far wiser and wider realm, to a point indeed where he might well serve as master to any writer in the world, in which connection it is as well not to forget the mature, indeed dying, Joyce, looking for Osiris Jones being reborn. (When Conrad sent me some 20 years ago a copy of the latter masterpiece, to my lasting shame I neither acknowledged it nor made any comment. Why should I? What was all this about Osiris Jones? After all it was not *Blue Voyage* and *I* had not written it. Worse still, it never occurred to me he might be hurt, so cruelly abstract is one side of youth. And weirder than all, one might have reckoned without one's own remote influence, even if not literary or direct, but beneficently springing rather—in so far as it sprang, if spring it did—in part from that very shattering and unsolicited faith in his work I had shown! But what did I see in *Blue Voyage?* Certainly something that was beyond my power rationally to see. Nor was I wrong. Perhaps what one might term Operation II of the daemon?) However it is no wonder I stopped the letter here, for the subject is hard to explain indeed, quite apart from which I had not even touched on what seemed to me the essence of the far greater subject that this began to adumbrate—

Then, after a while, I received yours of Aug. 9.

At which point I think it's time to take those shoes off and get into the flames.

(No joke either, if he didn't do it himself first, no one would believe it could be done and then there would be no initiation.)

I'll start with a few assumptions, in fact jump boldly to conclusions, all of them flattering to myself, and doubtless due to my great narcissism—though I won't waste time on this aspect of it—then make a few tangential observations, in the hope that even if inapplicable, they may some day, odds and ends of 2 x 4's though they are, serve well as reliable timber with which to build a bridge should you need one. For no wonder Dante found the straight way was lost. There is no straight way. There is no path, unless metamorphosed. Dante's wood was an abyss. Psychological—for the last time psychology!—as Kafka says—but true. Fortunately Virgil—since we all stand together in this world—was standing near and he had the common sense to make use of him. Dante didn't grow much happier, it is true, but perhaps that was his fault: and at least he finished his book. Perhaps he'd have done better still if he'd pushed Virgil into one of those swamps instead of another of his poor unfortunates and walked over using his head as a stepping stone but that's beside the point. Anyway Virgil was dead. If he'd been alive it might have been a different story. And I ain't no Virgil. Still I shall squelch along upon my feet of clay as well as I can—perhaps they will even turn into some kind of mottled marble in the process. Anyway:

(a) I'm going to assume, as I should, you mean the letter you wrote.

(b) That having written it, you now wish you hadn't: *i.e.,* perhaps you feel ashamed of so expressing your feelings, in fact you may even feel I've misinterpreted it, etc.

To (b) *don't* wish you hadn't written it. It is the best thing you could have done. And you are right, it *is* perfectly healthy. What would be unhealthy would be if you hadn't so simply and directly expressed your empathies on the subject. True—no doubt you could think—eventually you would have forgotten the said feelings, but here comes nature and the pitchfork again: more than that, a book is a much harder proposition than a human being—once truly recognized it is not in the nature of the thing to let you alone, though the source of its behavior is a reciprocal gratitude beyond human understanding, it's liable to turn into a kind of mantra yoga: old stuff I have to talk here, stemming from the last sentence but one— the feelings turn inward and what is worse begin to work against you: worse still, they can even give one a kind of persecution mania, one suspects necrophily in oneself, incipient paranoia, heaven knows what (and on top of that the mind, equally with the heart, is a lonely hunter—I once fell in love with an elephant—and it's certainly no use worrying about the downgoing and morbid "correspondences" of these things, they become ridiculous, when all one is trying to do is *live,* and God how hard it can be at your age: perhaps I am talking about myself, not you—no matter, still I can permit myself to suffer on your account feeling yourself to be misunderstood, or disregarded, or worse, understood coldly and *cleverly* and rationally and "psychologically," and so more than disregarded, when all one has said is something direct and sincere: [gap in the MSS]—well, I myself am extremely happily married, the luckiest kind of person, both in my wife and the kind of life we mostly lead, as one might say healthy—and by God it really is healthy—normal; what a word!—as if happiness were normal today, or this kind of life which has almost disappeared from the world altogether—note: Howard had no means and no words with which to explain to these simple men that business is the only real thing in life, that it is heaven and paradise and all the happiness of a good Rotarian. These Indians were still living in a semi-civilized state, with little hope of improvement within the next hundred years. *–The Treasure of the Sierra Madre*—but there are all kinds of huge life-giving feelings in the world you can't pin down: for prose, for elephants, for the sea, even for the ducks that swim therein: we are all here anyway.)

Well, it is healthy, your identity with the *Volcano* I mean, even though the book may not be worthy of you, though it might be worse (and I cannot say how moving to me, because I won't disguise from you that I'm extremely proud of most of it), but somehow all this must be used for your benefit; in fact it is yours, that's what it's there for. And whatever they say or don't say I think it's a good book probably.

However the full drama of what you have said has not yet emerged. Nor will it be lost on you. Here is the plot of the book lost by fire. (*In Ballast to the White Sea*—once the sort of Paradiso of the trilogy of which the *Volcano* was the first or "Inferno" section—now incorporated hypothetically elsewhere in the whole bolus of 5 books— I think to be called *The Voyage That Never Ends*. It was lost 7 years ago, June 7, 1944, when our first house went up in flames, not ten feet from where I sit, and written 9–10 years before that, in New York, when I was a little older than you.)

A, the hero of my novel, a young student at Cambridge, of Scandinavian origin, and with a sea-faring experience such as my own, feels such a kinship for a work as you have most generously expressed for mine—a novel of the sea, he has read in translation, by a Scandinavian novelist X.* The disorientation of A at the university is much the same as Hugh's at Cambridge in *U.T.V.* and for the same reasons. X's novel is an appalling and horrendous piece of work, a sort of *Moby Dick* in fact, but a *Moby Dick* that was concerned less with whales than the fate of the individual living characters of the *Acushnet* (that being the original name of the *Pequod*). Only in this case the more A reads X's book the more identified he becomes with the principal character in that book, Y—who supplies the one note of relief (in X's book)—(it is a book on the side of life though) the more so as the experience of Y—by extension he feels that of X too— closely—indeed supernaturally—resembles his own: not merely that, but X's book uncannily resembles the one A's been trying to write himself, which it seems to have rendered futile. (As a matter of fact it's more complicated even than that but let it pass.)

My hero is troubled, among other things (a stormy love affair with an older woman, the risk of being sent down for pursuing it, the invidiousness of being a man at the University and yet treated as a child, a Dostoievskian brother, the ghoulishness of his contemporaries, the ideology of the English faculty, the feeling of hopelessness that overwhelms him about his choice of a vocation when now he figures he perhaps isn't a writer and so no better than a child after all and so on), by the fact that he can find absolutely no parallel in *literature* to this growing sense as of identity with the character of Y—and the field of X's novel—save a rather minor, if good, but scarcely helpful book by Louis Adamic, a feeble short story by Aldous Huxley, and a

* Nordahl Grieg.

sinister German play running in London called *The Race with a Shadow* by one Wilhelm van Scholz, based on an idea by Goethe. All these, with the exception of the last, which is so horrible he can't take it, are almost parodies on the surface of an experience, by which he is bewildered because he cannot believe that it does not represent something universal and so of vital human importance; nor has it got anything to do with the normal experiences of hero-worship through which one passes: Y is not a hero in the usual sense, his experiences are not enviable, he is not even wise—he isn't even physically described in X's book, for that matter, so that he has no features or stature and is quite impossible to picture save as several kinds of person at once; on another plane he seems more like a voice that has commented upon a human experience with honour and an agonizing truth that is unique to A. (Y is not Melville's "handsome sailor" nor Conrad's ugly one—his virtues are simple and such as A's life in England of that period everywhere betrays and even interdicts: loyalty, simplicity, decency, and a capacity to be reverent, in the bloodiest of circumstances, before the mystery of life, and a hatred of falsehood. It would appear also that he has a faith, of a kind, in God, if not strictly according to Martin Luther.) Yet how can it be unique to A, when by God Y *is* A. And what's all this about a hatred of falsehood, when one of the things that most bothers A is that A himself is an almost pathological liar—unable to give any kind of rational account of himself, he invents the most fantastic tales about himself at every point that are so vivid they have a kind of life of their own. (It is important for you to bear in mind that though I, as you may have guessed, am by and large, more or less, with reservations of course, A—though X is not Aiken, albeit an individual too —I am not lying to *you*, even though it might be more comfortable to do so.) X represents the complementary and lifegiving operation of the daemon pleading to Π or perhaps—implicit in Π too—but without which Π becomes satanic. Something like that. My terms are all mixed up, and I realize that like this it sounds more than a little ridiculous. But bear with me. Probably I don't have to explain it. And how can A be A when he's Y? And yet this is not the half of it either. A is no narcissist. He has not caught paranoia. Moreover he is a tough baby, on one side (in my book, or ex-book) almost as extraverted as some character in the *Treasure of the Sierra Madre*, even though that is a side of himself he exploits with women and lies about, but this much is true, his ship has taken him smack through the first bloody Chinese revolution of 1927, etc., though he has only seen tragic glimpses of the real thing and his knowledge of what he has actually been through even so has only just ceased to be about nil. Nor has he some adolescent fixation or crush on X, because if Y is mysterious, X is ten times more so. (About X he can find out absolutely nothing at all, the Scandinavian's novel having been long since remaindered in translation, the publishers non-existent in England, and there is no blurb to tell him a thing—he's bought the book second hand. Strangest of all A doesn't even want to *write* like X. Not at first he doesn't, that is. A has a style all his own, and what A and X have in common—though A sees his whole life in that book —is something different.) A, though he feels like an old man, has either bypassed or not even reached the stage of adolescence. People like Whitman with an all-embracing love of mankind, and also Lawrence, put him off, save when they write about nature. His knowledge of how gruesome man can be is too close, and in Cambridge, on a flabbier plane, closer still. So his brother not being a type he can take into his confidence, and his father being engaged in a gigantic law suit with the Peruvian Government, and his girl friend rapidly growing fed up with him, he sits down and writes to X. In fact he writes letter after letter to X—they formed, intermediately, a large part of the book—but it never once occurred to him that almost any publisher in Scandinavia would forward his letters, if X is extant; he keeps his problem, as the letters, to himself, meanwhile becoming increasingly afraid of his thoughts as his identification with Y—and by extension with X—becomes more complete. . . .

(to be continued)

In order to keep my promise to get this letter off I have to post this right now to catch the Saturday mail—there is one mail a day only, none on Sunday, and the relative time the two stages of the letter must make to reach you are roughly as follows: From Dollarton to Vancouver, 15 miles—24 hours. From Vancouver to Albany, 3500 miles—12 hours approx. So if I delayed you wouldn't receive anything till the middle of next week. I shan't stop writing, however, till the letter is finished, if it ever can be finished. Plot of *In Ballast* has a triumphant outcome. So see exciting installment next week. On back of all pages save page 1 are some bits of the original MSS of *Under the Volcano* my wife and I dug out for you and thought you might like to have: when I say original, some of it is pre-original, dating 11 years or so back, though I can't find any of the pre-pre-original which goes back to 1936 save in typescript; as a matter of fact we can't even find any typescript to speak of; notes down the margin are due to a habit my wife and I have of exchanging MSS for mutual correction: some of the work looks as though one definitely knew what one was doing, other parts look uncertain and as if the author were out of touch, and the style flabby or derivative, other bits are no longer there—but in the main it's as is—sorry it's not in order, but felt it might please you. When I said confidential—of course that I leave to your highest judgment, because it might hurt someone's feelings. But I didn't mean that you shouldn't speak to your girl about it, if you feel like speaking to her. If you badly want any of it when I'm through for your thesis better let me edit it. In one way it seems like a dirty trick, on second thoughts, even to have voiced a bona fide criticism in these circumstances of Aiken, to whom I owe so much (though Aiken himself I am sure would be the first to give assent that I should write you like this) and you must be wise and see beyond the superficial envy and ingratitude that evinces, the criticism of myself and my own weaknesses it involves.

Sursum corda!
Malcolm L.

(Intervallo)

(Is, ah, Señor David Markson in the house? Will he proceed to the cantina—the dirtiest one—next door, where the gringo peon Bruto pelado Señor Lowry is lying seriously ill? Chocolates? Tequila? Cerveza? Gaseosas? Mescal? H'm. Buenos tardes, señor. How's it going, old man? Sorry, it wasn't that I was lying seriously ill, nor that I was ill because I was seriously lying—because I'm not indeed, though I find it difficult indeed even painful to remember certain details of the plot of my chingado novel—on the contrary I'm trying my damndest to tell the truth, fantastic though it may be—but because, in this intervallo, I have read your letter again, and I perceived, misericorde, hombre, alas, that I had not thanked you sufficiently from the heart—I hadn't mentioned I had a heart—for what you have so generously and above all simply said, and with a feeling, and trust, I was going to say, I didn't deserve: but if that is so, viejo, what the hell is the point of writing this letter? What kind of the hell reflection of yourself would I give back if I didn't deserve it? So, all right, I do deserve it. As certainly you deserve something back of equal sincerity. If I deny myself, I deny my book, and in denying my book, I deny you. For equally it is your book. So I shan't do anything of the sort; I will, on the contrary, affirm it, be proud of it. As I am not? But how have I answered—and this is what is making me at the moment sick, hombre—sickness is in that part used to be call: soul—moreover I hate to think that my silence, however explicable and non-invidious, made you suffer—this forthrightness, this frankness, this directness? Have I answered it with an equal forthrightness, an equal simplicity of feeling? Or with a concatenation of complexities, an evasion of gobbledegookeries—in short, for simplicity, have returned: psychology? And then on top of that have worn a mien of being so unco quid pure normal healthy and beyond reproach that perhaps it's unnatural in itself, as if my life, or anyone else's life, had not been wrested—and does not have to go on being wrested—out of the Molochian maw of errors often so destructible they make one's hair stand on end: so you would be wrong to think that the human being is not there, that he in turn is not sympathetic, or that he regards that life—despite a definite element of having *come through*—as anything purer or more upright than a collaboration between Strindberg, Dostoievsky, The Underground Man, a Ouija board, a talking horse, Joe Venuti and a Houngan: this on the one side, on the other you must feel yourself right to have trusted me, though not for reasons that are at all easy to answer. Still you *are* right to do so. The decency, the honesty is here, sprouting laboriously amid the indecency, the dishonesty. But immediately I say that the shadow of Melville's *Confidence Man* seems to fall upon my pen, that emblem of the worse than worst, warning one away from one's easy interpretations, one's facile optimism, and whose nostrums conceal who knows what hidden desire for power, even to exploit, even though on the face of it, it wouldn't be at all easy to see where he comes in. Very hard for yourself to see, who feel, if anything, you were exploiting me. Well, on both sides that is a risk one has to take. Simply for fear of error, of being self-condemned, of making mistakes, even ghastly mistakes, of sounding indeed like *The Confidence Man,* I don't think we should shrink from trying to be constructive, or rather to help one another, where we see the chance. And what is even God to do when if you ask for help the ambassador he chooses fails even to attempt to deliver the goods. Clearly His rating, even if unjustly, would go down. Which brings me to what I conceive to be the purpose of this letter. The best way that I can answer your own trust, can show my own gratitude to you as it were, can only be on the basis of the thought: "I wish to God someone had said something like this to *me,*" when I at your age said, or worse did not say, "I don't quite know how to say this." I insisted to myself for a while, "Do you have any idea what it means to me?" "Do you realize what I am saying?" I don't mean I have been unlucky in my friends or influences, exactly. In fact, in many respects, considering this and that, I've been a creature of luck all through. The few friends I've made in my life I've mostly kept, and still revere. I have spoken of the help Aiken gave me, sadly needed, because my father—who was by way of being a capitalist on the grand scale—good man though he was, rarely gave me any advice of much pragmatic value, though I'll always bless him for turning me into a good swimmer. But apart from that I often felt myself a kind of item on the business agenda, even, in some respects, an expendable item. It is natural, I think, to eschew giving, as taking, advice. I'm not sure there's any advice per se in this letter. Still there are times when the need for understanding is absolutely imperative. And it has been my experience that it is precisely among people of one's own artistic persuasion that one is likely to find the most crashing disillusionment. At least I often wished, at your age, should I say, or even not say, "Do you realize what I'm saying?" no matter what the subject, that someone older would have the courage to say, "Yes, I think so," and explain it for my benefit, even if wrongly, at least give me something to go on, at least *take the trouble*. But in fact—though there are exceptions as I've pointed out, especially in the good old tradition of poets—by and large these stuffed geniuses, this aristocratic proletariat of peacock, these sanctissima God donkeys, this Jesus man burro, say, like as not, nothing at all. Mean as so many stingy old gold miners sitting on a stake, they seem to think it too dangerous to open their trap, even if, like certain professors I know of, they're being paid to do so. And it's not merely that they fear to give away the source of the mine. It's how to work it—ah no, that would harm their bloody little conception of their own uniqueness. Ah, that contemptuous look that seems to say: "But don't you know that?" Even if they saw their best friend about to fall slap down the abyss, it wouldn't occur to them to say: "I've been there before, brother—in fact I'm there now—let me stand like a caryatid down there, while you step on my head and go round the other way, for you can achieve the same or a better result by doing that." Even if by saying that they would be achieving the only possible human good they were likely to do on this earth, they'd think of some way out of doing it. Still, if I'm not to be worse still, back to this letter. What? Señor Lowry is not in that cantina, but in his shack on the waterfront, drinking a friendly glass of plebeian gin and orange juice with his wife—and I'm not going to drink much of that at the moment, if this letter is to be right, and writing this letter, as from the Charlie Chaplin stove ascends the pungent aroma of frying horse, for inflation has driven us not merely to sharing, but to eating our archetypes too!)

So all this isolates the poor guy more than ever. So he never posts any of those letters, keeps the whole matter to himself. Meantime two other things are going on, on another plane. As he writes the letters he becomes consumed with an absolute passion—in one sense heredi-tary—to return to the sea. The sea begins to rise within him, haunts his dreams, and this longing that storms in him day and night to return to the sea was one of the best parts of the book—all of which makes it such a nuisance I have to write it again: (Do I hear myself aright? Well, perhaps your letter will one day give me the guts to do just that, not leave it merely buried, as it lies now, as so much exposition) for it takes a curious form: the longing for the sea emerges into a longing for the fire of the stokehold, for the actual torment—masochistic, though it somehow isn't, but above all for the fire (which being so the book could not have had a finer funeral—my wife rescued all *The Volcano,* I one of hers, but we had to let that go) the fire in which he sees himself purged and emerging as the reborn man. Which the absolute integrity decency and as it were purity of the feeling that overwhelms him whenever he reads X's book or writes—still with-out posting any of the letters—to X, it can scarcely but be pure for X is like an abstraction, but it has none of the evil either of absolute purity on this plane (albeit the White Sea itself is that, is death too) gives him to believe he may turn into. For, largely due to the suppression of this feeling, all is not well with him in almost every other respect. He neg-lects his studies, starts to drink like a fish, finds his own work increas-ingly worthless, gets through an exam on Dante's *Inferno* by consulting a blind medium who tells him what the questions will be, at last becomes, in spite of that, so closely identified with X that now when he does pull himself together and write, he can't be sure he isn't transcribing whole sections of X's novel which, whenever he is sober, which is not often, he has to destroy. Meantime he makes the mistake of taking his brother into his confidence who instead of being sympathetic is scornful of the whole business and accuses him of every kind of abnormal tendency under the sun, and several not under it. On top of this he—the brother—derides X's book which enrages A to such an extent that inadvertently he causes his brother to turn all his venom on himself in a Dostoievskian scene that leads to the brother's death. Shattered and sobered by this tragedy (there has to be a large gap in the MSS here if I am ever to finish) A makes a tremendous effort of will, and during the long vacation—he has four months in the summer—signs on, as a fireman, a Scandinavian timber ship bound from Preston, near Liverpool, to Archangel, in ballast. (His purpose, so he thinks, in doing this, is to gather added material for a play he proposes to make of X's novel, though incidentally he has arranged with his professor that this play will serve in lieu of a thesis for the second part of his English Tripos!) One of the best parts of the book I have to pass over too briefly here: almost on the point of sailing it turns out that A has to return to Liverpool according to law to sign on with the Norwegian Consul, this being impossible with the Captain, and there not being such a Consul in Preston. In Liverpool he runs into another brother, a criminal lawyer, who is tight and tries to stop him going: so the whole weary effort of will has to be made over again. The ship however does not go to Archangel but to a port in northern Norway that oddly *has the same name* as one of the principal characters, though not the hero, of X's novel. Here, seemingly by coincidence while the charter of the ship is held in abeyance pending a decision by the shipowners in Oslo, he falls in with a character in a cafe reading another book of X's. This book shows that X has been in China at the same time A has and it turns out that this character, a schoolmaster, has met X. Also there is a photograph of X in the book—this is the first indication to A's conscious mind that there really is in existence such a person as X. I had forgotten to say the most important thing, namely that while he took no human action at all (posting the letters would have amounted to that) some principle of tyrannic yet thwarted force in his feeling has worked against him, *à rebours:* now he does take action—and heroic action at that—mysteriously the thing begins to work for him in a way that alters his whole conception of life and human destiny. This place (where he is in Norway) also turns out not to be far away from the place where his own mother has been buried and he pays a pilgrimage to her grave, the ship meanwhile, for lack of orders—though as a matter of fact the orders are contradictory, paralleling the indecision in A's mind whether to take another job and go on to Archangel or actually try and meet X— being stalled in the fjord, and the crew paid off. Here we begin to get on to the theme of rebirth. On the day of his pilgrimage to his mother's grave he meets a girl with whom he falls violently in love. This love is returned and this in fact is his first real experience of mature love. Meanwhile, quite without his seeming to will it, coincidence after coincidence, obeying a kind of Law of Series of their own, combine to take him to Oslo and result in his actually meeting X, this meeting coming about through the shipowner who has been sending the contradictory messages and X is no easy person to meet, lives under an assumed name, and—though he has become a play-wright too—is a figure of great political significance (he is working against the conspiracy of Quisling's Nasjonal Samling, which consider-ing this was written in 1936 is a pretty good piece of clairvoyance when you think they hadn't even got wise to it in 1940, after the event). When he meets X though, X is on the point of going to *Cambridge*—the very place where A has come from—to do some research on Elizabethan drama, but because of a divided vocation, in a state of confusion and despair bordering on A's own original confu-sion and despair. It is too complex to describe in detail this part of the book—but the resemblances between A and X are almost as uncanny as the differences. The character Y turns out not to be X but an objective projection—though X has been to sea—whom X had imagined as very like A. However X's apartment, books, etc., though they are mostly Scandinavian, is an almost exact replica of A's rooms in Cambridge. X moreover tells A that the *real* name of the ship that had given him his experience is the same as that of the ship that A had used in imagination in *his* book (of which he has proof, having brought some of the more original sections with him to work on in between planning the play.) X gives him permission to make the play, and the absolutely glaring testimony to the existence of the transcendental in the whole business, finally restores to a man like X, who imagined up till then that he had created things out of cold reason whatever he made his characters say or do, restores his faith, which had almost been lost, in his art. Both men are realigned on the side of life. A's action has also resulted in his salvation by his girl; in effect both the life of the imagination and life itself has been saved by A's having listened finally to the promptings of his own spirit, and acted upon those promptings, rather than the analytical reductions of reason, though it is reason too—by virtue of harmony with the great forces within the soul—that has been saved, and on this note the story and the trilogy closes.

Well, what a hell of a plot, you say, a kind of Strindbergian Tonio Kruger, by Maeterlinck, out of Melville. That may be, but the point is that with a few exceptions like the brother's death, etc.—and in a few other minor points—I didn't make the story up. There was an X: I did write, did not post the letters. Some force did work against me when I took no action and then when I took some action, for me. The story of the name of the imaginary ship being the same as the one in fact is true too, and there are a lot of other even more curious things that are true which I haven't mentioned so that altogether one might say, as X did, in fact once wrote: Reason stands still, what do we know? I have said that X was not Aiken. Someday I will tell you the whole story. (X's full remark was: "Another spiral has wound its way upward. Reason stands still. What do we know?")

Tragedy in real fact comes in, in that after our first house burned down, we took refuge with a friend in Niagara who, not knowing I knew X, or that I had written a book largely about him that had been lost in the fire, was actually engaged in composing a broadcast on his death when we arrived, so giving me that news for the first time too—he had perished six months before the book of which he was the co-hero, also in flames, in a bomber over Berlin, on the wedding anniversary of my wife and self.

Meantime you needn't bother even to find out who X is. One day, as I say, I shall tell you the story. The reason I have mentioned it here is that upon the subject that makes up that story I have brooded, as you could not have known, half a lifetime. A's feeling—I want you to realize—is, in my opinion, above all, first and foremost *creative*. In that book I advanced the opinion that it was one of the most powerful and one of the most unknown—as to knowledge of what it is—feelings it is possible to have, and one of the purest as it were, even if directed at an object of blistering evil—though it is not exactly an object, it is something you share yourself, as you sooner or later discover: and anyway it is one of the most misunderstood: perhaps it is religious in origin or perhaps it has something to do with evolution itself; but it is certainly a *force* and as a force it obliges you to use it, obliges you to make an act of transcending. You have to go on from there. Aiken once told me that he considered it primarily an operation of genius. Genius knows what it wants and goes after it. He told me— this I say in strict confidence, though he did not swear me to confidence on the subject but admitted it freely—that he was once drawn to Eliot's work in the same way. Eliot himself—who owes a good deal to Aiken himself that has not been acknowledged—has called this identification "one of the most important experiences (for a writer) of adolescence." I'd like to know when adolescence stops at that rate. I surmise an identification on Eliot's part with Laforgue. On the tragic plane you have Keats' identification with Chatterton, leading, Aiken once suggested, to a kind of *conscious* death on Keats' part.

However that may be, it is a force of *life*. But also it is an operation of the soul. As you have observed—in fact as you have proved yourself —it can be clairvoyant. But it is only a writer, poor devil, who would ever imagine such a thing was unhealthy. I imagine that in the realm of music it is recognized simply and consciously absorbed as a process in composition, e.g. Berg and Schönberg. Leibowitz has pointed out that though Berg followed Schönberg in almost every discovery, adopting all his principles and reaching the same conclusions, he yet remained a great and original composer. Conversely, without doubt (says he), one can become a great composer after having had a bad master, but in such a case the very fact of becoming a great composer implies that, at one time or another, one has resolutely turned against one's master. I don't know why I have said all this, or what it adds up to. I started from an assumption—possibly quite wrong-headed— that you would regret having written me. I've tried to show that you certainly should not regret it. All this reckons without the human element, but since you unfortunately live some thousands of miles away, to write is the next best thing to our meeting, to which I look forward one day. Don't try to reply in detail though—it would be too difficult, if not impossible. But if I have said anything useful use it for your own good. One thing you could do is to look back sternly upon the impulses in operation before, say, you read the *Volcano*, the teleology that drew you toward it. For example I am drawn inexorably toward *Blue Voyage,* a novel which is the work of a poet, though I don't know that. I am also drawn toward the work of X, a novel likewise the work of a poet it turns out, but who is also a dramatist, though I don't know that either. I think both are novelists only. Sure enough, I become a novelist, whatever that is. But since the aim of my psyche seems to have been to make a synthesis of these two factors, and since my earlier passion was the drama, wouldn't it be a reasonable point to call sublime reason to one's aid in the person of someone like Ortega and assume I have some buried capacity as a poetic dramatist? It might. And something similar may be true of you. Anyhow you are much younger than I, and with time to decide what you want to do. And if you like my book that much, let it help you to get things in the right order. Perhaps they are, anyway. But still. Also send me what ever spontaneity you like. I have to work so hard now that I shan't be able to reply for some months save in monosyllables but don't let that put you off again. It is a pity there is so much space between us but perhaps there is not so much as there appears to be. Give my love to your girl and be happy in this order:

Health, Happiness, Sense of Humour, Art, Pleasure. My wife sends her love too. Hold that note, Roland!*

Sursum corda!
Malcolm L.

To Harold Matson

Dollarton, B.C., Canada
October 2, 1951

Dear Hal—

I am posting you today under separate cover a comic classic, or at least a masterpiece of nature, or at all events that is the only way of looking at it, at least for me, or I wouldn't have felt justified in writing it, so if you don't think so, don't tell me, at least not just yet.† I believe there is some chance some people will think it first rate in its genre though, if it has one, for it breaks all the rules, save that, I hope, of being interesting and amusing; on one plane it is no less than a kind of short short for Titans, a Moby Jumbo, a comic strip for the infant Panurge, of philosophic trend, and I do not need reminding that the magazine designed to accommodate easily such a Pantagruelian fancy, or *multum in colosseo*—for it is longer than the *Heart of Darkness*—is not yet, though it may be that its merit is such that one would stretch a point even to a bursting of the seams, or at least in two installments, to garage the monster.

However of this I am not sanguine, so please hearken unto my further intention. This enclosed new epistle to the Colossians was originally designed to be accompanied at the same time by another novella of the same length, though absolutely opposite in intention, locale, *sturm und drang,* etc., and of great seriousness (though it is a story of happiness, in fact, roughly of our life here in the forest, exultant side of) entitled "The Forest Path to the Spring." So far as I know this is the only short novel of its type that brings the kind of majesty usually reserved for tragedy (God this sounds pompous) to bear on human integration and all that kind of thing: though it isn't my final word on the subject by a damn sight, I'm mighty proud of it.

* A line from a Third Program B.B.C. production of *The Song of Roland* which the Lowrys used ironically as a slogan of encouragment.
† "Elephant and Colosseum," a story of *Hear Us O Lord.*

As a matter of fact this latter is in part an adumbration—though complete in itself—of a novel to be called *Eridanus* which, if things go well and I can get through the necessary ordeals so to speak which permit me to write the whole, will form a sort of Intermezzo or point of rest to the larger work of five, perhaps six interrelated novels, of which the *Volcano* would be one, though not the best one by any means, the novel you suggested I should write some years back, a sort of *Under Under the Volcano*, should be ten times more terrible (tentatively it's called *Dark as the Grave Wherein my Friend Is Laid*) and the last one *La Mordida* that throws the whole thing into reverse and issues in triumph. (The Consul is brought to life again, that is the real Consul; *Under the Volcano* itself functions as a sort of battery in the middle but only as a work of the imagination by the protagonist.) Better still: some years back I was not equipped to tackle a task of this nature: now, it seems to me, I've gone through the necessary spiritual ordeals that have permitted me to see the truth of what I'm getting at and to see the whole business clearly: all that remains is to get myself into a material position where I can consummate the ordeal by the further ordeal of writing it.

To which end this elephant and "The Forest Path" were intended —apart from a kind of practice on a few smaller peaks—to achieve among other things the practical end of getting a contract with Albert; these two would form part of yet another book to be called *Hear Us O Lord From Heaven Thy Dwelling Place* and would consist of:

(1) "Through the Panama." A story in the form of notes taken on going to Europe, partly on a ship in everything but final distress off the Azores; it reads something like *The Crack-Up*, like Alfred Gordon Pym, but instead of cracking the protagonist's fission begins to be healed. 60-odd pages.

(2) "October Ferry to Gabriola." Another novella, a first version of which we wrote in collaboration for you though it didn't come off. This I've completely redrafted and largely rewritten, and it deals with the theme of eviction, which is related to man's dispossession, but this theme is universalized. This I believe to be a hell of a fine thing.

(3) "In the Black Hills." The humorous-tragic short short I wrote which you have and which I take is for some reason unsaleable. While only tiny it's not quite as slight as it looks when contrasted alongside other themes.

(4) "Strange Comfort Afforded by the Profession." Ditto.

(5) "Elephant and Colosseum." 100 pages.

(6) "The Forest Path to the Spring."* 100 pages (about).

I could throw in a couple of other short ones, as a matter of fact I could go on completing short stories till all is blue, other things being equal, which they are not, and the point is I want to call a halt, especially if they're not too saleable in the item, as appears the trouble, and I don't seem able to help this, and get on with the novel. *Hear Us O Lord*, etc., is from the old Manx fisherman's hymn that occurs in 3 of the stories.

Of the above mentioned, three of them at least have the intent of being major productions in their class, and Margerie thinks "The Forest Path" contains the finest stuff I've done. What I meant to do was finish the "Elephant" and "Forest Path" simultaneously and this I've almost done but not quite. I should be through with "The Forest Path" in about a month. Though about the same length as the "Elephant" I feel it might sell, on the other hand this wasn't exactly the point so much as the "Elephant" and "The Forest Path" together would constitute (200 pages) something to show Random House and thus perhaps (together with a précis of my projected novels, etc.) give one a chance to survive the winter. I am sending you two copies of the "Elephant" but I feel it would be pointless to show it to Albert by itself, so bear with me till you receive "The Forest Path," for the two of them together have a wholly different effect, maybe quite electrifying, but the circuit won't come off the way I want for Albert with the "Elephant" alone. Perhaps the "Elephant" would be sufficient to get me turned down by Harcourt, Brace. Not that I don't love the "Elephant" myself, and psychologically you can see it as a good sign—my authority is Herman Hesse, the writer to whom I feel I bear most inner resemblance, though I haven't got that far yet, but the plan for the five, maybe six, goes as far as he in invention, maybe further. But more of this later, when you have "The Forest Path."

Meantime try and bear with me. Love to Tommy and yourself.

Malcolm

* Closing story of *Hear Us O Lord*.

To David Markson

Dear Dave:

The reason I'm long in replying is that I'm trying to secure a contract for another book (stories) before the winter is out. Also I have sprouted Zola's whiskers and have been preparing a public objection to a local injustice where a 16 year old boy was sentenced to hang (in a disused elevator shaft, painted yellow) for a rape he had not committed. Fortunately they reprieved the poor fellow (apparently to please the visiting Princess Elizabeth) but neither the ritual pardon nor the near-ritual murder on the part of our barbarous public, who has now sentenced him to life imprisonment, is something you would leave alone, if you had studied the evidence, the feeble and neurotic protests, the bloodthirsty cries for revenge, and you were the only writer in the community, much as one hates to risk one's position in it, even if one hasn't got one, and what is more does not care whether one has or not.

Apart from that I've been working very hard indeed on other things and have written a story called "The Bravest Boat"* I think you would like.

Meantime my wife wrote *Horse in the Sky* under name of Margerie Bonner. Don't even try to look for *Ultramarine* (the thought hurts my feelings) which is not worth reading and which I shall rewrite one day maybe. Did you see Louis Adamic of whom I wrote you tangentially died about a week later? More of this some day. Meantime God bless him—it's Hallowe'en anyway. Let me know news of your thesis. Many thanks for all your words and lots of luck from

Malcolm

P.S. Sunrise next morning, frost outside, tide high, just below windows. Seagulls having been fed. Coffee *being* made. Have you any advice for me re anything good to read? I agree *Miss Lonelyhearts* is an important book, and that Rimbaud had one leg, but where is the sunrise? Where is the frost? Where are my seagulls? Where is my coffee? Where is love? Where is your tennis racket? What has happened to Joe Venuti? They can't all be in the *Atlantic Monthly*

* Opening story in *Hear Us O Lord*.

or Bill Saroyan. And in fact there's a lot to be said for Bill Saroyan's *My Heart's in the Highlands* anyway. Don't forget that priceless possession, the author's naïveté. I will prepare you a more austere list, though yours can be austere for that matter. I would read Yeats' *The Vision* (second version) for your purposes, though it is scarcely Joe Venuti: of recent books I liked *The Catcher in the Rye* better than *The Barkeep of Blement,* which I am reading with some enthusiasm.

To Seymour Lawrence*

Dollarton, B.C., Canada
November 28, 1951

Dear Mr. Lawrence:

Unfortunately your much appreciated invitation, at which I am needless to say greatly honored, to write a word on Conrad Aiken, has only just come to light (due to no fault of your own or mine): now it is almost too late.

In a sort of frenzy therefore I hasten to attempt to get this letter in under the gun, begging you, where it appears too illiterate, to correct its grammar: for not only am I ashamed to write anything unworthy in haste upon such a noble subject, but I would not like the poet himself, who was once my tutor, to think that after all these years I was incapable (I am an Englishman too) of writing an explicit letter. But perhaps he will forgive me at that when I mention that I am still anyhow incapable of writing with critical detachment upon work that moves me so profoundly as his: "something about us doesn't like to share our favorite authors with anyone," perhaps not even with the author himself!

Not that the very fact of your winter number's being devoted to Aiken's work does not give me an immediate clue to a point of departure! For surely—as Winston Churchill might say—never has such a great author been for so long recognized as such by so many yet seemingly by so few! It is true that any bibliography will lead one to an impressive documentation of criticisms on the poet, ranging from the learned *Melody of Chaos* by Houston Peterson to the sensitive and painstaking analysis of Marianne Moore, but it still

* Editor of *Wake* magazine, now editor of Atlantic Press, Little, Brown.

feels as if he were but niggardly appreciated, especially in the domain of simple public information: misconceptions, both of the man, and his work, have been perpetuated: and then when a criticism appears in some quasi-authoritative organ like *Time,* how woefully uninformed it sounds: "But it is for his short stories that Aiken is most likely to be remembered"—what bloody unusual nonsense, if I may say so, fine though some of his stories may be. That is, that while there's no reason why half a dozen of his short stories shouldn't survive, as among the best of their kind, it is extremely unlikely that a miscarriage of justice in the realm of enlightened criticism (even if it existed on that plane, which is a puzzling point too, because in one way it doesn't—Aiken has of course long been universally respected as a major poet) should go for so long unredeemed into posterity as to result in the stories being remembered by future generations, while the magnificent body of poems was forgotten, even though every other kind of injustice—for reasons that are absolutely inexplicable, unless a Buddhist could explain them!—seems to have been done to Aiken's work in his lifetime.

It seems odd to me that *Time,* which in its art sections, at least, likes to give the impression it wouldn't willingly mislead its student readers, should make what amounts to a crashing boner like that under the guise, more or less, of established opinion, the more especially since it is to that magazine one was indebted—years before that, in its obituary, and a fine one within its limits, on James Joyce—for the information that, almost up to the very point that great man died, he was actually looking for, trying everywhere to purchase, expecting to receive indeed, Conrad Aiken's masterly dramatic poem, "The Coming Forth by Day of Osiris Jones." This, in my opinion, is an incident of literary history well worth remembering: in one stroke, it seems to demolish a whole bolus of misconceptions and injustices in regard to Aiken: while at the same time, to disengage my metaphor, it seems to sum up and contradict three decades of inadequate and wholly unfair repetitions and conditioned uncriticism—on that curious plane where this existed—of certain aspects of Aiken's work. Anyhow I like to think that there was that great author looking for "The Coming Forth by Day of Osiris Jones," seeking for it at the very end of his life with such persistence that there can be no doubt he had every expectation of being, should he manage to secure it, fructified by it, of learning from it. One lets the story rest, as "speaking volumes." The point does not lie in the eerie coincidence, even though it is one that Joyce himself would well have appreciated. In fact, after that bit of information, it seems almost unnecessary to add that saying that "Aiken was most likely to be remembered for his short stories" is much like saying that Shakespeare should be remembered for writing "A Lover's Complaint," or "Sonnets to Sundry Notes of Music," Eliot for "The Hippopotamus," Stravinsky for his children's pieces or—if one wants to grow really popular and international on the subject—that Henry Sienkiewicz was most likely to be remembered for writing "The Lighthouse Keeper of Aspenwall," as a matter of fact, and I have forgotten to bring in Sibelius "Valse Triste," which makes perhaps the most sensible comparison. But you get the idea. Aiken is, in fact, in my opinion, of least importance as a short story writer (I don't mean as a novelist: or that he is not—flukes and flames!—a master of prose); some of his pieces are wonderful, but often the daemon can almost be heard rebelling against the material involved, determined only to help him do his worst. (Nonetheless, both in best and worst, as the Canadian writer Gerald Noxon has demonstrated by some hair-raising and first-rate radio dramas he has made out of some of Aiken's stories, one is astonished at the enormous amount of sheerly dramatic material: in which connection I'm not alone in hoping that Aiken will take the daemon's tip and write some plays himself.)

But if Aiken's work has been seriously enough misprized sometimes in America this has at least not been, with few exceptions, at the hands of his creative contemporaries: it was merely the odd reviewer who, albeit in a place of authority, would give the impression now and then that a certain work was outdated or insignificant or showed "traces" of something or other: This opinion someone else would repeat almost verbatim in a given review, even though in that very same paper you would quite likely find a reference to Aiken as "perhaps the greatest poet now living," or "Aiken, the most majestic of all our poets," in other words though most of his works seem to me to have been more or less panned individually when they came out, there was always a growing body of authoritative and attentive opinion which paid no attention whatever to these verdicts and which existed independently and applied its judgement to the whole: in my own country however (I mean in this instance England), it was a very different matter. Here the poet was obliged to suffer for many years not merely absolute neglect or downright rudeness on the part of most of our so-called intelligent periodicals (even those to which he had brilliantly contributed) but an odd and inexplicable neglect

by the very contemporaries he was probably influencing at that time—
or should have been influencing, had there existed in England any
real independence of perception. Hard to believe though it is, nearly
a quarter of a century ago, when I was in my teens, there was even
an opinion given currency that there was one Conrad Aiken—they
liked to spell it Aitken, perhaps out of some obscure deference to
Lord Beaverbrook—a poet, who was already in some sense passé
(despite the fact that at that very moment he was engaged in a work
that if he had written nothing else should have been sufficient to
secure his position in world literature twice over, though it is true
that he had already written enough to make most people famous
five times over even on their plane), was probably dead—perhaps he
was even some mysterious contemporary of Howells, this Mr. Aitken,
so that it was not at all impossible that in picking up your monthly
Memoirs and Dead Letters, that then very modern journal, you
would find some such caustic statement (I don't mean by one of
our bullyboys remarkable for their cruelty, their emasculated phrase-
ology and their complete lack of any real creative talent, but by
someone perfectly decent, well-meaning, an author of many distin-
guished books admirable in themselves, and who probably was the
recipient of the Order of the Bath or something, but who liked
sometimes to write in that serene semicolon-technique-style for which
we are all so justly admired) as: "It gave me much the same sort
of faded impression, as if I had seen one of the poems of Conrad
Aitken in the yellowing—but once, ah, how new—*American Journal.*"

But contemporaneous with this sort of strange opinion, that "Conrad Aitken" belonged to another age or was dead, was another one
which caused people, on the contrary, sometimes to refer to him as if he
were about 15, as "one of the more bumptious and fractious of the very
youngest generation of American poets," a kind of latter-day E. E.
Cummings rampant, so that it was not impossible too, that in the
next journal you picked up for the same month, which likewise
lamented the state of modern culture, you might come across some
such considered advice as this given to the author of "The Divine
Pilgrim" by some wise old bird twenty years his junior: "Young
Aitken, for all his extravagance, and when he has put his poetic
excesses behind him, may yet be the poet to give us another 'Jack
and the Beanstalk.' "

Of course this state of affairs must anyhow have been long ago
corrected, possibly even the wise old bird in question having helped
to correct it. Though it was a fact that until I left England some

eighteen years ago about the only intelligent and fair appraisal I had read of Aiken was by the Scot, Edwin Muir (the co-translator with his wife, of Kafka, the good people to whom you may also be indirectly indebted for being able to find, in the New York Public Library, some volumes of Søren Kierkegaard beside *Diary of a Seducer,* which was the only one there in 1934 when I looked.)

Well (even though I have been partly joking) this kind of thing might have sorely dampened and even broken the spirit of a lesser man than Aiken—talk about being snuffed out by an article, at that rate one has to think of Aiken in terms of cathedrals of immortal and undying candelabras!—which brings me to the man himself. Here I must report, that though he would have been inhuman if such neglect had not wounded him to some extent, I never saw him bat so much as an eyelid at an injustice to himself. As for England, Conrad Aiken was far too chivalrous a fellow ever to criticize, as the Celts say, the bridge on which he had crossed. (That we English should have expressed ourselves long ago as more highly honoured that he should have deigned to cross on it at all is my only burden here.) Always willing to help his fellow writers, where possible, he was readier to find excuses for others than to criticize (as a matter of fact, as I have read is also true of William Faulkner, he never put up with any harshness at all about his contemporaries): while as for his own work, if it were in suspension, a half sardonic smile, and some such comment as, "Well, it's about time another book went spiralling down the drain," was often about all that in conversation it would elicit. (As against this he never failed to refer to his own literary struggles as having been on the whole a bit of fun and worth it.)

In this connection, however, I mean as a human being, I have often wondered how future generations would picture Aiken, and it is here that I can possibly render a small service by jogging the elbow of posterity in advance a little. Because for a writer who has been accused of being "subjective" as they say, Conrad Aiken has left, save in the very greatest of his poems where for that matter any picture of the man perhaps is irrelevant, very little impression of himself, and so much has been, I won't say written, but simply repeated of his "quest for a kind of absolute poetry," of his passion for the translunar, and his appetite for the expression of velleities, his "incorrigible mellifluousness," etc. etc., that one is liable to gain the impression of some one living eternally in a sort of Sussex or Cape Cod twilight. Again, some of his prose protagonists, however brilliantly drawn, can be the opposite of helpful should one be seeking therein any clue to the identity of their creator. Some of his work moreover is of such an appalling savagery that you might imagine the author personally resembled a cross between Abraxas Bahomet and Ahasuerus. Or again, it is of such transcendent beauty that you might imagine he did not live on this earth at all but had his hammock slung up on high somewhere between Aries and the Circlet of the Western Fish. Nor has Aiken himself, who has even written a poem called "Palimpsest a deceitful portrait," that is perhaps least help of all, ever pretended to be other than unhelpful.

Of course, what I say may be totally irrelevant to you, or to any consideration of his poetry. From an existential (perish the word, but let it stand anyhow) point of view, it perhaps is not so irrelevant. Nor from the human. In this connection anyhow a relative of Aiken's (I hope Mr. Aiken will not shoot me for telling this story, and if it has been told elsewhere, I ask to be forgiven for repeating it, moreover I can see another kind of irony creeping in here—when his old friends are asked to make a statement on his poetry, instead they recommend his name glowingly to the Society for the Prevention of Cruelty to Animals) once told me that when the poet was a lad he climbed a telegraph pole to rescue, from its crosstrees—and what is more did rescue—a stranded cat. Perhaps that doesn't sound so much, thus badly reported. Perhaps the reader has climbed telegraph posts when a youth. But however lately you may have climbed your last telegraph post, I think I can (the more especially as an ex-seaman) safely suggest that it is a very different business when you have to make the return journey accompanied by a cat that, having raised Cain in order to be taken down, is now striving its utmost to regain its former position aloft. Moreover the ascent of a telegraph post is perpendicular, and so the descent, it may be—all too perpendicular. You are not, as on board ship, climbing a sort of staircase: you are lucky if you have few spikes, and these don't carry you very far: you need both hands to hold on, but you don't have them, the cat demands both: and though the post may not be the height, say, of a mast, the invitation aloft to vertigo is very similar: while the ground below in your mental view makes no bones about being the ground below—and mends no broken bones—whether at a distance of a hundred, fifty, or twenty-five feet. So I imagine it. In Canada the custom rather more often is, on such occasions, to call the fire brigade, there being an extremely natural fear in the public mind in regard to telegraph poles, indeed in most minds, particularly in that of children, partly occasioned by the suspicion that the wires themselves may be alive, moreover unlike trees, or certain trees, they constitute something forbidden, dangerous—but without possessing the corresponding attraction for that reason ("Trespussers will be prosecuted," Aiken no doubt observed, quoting himself in advance, to the cat) and in short the majority of children, it is my experience, would almost rather climb anything else, even were there no cat in question. This act of compassion, just the same, I would say, was extremely typical of the man. It may even be that this concern for the indignity the cat might suffer at being rescued by other unskill-ful hands weighed with him almost as much as the animal's danger. Aiken indeed would not readily see any indignity or hurt afflicted either upon animals or human beings. He was capable moreover, as I recall him, of such an instantaneous grasp of a whole situation in all its permutations and combinations that you might have said that he had perceived it by some means of clairvoyance before it had been given a chance to develop. This empathy—of a kind that one associates also with expressionist painters, such as Munch—extended even to natural objects, so that he would point out even such a humble thing, say, as a piece of drainpipe, through which a cool stream was conduited, on a burning summer day, in such a manner that just for a moment you felt you were that bit of piping: listen-ing, looking, you partook, by Jove, for an instant, of that piping's cool feelings, even if it didn't have any before. So I didn't mention the cat on the telegraph pole from a sentimental viewpoint or even be-cause it was a pleasant thing for people to remember about Conrad Aiken—though it certainly is, for that matter—but the point is, it wasn't exactly an isolated incident, or something that gives you no clue to the man, such as that Edgar Poe took off all his clothes at West Point on parade, or Schiller couldn't work without a desk full of rotten apples: Mr. Aiken was, as the landlady of the Ship Inn, Rye, Sussex, remarked, replenishing my tankard, "a real kind thought-ful gentleman wot would go out of his way, you know, to be kind. Not many like 'im, sir!" What occasioned the landlady's remark I forget: probably it was no more than some minor act of courtesy, but courtesy of that true kind which is, as Keyserling points out, no empty form, but the assent to man's true being. What I think I mean is that you couldn't, no matter who you were, have met Aiken, if only to pass the time of day with the exchange of a few words, with-out mysteriously feeling, as it were, that your system had been "toned up": possibly it would not be until you got round the next corner that you saw the joke he had inserted tangentially into this exchange, whereupon all at once the day too would take upon itself a new, a brighter, or it might be a more bizarre, a more complex aspect, in any case became a wholly more amusing and sympathetic adventure; in some amazing way he had sensed *your* problem, made *your* own burden, whatever it was, seem lighter. In other words, to an extraordinary degree he possessed charity: in addition to this however he possessed a quality that, despite some richly comic scenes, and others savage and appalling, is not easily, or consistently at least, to be deduced from his works. That is to say he possessed about the most superlatively robust sense of humor it would be possible to encounter in a fellow human being. Very often, though more quietly, this combined with other qualities I have mentioned in a manner you did not fully appreciate till years afterwards.

For example, during one of his rare visits to America while he was still resident in England, I happened to be in New York myself, where "owing to certain auxiliary circumstances" I found myself living in the basement in the West Seventies of an old brownstone house, of which I had rented the room of the janitor, which he in turn had vacated because of the incidence therein (if I may say so without impoliteness, for they are after all international and know no boundaries) of certain rare insects. The other good roomers of this house all had the habit, with the maximum of conviviality, of playing pinochle all night in the basement kitchen so that, for that matter, had one wanted to, one couldn't sleep: as a consequence (though I learned happily in this way how to play pinochle) I often found myself working all night, that is, I was able to do so without disturbing others: on this occasion I had not only been working all night but for some enthusiastic reason for perhaps three nights and days on end, and the pinochle game having broken up in the early morning, I was, with the landlady's permission, continuing to type in the basement kitchen, having been driven out of my room by the aforesaid rare insects, not having shaved for four days, and sitting surrounded by a great deal of washing, some seventy empty beer bottles, the residue in fact of the vanished pinochle party, all of which I must certainly have given the air of having recently consumed myself, though it was not later than half past ten in the morning. At this point (I had stopped typing, to make matters worse) the landlady broke in upon my thoughts in respectful tones, in fact she whispered:

"Mr. Kraken is upstairs, sir."

"What!"

"A kind gentleman—very well dressed—his suit is made of real good material . . . Mr. Kraken would like to see you, sir, and is coming downstairs now."

It was indeed no less a person than Conrad Aiken himself, who finding himself in New York for a day had hunted up his old pupil in Columbus Circle, where having surrounded my whole position of embarrassment at a glance, he had metamorphosed himself verbally into the famed Scandinavian sea-monster, in order, perhaps, to blend himself the more unobtrusively with my cavernous, indeed monstrous apparent circumstances which, hinting to say the least of failure, if not of the abyss itself—without even the pinochle players to lend it all a touch of jovial humanity—however innocent in reality, were certainly not those in which one (immediately the pupil again, anxious to produce an illusion of steady work and regular hours) would have cared formally at first meeting to greet the great man in his own country.

Mr. Kraken! Well, well, sometimes, when feeling gloomy, I find I only have to think of this incident to start chuckling: finally the chuckle becomes a roar of laughter, and melancholy is banished. And then again I think to myself: who the hell am I? What an incredible privilege! Did I really know Conrad Aiken? And did he once actually come to see *me*? Or did I make that up?

Also I have sometimes wondered, as in a story of his, *Round by Round*, one of Aiken's characters wonders, as regarding a picture of the James family, their good faces "look forward at him with an extraordinary integrity"—where has that integrity, that kindness, decency, understanding, humor, as exemplified by Aiken equally—where have these qualities disappeared to in human beings? Were they perquisite of particular people of a particular age? What? Perhaps someone like Aiken was a link with a past age and at the same time is a link with a future one, that has not yet come to pass, when the cultivation and the possession of such qualities will again seem worth while to man.

I realize I have now finished this letter without having said more than a mumbling word about Conrad Aiken's work. I realize also I have spoken of him slightly in the past tense, when he is indeed very much alive, and with no doubt some of his profoundest work ahead of him. But this is perhaps because, as a matter of fact (though I have myself benefited from his generosity), I haven't, more's the pity, seen him for some fifteen years and I don't think, for that matter, we have even corresponded for some two, though we have conversed once upon the phone. As you see though, his memory is very much alive here, even in the Canadian wilderness.

Speaking of Aiken as a writer, from the time that, before I had ever heard of him, his work first slammed down on my raw psyche like the lightning slamming down on the slew outside at this moment, I have always thought that he was the truest and most direct descendant of our own great Elizabethans, having the supreme gift of dramatic and poetic language, a genius of the highest and most original order, and I have no doubt at all that in years to come we will do our best to claim him back from America as our own.

Yours sincerely,
Malcolm Lowry

To Albert Erskine

Dollarton, B.C., Canada
December 19, 1951

Dear old Albert:

Melancholy news about us: you've probably heard.

Harcourt won't let me out of the contract.* I have no choice—so it has seemed to me—but to stay with them.

All this time though I've been thinking *you* had the MSS of my projects but it turns out Hal had no choice either but to examine the Harcourt situation as an immediate problem before that could be done, with the above result, which is no one's fault, and though one cannot drink of it, it can't be helped.

I did not arrive at the sad decision without thinking of yourself, to say the least, for without the *Volcano* I would be a liability rather than an asset, the *Volcano* being, as you know, part of a sequence: and Harcourt wouldn't give up the *Volcano*. It had also occurred to me that you might not like *Hear Us O Lord From Heaven Thy Dwelling Place,* which tales were the immediate work in hand, or if you did, that others at Random House might not. I am still half of this opinion. I am also of the opinion that I would probably not have exerted myself to such an extent had I known the project was

---

* Harcourt, Brace had taken over the firm of Reynal & Hitchcock, which had published *Under the Volcano,* and decided not to release the option on Lowry's work in progress. (See Matson's letter of December 13, 1951, to Lowry in Appendix 8, p. 446.)

going to Harcourt and not to yourself, though this is hard to determine because as a matter of fact I had naïvely no notion at all that it was going to Harcourt albeit now I see that Hal, who had my own interests at heart, cannot be blamed for this. Robert Giroux has very highly praised some of the tales in *Hear Us O Lord,** referring to one as the best he'd read in a long time, for which praise I am grateful but the truth is that I have not sold a single bloody solitary one of these tales, whether they are masterpieces or not, and this seems to be the trouble, that though I have tried my best I do not seem able to survive in this way: and for the matter of that Hal has to survive in his way too.

Poor Margie has not sold a damn thing either so what with inflation, debt, the dead pound and the usual problems (we have not been to a movie, a pub, had a haircut in 6 months, nor a battery in our radio in a year), I actually had reached the point where I had no moral right to continue writing unless I was able to secure some kind of definite contract.

This is also the cause of my not yet having paid back your very kind loan to us though England's restrictions may soon prove less suicidal and indeed I think I can repay you soon now though it is something like doing it with your own property. Oh, shit. Excuse me. In fact, but for yourself not being there, I suppose I should be happy enough to be with Bob Giroux and the rest, for I am not involved with a "Reynal Current"—quite the reverse. They are most understanding and on this account I know you will be glad. For the rest you could not have thanked me for the position in which I would have put you should I have insisted on staying with you, in fact I argued to myself that I was saving you the embarrassment of your having to refuse to be put in such a position at all, for indeed I cannot see how you could have wanted me under the circumstances that would have accrued, under which everyone would have been unhappy. This does not mean I do not feel a bit like Judas Iscariot: I exactly do and I look to you to tell me I need not, though that cannot stop me feeling like Germany without Bismarck, not to say Enos without Fruit Salts,

---

* See Giroux's letter of December 11, 1951, to Matson in Appendix 8, p. 445.

In order to give proper perspective to the letters that appear in the text on pp. 285–303 and in Appendix 8, pp. 445–450, it is necessary to point out that Giroux favored Lowry's manuscript and says he felt as well "morally obligated" to publish it, and so proposed but was overruled by his immediate superior. Subsequently, in writing Lowry on behalf of his firm, he was obliged to suppress his own affirmative opinion and express only a negative one (see Giroux's letter of March 10, 1952, to Lowry in Appendix 8, p. 450). Lowry, of course, could not know this.

or Johnny Walker without the whiskey. Of course on one side we are grateful and pleased no end that Giroux is enthusiastic: on the other hand, because of yourself, one is heavy-hearted and has as it were a hangover before the celebration. For Christ's sake though do not let us fall asunder ourselves however. For another thing I am frightened by the appalling meaning of some parts of the book ahead and the character of some of the demons who have to be turned into mercies. All very well to say it's just fiction. This does not account for the fact —to hell with it. I'll tell you another time. But Bartleby in Mid-Atlantic is a jovial and social fellow compared with the company my character has to keep sometimes. Anyhow I hope you will still let me share some of its burdens with you. Also if I may I will dedicate some part or other—the best part when it comes along—to you. Do not forget there is always a shoulder here to lean on also. I hope your own serious troubles are not somehow too bad though how can they help but be bad: of course I know this but still I don't know what to say save that you have all our sympathies and prayers.

I now see this letter is psychologically one long piece of self-reproach for acting (or rather for not acting) in a way contrary to my higher self. Further to reproach me is a bit of pencilled letter to yourself that has just poked its way out of some papers, written last February, the draft of our S.O.S. last February that you answered so selflessly and immediately and generously. Alack. Thank you. Alas. Blast. Damn it. On the other hand I am convinced this is better for you too. For all God knows by the time I got to the end of the benighted work you may have returned to Brace and even be running it and so, what had started out from loyalty and friendship might well have turned out, from lack of long-sightedness on my side, neither loyal nor friendly enough: I may feel as though I've shot the albatross now, but I fear that you might have come to feel as though you'd been shot *by* an albatross. In short I would have abrogated some other responsibility of wisdom I left out of account. However, for purely personal reasons, if this is any good to you, I emphasize that I did not know (I even sent a Christmas card to Frank saying I was awaiting your verdict in fear and trembling) the course events were taking. In fact for once Hal's office even forgot to acknowledge the MS. I could not understand why you hadn't replied to my letter, and when I received Hal's with Giroux' report, we'd about decided it must have got lost. But by this time the ice was up to our door again. So there it is. Anyhow God bless you from us both,

Malcolm

PART VIII: *1952*

To Robert Giroux

1075 Gilford St.
Vancouver, B.C., Canada
January 11, 1952

Dear Mr. Giroux:

First let me apologize for my silence.

I hope you don't think it was due to ingratitude or improvidence. Also, right off, I want to thank yourself, Jimmy Stern, and Jay Leyda most sincerely for the superlative Christmas present of the latter's monumental Melville book. This is a triumph, a thing of obviously permanent importance. It is a triumph in many other ways too. Tell J.L. I shall write him the first moment I can. (As a matter of fact, his technique of cross-references spatially divided would be the only adequate vehicle by which I could express what has been happening here.) Give my love to him and Jimmy.

Now I want to thank you for so generously and promptly making it possible for me to have some money through Harold Matson. In fact this has tided us over a very hard spot indeed, though a most peculiar circumstance surrounds it at this end: it arrived here by wire on the morning of the 21st, but it was not until the afternoon of the 27th that we were informed of its existence. The fault, or aberration, lies somewhere between the Canadian Pacific Telegraph and our local postmaster, each of whom blame the other.

One reason I needed some money immediately was that if I was to get any work done at all this winter I knew I should have to get into town and into an apartment, for life in Dollarton in these winter months is—or has become of late years—largely a matter of cutting wood and merely managing to stay alive and keep from freezing. Moreover it was proving too hard on my wife's health. Meantime, a series of gales, hurricanes, blizzards, snowstorms, icestorms, sub-zero temperatures (the house has only cardboard inside walls, a small

[285]

cookstove, but no heater) and general acts of God (which calmed down yesterday only to descend tonight with redoubled force from the Yukon) made it impossible to commute from Dollarton in order even to search for an apartment in town. The flooding inlet with gales at the January high tides almost swept the house away altogether—you can imagine how kindly the former threat struck one under these circumstances. Somehow we slugged it out, without having to abandon the house at the very highest tides, and it is still O.K. (and safe with only half tides at present) though all in all there has been much havoc and anxiety. Finally we managed to find the only vacant hotel room in Vancouver 15 miles distant (it being full of wild loggers here for the holidays), packed up all my work—or what seemed the most important part thereof—into various brief cases and Mexican shopping bags and suitcases, moved in and started to look for an apartment through the continuing gales, snows, etc., during which my wife got flu, but it by now being after January first nothing in the way of an apartment was to be found—why go on? We did find one, and here we are, more than ready to get down to work, though it is not easy since I've not been able to do any since almost mid-November.

During this hildy-wildy situation (as it were "Under" Eridanus) I have begun this letter fifty times, for I not only wanted to thank you, but I felt a compelling need to be in communication with you, in some way, before I could begin work again.

In this connection, first of all, I want to say how sincerely grateful I am for your words of praise and that you wish to publish me. I certainly want to be worthy of this.

There are a lot of things I have to discuss though, matters peripheral or central to the work—not least, I'm not sure what to do next; it has been a sad disappointment not to have sold individually any of the stories in *Hear Us O Lord*, etc., before I can properly go on, yet I would like very much to complete it and publish it before finally getting down to *The Voyage*. Perhaps you could suggest to me how many more stories seem to you advisable to be finished and included in this volume? Yet our recent perils—and coming at what a time!— suggest to me that I owe it to you to get you a copy of even imperfect drafts or half intentions to cache away, which in any case might not one day be without value in themselves and in any case also would have been and would be pretty disastrous for me to lose without a copy. Of *Lunar Caustic*, I possess 2 versions, neither of them final: and I think a copy of these ought to be made and sent to you before I go on with *Hear Us O Lord,* so my wife will begin tomorrow to make these copies.

Re Albert Erskine: you will understand my position. I am deeply fond of him personally, so that the break hurts. Also I owe him a lot. I don't know which is troubled more, my heart or my conscience. On the other hand I don't wish you to believe that I was swayed by any financial extremity, even though that extremity existed: it was a fully thought-out decision. And of course I am likewise proud to be with you.

Anyhow we are now settled in the city until April first, having worked for three years in the wilderness; I have not been to a cinema for seven months or had a haircut or seen any kind of conveniences for some time so that civilization seems almost as strange to me as if I were Alley Oop. All in all I could not blame civilization refusing to give me a pew after I'd made such an ugly face at it. And that the events of the last month might compose, as a matter of fact, one of the best stories I could ever write does not make it easier to start again by reworking something old in a new place. (I am one of those fellows who when not deeply engaged in work immediately find themselves on the receiving end of some twenty works.) In short it is difficult enough to start again at all after our siege, though it will be done. The problem is where to begin.

These are a few of the things that perplex me. But first may I know if it is yourself I may address, not to say to whom I may unburden myself, in an editorial capacity? Or if I have not the honour, to whom may I speak? For I must speak at some length.

With every good wish to yourself and many thanks again.

Ever sincerely,
Malcolm Lowry

To Jay Leyda

1075 Gilford St., Apt. 33
Vancouver, B.C., Canada
February 27, 1952

Dear old Jay Leyda:
  Thank you more than I can say for the Christmas present of your book.*

  * *The Melville Log.*

It is a pouncing masterpiece, one of the best documented and dramatic and painstaking and altogether swell pieces of work that you or I will read in a generation.

I am sorry that I have not written you directly before, but this was due to the fact that the book's arrival seemed to occasion storms, Moby Dicks (an actual Moby Dick swam right past our window on the swollen flooding tide) of our own, that had to be weathered else we sank to rise no more; a little conjuration of climate you might say, but that the S.S. *Pennsylvania* should have gone down with all hands but one Seattle Ishmael, just after we had spoken it under the grain tips No. 2, crossing the Second Narrows Bridge, this and the absolutely unprecedented fury and disaster of this winter, in which more ships have gone down in five minutes than in all my seafaring knowledge, inhibited us, especially when we thought of the *Ann Alexander* and would have liked to speak Dana-wise of birds of summer and of wheelbarrows and watering cans and even whales of good omen—and anyway what with an editorial dislocation, I don't mean dislocation: merely I had to part from Albert, was (albeit happy and proud to be in your family) writing to Robert Giroux, out of a typhoon—inhibited us finally. I relayed therefore my admiration and thanks through Robert Giroux and I can only ask you to realize that my silence was not due to lack of appreciation.

On the contrary I was struck dumb.

With best wishes, and congratulations to yourself from my wife and myself. God bless you.

Malcolm

P.S. In case the S.S. *Pennsylvania* means nothing to you, she was in Chapter II of the *Volcano* (went down off here same day as *Flying Enterprise*—you can verify it from the *New York Times* or otherwise the press.)

1952

To Albert Erskine

1075 Gilford
Vancouver, B.C., Canada
Friday night
[March 1952]

Dear Albert:
  Goes without saying I thank you—and I have no way of knowing what you're going to say about the work since your letter not yet received—and I thank you God knows too for answering my telegram so promptly today: and with my surviving teeth, all 2 of which are screaming in sympathy and wisdom, and Margie's dividing though apparently so far still surviving teeth, with all the gold in my teeth which I would I could pluck out and repay you in advance and in retreat of your generosity, Oh Christ I can't go on.
  Various bits of information etc. will arrive your way within the next week or so which will buttress the situation—none of these ever sent to Brace—draw your conclusions.
  I am enclosing letters from Hal and Giroux* which explain why I was beguiled and forced into this situation.
  At that time with hurricanes threatening our house as well as floods, our own situation was desperate in that it was impossible to spend the winter (for Margie) in our house without freezing to death or worse and without being melodramatic I can't tell you how bad it was—we had tides that swept other houses away—sub-zero weather and our house has not yet been finished to stand such temperatures since we've been unable to put in any insulation, and inside walls are just paper. We have no heater at all and our old stove was literally falling apart and patched up with a mixture of wood ashes, asbestos and sea water, and we had less than $50 and in short, in December, the situation would have scared Dostoievsky, drowned Goncharov [and] Rimbaud, or frozen them, and sworn off Nanses (won't go into complicated reasons why this was so but Chekov would have understood very well, even though I did not read *The Demon of the Woods* till the other day, long after writing "The Forest Path to the Spring").
  But all this beside, the final thing was, as you see by these letters, Hal informed me that I could not break my contract with Brace and that they were determined to hold me to it.

---

* Dated December 13, 1951, and December 11, 1951, respectively (see Appendix 8).

[289]

Albert, I can only beg you to understand the complications of my situation and my divided yet undivided sense of honor to my work, to you, and Margie. What I did I felt desperately unhappy about yet it seemed my only path—it seemed indeed I had no choice. I tried to do what I apparently had to do and do it honestly. I tried to make the transference from you to Giroux and I wrote him as fully as I could and from my heart, yet telling him how hard it was to do. He never answered. Then I sent *Lunar Caustic* (which they requested as you see in the letter) and he never even acknowledged it—matter of fact I don't even know now if he did receive it and if you have it now. How could I go on working against this silence? What is the explanation? (1) Giroux declined the psychological gambit which is understandable, so his behavior is in effect sacrificial. (2) I am an untrustworthy bastard myself which I qualify with lifted eyebrow but surely the *Volcano* must underwrite this. (3) The office boy got into the machinery. I can believe *Lunar Caustic* was too gruesome for anyone's consumption. I can even now believe my unconscious made it too gruesome for anyone whatever but I cannot believe there is no merit in it.

Saturday night.

Ides of March have come but not gone. (Ides of March was a worse time for Wilderness in Mexico, in *La Mordida,* likewise for us in 1946, 2 weeks before acceptance of *Volcano.*) Your wire received yesterday, but not your letter posted Wednesday. The post office says that it may have been missorted in Seattle and if it does not arrive Monday must be counted lost, so I shall have to wire you to stop cheque. If this happens—and it is the kind of thing that has been happening all along—I shall almost suspect witchcraft, that Satan does not want me to write the book or something. Even so I shall have to hang on still harder. Instead of your letter comes an impassioned and overwhelmingly tragic letter about the *Volcano* from one Michael Montillon, a lawyer, of 33 E. 12 St., who says the *Volcano* means more to him than anything he has ever read, but how did I ever conspire to get it done? Yes—how?

Last night a night of grief and suspense—you do not say "love" to us on wire: and if you are fed up with me by now who shall blame you. We are now living in dread both of receiving and not receiving your letter. And how to explain? There is the sense of shame too in that we are trying to borrow money again without having paid back what

we owe you, and promised to repay and meantime you cannot know
I have not let you down essentially, even though it feels like it.

Sunday night.

Spring outside with people swinging tennis rackets and taking
photographs: a hell of a tension within, worst thing I have ever been
through, I think, I know, for reasons I can't explain in brief: worse
than the Consul, and it is not an alcoholic hell. It is the abyss itself,
or a taste of the abyss, and my job is to get out or symbolically to get
out, and my only way out in this case is as it were *back,* to Tiphereth,
as the Cabbalists say—but has this ever been done before? And even
supposing I did it, how to explain it, or its necessity, or its appalling
danger, or its validity, or its non-fictionality, or anything about it,
least of all how in this one spiritual case alone going back is equivalent
to going forward, or what the hell this has to do with the problem in
hand anyway, even supposing it were not a delusion, which on this
plane it is. Problem of commending to editors promise of author's
operating on astral plane. . . .

But to get down to brass, as they say, tacks.

(a) One explanation for everything is the power and truth—not the
reverse—of the total concept, which comes into a sort of being the
moment you postulate it, but also works against you, not wishing to
be postulated in such a fashion; the truth does not stand still, hence
one danger in making a précis of books of this kind. I won't go into
this any further.

The Brass Tacks. Second Attempt.

(1) The point of staying on here in town while there seemed any
reasonable hope rather than return home, apart from the fact that
we'd be involved with a breach of lease if we didn't, is: despite the
apparently added expense (a) I thought it was—ha ha—easier to keep
in communication here at this critical time (b) returning would mean
stopping work because of great damage during winter and necessity
of getting fuel, etc., (c) Margie's eyes badly need attention. In fact she
can scarcely see at all with her present spectacles. Physically too, all
this, that was to have given her some relief, has damn nearly wrecked
her nerves, since we'd paid half of this month's rent already, what
with trebled price of transport in this boom Province matters are
about equalized, save that of course we can't get groceries on credit.

The cheque Brace sent us last December through Hal was turned back as "addressee unknown in Dollarton." There have been no less than 16 related coincidences of this kind; should your cheque not arrive tomorrow that will be the 17th: but I believe it will, that you are— with Margie and the house—a link with the world of light and the powers of light and goodness from which I have not strayed either, to tell the truth. That it all sounds like delusional insanity makes it no easier to explain, had I a mind to, who thought he was not living in the world of Cotton Mather.

Nor is this getting down to those brass tacks. Of course that last was merely my imagination, working overtime.

Item: *The Shrike!*

Naturally it killed me a bit, a repetition of the publication of *The Lost Weekend* when I was finishing the *Volcano,* but you'll find it prophesied in the adumbration of the *Voyage,* i.e., that such a thing would probably happen (Law of Series). I didn't find out about *The Shrike* till after I had dispatched *Lunar Caustic,* the final plot of which so horrified me that I couldn't sleep properly for about 12 nights. You'd read one version before fortunately, or is it unfortunately? I imagine that it was at this point the office boy swore off. Perhaps I would swear off myself. Perhaps that was the idea. But this is not getting down to those brass tacks. I fail to see that *Lunar Caustic* even as it stands is not a masterwork, or a potential one.

Sunday night.

I have used the word *transference* in relation to Giroux—all that is absurd: I was still writing to you all along which is where the nightmare begins; possibly trying to write *against* myself at the same time, a damned difficult problem.

But the practical thing that was put to me was as contained in the enclosed letters: it seems to me that despite the "retaining fee" paid me I had a right—considering what I have achieved in the world at large (though largely certainly due to you) and the aim or apparent aim to achieve an editor-author relationship (ha ha), work out a financial program, etc.—to expect at least some kind of contract on *Hear Us O Lord*—quite disregarding the other work.

I did not (and I suppose I have to say immediately do not) mean to be a demanding author: at the same time even if *Lunar Caustic* failed with them and *Hear Us* was as good as they said it was I had some sort of squatter's rights, on the strength of what they said, to be bailed out even if on that book alone—but regard what happened.

Monday night.

Your letter and cheque gratefully received today—sent to wrong apartment number, arrived in Vancouver Friday and finally found us, after having apparently returned to post office, today, God knows how. Telegraph company must have given you wrong apartment number—just a sample of the 16 coincidences I mentioned earlier by which letters and wires have gone astray and been delayed. Also today an astonishing letter from Giroux.* Today spent writing night letter you will have by now.

(Re your letter I enclose your envelope as evidence just as it arrived. The apartment is actually 33, as I said in wire, and is sublet from some people called Rorison, which no doubt accounts for the "not known" written thereon, when it arrived on the 13th for No. 30. Had we not been in touch with the post office about the possibility of its having gone astray in Seattle probably we wouldn't have received it at all.)

Tuesday night.

This letter will be posted tomorrow even if still unfinished. Hitch occurred re stamps (!) this time.

Giroux letter to me appended. In one sense it would seem extremely reasonable. That is, had it been preceded by any reply whatsoever to my previous letters to him. *But this letter is the first and last I have had from Mr. Giroux: the alpha and omega of that wonderful author-editor relationship state.* And it was they who were inquiring about a financial program, not myself holding them up in that respect. I had sent them the copy of *Lunar Caustic* you probably have of my own free will and it had never been acknowledged. So that Giroux' letter coming after that long silence and suspense was a cruel thing, whatever the happy outcome.

But the point I want to make is that it is based on a complete misunderstanding, that if not cleared up might wreck things between ourselves too, supposing you and Random House think me worth publishing, a misunderstanding that my already having had to borrow money from you will not help. Harcourt, Brace seems to have been led to believe that I am completely broke and that I was

* This letter dated March 10, 1952, appears in Appendix 8, p. 450.

putting out for some sort of complete support or something for two years. That is bloody nonsense. As I wired you, I expected and hoped to publish *Hear Us O Lord* this year, so all I expected was a reasonable advance on that. The *Volcano* has been such a success in France and Germany that my publishers there are asking for my next book practically sight unseen and will give me an advance. The point imperative to make to you is that I only want to *work,* and that any such misconstruction could have been applied is appalling to me of all people. I have, as you know, a small income from England (it comes to about $90 a month at the present exchange) and had— and still have to some extent—hopes of a great deal more when my father's estate was, is, finally settled. If the pound gets back to normal and restrictions are relaxed a bit—as seems just possible within the next year or so—I'll be positively well off. So it is only this immediate period, until I can get a book finished, that is difficult. We live in a shack we built ourselves in the country as cheaply as any two people could live. When we shifted in town this winter we not only had the expectation of the Brace contract—they had given us $500, less taxes and commission, etc.—but a notice from Correa in France of $800 royalties there and a contract sent us on a German film of the *Volcano* (they offered me 50/50, we sent the contract to Hal, no further word). The Correa money has been presumably held up at the last moment due to the falling franc. With all this it seemed that for once we could afford to live in a place over the winter that had some hot water and where we could get on with the work instead of spending our time cutting wood and trying not to freeze. So we committed ourselves until April first. Giroux never replied to me and everything else seems to have fallen through. I'll get the money from France eventually but much less because of the devaluation of the franc. But the most cruelly ironical thing is all this having been placed in the position of some sort of potentially mercenary or grasping author! I've got to make this clear to you, even in the face of having had to borrow some more money from you you couldn't afford and then asking for more. (We are already trying to devise means of paying this back by the way.) Naturally I feel the laborer is worthy of his hire but I expect to deliver more than value received, and you know this. I hope I've made it clear why I had to shout for more help but if I haven't I'll make it so in the next letter. This has been and is a period of excruciating torment for us, as you can probably gather from the style of this letter—and the agony of suspense continues.

1952

Thank you for bearing with me, and thank you again for your belief and friendship.

What is the news of you and Peggy?

With love and gratitude from us both,

Malcolm

P.S. Frank has a masterpiece of ours, by the way, did you or didn't you know? That too is publishable perhaps.

P.P.S. In your own good time please return the enclosed letters for I have a story cooking on the subject—possibly to be part of the novel—called "In the Abyss." Also please hold on to this agonized unbalanced and demoniac missive for the same reason.

M.

To Robert Giroux

[Vancouver, March, 1952]

Dear Mr. Giroux:

Let me say right off that I believe you when you say "It is painful to me to report . . . ," that you mean it and that it is, just what you say, painful to you. More than that, I even sympathize, for you must know what complicated bewilderment, even anguish, your decision has caused at this end, both to my wife and myself, and it's often seemed to me that the only thing worse than suffering is the knowledge that one has been unwittingly forced to inflict pain on other people.

Though it may sound as though I have phrased this half cynically it is not really so: I feel that you must know there is wrong, that you hated to be the instrument of it: even if you had to tell me to the contrary, I couldn't believe you. Even if I didn't feel I know you, the formality of your first communication would seem to belie it. Otherwise, if I didn't see this, this author might find himself saying something like: "It is likewise painful for me to report that the action of your firm in suddenly casting this author adrift without warning or word after insisting several months ago he be made fast, months of complete silence on your part, would seem to any impartial observer unscrupulously inconsistent with the highest traditions of American publishing, or whatever, not to say the sincerity with which you, as a representative of that firm, sign yourself." Lots of fine sarcasm of that kind springs only too readily from my brain, or from the demons that inhabit it—I hope in lesser part than the angels— let it go: if I get mad in the course of this letter, the anger is not directed at you personally, but at a situation, the apparent cruci-ficiality of which the work itself might just as well have brought about for some mysterious reason of its own, though at the moment it's rather hard to see what.

In any case (to return to the human side) I was brought up in a milieu in which I learned to know pretty well that the fellow in command, be he general or sea-captain, may have to take things that he doesn't want to take, do things he doesn't want to do, contradict himself and at the same time have to take the contumely for it, if any, out of a loyalty to the situation which he perhaps doesn't accept but at the same time is honorably committed to (I even seem to recollect, though it's quite irrelevant, a famous point in maritime law "where the privity of the owner be not the privity of the master," etc. etc., the clause that the latter so rarely avails himself of even though entitled to—recollect, incidentally from my father who, not without a certain observance of poetic justice in this, since his father-in-law was a skipper who'd gone down with his ship, was, among other things, a director of Lloyd's; the wrath will be piled on the master's head any-way); you can say no more than that "I personally regret this . . ." or "It is painful for me to report . . ." etc.

However it is a pity indeed you should have to find "painful to report" anything that could have such melancholy consequences as this when it seems to be based on an inexplicable misunderstanding. I take my cue from your letter to me—your complete rejection of me— in which you intimate, and it is courteous of you to do so, that at least there is some compensation in that the relationship must termi-nate (though another might be pardoned for wondering how a rela-tionship which never exactly began can terminate) on what after all is a publishing matter rather than an editorial decision. Yes, but who would not be forgiven for thinking that your decision—or lack of it—not to get in touch with me at all—and here I go, so pardon me in advance—or even acknowledge the receipt of *Lunar Caustic,* was not an editorial decision. That was not a publishing decision. I was not holding you up to reply to each facet of my letter—indeed I asked you not to hurry, knowing you were probably hard pressed at that time— but I did emphasize, in attempting to cooperate wholeheartedly and simply, the need for contact and advice—and surely the obligation at least to acknowledge the arrival of a manuscript cannot have escaped you, even though no obligation was laid on you through its reception; to spare you any feeling of being saddled with extra responsibility was one reason I sent it direct and not via Hal. It was in one way simply a *copy* of stuff I didn't want to lose, of material for future work, and at the same time a sort of earnest of future work, that you had besides asked to see: I asked no editorial decision exactly upon *Lunar Caustic* per se, though I thought it would be self-evident that that material could be regarded as pretty complete and that it could be seen—even if not publishable as it stood, which I'm not sure it isn't—that if I pursued a not too elaborate policy toward it, it wouldn't take so long to finish, albeit on all of this I required advice. It would have been no disaster had not *Lunar Caustic* arrived, for I have a copy, but it would have seemed a very irresponsible beginning to the editor-author relationship from this end, and the failure here from your end would seem inexcusable, considering the torment of suspense it caused me and the psychological effect you must have known it would have—for it *was* all important to me to know you had it, as it was important to me at least to *know* you had at least received my letters, which I didn't expect or ask for—did I not now believe that part of this whole thing must have been some tragedy of misplaced ethics. You possibly acknowledged the receipt of *Lunar Caustic* to Hal rather than me: Hal for whatever reason did not get in touch with me, or his letter went astray: in fact, up to the moment of writing, my last letter from Hal was dated January 14,* in which he assured me that you wished to establish a good author-editor relationship, that he believed you were the man to hold up your end, and that he was seeing you that week (though the next information we have is a wire on the 6th of March saying "Brace decided today no more advances on basis of work available"). Still, I did not feel, in default of any reply from you either to my first long letter, or the letter accompanying the MSS of *Lunar Caustic*, that it was right to pursue this matter behind Hal's back, supposing one had not been by then so completely confused and heartsick at the silence that one had been able to pursue it. In this limbo—or perhaps oubliette is the better word—I eventually had to appeal to Hal by wire, after letters brought no reply, mentioning that I had a right to know what was going on. But from this only grew what is in fact the further misunderstanding on the basis of which came your report, which it was so painful for you to make and me to receive. Yet even supposing there had been no misunderstanding, was it so unreasonable under

* This letter appears in Appendix 8, p. 447.

the circumstances—which circumstances would readily have been explained to you had you replied to my letters—to have expected some further assistance at this particular period, even if on the basis of *Hear Us O Lord* alone? I don't believe my worst enemy—and I have sweated with fright to think who *he* is—could say that there was. (I didn't mean he was in your firm, I was thinking that Old Scratch himself might have been getting his oar in, not liking—as well he might not—the theme of my work.)

First allow me to quote from your letter of Dec. 11 to Hal, who for his part carried out your wishes immediately as per the last paragraph in communicating your desires to the said Mr. Lowry.

From this—even your own most inveterate supporter must admit— one would deduce, logically speaking, a feeling that (a) one was wanted as a writer by your firm (b) that you wanted to work out a publishing and financial program for the whole body of Mr. Lowry's work. In fact the latter clause you repeat twice, insisting on it again at the end, saying, "We should very much like to work out a publishing program and we should appreciate your communicating our desires in this regard to Mr. Lowry."

Mr. Lowry was so communicated with by his loyal agent, with what result of hope to a couple of writers who've been slugging it out in the wilderness with diminishing returns and little success for years or compensation to their agent, you can imagine.

This joy, however—as I later tried to point out—was not unmixed, to say the least, because of the wrench of having to leave Albert Erskine, but I now proceed to, before I return to the other, a further point, that is made after the first mention of this noble publishing and financial program for the whole body of Mr. Lowry's work: that "He has many admirers here, and indeed friends . . . to be published here." All this, I submit, quite logically would lead the said writer to believe that not only was a publishing and financial program for the said writer to be evolved—and that it was your desire it should be evolved—but that in addition to the financial background, there existed yet another, subtler background, where, as in a shadowy ballet, could be described a kind of dance of devoted and faithful friends, all of whom might be imagined, as it were, cheering on the author and providing him in his frozen retreat with a sort of warmth and security, as his work beautifully evolved with the beneficent assistance of the other, the more material financial background, with which in turn was related the publishing program you had expressed yourself as so very much liking to work out. Now before I return to the other point I think I have some right to communicate the words written to me two days later—by a coincidence upon the day of the Virgin of Guadalupe, that is so significant in the work itself—by the said agent:

"Let us assume that editorially you could have a satisfactory relationship with Harcourt: what kind of financial program would meet your requirements? Is there a first draft of *Lunar Caustic* available?"

Now at this point I was faced with a very hard decision, as I tried to explain to you. I had thought the MSS was going to Albert Erskine, but instead it turned out it had gone to you. If you were refusing to bow out and had decided to stand by your moral and legal rights as I was informed, and I was going to insist upon staying with Albert Erskine, obviously I wasn't doing anybody any good, least of all Mr. Erskine, who under those circumstances could scarcely have been other than embarrassed by my loyalty. Indeed it was also difficult to see how one would be proving a friend by insisting that that friend maintain an imaginary freehold upon property that it turned out was within the tenure of another. Moreover having emphasized the importance of the *Volcano* to the whole in the outline of the Work in Progress, it was yet further difficult for me to see how my work's attractiveness as a commercial proposition was going to be precisely enhanced by the fact that you owned the *Volcano* too, as a part of those rights, the more so since now it turned out I'd emphasized it to you rather than to him. So I made my decision then and there, if indeed it could be called my decision and not a case of *force majeure*, and wired Hal to that effect. I also wired him that I was in desperate need of immediate cash, something that merely looks as though it had something to do with your or my decision at this time, but in fact had none, and was only relevant to it, if at all, in this way, that I could justly have been swayed by the fact that in Dollarton conditions were such this winter that I had not the faintest moral right for my wife's sake to allow her to endure them a day longer than absolutely necessary, though that as I have suggested does not mean that the situation was Biblical in its simplicity by any means. For me to raise what seemed thoroughly impractical objections to what Hal was after all trying to carry through for me, objections which could do no good to Mr. Erskine, was extremely unfair to Hal, who has labored long and faithfully on my behalf. I think he would have had an absolute right indeed to tell us to go to hell, I felt I had no right to let the matter drag on into an impasse over and into the New Year but so far it had only occurred to me that your approval of my work must have sent up my stock with Hal, for at least here there seemed the prospect of some money and possible success in the future again. But my plea for immediate cash was only in part based on this prospect, and it wasn't a plea to you, or was not intended to be, but curiously enough was an appeal to *him,* all of which would be excessively funny if it had not had such complicated and sad results. No, the idea of appealing to you right off for an advance—and on my side I can say quite honestly that this is the only near hypocrytical part of the whole business if indeed even this is hypocritical—horrified me; I deplore this English trait, but there it perhaps is: when I realized at last it was you who had sent it to me through Hal I was not sure my gratitude, which was and is sincere, was not outweighed by a kind of nightmarish foreboding, for I said to myself, "There goes the whole thing—for they will say, you offer an Englishman admiration, friendship, and belief in his future, and the bloody man asks you for 500 bucks even before you've had time to down your Scotch."

I daresay there's something equally English about this kind of self-deprecation too—it's as if we never like to think of anything being transacted on the material plane, even though we've been transacting it, and moreover are perhaps quite capable of carrying through the transaction to the benefit of all. *We are not here to ask for dollars.* Of course not, Winnie, old boy, how could one even suspect you of such a filthy trick?

But as a matter of fact, quite apart from all this, long before the money arrived, and immediately I had sent my telegram of "acceptance" of what looked like *your* "acceptance" to .Hal, yet another obligation had arisen. This was of course to yourself, or selves, as well as to Hal. If you were going to take my work, the sooner it was got down to again the better, in addition to which it seemed to me that considerable correspondence, and that of an intricate nature, would have to be entered into with yourself. Such work, such correspondence, was becoming more impossible where we lived by the hour. The typewriter was frozen. It is hard to write with gloves on, still harder, perhaps, when you have no gloves. So for this reason alone we had to get out. In order to get out we needed money. And in order to get money, other sources having not yet come through for us, we had to wire Hal. It now strikes me I may have erred in not acceding to Hal's request to outline just what kind of "financial program" I *did* require, merely saying I left that to him, erred both in this and in not making it clear enough to him what our *exact* financial position

1952

was, though my excuse is the unassailable one that I didn't *know:* from being blackly pessimistic we now had every reason for optimism, but I should have made it clearer that under *normal* conditions we had enough that was gilt-edged barely to maintain ourselves in a fashion, even if in poverty, provided the pound did not crash further, and at that even if all our other prospects collapsed though under these conditions of course work gets slowed down in a crisis by attempts to earn money in a different way.

And to throw some further lightning of sincerity through all this. We owed—and still indeed do owe—Hal money himself—about $250, to be precise—but for once most certainly in my life I was sure that I had some excellent security to borrow some more. There was yourselves, but that was in the future, not at that moment, for almost simultaneously we had a letter from France, from Correa, saying the *Volcano* had earned nearly half a million francs, and there was some $800 or so owing me in royalties on the profits of the French translation, and where should they send it: we told them to send it to Hal. Simultaneously I received a contract from my German publishers of the *Volcano*—which was a sensation in Germany—offering me 50% of the profits on a movie they wished to make of it involving Peter Lorre, who'd already been reading bits of it with great success over the Munich (God perish the word) radio. And then there was yourself, or rather selves.

But alas, though I sincerely believed in these two former possibilities, Hal was only too right to be sceptical: he has informed me that the French money will take at least 10 months to get through to me—and now the franc's begun to crash—and as for the film, it looks as if it were a chimera. So you sent me the money through him and I have explained how, inexplicably, through carelessness on the Canadian side, it was delayed till after Christmas, which might be termed Favorite Special Trick of the Fates No. 2. This ominous delay turned out to be a fatal proposition all round (I qualify this later) for we couldn't find a vacant hotel room till New Year's Eve nor a practical hole to crawl into till January 6. It put us to a lot of unnecessary expense and in that weather nearly drove us off our rockers. But yet it was necessary, somehow, to find that hole, if I was ever to begin to deal with what seemed now to be my commitments.

For now behold again the appalling situation then existing here. I don't want to complicate this letter by making dramatic descriptions of the scenery. You only had to look at the *Times* building to discover what was happening here. There never has been in all living

[301]

L

history of the Pacific Northwest such awe-inspiring weather north of Cape Flattery. Ships had been going down every day all around us, including for the record the S.S. *Pennsylvania,* out of Chapter II of the *Volcano,* with all hands off Vancouver Island—all hands save one, a Vancouver Ishmael, I should add, as if to report the matter to old Jay Leyda. Tides rose 5 and 6 feet beyond any hitherto known levels. What you think this was like living in a fisherman's shack, though built by ourselves, right in the sea, even though we are supposed to be in an inlet, I can only ask you to imagine. Huge seas, blinding snow, flooding tides, gales of hurricane force, uprooted trees threatening you, shakes falling on their knees and havoc everywhere, certain death if you slipped, etc. etc. etc., in short a kind of D. W. Griffith melodrama of the weather such as had never been known even in these parts.

Naturally the work was in danger too, as I later told you: hence that anxiety—only two fishermen (once some years ago we were the only people to stick it at all, population of Dollarton went down to 2 at that time, my wife and myself, though it wasn't so terrible as this and we were younger) stuck it right through, and themselves were bachelors: the rest you more or less know from the middle part of my letter.

But to return, one of our main reasons for coming into town, as I said, was to enable us to get on with the work and fulfill the times suggested in the work in progress: in short, I had hoped and expected to publish *Hear Us O Lord* late next fall or early winter, and *Lunar Caustic* the following fall, though if you preferred *Lunar Caustic* could have been finished and published first: i.e., next winter, and I was preparing to work, as I have in the past, 12 or if necessary 18 hours a day to that end, which was utterly impossible during the deepest part of the winter in Dollarton, as we have discovered in the past years, for there seems to have been a real and startling climatic change here.

But primarily I am not broke in the sense that you seem to have been led to believe, far less was I expecting you to support me on the basis of a chimera (not that it is a chimera) for 1, 2, 3, or 4 years, or even for that matter—it would be something that would make me decide against you and *go* broke rather—for one month, were business to be conducted as inconsistently as this appears to have been. My financial reverses were and are, I have every reason to believe, temporary. I have an income at worst of just under $100 a month, and when my father's estate is settled I shall be, in these days, well off for an Englishman; certainly enough that I shall never again put myself in such absurd position with any publisher. My French and German publishers are eager for my next book sight unseen and will give me an advance (which would presumably take some months to get here however): once back in Dollarton, where we shall be moving this week end, we live very economically indeed; I was merely at a point where I required some assistance in order to finish my work that much sooner. In short, I must repeat, I have perhaps not brought out the point sufficiently that in order to do anything at all, and fulfill my promises and the time schedule, I was bound to behave as I have behaved, to have moved temporarily to town in order to continue writing, despite the added expense. I have not concealed from you the obligation I still owe and still hope to fulfill to Albert Erskine, who was, to the best of my knowledge, the only one who really believed in me or did anything for me at Reynal and Hitchcock, except Frank Taylor. What remains of this moral obligation I now apply to yourselves, to think of at 4 o'clock in the morning, which I had not known Fitzgerald had advanced as the real dark night of the soul when I wrote the *Volcano,* and it may be that it is 3 o'clock or even 5 o'clock.

However this letter is not written in the realm of public, nor ethical, nor any other kind of relations but those called human: and it is only because I value human relations, and even in default of it treasure your invisible friendship, and believe that what you have said, as what I have said, operates outside the mechanical march of events, and if not now, 10 years from now will give you, as me, a peace of soul that I write as I do.

And so—because I believe in the preservations of human relations and human decency—I sign myself, not merely sincerely, but yours, without hypocrisy, with true affection, and belief in what you sincerely said to begin with, and again later, as well as you courteously could— as I not merely courteously but sincerely dare to call myself, your friend,

Malcolm Lowry

To Albert Erskine

Dollarton
Thursday
[April, 1952]

Hooray, Albert!

Just a line to reciprocate joyousness, and try to express my gratitude and relief.* Inexpressible, so can't do it at the moment. Everything has been held up here for the last week due to exigencies of moving. Your first letter arrived Monday in Dollarton but your telegram went to Vancouver, and so was delayed. The fault was entirely theirs, not yours or ours. There is terrific damage here in Dollarton, though our house has come through practically—or rather relatively—unscathed. Nothing has been lost though and it was a wonderful homecoming. Margie is dancing a saraband. There is much manual labour—house cleaning and wood chopping—to be done in next week so forgive if there is slight letup in correspondence. Will write tomorrow more fully. Hooray again and all gratitude.

God bless from us both,
Malcolm

To Albert Erskine

Dollarton
Ash Wednesday (with reservations)
[1952]

Dear old Albert:

This, an interpolated note of affection and gratitude merely, with the knowledge that you have not time to reply. (But also with the intention of explaining a few peripheral things.)

A clean house, at last, even a clean soul, what is more; a full moon over the inlet, the mergansers gone to rest and the mink returned to her hollow tree. Never was anything more miraculously well nor more peaceful in our town—population three—perhaps four if "Kristbjorg"† is still on deck: he swears, or swore the day before

---

* This is in reference to a Random House contract.

† "Kristbjorg," a local fisherman, and "Quaggan" (Jimmy Craige), both turned into characters in "The Forest Path to the Spring."

yesterday, that in the 60 years of his experience he has never seen the sea do anything worse than it has done here: it has cut away about 20 feet in depth of the entire forest sea bank, dropping whole gardens into the sea, not to say houses, while the entire shore has changed from about $\frac{1}{15}$ gradient to about $\frac{1}{6}$ in places, with the corresponding undermining of foundations. "Quaggan's" big float in front of his boathouse—the whole two hundred feet of it—carried away completely: but our pier still stands—absolutely undamaged—as do our foundations, despite the fact that we have four and a half whole uprooted trees terrifyingly *under* our house. Since our pier is made only out of light two-by-fours and 2-inch planking, is now ten years old, and has stood the brunt of the worst furies of wind and sea ever endured here, we have not met anyone yet who has even bothered to think of a material explanation for its survival, though there might be one, namely in its simplicity, lightness, and freedom from top hamper: thus in a terrific sea—and it was overwhelmed, under water when we left—instead of giving way to the sea and lifting from its foundations, it simply and calmly clung to the beach and stayed where it was, the foundation being just slightly heavier than the overall plankings: nearly all professional jobs gave way in this vicinity, for not having recognized whatever principle there is in this; they figured that the heavier and stronger the planking the more weight it would place on the foundations, and hence the foundations would be the securer and the whole safer in every way in any emergency. But it ain't so—wood *floats* and will try and float even if nailed down, and if overwhelmed by water the heavier it is, the harder it will pull at the nails—and all round guess there is some sort of lesson—apart from an image—in this, the more so since the foundations, in this case, simply and contrariwise adjusted themselves to the undermining of the beach, instead of vice versa, and became securer than ever: naturally we are very proud of ourselves. Our subsidiary house was not so lucky as we said, but then we didn't build it; even that has stood up though, minus a pile, it is sagging badly at one end and we have to prop it up.

I have interrupted another longer letter to you to write you this—because of changing circumstances—but will try to supply you with a sort of log. Friday, March 28, two days before we left the apartment, we ran into a typhoon and damn nearly foundered almost in Falmouth harbour—very eerie and dramatic, albeit with a happy outcome—I'll not tell you of it now, though God knows it's worth the telling, it left Margie, who was taking sulfanilamide for a throat, unable to type and almost completely shattered, coming on top of everything else. I can type, but not well enough on her typewriter to transcribe the job I was then doing, which was a letter to Giroux, especially as I proposed to give you a carbon. I was trying to make the point tactfully that while I did not blame him personally, since they had made such a to-do about moral rights, where their or the office boy's moral rights to the *Volcano* came in: so this letter—though almost finished—I had to abandon or leave in abeyance, and since Haas'* decision and yours in my favour, the Case is somewhat Altered.

Sunday we came home, by a coincidence "Quaggan's" birthday—which he had celebrated in part by putting hot bricks on our soaking mattress and chopping some wood for us: so we had a warm as well as a happy homecoming. Of course we do the same sort of thing for him when we can and when necessary, each for the other, but I hadn't known the efficacy of hot bricks till then. He had lost our poor cat though (which has gone wild) so you might say—horrible image on second thoughts—we had the hot bricks without the cat. I guess he'll come home though, that is the cat; at least he has been "reported to have been seen."

Monday the 31st we got your airmail letter written to Dollarton saying that things were still in abeyance, but since Monday was a kind of crucial day with Haas so far as I could gather, we (expecting as it happens correctly a wire from you were there good news) felt some gloom and prepared to fight the rearguard action still further: e.g. letters for paying your debt, etc., though we had become in transit confused about the poems, and what to send: so preparing for the worst began to "dig out sails." Margie meanwhile was rallying nobly.

Tuesday April 1st. Your wire came through to the store, eventually, by telephone: it having been sent to the apartment the day before. They said oh well, they thought that was our address, and the note had been put under Number 33 at the apartment. *But the telegram had meantime been lost,* they said. Finally they found a copy of it and phoned it to the store and Margie came whooping through the woods with the best news I ever heard in my life. (Actual telegram, which we now have on the wall, did not arrive till 2 days later, but it was a supreme moment and bless you for sending it.)

Rest of the week—I received the general terms of the contract both from yourself and Hal, who expressed his unqualified admiration for what you have done for me, as I do ten times more, my unqualified gratitude. Hal's letter though went likewise to the ex-apartment in Vancouver, and not here. Though we might seem to be to blame

* Robert Haas, editor at Random House.

here for not having informed Hal directly of our change of address, this is actually one of the strangest of coincidences, for the general post office had our change of address by postcard well in advance; in addition to the P.O.'s error Hal failed to put the apartment number on the envelope so it was surprising it reached us at all, though it did, if delayed. In the case of your telegram going to the apartment, while we hadn't thought it necessary to inform the telegraph company of a change of address since we had informed you, they simply and inexplicably disregarded the Dollarton address you'd given, as I have explained, so I felt obliged to reply to Hal first.

I told him I was not sure of 2 *absolutely completed* novels and 1 book of tales i.e. three bona fide books, 2 of them novels, in 2½ years, as seemed called for, despite your more than generous terms, for which terms please also express my deep gratitude to Mr. Haas: though I could guarantee *Hear Us O Lord* and *Lunar Caustic* in that time, or even in 2 years plus (as I said in the telegram) the detailed scenario of the whole, albeit this last entails no obligation to yourself, on the other hand I feel it a necessary item: on the other hand this *detailed* scenario of the whole might seem to many novelists to subsume several more completed novels, but it all depends upon what the hell one considers a completed work of art, and it is on this point that I really desire some leeway for consultation with yourself, and advice. It is possible that *Lunar Caustic* could be finished way ahead of schedule, and that "The Ordeal of Sigbjørn Wilderness" both parts I and II would make a novel that could be completed in the remaining time. But *Dark as the Grave, Eridanus* and *La Mordida* are together a trilogy and though they might well be published separately—as will probably turn out to be the best idea—I can't *think* of them at present separately, a problem you will readily see when you receive the material in question: two years hence, if all goes well, with *Hear Us* already published and *Lunar Caustic* in your hands, it might be that in the remaining 6 months I could finish *Dark as the Grave,* say, but I can't quite think that far ahead with any degree of feeling completely honest as to what it is possible to achieve —and naturally I would like to achieve more than I promise. What I am chiefly anxious to do, presented with such generous terms as you have offered me, is to pay my way, fulfill your trust in me and not to let anyone down. So please don't think that I am beginning to hedge or chisel on the contract: the last thing I want to be is a "difficult" author in that sense. On the contrary I really am motivated by a feeling that once I've got going with any luck and God's help I may be able considerably to exceed your expectations.

Re the financial end of it, it is more than generous, as I have said, but since there seemed some possible flexibility in the arrangement, while accepting it gratefully on whatever terms seem likewise most convenient to yourself, I asked Hal that in case of some kind of untoward accident to wife or self I might feel I could ask to apply at some time for a couple of hundred dollars or so in advance, if and only if, I really mean and add now, it seemed absolutely necessary to the fulfillment of the contract, though I qualified this by saying—which is true—that such an eventuality does not seem likely, and so shouldn't necessarily be an item on the contract: the reason is that my whole financial picture seems likely to improve. I had another letter from France that so far as they know that 800 dollars *is* coming through after all without the franc having fallen: and though England is still stalling for time I expect confirmation of similar good news from that quarter. So with your generous lift and these other items I expect not only to pay my debts but to be well in the clear in regard to emergencies. For we do have a hospital insurance scheme. What was nearly tragic for us when we first borrowed money from you was (one) that the premium was compulsory and so high that one couldn't afford to pay the ordinary doctor's bills or buy medicine. As for me, my health is excellent.

The other item was there has been a question of a film of the *Volcano*, with Peter Lorre. Whether this is going to come off or not, I don't know, but if it did, I asked for a few months' grace or leave of absence or something during which I might assist with the script. Naturally one would not expect to be supported by Random House during such a period; I would not want it to interfere with the final fulfilling of the contract, but naturally such a thing might prove circumambiently a factor in paying one's way.

Finally I said if the third book couldn't be within that time a novel I have a collection of poems, *The Lighthouse Invites the Storm*, that could be got in order almost any time: one would not expect this to sell, but if *Lunar Caustic* was going good and more than paying for itself, it could act as a stop-gap.

Finally I have something I hadn't thought of, namely the film we did for Frank, which is still supposed to be secret, though the secret now seems absurd to keep from you, albeit I haven't told Hal its name. Whether or not this would be feasible as a quid pro quo for a third completed book within that allotted period—what with the difficulties of copyright and the joint authorship—I don't know, but its existence is at least an earnest of what one can do. We did it in seven months and have not ever accepted or borrowed any cash on it and indeed it, alack, did not do for Frank what we had hoped: but perhaps that wasn't its fault, and it may yet. And certainly it wasn't Frank's fault. Shall I write to Frank to send it to you? I dropped *Dark as the Grave* to write this—and eventually I had hoped, among other bright results for Frank, it would prevent our getting into precisely the sort of situation we did get into. I enclose some comments by Isherwood, Leyda and Frank himself. It is by no means an ordinary kind of script. The film of course is *Tender Is the Night* and I know Frank won't mind my mentioning it. In fact by writing it for him we felt we were in some sort "keeping in the family." The result was just the beginning of our three years' heartbreak: but at least we keep a-tryin'.

I have two hundred more French reviews, panegyrics of the *Volcano*, Teutonic headlines, Norse encomiums, and even caricatures of the author—but perhaps those are now somewhat beside the point, so I am not bothering you with them for the present.

A Happy Easter to you from us both and loads of gratitude and love,

Malcolm

To Mrs. E. B. Woolfan

[Dollarton, 1952]

My dearest sister Priscilla:

We went to see *The Strong Man;* being privileged to be related to the star,* to say the least, we were invited as honored guests to see a private showing albeit it is now wowing the audiences again in the theatre proper. I think you should know too that of all the cinematic consummate masterpieces in demand *The Strong Man* is about the most popular, if not the most popular, and consequently one of the hardest to obtain. That it was got in time for us to see it was due to the courtesy of the Museum of Modern Art for the same privileged reason as above. And before I say anything else, Priscilla—though I have seen the film before—I want to say immediately that your performance is one of the most profoundly realized and inspired—one of

* Also starring Harry Langdon.

the greatest and most permanent things in short that I or anyone else have seen in a movie. The audience was certainly of the same opinion.

That Chaplin seems to have borrowed liberally and literally from the general idea in *City Lights* was something that occurred to the audience too, to the grave detriment of one's memories of the direction of Virginia Cherrill therein, but perhaps this is a minor point: or one that could have been more literally minor had not your performance in *The Strong Man* been so absolutely major.

I myself have to throw myself forward rather than backward to get any comparison in terms of excellence for your acting, recently, to Barrault, etc., and the drama of the mime: though when we were in Paris we never saw any performance comparable to yours. I don't suppose such a one as good will occur again, though I don't see why it shouldn't, should you yourself choose even if tangentially to return to one or the other of the departments of drama.

The film itself—though we saw it under the worst kind of circumstances in one way, 4 or 5 people in a room, recorded thunderjug music that was far too soft and rarely varied and only once really imaginative, when they shut it off altogether when you were playing the terrific scene with Langdon on the garden seat—struck me as being colossal too: its revelation of the human soul was profound. Not to say the present situation, even if partly unconscious on Capra's part, though it must be said that he has not failed to continue to mine that apparently inexhaustible gold mine of the American consciousness of decency and wisdom against the forces of hypocrisy. Perhaps it wasn't meant to be profound, but even if not, your own performance would have made it a pioneer work in cinema. In short, as a film, it must strike anyone who has loved such things as important.

Your affectionate brother,
Malcolm

To Harold Matson

Dollarton, B.C., Canada
April 7, 1952

Dear Hal—

Sorry to be so long in answering your letter re the contract, but as you see by the above address we are back home in Dollarton and the letter took 3 days apparently to be forwarded out here from town.

Now, to get straight down to business so I can get this off to you today by our one post. I am more than happy about the contract as of course you must know. I think the financial terms are most generous and I accept them without any alteration. I should like to feel though, whether it's in the contract or not, that in case of some real emergency, say an accident to Margie or myself entailing hospital, or something, that I could draw up to 2 or 3 hundred if it was absolutely necessary. As things are shaping up at the moment though, this looks unlikely for my whole financial picture re England will eventually improve and it may not be much longer. Yes, I most certainly am interested in your plan of funding the money in case of any success, and please do whatever is necessary about this. I certainly should never want over $10,000 in one year, and I'm almost inclined to set this at less, say, $7,000 or so.

Now for my part of the contract I must say that I don't honestly know how I can deliver 3 books in 2½ years. Two books I can guarantee and I'll do my best about the third. I can finish *Hear Us O Lord* and *Lunar Caustic* all right, and if the third could be a book of poems they can publish that any time for I have sufficient for a volume now. But another novel I can't absolutely promise—that is, I could get out something or other of course but it might not be my best work; but then again I don't know until I see better how things shape up. We have concurrently an enormous transcriptionary job of material in hand facing us which must be done and I am very anxious not to let anyone down, so am reluctant to promise what I'm not completely sure of. This material of course covers all the books and I could certainly guarantee to get this in, in addition to *Lunar Caustic* and *Hear Us O Lord,* well within that period. I can deliver the first book within a year. I hope to have finished *Hear Us O Lord* by this fall, but just to give myself leeway you'd better say a year. Actually, I'd like to publish *Hear Us O Lord* next spring anyhow, though again this depends on correspondence with Albert, etc. What I would like is to keep the thing as flexible as possible and then exceed, rather than fall short of, the publisher's expectations. On the other hand I rewrite a lot and don't want to be tempted to let anything but my best work get by.

One last question for my part: suppose something came up about making a movie (and did you write Klett, by the way?) of the *Volcano,* say, would something like a few months' grace be granted so that I could work on the scenario? It's not impossible the scenario itself might be publishable, and I'm not sure what I mean by grace either.

deep worries of your own to which I would not like to add by my seeming neglect.

One thing I had said was that if you found yourself absolutely spiritually spiralling down the drain at this period you might do worse than work your way west: my wife and I live—à la Chapter I or IX *Volcano*—in a place as described there, in a shack built by ourselves. The town, composed of fishermen's huts along the granite-strewn shore, is falling to pieces, is largely abandoned, and at the moment contains only about four diehard inhabitants besides ourselves. You have to hew wood and carry water, the conditions are those of the utmost poverty, we have nothing to offer save our friendship, there are no conveniences of any kind, and you might hate it like hell. Nor, since we only have two inhabitable rooms and a stove out of the Gold Rush, could we put you up for more than a few days without the maximum of misery to yourself. But I could probably find you another neighbor's shack to crawl into for next to nothing, or possibly even nothing. The advantages are a primeval forest to wander in, incomparable scenery (though you may hate mighty fine prospects), wonderful swimming—though extremely cold —and a fine way of life that seems dying out of the world. Likewise we have a rowing boat we could lend you. Sometimes the place fills up a bit for the summer months though it is nothing like anything you ever saw, probably. In general the real life is a cross between the Sea of Galilee, *The Wild Palms* and Paradise: and sometimes in winter hell itself. It is our home, we pay not rent or taxes, and the anguish is always the danger of eviction, sometimes near, sometimes far, sometimes non-existent. But there is always the risk. It can be a wonderful place to work, or not, according to temperament. If the Random House contract comes off we would be hard pressed to fulfill its first year term and so working hard. We have no or almost no intellectual friends, we are nearly always hard up, but that doesn't mean that we might not all help each other in some sort and even have a fine time. I leave the suggestion at that, as a sort of risky beacon. But if you did work your way west and back again, hitch-hiked, by bus or what not—with the expectation of nothing but ourselves as the perhaps evanescent and unworthy gimmick—and took notes all the way, of street signs, bar signs, people, animals, houses, flying bedpans piloted by a celestial race of humming birds, you might get a fine novel of withdrawal and return and a memory of an adventure not wasted, utterly impractical though it sounds. Also I have a pal, Ted Roethke, of the University of Washington in Seattle

1952

who might help you to a job—he's a first-rate fellow in every way. Anyhow we throw out this shredding lifeline of a suggestion (though with no right to do so) in case the prospect of New York in summer is too much for you, and there seems no hope at all at the bottom of the glass.

Love from us both,
Malcolm

To Albert Erskine

Dollarton, B.C.
[May 1952]

Querido Alberto Bueno Excelentísimo de la Justicia y Ley—
(Buen suffragio y no reelección!)

I don't think I'm going to have time to say anything very considered, i.e., grammatical, about *Invisible Man*—unless that is important to you, in which case I shall, but I've read it carefully, some of it several times, and have come to the conclusion that at best it is a really electrifying piece of work, and that the author is probably a real rooting tooting double-barreled first-class writer. In fact my opinion of him is higher that that of the book as a whole, though when this is said it must be admitted that though I suppose that book has some of the faults usually attributed to first novels, it also has some absolutely bran new virtues that have not to my knowledge shown their nose in any novel, recently I mean (at least of recent date, if that makes sense). In parts it really seems—whether devilishly or not I can't make out—actually inspired. And his technical facility is such that in one astonishing brilliant and wonderful-horrible scene the reader finds his sympathies and antipathies engaged in so many different directions at once—and in directions one would not have thought possible—that like the loathsome character on the receptive end of this scene, the reader may find himself crying aloud faintly for a stimulant. Yet the author is really a bit diabolic, however much one may like him. My sympathy for instance—indeed complete empathy—for the man who has committed incest, because he couldn't (1) help it and (b) his subsequent behaviour establishes his real integrity since he accepts that he is what he is—could not, as I apprised you just now, be more: but subtly you feel you're being shamed, by identity with the odious Mr. Norton and the other

[315]

"benevolent" whites, when you want to identify yourself with the Invisible Man at this point whose behaviour has not been any too simon-pure either, but whose standpoint of condemnation (though subtly he was a Judas at this point) is clear, or seems to be. Actually this scene abounds with the most ghastly and new insights and by and large may make one as a writer oneself want to go out and buy a new set of brains, and if possible a new set of eyes and ears too, before writing another line. Purely as a scene it's comparable with some of the best in Faulkner, and it's not the only scene that affects me that way by any means—there're five or six others almost equally inspired in the midst of the utmost complication of intention, but this does not mean it's a successful book: it might mean your author is a genius, or something, but that's rather different. "Nonetheless that it is besides so interesting and easy to read should not blind one to its extraordinary complexity nor the solid intellection that is behind it. Nor should this in turn blind one to its texture, its real beauty as a work of art." If as a reviewer, say, overcome by enthusiasm, I'd stopped at about page 245 and written my piece right then without reading the rest I could imagine myself saying that or again something like this: "*Invisible Man* makes comment, like a kind of benign and diabolic atom bomb, upon all forms of oversimplification in regard to its central problem, on which the author goes to work not only with all the skill of a first rate story teller, but the resource and wisdom in complementary thinking of a nuclear scientist." Anyhow it's certainly a book to recommend to those who imagine that modern fiction is lying or unimportant, and it should satisfy Ortega himself on that score, not to mention the damaging Mr. Barzun. Sure, adaptations of the book—play, movie, whatever—will no doubt be made, and at that successfully. But in what other form than the novel could so many hard and—for the world—necessary points be made so tellingly? So my hat is off to the author, his overall skill and—with some reservations—to his most original conception, as also to his guts and integrity. But alas, did I say it was interesting after, say, page 245. I wouldn't quarrel with its necessary complexity, but in my opinion the book itself—with a few miraculous cloudbursts of recovery—begins to fail and become arider and arider, even fall to pieces (pardon my mixed metaphors) approximately from this point on. I more or less dissent too from the opinions expressed by certain reviewers of the book in this regard. However noble the multiple intention, the book itself begins to fail as a work of art, in my opinion, though fragmentarily still it can still show itself a hell of a sight better than many or most novels. Possibly this is because the beginning, likewise the enclosing theme, is so good. Either that or he leads you to expect too much of himself. But the irony utterly ceases to be out of the top drawer, becomes somewhat derivative finally. The reporting of the communist brotherhood is as boring very often as their dialectics probably were in real life. One has been invited so often to these cocktail parties of well-heeled communists before and the essential and important points are too often clouded as a result of the technical out-of-touchness of the writing. One thinks (though only in relation to the satire) of Orwell and says no, and what is worse, the suspicion arises that—if not the author—the book is somehow trying to curry some obvious critical favour from certain people and interests, who would have to be promoted into another spiritual sphere, in my opinion, even before they were honestly damned. The white world—I feel—is wickeder than he, Ellison, dares to let on: the "point" he makes, that the black can be equally black, is tremendously important, though he makes it with least effectiveness here at the end. I think this part should have been cut considerably because Ralph E. seems to have forgotten that the nearer a thing approximates to a true work of art, the nearer it gets—or may get—to the "truth." (Not vice versa.) *Invisible Man* ceases—or very damn nearly ceases, in my opinion—to be a work of art roughly after about page 245 and consequently the truth suffers. But the saving grace of this is, I believe, or may be, that Ellison realizes that himself and makes a near-heroic effort to save the thing itself in terms of art and damn nearly succeeds. For instance the speech at the funeral—tremendous! Though the book had begun to go down the drain on one plane after the wonderfully humorous as well as savage and dramatic business of trying to get rid of the Feed-me Americana emblem in the various garbage cans —a scene as good as Chaplin. But his trouble, I think, is involved as I say with his brave endeavour to keep his theme consistent: i.e., to bring the thing off with flying colours as a work of art. Maybe I contradict myself but it seems to me that perhaps it is here that the very disciplined strictures imposed by his own form begin by their inevitable contraction to render the whole body a bit morbid. To put it another way, the book seems to shunt ill or uneasily between its prologue and epilogue: the couplers, the drawbars, begin to fall, or sound as if they were falling, apart: while it still makes a terrifying noise from time to time the train, you are reminded, seems nonetheless stalled: the prologue (that I read before in *Partisan Review*) seems no such brilliant observation car on close inspection as it did, and the epilogue does not show any signs of taking us into any final truth, and when the train you feel is beginning to move, whether to shed or station, it is with the uneasy feeling that it's been partially un-coupled and at least some of the passengers—including perhaps even ourselves—have been left behind. Above all, it is a bit too fantastic at the end, too unsuccessfully dada, too would-be (though with some miraculous recoveries and exceptions) nightmarish. The characteriza-tion seems to me likewise—even allowing for his anything but conven-tional or easy purpose—pretty feeble, though again there are trium-phant flashes and insights. The race riot, so highly praised by others, strikes me as at worst resembling one of those very early Soviet futuristic films such as *Arsenal,* where symbol and the thing symbol-ized, man and meaning and photographic virtuosity are so confused that it is only your respect for the ingenuity of the director and the hope of what he may do at the next moment that keeps you from leaving the theatre out of exasperation with the sheer inertia and muddle he imposes: but above all this I had the feeling that here Ellison was not writing what he wanted to and knew it. My final feeling is, though, that his final remark is universally justified and that in the main he does, like Kafka, strike at the soul of man himself. At least he strikes at mine, and I shall certainly prize the book as the work of someone I feel may be important indeed.

As for *The Shrike*—for which thanks not so very much on the plane of its merit, but still thanks very much—while it has an Ibsenish sort of purity, I don't think it is so hot, as you generously intimated yourself. It has the purity and the architectonics but it doesn't have the final honesty or understanding. The Shrike herself— shade of a shade of shades of Ethan Frome!—may be a theme in her-self (there is something like cowardice in the way official man blandly ignores woman's lunar capacity to drive folk insane, some-thing like a perversion of the chivalry of pioneer days and an implied Mom worship in their so blandly taking her side in cases where they responsibly shouldn't, while one can see in modern North American and Canadian men often a victim of penis worship and pitiably a true Wylieish subject of tragedy as a result) but the Shrike's be-haviour in bitching the protagonist's possible job is worthy only of the comic strip and the psychoanalysts are no better dramatized, should truth and not effect be in mind, and dramatic honesty would surely have involved more of these characters being in the right: the brother struck me as especially banal: as it is a certain kind of pseudo-good theatre, though perhaps better than nothing, wools the truth of

the matter. Nonetheless I found the best parts expert, such as the
Calypso singing bit (though the song was not specified) and under
the circumstances a bit hard to take. But what the hell. God bless
from us both.

Malcolm

P.S. Though you won't believe me, I read (your gift of) *Ulysses*
through—essentially—for the first time, when I had a fever recently.
Le gusta esta Dujardin? Why is it Joyce? Since it really was my first
intelligent and complete reading (why I was inhibited I know not, in
the last 12 years here no doubt by the censorship and sheer lack of
time) some of my perceptions I feel may be unusual though I won't
go into them right now.

P.P.S. Just received your letter of May 1 to which I won't reply in
detail—only to say how deeply I appreciate the thought, consideration
and generosity within the contract to come and to thank you again
most deeply, Albert, for the trouble you have gone to and time spent
on my behalf. Needless to say I'll do my damdest to make you feel it
was worth while. There are several immediate points. Unless England
goes bankrupt or we have an extreme government or the pound
crashes further my income should be more than doubled, if the
pound goes up perhaps tripled. I already have had to pay taxes this
year (without receiving any of the said money) on what looks, from the
trustee's statement, to be an income of nearly a thousand pounds a
year, and this is without my one fourth share of the actual real
estate, so to say, of the estate. This sort of thing was what fooled me
when I said in good faith I thought I could repay you right off for
the first money you lent us, i.e., the will (though not everything
connected with the estate) was probated, it seems: I received a certain sum as I told you, much diminished by the exchange: but the
law still does not permit the transfer of even the income from the
whole to a dollar area even after taxes (current part of the income
comes under an earlier jurisdiction): however the change in government does mean this much, that the money seems to belong more
legally and forthrightly to me (hence the taxes, fortunately mostly
deducted at the English end, but still leaving me here in a higher
tax bracket than is warranted by the specie received—i.e., in no tax
bracket at all here—though fortunately we caught them in an error
which reduced the spectacular injustice at the last moment): therefore
(though it is too complicated really to explain) I have discovered
that if you, or rather Peggy, for example, or for instance, were think-

ing of taking a trip to England, empowered by a note to my bank from myself, you, or she, could draw the money owing to you (on the first debt) at my English bank. I mention this only because probably its purchasing power of $200 (our first debt) is—being nearly £70—in England far greater in pounds than dollars here. Or is it? It certainly was. The money owing me from England will in any case probably come through for me here sometime, and as for this particular debt, as I intimated, it can now be paid back from other sources, such as the French money, to speak of nothing else, but I just mentioned this curious fact in case you by any chance wanted to avail yourself of it. Since the money would come to me here only via income, presumably—though there might be an exception—the main capital would still be there, whether the former were paid or not. Of course I know you are not taking a trip due to exigencies of molars but it could be that Peggy was peripatetic—and my dear fellow, how is all this bloody anguish with you now? I can hope only as well as possible, and beyond that hope for your happiness. I only mentioned this in case something of this kind arose with you suddenly before I was able to pay back the first debt in the usual way: as things stand —if this is O.K. with you—second would be paid before first, i.e., well in time for your summer session with the dentist.

Re the order of the books, while I agree that it would seem on the face of it strategically and financially better for me and you to have you publish the stories second and *Lunar Caustic* first, I've been more or less proceeding rightly or wrongly on the other assumption, and though it isn't absolutely too late to change this plan, certain minor considerations have accumulated into a larger consideration that might not in the end make my plan the more feasible after all: first there is a good chance now I can complete *Hear Us* well ahead of schedule, so much so that a year and a half from now I should with luck have completed or at least be in clear sight of the end of *Lunar Caustic* too. There is a mechanical problem here. *Dark as the Grave* in its early drafts is still going along being typed by Margie from my execrable pencil notes and until she's got to the end of *La Mordida* it would be much harder in the circumstances of 2 rooms in which we live for me to concentrate on *Caustic* than on *Hear Us*. On the other hand though *Hear Us* is much easier to write with its less interrelated problems, it seems to be shaping up less like an ordinary book of tales than a sort of novel of an odd aeolian kind itself, i.e. it is more interrelated than it looks. And so, I suppose, while it might not sell, what if it were an exception and did? Perhaps unlikely. But para-

doxically I am not polishing anything in it that looks as if it had
much chance of selling individually though it would be pleasant if
it did, nor do I offer the converse as an earnest of its possible success
as a book but what I mean is that you certainly have delivered me
from that feeling of necessity of trying to pick up money from the
magazines so that *Hear Us* is not being proceeded with with the idea
of specie always getting in the machinery so much as with the idea
of getting into training for the Popos and peaks ahead and also
because I hope it will be a worthy book. This doesn't state the whole
problem by a long shot which is one really of getting the greedy
daemon in line and forcing him to do something more lowly and
unpretentious as a discipline even at the expense of working with
logic and simple motives rather than with more gluttonous danks
and darks until the material at least of *Mordida* be transcribed. I
hope the whole thing will have been transcribed by about the time
I have finished *Hear Us,* meantime he will have to scream in vain
(though I shall feed him morsels), for until there is a copy of this
material in a safe place somewhere I shall not rest easy, for if it
were lost I could scarcely do the work I have promised in anything
like the time allotted; I don't always share his memory, for one thing,
and I sometimes fear he could not care less, for having already
written the book, as it were, he has no time problem, and for things
that still continue to harry us—such as that our position on the
beach with the boom and election time may be in revived jeopardy
while this is part of the plot—no consideration at all. (Though I
hesitate to set this down I think it only fair to assure you that if
worst comes to worst in this regard I'm not going to let it throw me,
or even much delay me: a Norwegian-Canadian friend has offered
to let us squat on his beach some 50 miles away on an island in Howe
Sound in that case, though in that case too a common-sense problem
might arise of leaving the dollar area altogether—for our dollar is
higher than yours, consequently we doubly lose—and seeking a ster-
ling one eventually, such as the Bahamas, should England come
through with a lump sum to get us there: this is about the worst
delay I can envisage, but why anticipate trouble: one's luck has been
phenomenal. Just the same this element of insecurity or uncertainty
increases the responsibility of giving the copying of that material
priority over the longer haul and only Margie can understand my
handwriting: not even I can always understand it.

Malcolm

P.S. The contract has now arrived, it is: wonderful, and I have signed it and dispatched it. I thank you from the bottom of my heart for everything. Can we let the matter of short stories or novel first ride for the moment? God bless you from us both.

To Albert Erskine

Dollarton
August 12
[1952]

Dear old Albert:

Did you get the $100? Hope you are O.K.

Dark as the Grave—700 pages of notes and drafts—is deposited in the bank (it hadn't occurred to me till very recently that there *were* things called safety deposit boxes): *La Mordida* has been started on the long haul of typing. I didn't send you any of the former because in toto it is not in a fit state to read and it would take a lot of time to make "suitable selections." But if you wish me to take this time I will do so. In a moral sense the material belongs to you but in any case it is now safe.

I am having to rewrite—for the umpteenth time—the penultimate novella in *Hear Us,* due to the appalling difficulty of trying to render overlapping material consistent: the number of false restarts and hen tracks on the page I have made has me half dead with discouragement, I don't feel I've earned my hire for the last month despite a more or less sizzling (though still imperfect) "Pompeii," I feel lamentably out of touch with the contemporary world of fiction. England seems too busy going down the drain—or pretending it is—to answer any of my letters about my interests there, I often don't think I'm even a writer, and all in all I am suffering from the Desconsolado blues; but somehow the work *does* seem to be getting itself done, even without me, and perhaps even it. Love from us both,

Malcolm.

P.S. I've forgotten what I was going to say but it was something more cheerful. Am reading Flaubert's *Education Sentimentale,* just to keep up with the times—a book so marvellously boring it induces in one a kind of ecstasy.

1952

To David Markson

Bayview Apartment Hotel
1359 Davie St.
Vancouver, B.C.
[November 24, 1952]

Dear old Dave:

I am a bastardo for not writing. I am glad you are writing. That is more than I can do. So please write. We are living opposite a convent with stained glass windows. Nearby is a Catholic church within which it says: "*We want girl-power for our convent.*" A little further away is a haunted house, with tall chimneys, drawn blinds, a sagging stoop, and, mounting guard upon a high window sill, a stuffed decaying owl. What comes out of the chimneys? Smoke comes out of the chimneys. Alternate exercise for more advanced students: What else comes out of the chimneys? Nothing comes out of the chimneys. How can nothing come out of the chimneys? Because my uncle said that the postman saw nothing coming out of the chimneys. Has the postman been? The postman has not been. Why has not the postman been? In order for the postman to have been it is first necessary that the postman be. The windows (les fenêtres): the girl-power (batterie de fillettes): the haunted house (   ) the owl (l'hibou): the postman (der Brieftrager): Where is my uncle? My uncle is in the garden with his good strong stick. We send you our sincere love. So send us the same and a word. Writing goes hard. So I think to have sended an angel— or perhaps even a saint—after you to find out if you are not dead already.

All the very best from both of us and everything in Dollarton.

Malcolm

P.S. News from there is we were practically alone with marvellous weather since you left. Cabins on both sides of us are now for sale— including the one to the right on our old site. But the isolation gave us for once a slight case of the cafard so we've shifted to town earlier than last year (the two previous winters we took it out there) and are enjoying the change hugely.

P.S. A seagull has shat on the roof of the convent.

P.P.S. We visited a spiritualist church where we learned (from what seemed to be a genuine medium) that there are some spirits who live only 17 miles away up in the air. These spirits are borrachos, etc., and love to haunt pubs and bars. They are not, however, good spirits (though there are also good ones who like to drink) and drunks they will sometimes utterly possess so perhaps there is something in the Consul after all. All this was uttered by the medium in a kind of trance state and was presumably directed toward me. She went on to say in effect (the very sober audience seemed a bit taken aback by all this) that this was the only reasonable explanation why a drunk who has one drink in his hand, and another on the table, and who could not possibly drink another drink if he tried, nonetheless says: gimme another (i.e., he doesn't say it).

P.P.P.S. Another seagull has shat on the roof of the convent.

PART IX: *1953*

To Harold Matson

1359 Davie St.
Vancouver, B.C., Canada
January 8, 1953

Dear Hal:

Very happy to hear the news re "Strange Comfort." The revision I've done on this particular story is negligible as affecting it as a story per se, and pertains rather to its interdependent position within the volume, and I'm not sure I won't have to revise the revisions: minor points were that I was uncertain whether or not to turn him, the protagonist, into a Canadian—also that his name is Sigbjørn Wilderness, which is the same name as that of the hero of the whole bolus, though the Sigbjørn of "Strange Comfort" is not the same person as that hero. Tant pis! Unfortunately we don't have a copy of the story here in Vancouver, having left it on an island over Christmas with a fellow who wanted to make a tape recording of it, so I shan't have time to get hold of it and make any last-minute corrections if such be needed. But I think I'm only too delighted for the story to be published exactly as it stands, or rather as *New World Writing* has it (psychologically immoral though the story may be called) if Arabel Porter* feels the same. Only please ask her to be good enough to see to it since it must be (even though as I have said in another sense strictly it isn't): Sigbjørn Wilderness. (i.e. I am infatuated with the line through the O) and also for God's sake to look out for my possibly faulty Italian. Other small points: Gogol's last words—repeated several times—come from Nabokov's authoritative and wonderful book on Gogol, though acknowledgement is made to Nabokov *within* the text of the story and I hope this is sufficient for after all they are Gogol's words not Nabokov's (though one be indebted to Nabokov for them): if not, further acknowledgement could be made in a small footnote.

* Editor of *New World Writing*

As an afterthought, what I *do* regret not having put into "Strange Comfort," since part of the story is in Richmond, is:

Mem: consult Talking Horse Friday.

Yes, that really *ought* to be in and it's too bad I don't have any MSS to hand to suggest just where it should go: do you suppose Arabel Porter, if she agrees, would obligingly find a place for it?

Other work accomplished outside to date is huge and has been reported to Albert: i.e., thousands of pages mostly in first draft and notes, typed, and placed in a vault at the bank. This takes care of the whole thing to the end, however, with the exception of the short intermezzo *Eridanus* from which "October Ferry" (see below) has to be prevented from greedily gulping the material. It's no easy task but we's a-gettin' there, not too far behind schedule either. Work in progress is still last 4 novellas of *Hear Us*, and their interrelation: with a rewritten (and I hope terrific) *October Ferry to Gabriola* as the current and besetting problem that has engrossed and forestalled obsessed and delighted me for months and is still a problem child for it grew almost to a novel on its own and is still not quite subdued and cut to size, though I hope to have results soon. Mem: Consult Talking Horse. Health is good, hope you the same. Very happy New Year to you and Tommy and the children from us both.

Malcolm

P.S. Has "Bravest Boat" braved the Atlantic yet?

To Clarisse Francillon

1359 Davie St.
Vancouver, B.C., Canada
January 20, 1953

Dear Clarisse:

Hope you received our Christmas card O.K.?

I hate to importune you again, but I wonder if you could do me a favor, which shouldn't be much trouble for you and would be of absolutely ineffable help to me. I still haven't received the money you wrote me about over a year ago from Correa and the Book Club. My agent in New York is trying his best to collect it for me through a Mrs. W. A. Bradley (a French literary agent) whose address is 18 Quai de Bethune, Paris 4. They are now holding it up because apparently they cannot locate any contract between the Book Club and myself. To the best of my knowledge there never was any such contract, as I have repeatedly told them, and the only evidence I have regarding Correa is your letter to me, of February 23rd, 1950, in which you said that Correa was taking over and you will remember I replied to it at once agreeing to completely. Is there some way in which you, as the witness and go-between for all these deals, and being *there* (and not ten thousand miles away as I am) could do something about this? I would appreciate it more than I can say, for I'm working desperately against time to get my new book finished, these delays are driving me crazy, my estate in England is still held up, we are in debt, we live on one hard-boiled egg (bad) every three days, and I've been expecting this money every day for the last year, and having made commitments on that expectation (which I felt I had every right to do) I am now so harassed on every side I don't know which way to turn.

We're still hoping and looking forward to returning to France some time in the future, perhaps when my next book is finished. What is the news of your novel? How goes Mike? Should you see M. Nadeau, please thank him very much from me for his letter and say I'll reply as soon as I can.

A thousand thanks in advance, and all best love from Margerie and myself, and every good wish for a prosperous and happy new year.

Best love from
Malcolm

To Albert Erskine

[Dollarton, Spring, 1953]

Dear Albert:

Your letter arrived without hitch—many thanks, though it was some time before I could read it, so apprehensive was I, albeit Margie assured me it was hopeful and encouraging—as it was, heaven reward you—though be assured I appreciate all your difficulties and shall understand should things go awry. But I am praying they won't. Meantime *quam celerime* my feelings and prejudices—which I hope will dispel some doubts—in regard to fiction about writings and writers as such:

(a) Your feelings and prejudices are shared by me, almost un-qualifiedly, on the more general plane, as indeed probably by most other writers, though one occasion I feel that most other writers share them is that they have been taught since they began writing that all editors and producers have these same feelings and prejudices, so what's the use of writing about writers, etc. (even though they, the writers, somehow so persist in doing so in one disguise or another), when they would be rejected, etc.

(b) Against this I strongly believe, as I strongly believe is the case with dipsomania—"as dull as dipsomania," an impossible theme etc.: this sort of thing was said to me again and again well over a decade ago—that it has very rarely, if at all, been done properly. (It hasn't, despite Zola, Baudelaire, *Ten Nights in a Barroom*. That's why *The Lost Weekend* nearly slaughtered me.)

(c) But I don't believe the general public shares the prejudice, for there is an artist, a poet in every man, hence he is a creature easy for anyone to identify themselves with: and his struggles are likely to be universal, even on the lowest plane. Even kids, and our forgetful grocer and postmaster—perhaps especially our forgetful grocer and postmaster—can identify themselves with such: as can Jimmy Craige, the boat-builder, and Guldbrandsan the fisherman, etc. But this is by the way. My own prejudices and feelings remain on this plane no different in essence, let alone from your good self; but from those adumbrated by bloody old Bernard de Voto in his truly horrendous excellent little bits about Mark Twain and his malicious bits about Tom Wolfe.

But I note that even Bernard de Voto had to interpolate that he was "a good Joycean—he hoped"—and where on this line of his argument *The Portrait of the Artist as a Young Man* has always partly failed (while one recognizes its—ha ha—importance of course) for not dissimilar reasons to those that made Wolfe fail with de Voto.

(I have cut out what seems to me now a first-rate digression on Joyce at this point, in the interests of space.)

So I daresay I am even "left" of de Voto on the subject, and as a consequence even more prejudiced than yourself, and for most editors or writers against such writing, and on that point that does in the end perhaps begin to involve the whole of autobiographical fiction and much beside—particularly it would seem to depend upon the technique—moreover what if one should give a real turn of the screw to a subject that is so often treated half-heartedly? I think unquestionably what one is after is a new form, a new approach to reality itself; though I would submit I think those works that treat of the matter tragically or philosophically rather than romantically have suffered in acclaim for that reason. Chekov's *The Seagull* is a case—perhaps irrelevant—that comes to mind, and *Six Characters*.

Of course you can say these are single works, but in fact virtually the entire basis of Pirandello's work involves a not dissimilar theme (in this case that art, the theatre, is somehow realer than life). My reasoning may seem slightly cockeyed here or irrelevant again but I know what I mean. Nine out of ten people who saw *The Seagull* would scarcely remember that it is almost entirely about writing and writers or art in one way and the other—what they would take to heart is that a talent not put to proper use and divided can destroy its owner, and apply that melancholy truth to their own talent, whatever it might be. But I digress. The real protagonist of the *Voyage* is not so much a man or a writer as the unconscious—or man's unconscious—and at present it's a little difficult for me to see how I can swing what seems to me the superb irony of Wilderness living in Laruelle's house and the death of "Vigil" unless Wilderness has written, so to speak, the *Volcano*. Apart from this though, both *Dark as the Grave*, and *La Mordida*, especially the latter, should exist as powerful novels in themselves, if done aright, without obtrusive reference to writers or writing. There are emotional and sexual and alcoholic and even political dramas which overshadow these matters; albeit I would lose what seems to me one of the most potentially masterful scenes, i.e., when Wilderness has his novel accepted in Laruelle's house while technically under arrest, if Wilderness hasn't written the *Volc*. Even so Wilderness is not, in the ordinary sense in which one encounters novelists or the author in novels, a novelist. He simply doesn't know what he is. He is a sort of underground man. Also he is Ortega's fellow, making up his life as he goes along, and trying to find his vocation. In this regard some of the notes to the "Path to the Spring," though chaotic, may prove helpful re the treatment I propose. According to Ortega, the best image for man himself *is* a novelist, and it is in this way that I'd prefer you to look at him. He is not going to be the self-conscious author himself of so many novels, if that was what you rightly were afraid of, even though I have to make him responsible for the *Volc*. Moreover he is disinterested in literature, uncultured, incredibly unobservant, in many respects ignorant, without faith in himself, and lacking nearly all the qualities you normally associate with a novelist or a writer. As I've said he doesn't even think he's a novelist himself.

The *Volcano*—which "Laruelle" doesn't think much of at first—or rather *The Valley of the Shadow of Death*, appears less as a novel than as a sort of mighty if preposterous moral deed of some obscure sort, testifying to an underlying toughness of fibre or staying power in his character rather than to any particular aesthetic ability of the usual kind. His very methods of writing are absurd and he sees practically nothing at all, save through his wife's eyes, though he gradually comes to *see*. I believe this can make him a very original character, both human and pathetically inhuman at once. I much approve of him as a doppelgänger and am reluctant to turn him into a steeplejack, a cartoonist or a billiard maker, though he can be all these too, for all it matters. What does he know? What he suspects is that he's not a writer so much as being *written*—this is where the terror comes in. (It came in, just then.) His tragedy or his fable or whatever is less that of Faust than that of Aylmar, the water diviner—whose story should be told briefly somewhere or other: a character of the Middle Ages who, with his wand, was used by the French authorities to track down murderers; half fake, because his talent kept failing at embarrassing moments, wouldn't work at all under certain conditions, yet he had to pretend it *was* working; half genius, because he nearly always got his man—a sort of Aylmar, latter-day underground Aylmar, looking for himself or his soul. I'm damned if I don't think him an original fellow, not to be confused with the ordinary novelist, and I would have told you all this already, had *Hear Us* only gone to you and not Giroux. (Magic didn't seem to be working very well then, or maybe it'll turn out it was working overtime and was just a bit too subtle for once.)

Well that's Pat 30 for now and by the way it wasn't because you wrote Pat 30 that your first letter didn't arrive but because it was Pat 33 not Pat 30 at all.

I read some of *The Invisible Man* already in *Partisan* and thought it pretty extraordinary but don't talk to me about *The Invisible Man* until I've ceased a little more being The Superfluous Man.

Meantime: I need all the *coraggio* you can wish me. Am pretty scared, if still on deck. God bless from us both,

Malcolm

P.S. But one beautiful bit of Law of Series was that the day after I had written "you" as I thought, together with a *Hear Us O Lord* batch of MS, that I might find myself having to split off *Gabriola*, I received a letter forwarded by Reynal from one Malcolm Lowry, an engineer, of Kansas City, who said that his father had been President of Erskine University, South Carolina, that he had been congratulated frequently and erroneously on writing the *Volcano* but that he was interested in tracing the family history. This was followed by a letter from my brother in Liverpool who reported having met me and had a conversation with me in Bayswater, England, though I was in Dollarton, and also adding that the old family house, recently sold —though I have yet to receive my share or I would have paid you back ere now—was haunted.

I replied, since we were finding the wilderness tough just then, that it was probably the bathroom that was being haunted by me.

M.

To Albert Erskine

Castle of Udolpho
Sunrise
[*Dollarton, Summer, 1953*]

Dear brother:
Herewith an instalment. Rest will follow *quam celerime*. Instalment on debt I mean. But re work, health, all news good. We are going like a bat out of. Not to say just like a house on. Love from us both,

Malcolm

To Albert Erskine

[*Dollarton, Early Summer, 1953*]

Dear Albert:
Here is a bulletin. Margerie, on top of everything else, now has worms. At this point we decided to laugh, she being gallant enough to join in. We decided also to laugh about the house, repair what has to be repaired, accept what has to be accepted, enjoy what can be enjoyed while we still have it: and we do still have it. After all, one cannot tie oneself to the bed just because there is death in the world. And perhaps Robert Graves's attitude is the best one to

[333]

M

preserve toward such confections as the hydrogen bomb. And so the stiff—but not too stiff—upper lip, and a dose of Kipling's "If," though not too smug, each morning before breakfast, seems the watchword. But despite all this Margerie—not unnaturally!—cannot help feeling like "letting the potatoes rot in the fields," as she puts it: she can't type (and I can't either, at least not on her typewriter, and I can't take time off to learn) and she is temporarily more or less disengaged from the work, and in fact, although she is getting better, I should not even discuss this or anything else serious with her until she's improved. Naturally it's hard to obey this rule, and in any case the work has suffered. And so has she. And so, by God, have I. But that the work has suffered does not mean it's suffered to its detriment, at least so far as *Gabriola* is concerned. This damned thing—which is now, as I say, a short, perhaps even not so short novel—has cost me more pains than all the *Volcano* put together. And needless to say I am suffering agonies of conscience because it seems to have thrown me off schedule. Nonetheless I still have the hope it will fit into *Hear Us O Lord*. Having gone so far there is only one thing to do which is to finish it. Meantime the perilous chapel section obliged me to rewrite the "exposition." But by the time I had done that I realized that what was required was not one, but two expositions. In case you think (I do) that this is not obeying Robert Penn Warren's excellent rule of thinking straight through before one sets pen to paper I must find excuse in the originality of this notion. The first exposition, though objective, is nonetheless being *composed* in the protagonist's mind. A shock suddenly makes him see that he's lying to himself, merely "goofing" in fact, and a totally different consciousness arising in the same person works diabolically back through the same material, putting a completely different construction on it. I am hoping that the reader's sympathies, far from being disengaged or bewildered, will be intensified by this odd treatment which though I feel it artistically justified might certainly give many a psychologist pause, I fear. What crisis was the author himself passing through, he might ask, that would cause him so to deliberately hebephrenize his apparently objective data, and did he come through it successfully? The answer to this question I can only say must be found in *Gabriola* itself, which I more and more see as a challenge—though perhaps half humorously—to the author's actual personal salvation, which I had been a little forward in already assuming maybe. Hence the story's importance. We shall see. But I'd be glad of a comforting word. Some time last November

I began to be uneasy lest the whole work itself was in places not consonant with the best mental health and spiritual economy of its benighted author so I took some weeks off and read nothing but psychology. What I learned about myself was not very encouraging— but then at that rate and in those terms the *Volcano* was a sheer psychologic impossibility to begin with, so perhaps I can take heart after all, even though in those same terms, however, I may succeed. However perhaps miracles may be wrought with the pen even while actual catatonias seem to vampire the mind. One catatonic and besetting nightmare worry which has had me counterwhored from time to time even to the point of creating a psychic block in the work, even though I sat down a regular number of hours at the desk (one part of *Gabriola* moved so slowly that in the original you may see invocations to everyone from St. Jude, the Saint of the Impossible, to the spirit of William James, not to say God, to help me get on more swiftly, at the head of each page) was that I had made a mistake in trying to cope with *Hear Us O Lord* at all, and should have taken your advice and got right down to the novel, or *a* novel, instead of wasting my time on short stories that began to seem more and more inadequate the more I thought of them and which in any case had been originally written with the not unnatural hope of selling them; now I seem to have compromised on this advice with *Gabriola* but my fear now is it will make the whole damn thing too unwieldy. On the other hand if I can get some of the nonsense out of "Through the Panama" and perhaps the "Elephant" the *whole* thing does have a very beautiful form, and makes a very beautiful sound when taken together: and it is a form you can only see when you see the book as a whole. Then: but at my back I always hear Time's winged chariot changing gear. And now even while hearing it I am perhaps wasting more time with more worry. A veritable octopus has fastened its tentacles to our conscience at the thought we have not yet paid you back the money you so generously lent us and the procrastination on this promise seems to merge abysmally into the procrastination on *Gabriola* and the procrastination on the worms and the eviction— We evict those who destroy!—and God knows what else which maketh in the night watches an incantation to the mournful refrain, "We are letting Albert down." (Not that we are: but this is the dismal impression we fear you may have formed.) The procrastination, to be sure, has been nine tenths due to the even worse procrastinations of perfidious Albion, and unforeseen expenses due to illness, but it has also been due, in one unlucky instance, to perfidious

Malcolm who finding himself recently with sufficient specie to make matters good proceeded to invest some—unwisely, to put the kindest construction on the matter. . . . Not a word, as Mynheer Peeperkorn would say. Despite this, however, we are still pretty well in the black, so let us know if there is any immediate urgency. For actually our continued delay is only caused essentially by the fact that we still are not quite sure where we stand or how we shall have to act and this at least is not our fault: we have repeatedly tried to find out. My brother's letters do not answer many questions and are written in a style which I find difficult to understand. This means that for our protection I may have to approach the whole matter through a lawyer, as I have been strongly advised to do, though I am naturally very reluctant to do so. What a position for me of all people, the *mouton noir* and the youngest, if I should have to refuse power of attorney to the eldest one whom I have always regarded as more reliable than my own father, and what if I did? I can't manage my own estate from here. In fact I'm not legally empowered to manage it at all; and if I did, how could I do it without mortally wounding or embarrassing him? And, meantime, time has been bitterly consumed by meticulously having to answer or take up questions with the other trustees.

Then there is always the old hypocritical business—though this receptacle has acquired by comparison recently almost a distinct sheen —of the pot, or the ex-pot, calling the kettle black. And so it goes. . . . Another and very important factor is that we are still uncertain— though we should hear any day now—whether the Canadian Government are going to give me a fellowship on my second application, my optimism being reinforced on this point by the fact that it was they themselves who suggested—though they are aware that I am not actually a Canadian citizen—that I *make* a second application. The situation is a bit peculiar. Under the old dispensation, so I was told, I was automatically a Canadian, without for that reason having to forfeit my British passport, or lose my English citizenship. Now they have a sort of American Plan, whereby you do lose it, take out citizenship papers, swear a loyalty oath, etc., that would exclude my allegiance to England. Naturally I was not going to do this simply to qualify for the fellowship. And equally, though they want artists of my type to stay in Canada, which is partly the object of the fellowship itself, they can't very well let me think I'm being bribed as it were by a fellowship to *become* a citizen. Odder yet, though I could in good conscience swear allegiance to Canada itself (little Malcolm has supplied a national deficiency by writing them a national anthem

—not performed yet, though it will be, and very good too though I say it), British Columbia—which is the only place we want to live here—has a political set-up of a nature that does not encourage an Englishman, to say the least, to give up that old blue passport, that emblem of freedom. More properly, B.C. at the moment has no government at all, though both of them are totalitarian. This is the way George Orwell would put it. Or quasi-totalitarian. B.C.—though not me, I couldn't see anyone to vote for at all—actually voted in a Marxist government, if of a non-violent type, the C.C.F., but by some political legerdemain or other, an even more fantastic government— whose protagonists were not British Columbians at all but had sneaked down on well-oiled roller skates from Alberta—managed to capture the most important seats in the house and so became a minority government. This was Social Credit, and whatever may be said for that economic experiment in its ideal state, our premier hereupon gave as *his* ideal of government that of Venezuela! (a bloody-thirsty fascist set-up if ever there was one), whereupon the Social Crediters fell, after having made some demonstrations of power that were enough to make one's hair curl, if one saw them for what they might promise under other circumstances when they were not trying so hard to please. The C.C.F. (who are vowed to the destruction of capitalism but nevertheless had to make less than a polite promise to the Lieutenant Governor to do nothing too serious about it) now have taken up the slack, so to speak, are a sort of stop-gap govern-ment now, and soon there's to be another general election. Sure enough, it's comic-opera Marxism, comic-opera Fascism, so it seems: but Canadians can be tough and intolerant babies when they get going, they have an ominous predilection for the use of informers, the Mounted Police have a power and ubiquity that can be considered in anything but the romantic terms of *Rose Marie,* even if they are no doubt decent guys personally: all in all it seems to me British Columbia is a hell of a paradoxical place to ask any Englishman to give up his English passport in, with all that means, no matter how one might believe in or love Canada per se. It's almost a contradiction in terms; and so hence is my position on this score. . . . And so, come winter, if we can afford it, if England comes through, irrespective of whether we have the fellowship or the house or not we half con-template making a large move, if temporary and not irrevocable, where to—whether the Barbados or Sicily—we have no idea: all this is still in the realm of contemplation: I have been contemplating carrying on the work (how Hugh would like that) in a monastery in

Majorca. But before anything like this naturally debts must and will be paid and work delivered. My first deadline for you is November —and here again the position is complex and worrying and I can't do much more than cast myself upon your mercy and advice. If I succeed in getting the fellowship that will mean I can cease long before November taking your cash for a considerable while and so presumably that deadline could be extended. (The excellent thing about the fellowship is that though I'd have to live in a foreign country, France or Italy, I would be permitted to go on working on the work in progress for yourself, though I'd probably assist in the translation at the same time—and here again I would be able to live without taking your cash—but here too the hebephrene of the situation is without end. Well, let it not become hebephrenetic dilapidation, is all I can say. One thing at a time, Mr. Jorkens.

Perhaps the deadline does not need to be extended. For in one sense I—have I?—have already exceeded the terms of the contract by in an interim producing an unscheduled novel in *Gabriola*. But here is the rub. Does *Gabriola* make sufficient sense or lose too much without its symphonically adjacent companions? As things stand, *Gabriola* (I seem to have said this before) is—or will be—a novel. But so is "The Forest Path to the Spring" another short novel. *Gabriola* and "Forest Path" taken together make, as you will see, *another* kind of novel. "Ghostkeeper," "Pompeii," *Gabriola* and "Forest Path" make yet *another* kind of novel. *Hear Us O Lord*—with its 12 chapters—would be, if done aright, less a book of short stories than—God help us—yet *another* kind of novel: a kind of—often far less serious, often much more so—*Volcano* in reverse, with a triumphant ending, but ending (after "The Forest Path") in the same way, with the words Le Gusta Esta Jardín, etc. You will see the point of this in *Gabriola*. But what—terrible thought—if you don't *like Gabriola* etc. . . . . I don't want to palm off something second-rate on you simply to be able to say, "Well, you see, I've kept my promise." Or my promise, a part of it, only kept in another way. So far—with the triumphant exception of the typing and reordering of the entire material of the Mexican trilogy (much of it in its present form is far too intimate in nature to send even you, supposing it had been possible to do so)—I have willed one thing and the daemon has decided another, since I've been under contract to you. I can master booze, my bad temper, my self-deceit, and to some extent my other myriad bad habits, but I have not yet learned how to master that bugger. And if he was a good one it would be different. But he is slow, confused, paranoiac, gruesome of mind, as well as being completely inplacable, and he seems to have some vices unknown even to me. And in *Gabriola* he has turned out what set out to be an innocent and beautiful story of human longing into quite one of the most guilt-laden and in places quite Satanically horrendous documents it has ever been my unfortunate lot to read, let alone have to imagine I wrote. One saving grace is that it is in places incredibly funny, I think: but here again I have a feeling you don't altogether always approve of my humour, alack.

But to restate some of the themes at the beginning of this letter in more positive and hopeful form. *Gabriola* may not be the artistic triumph I sometimes think it is, but if I have any knowledge of the human psyche at all it is—or can be, for I haven't finished it even yet, even while I speak of it as *un fait accompli*—a psychological triumph of the first order. True you have not been paying me to achieve psychological triumphs of the first order, for my own benefit: but here the challenge seemed—and seems—ultimate, a matter of life or death, or rebirth, as it were, for its author, not to say sanity or otherwise: perhaps I overstate the case, but my love for this place and my fear of losing it, nay actual terror, has begun to exceed all bounds; moreover the tactile objective threat has been horrible for me beyond words—which is part of the point, alas: not Dante's personal spiritual position when he wrote the *Inferno* was worse, and I shall have no *Inferno* to show for it, only with luck a piece of prose which if it manages to live at all—and it just might—will no doubt do so for the wrong reason, and for a reason which might well condemn it as a work of art (Though it must be said you might have to go to Genêt or, as some French critics said recently—where they are calmly and enthusiastically translating *Lunar Caustic*, the first version, without permission—to Villon sui-même to find anything more extreme. So they say.): namely, the bloody agony of the writer writing it is so patently extreme that it creates a kind of power in itself that, together with the humour and what lyricism it may possess, takes your mind off the faults of the story itself, which, incidentally, are of every kind—in fact it possesses perhaps not one single conventional virtue of the normal story—its character drawing is virtually non-existent, symbols are pointed at blatantly instead of being concealed or subsumed in the material, or better still simply not there at all, it is—or is as it stands—repetitious to the point beyond that which you can believe. It's all done on purpose, and some readers—if they read it once—might have to read it 5 times before they could be convinced anything has happened at all. But I make it sound too interesting. I have to accept the possibility that you will consider it a total failure and my remarks prompted by self-delusion. The important thing though is that I should have written it—touch wood!—at all. For it represents—but you will see only too clearly what it represents. . . . And it does have some aesthetic virtues. It starts gently, so gently. . . . So the important thing, as it seems to me, is to rise every morning with the sun, have a swim, and making all allowances at this moment for the typist on the sick list, get down (as I am doing) to my desk and (I was going to say) write it *again*. Fortunately it won't be quite as bad as that—but so, anyhow, *get it sent to you.* Otherwise I might as well shut up shop, pay Random House back what you have already paid me, which I should be well able to do if things go only half right—right!—admit complete defeat, abandon writing altogether, and in order to save my by then unsalvageable soul, enter Gurjiev's nursing home in company with the beneficent ghost (perhaps) of Katharine Mansfield. Which would mean admitting that the office boy was right too—a bitter pill indeed. In short, if I don't finish this—and that right *now,* and in these exact and excruciating circumstances of being on the one hand damned Ahab-wise in the midst of Paradise and on the other still mysteriously given the grace to live there even if it is only the privilege of great guilt to which is added, by the way, the privilege itself—such grace has fallen on us now the Powers that Are (as the French used to say) seem to have decided this part of the beach is under a special providence or haunted, probably by me, so we are the sole inhabitants, the bulldozers crash everywhere else, I can look a mile on either side and see only uninhabited houses, they having evicted themselves out of unnecessary terror or horror at what their lives would be like without this, but they take it, since that, what they say, is to exist—while I don't. *Tant pis.* The story was to tell you and I did.

Malcolm

To Albert Erskine

[1953]

Dear old Albert:
News of the rich and strange. Dispatch of first instalment of *Gabriola* was inhibited as follows: just as it was about to be dispatched

two things happened almost simultaneously (as in XI–XII of the *Volc*)—I fell foul in the dust in the forest of a children's cops and robbers and Indians' snare, a deliberately upraised root (not deliberately upraised to catch me, of course, but stretched as to create a murderous stirring I saw too late) and shattered all the bones in my ankle, as well as dislocating the joint of the same organ, and fracturing both bones in my right leg (this in almost the exact spot in the local *bosca oscure* where imaginatively, not being in Mexico at that time, Yvonne was killed by the horse, as we plotted it out then): Margerie, upon going to the store to ring for an ambulance, was suddenly sprung upon by a "beast" (as she describes it) half husky and half wolf, who went for her throat, horribly tore her thigh and leg (which still after 10 days is exuding pus), [and] was finally choked off by a bystander. She returned half crazy with fright and pain and dripping with blood and Grand Guignol, and when I went to the hospital finally, she having come along in the ambulance, was ordered by the medicos to stay there hospitalized too; her life was in balance (or seemed so) a couple of days, meantime my injuries were so complicated they were afraid to give me a general anaesthetic to set the leg, or a spinal one because I had formerly broken my spine: finally they risked the latter (the spinal fracture—only a percussive one—had been between the fourth and fifth vertebrae) and from that point on luck was magnificently with us, even though at one point, formerly unable because of a hospital ruling even to see Margerie or know how she was getting on, I was in such general anguish (equally over the undelivered work) and pain that apparently I *ate* the goddamned thermometer in rebellion. That is to say that under sedation I apparently angrily bit it in half: however I evacuated it all two days later, or most of it: temperature unknown. Maybe Mercury stays with me. So now we are back, I having meantime forgotten everything I wrote during the previous months. It comes to comfort one a good deal, however, for it is some of the more powerful and original stuff in its way I've read in a long time. I must say that I have disciplined myself like an ascetic (approx. 15 hours a day up till the mishap and thoroughly enjoying it. Accident was only a fortnight ago next Sunday, so considering the relative seriousness of M's injuries one hasn't lost too much time. The Spartan medium is this newly developed "walking cast" I mention—hell on the patient but undeniably an innovation. In former days one would have lost months), allowed myself no drinks (whatever that matters!) not even a beer. So that's something. I have to finish the flaming bloody thing in considerable pain though, which is something else. My leg is in a cast, the weather wonderful and hot, and I can't swim (or the cast would melt). That's about all, brother. Horrible: but also damned lucky. Margie is well, and myself a pegging Ahab (they thought they'd have to take off the leg too but it's still here)—nothing has been wasted, not even the experience in the ward (continuous Grand Guignol that fitted in beautifully, and I had the sense to keep my pencil to paper too)—you will get the first instalment, though, or it will be dispatched, rather, end of this week or beginning of next instead. (I perhaps should not say that when the accident happened to me I was trying also to do two things at once for an aficionado of the *Volcano*—a well-known Canadian architect—who had visited us: a) explain the symbology of the "Fog" throughout, and b) show him the locale of Yvonne's imagined death.) This is about all brother for the moment. Accidents to me might seem psychologically suspect: but how explain the dog? And the good luck? Please forgive bad writing which is due to exigencies of leg: cast is a "walking cast" I have to wear ten weeks, dying each night in bed with my boots on so to say. It's all right quite often save that one's toes get red hot. Apart from this our health and spirits are good. Today am working in bed. Well: through those weeds! Over those falls!* Love from both,

Malcolm

To Albert Erskine

[*Summer, 1953*]

Dear brother:

I'm sorry you still have no instalment but I reckoned without certain difficulties of adjustment, on top of which Margie, with her hands full with me, has little time to type recently, while I at about page 12 went and had another inspiration, a lengthy insert which in any case would have held up matters slightly, even though on the further bank there is a more or less lengthy stretch of pretty final draft. The cast (no reference to the play I haven't written yet) got loose too (as I think I intimated in my other letter) and I had to make a trip to the hospital the Friday after I wrote you to have a new one put on. (I thought I'd greet some of my old pals in the ward, only to discover ¾ of them were dead.) The new cast having been put on I was then instructed (there being no room for me in the

* The Lowrys had seen the film, *The African Queen*.

hospital to stay overnight) I'd have to make the return trip on crutches without putting my injured foot to the ground because the cast was still wet. Such a return trip through the forest to our house is physically impossible, but it being equally impossible to explain to anyone how we lived we had to make it anyhow. I would still be making it but for Margie herself, of course, and a shining Christian deed rare in my experience which emphasizes how all ex-Consuls in the Lowry psyche should behave in future toward their fellow man and I hope will. A bloke had spotted my—our—plight from the road, stopped his car, and followed us into the forest. I—and we— were going well at that stage, had renewed optimism and declined further help beyond the steep hill I was going down, but the bloke insisted, saying that it indeed was, as we had earlier thought it was, quite impossible, even with one person's assistance; he knew, because he'd been in a similar predicament himself, he said—the ground is in places too spongy to take crutches, which simply sink in, and there was worse to follow. True I had made the frightening trip up the hill through the forest earlier in the morning on the loosened cast but then I had a stick and moreover could walk after a fashion *on* the cast, it had not been so bad and there was no pain to speak of, *now* the pain and strain was so God-awful the sweat was pouring off one in cascades and one had to stop every ten feet or so.

"Well," I said. "This is really damned noble of you, sir. . . . Our name's Lowry." "And mine Budd, William Budd. Just call me Billy. You haven't heard of Billy Budd?"

We said yes and Moby Dick too, but since he evidently did not understand us did not pursue the subject. The worst part was not the forest, but just before reaching the house, which, because of a cave-in in the forest bank, now has to be approached by a plank running five feet or so above the beach and about ten feet long. Well, not even Billy Budd could walk the plank on crutches, I reflected! I had to make this last part of the journey, to the great danger of the others, on my seat, and I was so demoralized finally it took me a week to recover, during which period it seemed to me from the pain that the leg was getting worse, not better, while the new cast didn't seem any firmer than the old. However, I'm glad to say that now the pain is very much less and I seem definitely on the mend. The only bad factor has been that if the accident—as some unsympathetic psychiatrist might aver—was a form of device on the part of my psyche to produce a situation in which I would be physically incapable of doing any difficult chores at all—or even to sit in the sun (which I can't else the damned cast might melt)—and so give me that much more time to work, it wasn't a very successful device. I had had so far extreme difficulty in working for more than 20 minutes at a stretch, after which I have to rest for about an equal period: moreover it's disrupted my methods of work to some extent; I'm used to working on several drafts at once, which involves much standing up and walking around, and that I'm not physically up to. What would have become of us in this situation for all Margie's stoicism (not to mention my masochism) without our neighbor, the Manx boat-builder, Quaggan of the "Path to the Spring," I don't like to think either: but somehow it all is working out—but I'm very sorry indeed for the delay. For the rest I'm glad to say that despite dog bites and all (which I didn't tell you produced in Margie for some reason the exact symptoms of angina pectoris) Margerie is definitely very much better in health and getting better all the while so that all in all I feel pretty optimistic about everything apart from the original plan of *Hear Us O Lord* in regard to which I'm going to need some advice from your good self.

Everything very much better since this was written! Through those falls! Over those weeds!

Love,
Malcolm

To Mr. and Mrs. William McConnell*

[Dollarton, Autumn, 1953]

Dear Bill and Alice:

I'm terribly sorry we haven't got in touch, but I broke myself a piece of leg and dislocated an ankle and broke that too, while Margie got simultaneously chewed up by a dog (one might think one was accident-prone from this but in fact it was too much of an accident for that, though it certainly left one prone all right), so all in all we've had a bit of misery-grisery this summer, as the Sultan of Zanzibar remarks in this week's *New Yorker*. However I've practically written another novel in the meantime. Hope you are working well and successfully. Your returned books arrived naked of word: I hope not an implied rebuke. Above is the reason for our silence, pure misery-grisery. But we are quite recovered and in fine form now. We are thinking to move for a month or so into town soon and get around

* Vancouver friends. Mr. McConnell was the Lowrys' legal adviser.

a bit and hope to see you then. I hate to return *The Seven Pillars of Wisdom* but I've kept it too long already, Alice. It's wholly marvellous and makes most prose look silly. I read the Darwin with fascination too, just to keep up with the times. We'll give you our address in town when we know it for sure and know it's a good one. Our last one in town turned out less a place to invite a friend than ambush your worst enemy and even that's an understatement: misery-grisery.

Blessings on your heads and not forgetting the boy's from us both,

Malcolm

To Albert Erskine

Castle of Otranto, Hallowe'en [1953]
Clocks striking midnight
Enter Gower ghosts and others
Tucket within and a flourish of strumpets
Enter Ariel and Caliban singing in unison:
Ah gotta shake a wicked tail to get to
Liverpool

Dear brother,
Yippee!
—Or maybe that's an inappropriate remark to make when we're already running shamelessly overdue, but maybe not so much. All's a-taunto save that we have our starboard engine snaggled in a wisdom tooth, the chief engineer has an ulcerated throat, and the ship itself is running on sulfanilamide. So the main trouble is still typing; there's more completed than this too, and of course beyond, but there's a snag on the next page (the more so since it is a "snag" literally), so thought this was a good place to break off, as for being sent round Hallowe'en and to arrive over All Souls, with the other batch to follow the beginning of next week. After which there's still another 50 pages or so to go till I reach my old final draft, which will need some overhauling too when—touch wood—I overhaul it; perhaps you better reserve your judgement in the meanwhile, but I can tell you this, the book gets much better as it goes along—brother you just wait till that old tide starts a'coming in, a'roarin' and a'growlin' and it does too, a bit: in the next batch, and then what rugs and jugs and candlelights; and corpses and last judgements and perilous chapels; I

suppose I ought to tell you for your peace of mind that I *do* get my bloody hapless characters off the bus eventually and *on* to the ferry. That is to say, though the temptation may be great, I do not avail myself of the priceless opportunity, no doubt offered by the progress in the meantime since I began the book, of taking the bus *on the ferry itself*, where, thus still seated in the dimensions of one element and floated off on the bosom of another—that's not quite what I mean but still, let it pass—they may reach that destination, without having once set their foot on land, or in fact wake up again, or the reader either, or the author come down to terra firma. You will be wondering at the length of this first chapter too—if it is a first chapter and which, if so, threatens to be the longest on record, so I will expound thus far the magic of Dr. Lowry's dialectical-Hegelian-spiritualism-Cabbalistic-Swedenborgian-conservative-Christian-anarchism for ailing paranoiacs: the first chapter (whether visibly such or not) is as the base to a triangle or a triad (and/or a radical having a valence of three): viz

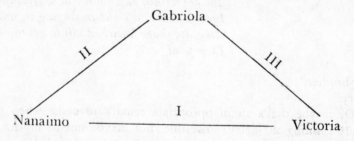

As you observe, in this configuration it is difficult for Chapter III not to seem to be going back to its starting point—or both ways at once—and in fact where does III start? And how is it solved? H'm; something that must have puzzled mightier minds than mine—but no more. On with the work; over those falls! through those weeds! Love from us both,

Malcolm

P.S. Which is meant to illustrate no more than that Chapter I might be 180 pages long, Chapters II and III each half that length, without its form being overbalanced—to the contrary. Anyhow I'm having a bloody good time writing it and—if you're having an anxious one reading it—which is more than I could say a year ago, when every page was covered with invocations to St. Jude the Saint of the Impossible, and once it took me 3 months to produce as many readable pages, and even so some of the writing seems slack or matey in places or redundant (though sometimes later it is meant to appear redundant on purpose—as to give the effect of the man *caught*, washed to and fro in the tides of his mind, unable to escape) and can stand tightening.

P.P.S. Just received at this moment your very reassuring letter for which many thanks and contents duly noted (and thank you very much). I think it's better for me to behave as if I were overdue, though. It gives the fireman something to think about. I think this letter anticipates some of your anxieties too. Perhaps if I were to tilt the triangle on its side it would be more helpful? Especially if you got out your atlas?

To Albert Erskine

Dollarton
November 24, 1953

                    Part IV
46. when a black storm came drifting round the point.
      "   "   "   "   crept round the point.
His ship had been lying peacefully out in Yokohama roadstead, when a storm exploded over the harbour.
His ship had been lying peacefully out in Yokohama harbour when a black storm exploded round the point.
His ship was lying ditto. Problem of suddenly.
47. There was a collision of thunderclaps, and a gigantic discharge of lightning in the brilliance of which a Japanese fishing boat they'd been watching puttering in for some time, (amused, because it was strangely equipped with a motor-horn it tooted proudly at intervals)
(I'd like to get this note, though more briefly—it adds pathos: besides it's true.)
the lightning blazed a little longer
                                        Oh to hell with it.

Dear old Albert:
    Bear with me. Am reading a book. But am also working night and day on two short novels, one, comic, above, about an elephant, hope may form basis (elephant is part V)—well, form basis anyway of coming on your wing again. Am very disappointed no go by you with Margie's book. Passion comes from such deep source—makes interest-

ing corollary to Myrer's—however see complicated point. If you truly like it personally though, if you see collateral way, give it helping voice. I myself love it: all she needs is some encouragement to do big things. Hope someone will see it.

I also love Myrer's book in many respects so far, though stylistically often Joyced in own petard. So my reaction is divided a bit between what I feel you ought to say to *him,* and conviction it deserves wide audience (not much doubt—perhaps all too little—it will get that)— but make no mistake it *does* deserve sincere salutations. Indeed it makes me feel like Father Mapple. And it has sent me on several long swims already. Will try and come back with some clams—if not giant ones. (Though there is no reason he shouldn't receive giant ones.) Other financial clams seem still covered with Iranian oil. But I have just seen 7 mergansers outside window. Our favorite birds of good omen. So bear with me yet. God bless and both our loves to Peggy and thanks for reading *Malatesta* promptly too despite sad result.

Love,
Malcolm von Steppenwolf

To David Markson

[*Postmarked Vancouver, 1953*]
Castle of Otranto
Tuesday November Moonlight
Wind Thunder Enter Gower and others.

Dear old Dave:

Started this a week ago but have had one interruption after another, being both in the throes of a temporary move (our new stop-gap-roast-beef-of-old-England-cum-Jacobite address: The Caroline Court, 1058 Nelson St. But maybe we'll enjoy it, have a bath anyway, other than in the inlet, getting a trifle chilly at this time of year perhaps though I've had a few fine swims lately) and trying like hell to finish *October Ferry to Gabriola*. I'm very grieved to hear old Dylan's under the weather,* if you see him give him our love and best wishes for a speedy recovery. (You mention he is in hospital with a *"brail"* ailment. Without conceding this to be a matter of humour exactly or necessarily any way you look at it may I ask if you intimate an

* Dylan Thomas—who was already in his fatal coma; of course, the Lowrys were not aware of this.

ailment as of one slightly blind or that the old boy has actually got
stranded in some Rolando's fissure or island of Reil? Anyway I
wouldn't trade his brain or braille for most poets, drunk sober blind
alive or dead, or all five simultaneously, as is more likely: one imagines W.S. at moments not without his limbos and brails also—and
you couldn't attribute that precisely to society either for he made
pots of money. *Es verdad.*) As for ourselves, we are very well, though
Margie hasn't understandably reacquired any great love of dogs or
myself of children playing Indians. I'm pretty lucky to be about
again, for I smashed all available bones in the right leg and ankle
and dislocated the ankle on top of that with the foot pushed right
out of line—basta. But I ran in one cwt of coal from the store today; do everything more or less normally with it, including swimming (and occasional, as I think, writing) though the damned limb
will be a bit weak for a couple of years; though I don't advise the
experience on the whole, nothing in it. At any rate we still *got* it:
touch wood, or rather the ivory of the revered gent from Nantucket,
so we ought to be all right awhile, unless one of Margie's dogs bites
it off, or I bite it off myself, all for the fun of having to chase myself
to the Marquesas with a harpoon. Nothing else of note: save when
half through the first attempt at this letter, Margie being in town
and myself alone on the beach, on observing what appeared to be
flames issuing round the point—well, brother, I hightailed it thither
anyhow, fire-extinguisher in hand (and not forgetting the notebook
in pocket): it wasn't a house, as I thought, but a ship, already burning down to the waterline, and which had been beached thoughtfully
under the trees where a land fire-brigade (the fireboat from Vancouver
having refused to come) had already failed to save it: when I say
ship, it was a fishing boat, but with a great deal of top hamper, alas
all came crashing fierily down, and in fact it was a sad sight, as you
can imagine, just before darkness, with the wind driving clouds over
the mountains, and the mast-head lights of its companion fishing
boats going on one by one like mourning candles, and the ferry
passing "silent as Charon's boat" though nobody we knew—which
reminds me that the boat of happy Port Moody memory (before I
forget, Port Moody was the terminus of the C.P.R. before Vancouver
was built) has to be brought up on to the platform tomorrow at high
tide—she is banging away merrily down there, but it's too much of
a good thing in the winter: said craft sends the best of love as do
Margie and myself, not to mention the house, which is leaking, as is
the boat for that matter.

Malcolm

I wrote this Tuesday night—yesterday—did not find out till just now, Wednesday, to our great grief, Dylan is dead. Sad news was brought by a Canadian writer who has settled transiently some doors away and we drank his health and poured a libation of gin to his memory on the platform and for some reason cut down a tree, likewise dead and an old friend, but which has long since seemed asking us to pluck up the courage to cut it down, rather than let it fall down, since the only way it could fall was through our roof. There is no symbolic significance attached to the tree: unless one had felt as a reaction to the black news one had to do something exhilarating lifegiving painful deathdealing dangerous and useful all at once. Selah. I see no point in changing the letter to you, though we sense how you must feel his loss hardly on the spot and sympathize deeply. God damn it all, what a misery-grisery it all is sometimes, as the Sultan of Zanzibar says in this week's *New Yorker*. (About five minutes after that bad news to descend from the immortal to the unusual, we get our first good news in years: Philip Rahv of *Partisan Review* takes "Bravest Boat"; Dirty Degenerate Bobs anthologized in Italy, etc. etc.)

P.S. No I haven't read *Augie March*. And I'd be very grateful if you'd send me a list of books, poets, mags, authors, to read—of what you conceive worth reading during the last years—some time when you have a mind to, for we're both falling badly out of touch, all too easy in these parts, and quite apart from anything else, as Gandhi once observed, "I see no virtue in being ill-informed."

P.P.S. Received your last and very good letter just as we were moving to town, taking this letter with me—but by mistake (or as a protective talisman) leaving yours behind on the table of the shack together with your address, of which (since I'd got used to the old one) I'm not absolutely sure. Margie is going out over the week-end to collect some things and your letter so, damn it, this must wait till then.

P.P.P.S. Margie just came back from the shack, bearing your last note, for which thanks, but not your other letter, which *still* remains there as a talisman. Your last note hasn't your home address on it, so I'm sending this to the Printing and Litho.

T X: *1954*

To Albert Erskine

1058 Nelson St.
Vancouver, B.C., Canada
January 4, 1954

Dear Albert:

I have received a letter from the Westminster Bank, dated 23rd December, saying in part:

"The Bank and Mr. O. S. Lowry have now been appointed Trustees of your settled share of your father's residuary estate but unfortunately the transfer of the investment certificates into the names of the new Trustees has not yet been completed. The Trust Solicitors hope to be in a position to send all documents during the next few weeks. In the meantime we have asked them to make you a further payment out of income held by the previous Trustees and they will remit you the sum of £500 within the next few days. As soon as the investments and remaining cash have been handed over to us, we will make you a further payment of income on hand."

So far the £500 has not arrived, but the news seems straight from the horse's mouth this time, and undoubtedly the money has been just held up over the holidays. I have been expecting this news for some time and it would have saved me a lot of worry if it had come before: the delay was caused in part because my mother died intestate: and there have been so many changes in the trusteeship. And of course there has been England's policy of making everything as difficult as possible for the ex-landed gentry—not unpoetic justice, on paper, so long as the cash doesn't happen to be one's own.

However it appears that I am in a position to propose what I have long planned under the circumstances: to make some guarantee of good faith by "buying some time," I mean by voluntarily requesting that your monthly payments to me be suspended for a period of time, while I go on working on my own hook, and I believe there is a clause in the contract something to that effect.

Last year, what with getting out of debt and the unforeseen expense of "neck and leg break" (as Christopher Isherwood somewhere calls it) what money I did get from England was not sufficient to allow me to make this proposal, and my other auxiliary efforts, such as the Canadian fellowship which would have left me free to work, came to naught.

This year it looks as though I shall be able to carry on, though *how* long I could carry on without anxiety depends on the last sentence I quoted from the Bank's letter. At any rate I propose that you suspend payments to me from next month until at least you've received delivery of *October Ferry,* and some more practical earnest of what shape the work that follows will take.

For one thing any estimate of *Ferry* made on the basis of what you have received may be unfair to the work itself, whose form is of necessity bizarre, and goes on getting more so for a while; moreover I may have got one chunk—the next you will receive—in the wrong place, moreover there'll naturally be some editing necessary when it is completed. Anyway such a proposal as this will at least have the virtue of putting me on my mettle not to break another leg, at least until *this* work is in. I hope I haven't meantime put you in the unpleasant position of having had to write me yourself that this, or something even more stern, is what has already been regrettably—or even regretfully—decided by Random House, with the result that these letters cross.

All the very best from us both,

Malcolm

To Albert Erskine

#73 The Caroline Court
1058 Nelson St.
Vancouver, B.C., Canada
January 4, 1954

Personal P.S. for Albert

Dear Albert:
    Enclosed speaks for itself; is pursuant on the other, that I hadn't perhaps kept *im*personal enough.

or:

TEN FIFTY EIGHT *MAY* ARRIVE
    ON THE DATE
BUT FIFTEEN O' EIGHT WILL
    ALWAYS BE LATE

[354]

1954

Meantime I'm just hoping to God all this hasn't embarrassed you too much. By ill chance—see poetical explanation opposite—your personal letter didn't arrive here till today, January 4. You read-

LAND ON NOBODY'S PLATE
SAVE ITS SENDERS WHO WAIT
—OH INDIRECTORATE
WITH A HAND ON'T LIKE FATE!
—OR SOME BARTLEBY FATE
FOR PO' FIFTEEN O' EIGHT!

dressed it also *1508*—but with sage afterthought also The Caroline Court. (Technically The Caroline Court, Nelson Street, ought to do it without any number or vice versa, but not *1508* by itself which is an unfortunate combination that doesn't exist in Nelson St., else might have found me.)

Perhaps all the work on *Dark as the Grave, Mordida,* etc. was worth mentioning: there's at least 2000 pages more of stuff, Margie estimates, reposing now in the Bank Vault, done contemporaneously, impossible to send as it is, but it was impossible to proceed before it was at least as safe as that. I'll have more to say on *Gabriola* later: and more to send. Meantime I'm more concerned, as I say, that your kind concern for me may have embarrassed you.

So this in haste. All the very best love from us both,

Malcolm

To Harold Matson

The Caroline Court
1058 Nelson St.
Vancouver, B.C., Canada
January 25, 1954

Dear Hal:

This is in reply to yours of Jan. 11, though I had already begun a letter to you re Random etc. Yes, thank you, we received the January instalment.

The situation as it has arisen with Random House is a complex one which has been brewing for several months and about whose possible onset I had, in fact, repeatedly written Albert. In the light of what has happened I would have finished my letter to you but that I was awaiting a reply before doing so from Albert to an important official letter I wrote him on *Jan. 4th:* moreover I was too deep in work to write any more letters if I could avoid it. There has been no reply, and there being no evidence in your letter that Albert has explained my side of the question to you (I don't mean this in any derogatory sense to him) I'm put in the ungrateful position of having to explain it myself. Since it seems to me I am more in the right than the wrong, and even the object of some injustice, while my gratitude to Albert remains great and we are of course friends, I'd therefore be obliged if you'd keep this confidential—I mean as between Albert and yourself—the only thing not confidential presumably being my official letter of Jan. 4, which I'm including a copy of. You may wonder why I hadn't written you before, as normally speaking I should have, as I said, but now, in any case, I owe it to you, and myself, to give you all the facts and factors, but I want it understood that I do so with no implied disloyalty to Albert. Now I'll be as brief as possible.

I'd intended to complete the collection of short stories and novellas, *Hear Us O Lord,* as the first book, and for this to be delivered, being conscious of my obligation, on Nov. 1. However, when working on the penultimate story I found, as I told you, the material developing and growing and presently I realized I had a full-dress novel on my hands which I was so deeply involved with by that time it would have been fatal to stop. Moreover, this together with the last three novellas, more or less completed, made yet another sort of novel, and in *Hear Us* itself, the stories therein began to take on an interrelated form as a work of art it had not possessed before: and some of these pieces might be publishable by themselves, particularly *Gabriola.* Albert seemed pretty tepid about the stories and I gained the impression, or formed it, it might be better to kick off with a new and finished novel, whether this later would form part of the collection or not. Moreover in this way I saw myself eventually considerably exceeding the terms of the contract. (Meanwhile it is important to remember that I never, consciously, gave either you or Albert the impression—and I think my former letters bear me out in this— that sooner or later I might not choose to go on by myself for a while, without the payments, to gain time, and without the clause which gives me that right I never could have honorably signed the contract, especially after the discouraging experience with Brace. And to this end I have kept hammering away at my English bank to hurry the settlement of the estate and send me the money owing me.)

Meanwhile *Gabriola* continued to develop and grow more serious, and about this time I (we, for Margie was bitten by a dog the same day and was in hospital with me) had my cursed accident. Despite a broken and dislocated leg and ankle I tried to keep on working after the interim in the hospital, as I had even in hospital, but I'd lost the feel of the work, it was a ghastly and painful summer and altogether I'd say this set me back at least 3 months, looking back on it now, and whatever I may have said or felt at the time. You'll remember when signing the contract we suggested there should be some provision in case of serious accident or illness, and you and Albert decided this should be left up to the understanding or whatever of the publishers. I think I ought to point out that no one seems to have taken any account either of this time lost, or that I did not invoke any such unwritten contractual provision, though my accident could scarcely have been more serious, especially coming at that time, and one reason I didn't invoke it was that one's own anticipation of such a thing had seemed too much like clairvoyance, the accident itself too diabolically pat, psychologically suspect to another, though there was really no damn psychology about it, as I should know! However I had and have no intention of using this as an alibi. I merely state I don't find it sporting it should be entirely overlooked when there arose a question of the deadline.

During the summer I wrote Albert two or three letters re the general situation, not losing sight of the Nov. date, and received no reply. (He was away and the letters weren't forwarded.) This was discouraging, but on emergence into convalescence I may have grown too optimistic again (this time to yourselves) about my chances of getting it in on the dot. By the end of September, realising now it might not be possible to have it ready in final and negotiable form, I wrote Albert again and received a reassuring reply not to worry. Finally, in October I think, after I'd delivered an instalment of over 100 pages, Albert wrote saying he'd thought the November date was merely a date I'd set myself, but had looked up my contract and discovered that Nov. 1 was there all right, but that there was a three months' grace period, and *they could not "call me" before February 1.* I felt confident that by February 1, I could have enough in that would put their eye out, even if it were not quite finished.

However, and this is important, having been in touch with my English bank, I felt I would be in a position by February 1 to buy some time—a supposition in which I've proved right, as you'll see— and my intention all along was to show my good faith by buying some time *anyway,* even if *Gabriola* was finished. Had Albert's letter been urgent re the deadline, I should have taken a chance and asked you to call the changes there and then and stop payments, and would have done so anyhow before that, had not the accident taken most of my ready cash.

I hope this makes it clear that I have been extremely conscious of my obligation to Albert, Random, and yourself.

Just before Christmas I received an official letter from Albert written a week before that, saying that the Keeper of the Contracts had questioned him, and that the material in hand seemed to need more buttressing if they were going to extend the payments beyond February 1, the killing tone of which letter made us want to fall out of the window rather than take anything off the Christmas tree. I immediately replied, outlining the novel and saying I expected to have another 140 pages in by February 1. The personal letter (which of course mollified matters somewhat) further qualifying the situation Albert had sent to the wrong address, was returned to him, sent back to me, and didn't reach us till after the first of January. A stroke of evil luck, and we may have been to blame for putting the wrong number on the envelope.

By this time I'd heard from my bank, promising me some money in a few days. I therefore, on *January 4,* wrote Albert another official letter, with a covering personal one, voluntarily suggesting that they suspend payments at least until I'd finished *Gabriola* and they could see better what I was doing. This letter I enclose. Personally I have a high regard for the work sent in, as I do for *Gabriola* as a publishable entity, but I felt it extremely unfair *Gabriola* be judged on those 159 pages Albert had, and a hundred times unfairer that all the work be judged by it. More of this later.

The immediate point is, Albert must have received this letter by the 6th of January. But now, on the 8th of January I received another official letter, with a covering personal one, saying *they* had decided to suspend payments, and of a chilliness beyond all chilliness. It appeared I had not only laid a Great Auk's Egg, but where, even, was the Egg? Your letter is dated January 11, and I do not understand why Albert has not informed you of having received my letter, written two days *before* theirs, asking them to stop payments, for it makes a serious difference. The reason why I didn't inform you myself I hope you'll now understand. It was all sprung on me at once. Having completely accepted Albert's former reassurance I thought, even after the first official letter, I had until *February 1.* I thought too, even now, my own request to buy time would be well *in time:* as it turns out I was mistaken, but too late as it was. I hope you'll understand all this.

Naturally it is distressing, as well as psychologically mortifying, not that payments should be suspended a while—for that is no more than I have consistently, even wishfully anticipated, could I carry on without—but that it should be done in such a fashion that it carries the direct implication of irresponsibility in this regard on my part, when the fact is I have been writing Albert about it since last summer and even before that. Against this is the fact that Albert has been motivated, amid many troubles of his own, by great kindness and understanding in trying to mitigate just such worry; once having helped so generously to get the boat launched, he didn't want to rock it.

Without losing sight of this for a moment, or that I am sure he thought he was acting in my best interests, all I can say is that in this instance he didn't think *enough* and I shall say this to him. For though I speak only of the embarrassment to him in the letter enclosed, should what has happened happen, what about the worse embarrassment to me? There was plenty of time in the interim to have given me an opportunity to do it myself, which was precisely what I did do, the first moment the final urgency of the situation became clear. Which leaves me with the feeling that they weren't even acquainted with my willingness to do it, if necessary and possible, otherwise what point was there in making it appear something like a punishment, as well as an impugning of the work in question? I don't see that it's even good business. For how the hell did they suppose I was going to finish it at all, since they didn't know I would have the money to carry on? Perhaps they thought discouragement of this kind, all of a sudden, would give them a better opportunity of getting their money back. For bear in mind that, after Albert's letter relieving me of the tension of the November 1 deadline, up to the time of his letter received roundabout Christmas Eve, it was our impression gained from that letter there was nothing in the contract that obliged me to have sent in a goddam page until the deadline, which was (now) February 1. Who knows what I couldn't have finished by then hadn't this happened? One consequence has been I've had to write so many worrying and complex letters that the section that was actually finished before the New Year is only reaching its final typing now. And then on top of this to be *judged* by what I'd already sent in, which so far as I knew I didn't have to send in at all!

Perhaps I could have laughed this off but on top of this to receive no reply whatever to the letter cutting myself off seems a little too much. For I think morally this is where the situation should stand and I repeat it makes a serious difference. That finally they did not cut me off. I cut myself off. My letter to them concerning this is dated

Jan 4. Albert's to me the 6th. What arises to us from this is that if the author is a gentleman enough to ask the publishers to suspend their payments on his work, the publishers should be sporting enough to suspend their judgement on it, if only that some damaging gossip doesn't get round through the grapevine that might injure one's chances of selling anything, say, to the Signet outfit.

Of that judgement, which is so far unfavorable, or non-existent, I'll speak briefly. It is discouraging, but I'm not really dismayed. *Gabriola* won't admit of any stock responses to it, as a novel of situation, character, et al. It's probably hard to read, as the *Volcano* was, and for some people harder, if they're not to some extent presold on the reward they may have should they read it. Probably they're quite right that it isn't a "good" book. It isn't. It doesn't aim to be, but thinks of itself as a classic. (Especially and/or also in conjunction with its fellows.) The impression arises from the dim view so far taken of it (in my more humble moments) that I may have made some elementary mechanical mistake as to the disposition or order of narrative, but I'm not particularly worried about it since, if so, it should be easy to correct. The part I'm just sending in, of which you'll have a copy, should convince you that if the narrative doesn't move horizontally it certainly can move, if in a bizarre fashion, vertically.

For the rest the *Volcano,* when so viewed in bits and pieces (or even—er—not viewed in bits and pieces) might have caused anyone to take a dim view of it. I hate the feeling, though I may be wrong, that Mr. Haas himself rejected the *Volcano.* On my side I'm not impugning anyone's powers of reading, least of all Albert's, who must express his honest opinion, but I can't see it would have been much different of the *Volcano* under these circumstances.

As for the rest ingratitude is not among my vices, and I remain extremely grateful to Mr. Haas and Random House for their financial assistance. Deo volens, they will more than get it back in the end.

The section sent off to Albert simultaneously with this letter which was finished before Christmas brings the final typed *Gabriola* to 206 pages. But for this we should have reached about 350 pages by now. The complete *Gabriola* as it stands now runs around 500 pages. Margie is making you an extra copy of this last section, a story in itself, called "The Element Follows You Around, Sir,"* and you'll have it in a few days, I hope, though we're snowed in, the planes are all grounded, not even trains are running, and in fact the elements are following us

* Published in *Show Magazine,* March, 1964.

around, sir. I'm very sorry indeed for any collateral harassment any of this may have caused you. With all the very best from us both,

Malcolm

To Albert Erskine

The Caroline Court
1058 Nelson St.
Vancouver, B.C., Canada
January 26, 1954

My God, you old rapscallion. I don't mean that I'm really distressed by the set-back, am not over sensitive (like hell I'm not, as you once observed, in fact my throte is only cutte unto the nekke bone) but if it was all going to be done as rapidly as that, and *like* that, couldn't *you* have called *me* somehow, so that I would have been given more of a chance to call myself, been given credit at least for trying to move hell so to do, and then, in fact, finally for doing it, which I morally did, for my letter was posted on Jan. 4, yours to me on the 6th: or if not for doing it at least acknowledgement that I'd done it, or if not acknowledgement that I'd done it, at least some to Hal, who writes me on the 11th, and is still in the dark, though I can see opposing ethical obliquities there that might have prevented you. But which (I've postponed writing him till today, awaiting some answer, the 25th) has given me no choice but to write him a letter (but to be strictly confidential between him and yourself) saying that though I love you only second to Jesus, and will always be grateful to you to my dying day, as I am, blow me down—complete shit though I felt in having to say so—if I don't think you much at fault in letting this happen like this, so that such shades of ignominy surround your ambassador to oblivion, who was not even given the opportunity to save his face: (but what of Hal's face?) or if you couldn't help its happening like this, it seems to me, as I said, you should have replied to my last official and personal letter, of too clairvoyant eye, suggesting the suspension myself. On top of this—though I haven't looked at the contract again—and though technically I may be (as I thought) at fault—or even completely at fault—in not having the thing ready for publication by Nov. 1, does it seem altogether fair to judge a fellow on merely what he'd sent under the new impression it was Feb. 1, on stuff (in that context of belief) which he was not obliged to send in at all till the deadline, whatever that was, making allowance for this, after all—especially under the circumstances—very understandable error? It does not seem altogether fair, my brother. Nor do your strictures on even what you have of the work in question which looks to me as though you didn't have your reading cap on, nor Mr. Haas' strictures, whose "dimmer view even than mine, perhaps because more objective" looks anything but objective to me, in fact much as if he'd borrowed the Consul's dark glasses in order to read it, or perhaps Mr. Reynal's, or even Jonathan Cape's. Well, we have spoken of my face, and Hal's face, but there remains, I haven't overlooked the Random House's money either, or, more importantly, yours. Here I feel truly woebegone at the possible implications, already chasing themselves, or half chasing themselves, with 7 league boots through whatever circles they chase themselves, that you have been let down, have backed the wrong horse, that possibly there was no horse in the first place. But brother, wait, hark, what is that sound of hooves I hear? It is a sound: unmistakably it is a sound. Perhaps this next instalment, here before you, will begin to change matters slightly, though regarded, even now, with some if not complete loathing by your good self, and more dimly still by Mr. Haas. Re this, all I have to say is that it was finished, as I said, before the New Year, but because of these new auxiliary circumstances it has taken till now to type finally. The objection will arise to what it is like—but read on, read on—Mr. Fort (it would be amusing to receive the verdict that it was apparently *only* just like Fort, even though it were, for that would prove that only the first pages had been read). It is founded, I am horrified to say, upon a personal experience and the only official part of this letter are the following words directed to Mr. Haas, to whom I shall always also be very grateful (and not being unmindful of my gratitude now): "that the author wishes to demonstrate for Mr. Haas therein that if he can't make his novel move horizontally, he certainly feels that here he proves he can do it vertically." Other minor matters: the thematic collision of the material and the immaterial. Shadow and substance, reality and unreality. Hence of amalgam of "fact" and fiction. Also the other side, with a vengeance, of any "back to nature" theme. Another small note re the whole. Poe didn't die on October 9th (1849) but Oct. 7—curiously enough the same date in which we visited Gabriola in fact (Oct. 7, 1947): I still have the bus ticket. It would be more proper to refer to this date then as the "centennial" rather than the centenary of Poe? Curiously enough I found myself putting the last finishing touches on this bit on Jan. 9, that 1809, was Poe's birthday. Perhaps you would do me a great favour and look at the copy of *Life* for Jan. 11. *The Case for E.S.P.* by Aldous Huxley pp. 96–108. But on the next pages 109 *passim* is an illustrated article called *The Mission of the Shantymen*. H'mm. Some of the photographs might be exactly of Eridanus—or Dollarton— especially the second one from the bottom on 110 (ask Dave Markson) is indistinguishable from it. Men like John Rudd on 114 are the neighbours described. And as for high tide? I enclose a few cuttings. (Deep Cove is round the point from Dollarton.) We are now completely cut off (the bridge caught fire among other things and blocked shipping) from home by the worst—I thought they were the worst in 1951–52—blizzard in all Vancouver history. See also the section sent in, that I am offering to Matson as a story, under the title "The Element Follows You Around, Sir." Or, the elements. In short, never a dull moment. So perhaps it wasn't so irresponsible after all to take Random's time getting a copy of the notes of *La Mordida* in the bank.

For the rest I hope (a) the tone of injured innocence (b) facetiousness of this letter, will not blind you to the fact (a) I'm deeply sorry I've put you in this situation (b) deeply grateful (c) your friend (d) more than ever on the job. For the rest again while I have every regard for Random's business side of it, and intend to respect it, am grateful again, I can't see the slightest point from a business view in their doing what they have done in this manner. After all, with *Lunar Caustic* practically finished, it doesn't seem to have occurred to anyone how easy it would have been for me had I chosen simply to fulfill the minimal terms of the contract. And since at the time they thought they were cutting me off they didn't know I'd have the money to carry on, how the hell did they think I was going to finish the novel at all? Or did they think, by some legerdemain, this callous discouragement and schoolboy punishment technique was going to cause me to suddenly finish it overnight? As for you, brother, let us have less stock responses. Get out of your rut. You sound like Mr. Reynal. (These last sentences were written by Margie and I disclaim responsibility for them. She may be forgiven in that no publisher has ever kept a contract with *her* in her life.) Vancouver's only snow plough is stuck outside. Love and God bless from us both,

Malcolm

P.S. So far as I can see the only real casualty at this end is time—all this having put us another month or so behind, in terms of final typing that is, having had so many letters to write. I'd like to see your face if one day you found yourselves putting *Ferry* into the Modern Library. Perhaps not quite in this order to be humble. Further note: my source for the dialogue in the movie of *The Wandering Jew* is Rallo's thesis, *The Haunted Castle,* and not the movie itself or the play. For the rest I don't want to spoil the story, and can only hope that no one else has noted the appalling coincidence I cite and reported to the Fortean Society, whose published organ I have never read.

M.

To David Markson

Vancouver, B.C., Canada
[Postmarked February 5, 1954]

Dear old Dave:

Thanks very much for your letter, now yellowing with age in the Lowry pocket. Many happy returns on your birthday; we hadn't known when it was, or we'd have sent you a birthday card with a picture of the Absolute on it or something. Your dreams of stormy weather besetting we ducks didn't seem to have much more than magnificently diverting pertinence at the time, when we were riding fairly high, all things considered: since then, as it has turned out, those excursions of our somnambulant consciousness, as you put it, have taken on, so to say, a more parapsychological or psychic significance. Nothing serious: no untranscendable gales, but just lots of discouragement and misunderstandings from various interrelating sources, and all of a kind rather harder than not to take at this point: who invented the phrase "throw up the sponge" I wonder? It has always seemed to me that anyone with sufficient indestructible intestinal eccentricity to want to swallow a sponge in the first place would have a corresponding reluctance in wanting to vomit it forth: anyway we haven't thrown it up. Maybe because, like Hasbrouck's rose, it is digested. (Margie tells me it was to throw *in* the sponge but I thought that was a towel.) There is no sponge. All of which has not prevented one's interior life from becoming all of a sudden rather to resemble Balzac's with the difference that, to all appearances, there is no *Comédie Humaine* either. Oh well, Malc, Malc, what the Halc, as old Aiken used to say. Or one could always go to Sardinia and promote a silver mine. I recommend Stefan Zweig's posthumous

Balzac in this connection, especially if you want to read about my childhood. Or Stefan Zweig's. Or whoever's. Who cares anyway? Illnesses too, many dozens: fevers, rashes, flus, fleas, and the all-dreaded thunderstone. But the finances look up. And the little house, all alone, together with the pier, has withstood (again) the worst gales in a century, Deep Cove, round the corner (and where we nearly went, by mistake, under my faulty pilotage, after Port Moody) having been blown to hell and gone. Meantime we have a fascist government; books are burned in the libraries, or are threatened to be, and they have banned *The Wild One*, why is all too obvious: McCarthy is their hero (though even Ezra Pound wouldn't have recognized these Strongarmed Stinkweasels—they are Social Creditors). I threaten to make a stink that will resound from one end of the earth to the other, but so far I haven't got further than making myself ill and losing my temper. Besides (after seeing *The Juggler*) I am seized with a desire to go and die in Israel. Or perhaps even live. We went 25 miles in a blizzard to see *The Great God Brown*. Very good. And worst of all we have received a notice, directed to Apartment 73 specifically, saying, We the Caroline Court Apartments Ltd. respectfully request you *not* to feed the seagulls or pigeons . . . whose habits have the result of attracting mice and other vermin . . . and otherwise rendering the surroundings unattractive . . . to the distaste of the other tenants . . . *besides it is contrary to the City's bylaws. . . .* To which I replied: *We seagulls and pigeons* respectfully inform the Caroline Court Apartments Ltd. that we have been here a great deal longer than you have, that far from rendering your surroundings unattractive, we claim to be the only aesthetic attraction within twenty miles that renders your premises attractive in the least degree, and while not inpugning the "mice and other vermin" we are said to attract, we must presume that the other tenants whose distaste is referred to are the 1450 sparrows who have nested here in these walls without molestment since 1905, according to those City bylaws you invoke by which we are also protected (see Clause 73 Ibid 6 p. 3) and with whom we have always lived in a state of amity: as to the pigeons our own sporting instinct forbids us to ask what other kind of pigeon informed on us: meantime we shall continue to sit (and shit) upon any damned window-sill we please, especially that of Apartment 73, giving notice respectfully to the Caroline Court Apartments Ltd. that any wanton interference with our so-called habits—the more so since in this bitter winter we have no choice unless we are supposed legally to die at the hands of "those legally bound to protect us"—will be duly reported to the proper authorities and the culprits punished with the utmost vigour of the law, by which we merely mean that we shall with-draw our society from you altogether, with the result that your so-called premises, so far mortised and tenoned with our bird-lime, will not only become, as you term it, unattractive, but, having fallen down, cease to exist.

Something of that nature. Meantime, old man, I want to say on be-half of us both, how good it is to hear from you, how loyal a friend you are to write to such rotten correspondents. It is always a fine and cheering thing to hear from you. Send a manuscript. Pay no attention to premature discouragements, or, for that matter, the misery-grisery implied in this letter. Actually, we hope to present you in the not too distant future with some work that will make the top of your head blow off. But, if you have to blow mine off—ours—it doesn't much matter. Or not so much but that we should keep somewhere a nucleus of peace where the heart's velleities are clean, its cormorants dry their heraldic wings, its seagulls, in sunlight, fly. They'll drop some-thing on your head, of course, but that's where the sense of humor comes in.

Not to mention where the mixed metaphors, perhaps, go out. See you in Port Moody. Great love from us both,

Malc

To David Markson

Dollarton. 3 golden-eyes,
2 mergansers, 3 gulls,
7 grebes, 1 cat.
[Postmarked May 10, 1954]

Dear old Dave:

I should have written you weeks ago—and indeed I did write, and more than once—but owing to certain auxiliary circumstances. . . . Yeah. Well, the first auxiliary circumstance was that a pigeon nesting in the airvent head on the apartment roof fell down the said airvent shaft and got trapped in the wall behind our bed, which bed came out of the wall like a drawer. I was going to make the rescue of said bird coincident with the second circumstance, though in fact the latter preceded it; a cut forehead, no more than a scratch it seemed, while messing about with these city chores more unfamiliar than trapped

pigeons: but suddenly the scratch had turned into Grand Guignol—
I'd severed a bloody artery. Worse to follow: Margerie, on going to
the rescue, got trapped in the elevator. I mean that the elevator chose
that very moment to stop between floors when her benighted husband
was bleeding to death in the bathroom. Pandemonium: save from me,
who having let out the third bathful of Lowry gore felt at the top of
his form, and even less disposed to holler for help myself than I was to
put a tourniquet round the wound in question: I have not, I said to
myself, got an artery in my head, so how can I put a tourniquet on
it? Perhaps what I meant was any brains but at all events there was
a happy ending and we were saved in the nick, on the stroke of
midnight, in St. Paul's Hospital, having been conveyed thence at
117 miles an hour by an air force officer who up to then had been
slightly drunk in the corridor below when he'd been having an affair
with his half-sister. "And did you do this yourself?" asked the midnight interne grimly, to which I replied, "Christ no, it was that bloody
pigeon." All went well for a week or so, when someone supplicated
our own aid in a manner almost as urgent as we had—or Margie had—
the air force officer, though the urgency in this case was more psychological or interfamilial, and implied a journey, through the wet and
wilderness—long live the wet and the wilderness yet!—of some
seventy miles to a remote island—the very island upon which lives a
friend of yours by the way, should you ever need him, and whom I
once mentioned to you—and with a couple of cracked ribs, I mean
mine, also perhaps suffered as in combat with the holy bird, and
growing increasingly more painful, the more so since to reach our
friend's house, one has to descend a precipice some six hundred feet
in depth and at a gradient—where steps go down—of about 1 in 2.

Back in the apartment of the holy bird (the janitor suggested that
despite the rules we might feed the poor thing on the window-sill
after its exertions that night) it was to discover that the cracked ribs
had succeeded in apparently paralyzing my innards: in endeavouring
to remedy this in the approved Gandhi-esque manner—my enema
the Douche, as Haile Selassie put it—there was, after many fruitless
attempts, suddenly a sound of breaking and crepitous (though alas,
not crapitus, had it been crapitus might have been better) enough
to awaken the dead, the dead being me, to a sense, again, of the
illogical or brute fact: ribs (and I have broken them all before)
seemed to me malleable creatures, designed for give and take—and
sway and scend and every kind of pressure from the outside: but

apparently not from the inside—horrendous thought (one red-throated loon, one foolish seagull trying to steal a fish off one beautiful merganser, burning oil waste in the refinery, the first star—is the scenery outside from the room you know) like those dams in Holland during the floods of yesteryear, the ribcage was giving under the water-pressure, and it wasn't any use sticking one's finger in the dam. Or up one's arse for that matter. This time Margie got her instructions by telephone, nobly—and embarrassing though it must have been (our doctor lives in North Vancouver)—bind sheet tightly around patient to give support: more enema the douche: cascara: 2 tablespoonsful of epsom salts: an infusion of rosemarine: and caper several times boldly about the room, taking deep breaths of smog. And brandy, said I, should be given to the dying. It was, but by Monday night—that had been Sunday—it still hadn't done any good. "If nothing happens by 8, get to the hospital." Our last call was cut off by the cry Emergency! from somebody else: so I made my own emergency this time under my own steam—I mean I walked—nach dem Krankenhaus. St. Paul's again: (the first and last scenes of the whole *Volcano—The Voyage That Never Ends*—are supposed to be there too, but this was nightmarish a little: I ought to have been writing this, not living it or dying it, mutters Malc to himself, chuckling thoughtlessly—you oughtn't to chuckle thoughtlessly, old man, with broken ribs under such circumstances, and I warn you not to try it should you ever be unfortunate enough to be in the same position. So our North Vancouver doctor sent an emergency doctor after me, x-rays were taken, drugs given, and suffice it—with a temperature that was now rising much as it does when you go down into the engine-room of a bauxite freighter—

Several mescals later . . .

FASTING

behind the bed.

And at the foot a picture of the infant Jesus, apparently being instructed, with a view to the corollary of constructing a cross (since there was one above) while he looked rather like Dylan, when absolutely blind tight, being instructed, as I say, by his father Joseph, in the art of what can be done with a hammer and a nail—a truce to this. (unposted)

Our very dear old Dave:

I am terribly sorry not to have (unwritten)

Very dear old Dave:

Extremely sorry not to have written for so long, or rather not have posted any letters to you, especially when you were so sporting to write us para-psychologically suspecting some Lowry misery-grisery, and at that so entertainingly, brilliantly and sympathetically, so often at that point—(unposted)

—to cut a long story short (and incidentally I wrote you another long unposted letter, which didn't mention our troubles, but concentrated on what we thought might be your own, not posted, because of the supernatural idea that perhaps the troubles didn't really exist but stating them might somehow and obscurely beget some of them for you, god damn it, all this when I know very well that all you might have wanted was for a fellow to say oh or shit or something (as you see I couldn't say shit very well, as the poet said when he shouted Fire, having fallen down the sewer)—to cut that long story short anyhow, we are thinking of coming east this summer, in fact with the object of seeing you before we depart for Tel Aviv up the S.S. ΟΙΔΙΠΟΥΣ ΤΥΡΑΝΝΟΣ, though actually we are bound for Sicily, or at least the kingdom of the 2 Sicilies—if not under dat ole King Bomba (who made a law that stopped the trains every night at 6 P.M. making it obligatory that they hold a religious service on board)— there to live, if not in turn like that old Typhoeus, beneath Mount Etna. Previous to this, Prospero-wise, we aim to return to Milan, in which city the Volcano of your own better (or bitter) discovery is shortly to erupt: or fizzle out. We wondered if you could put us up in New York for a few days previous to this, under a bed or wherever, while we were on our way: said request not being made for financial reasons, but rather from love, whatever that entity is. If you want, you can have our house when we're gone if you want to go west though don't swear we won't haunt it and sing hot teleported tunes at you: but more likely you won't want and more likely still you'll be crossing the seas like us or whatever. Actually we don't know exactly what ship we'll be going on from New York: whether a Greek, Egyptian, Israeli, or Italian freighter. Or the exact date. But the Italian Consul is letting us know. As the said Consul remarked to Margie the other day: "This ship for lady-nice—I haf a friend who know the Commandante: the captain: but I must see friend. But maybe wait 5 or 6 day New York. But is friend I will try. . . . No, it is my privilege for lady-nice and friend-boy, or is he your housebound?"

At all events, you won't be too far away even if you are; but let us know, as we shall: and meantime HOLD THAT NOTE, ROLAND! BLOW THAT HORN! Hold that note! God bless from us both,

Margie and me, and from the shack and many mergansers and other wild and profound sea-foul (not written),

Malcolm

To Albert Erskine

Dollarton, B.C., Canada
May 22, 1954

Dear old Albert:

I feel I ought to make some sort of report. Before I do though, I want to say how sorry I am the letter I wrote last January angered you or may have hurt you. In fact I am sorry, period; that is, from the personal standpoint. Please forgive me. Before you write off that behaviour as being the ultima thule of ingratitude however—if you haven't done so already—try to understand the effect your news from Random House had on me coming in that particular way at that time. Well, a truce to it all.

Meantime, I'd overlooked several things myself: one was that I had to pay $400 income tax this year on the Random House payments themselves. Moreover, by mid-March my English bank still hadn't come through and we were living precariously on an overdraft on our Canadian one; neither had the Liverpool solicitors, despite their promises (in fact they were behaving quite like certain authors) and things for a while looked pretty bleak: the money did come through finally (just in time to pay the income tax), though not before I dispersed many further energies wrestling with these people and was, in fact, in hospital; not because of any more accidents, but simply some old broken bones aggravating a yet older, indeed hereditary, minor, and very English trouble: colonial anyway, vastly uncomfortable, but not very serious it turned out. (The only accident I've had this year to speak of was to sever an artery in my forehead while rescuing a trapped pigeon from an air vent in the apartment, which is a good excuse to give one's maiden aunt when late to tea.)

As you see by the address we are back in Dollarton, and so far as the financial situation is concerned things look rosy—touch wood—so much so that had you continued the payments I should by now, I think, have returned them, not out of nobility; but to avoid income tax. Not that I may not be grateful for their resumption again at some future date, if I'm still on the roster, but as things look at present I shall be, as I intimated I would, able to continue on my own, or without having to get another job, at least, I hope, until something is completed to all our satisfactions. Which brings me to another point, very important to me: it would seem better, all round, that so long as I continue on my own that the status of the work remain, so to say, my own, or more my own, stage secret. In other words, I don't think I want to send you any more bits and pieces (any more than you necessarily want them, after all, you didn't ask for them) for two reasons at least: one, I can't risk any further discouragement, not in the usual sense, and I don't mean this in a carping spirit, only that my self-critical faculty tends to be slightly manic-depressive, and to be frank, there are times when in process of creating I seem to need encouragement even if I think myself what I'm doing isn't entirely right, which certainly isn't fair to you; the second reason is that because of the peculiar way it seems I have to work, it's unfair to the work itself; for instance I honestly don't know at the moment whether I shall cut 200 pages out of *Gabriola's* 500-odd and I won't know until it's finally (sic) typed. So at the moment I don't even want to tell you how its going or its present status; and that's purely a sort of self-protection.

Which brings me to another point: the immediate outlook betokens a further change of plans, a further diversion of energies: I mean we have to move. Just as the work itself predicted of Eridanus the evictions so far have stopped at the lighthouse, but we are nonetheless now completely surrounded—the aspens all, all are felled, save in our little oasis of greenwood and sea—by sub-section and oil refinery, and though this oasis last forever, sanity and health dictates we should this time go: if only because if we stay next year I shall have to pay $1000 income tax, which we could just as well use to get to Europe and find another pied-à-terre less anguishing and even, in the end, more economical. We have for the moment fixed on Sicily. We of course hope to come back, but all preparations have to be made as if we would not, and these preparations are many and complicated in a place one has lived in for fourteen years.

Now finally as to my contractual position with you, I find it a bit obscure. Although I felt sure there was some agreement on this score I can't find any clause or rider in the contract that says I may "buy time" in this manner. As things stand I have another deadline a year hence, and a third Nov. 1956. It would simply be an impossibility for me now, under these changed and changing circumstances, to attempt to itemize what I think I can or can't do or in what order, or by then

(the way it looks at present I shall have three books for you all right
—or more—by the last deadline, but all of them a little outside the
general main scheme: meantime you haven't had the faintest indication of all the work that's been done), and I don't want to make any
more promises I can't keep, or, more accurately, ones that may look, to
Random House, as though they're not being kept to the very best of
my abilities. I don't seem able to work that way anyhow: I have to
let things gather more dust apparently. But I am assuming that The
Case Is Altered. Or, to put it another way, I'm hoping I may consider
myself to have stopped the clock at 11:59 P.M. on October 31, 1953—
or January 31, 1954, whichever way you prefer to look at it. Please
inform me on this because it worries me to death. We think to be
passing through New York on our way to Sicily in September, and
we hope very much to see you then, when the situation may be
clearer, or we can clarify it, or anyhow have a good—pow-wow is
perhaps the good word, about it. Anyhow, dear brother, we want to
see you. I hope you'll convey my real gratitude to Mr. Haas for
having tided me over and assure him I mean to come through. All the
best love from us both,

Malcolm

To Arthur A. Sprague*

Dollarton
June 1, 1954

Dear Scipio Sprague
    sans plague sans blague
    (if I seem vague)
    I'm extremely beholden
    for your words golden
    as bourbon olden
    in which prosit to you
    as you sail toward the blue
    on some Pequod gaily
    or Behemoth sprightly
    from Malcolm Lowry
    late of the Bowery
    whose prose was flowery

* A friend of David Markson.

if somewhat glowery
who worked nightly
and sometimes daily
and died, playing the ukulele. . . .

Malcolm Lowry

To David Markson

[Postmarked Dollarton, July 10, 1954]

Dear old Dave:
Your Modigliani caryatid from Milan received, speeded by the imposing Columbia University stamps, but with some misgiving as to the long silence. . . .
All is half gaily bloody and schizophrenic here but hopefully and even gaily forward; oddly enough your card caught me at a moment when I too was reading *Ushant*—for the first time more or less objectively that is: I found it somewhat too productive of underground bleeding for certain participants therein to make much intelligent comment at the time its creator sent it to me; an oversight which I fear may have somewhat hurt the old master: something which will now be corrected. It is though, you will admit, a hell of a difficult (and not merely in the sense of its being profound, which it frequently is, but of its *moving away* from one while one reads) book to grasp right off in its entirety of evocation or of which to say "Jolly good job, old boy," or something: especially when oneself is supposed to be one of the protagonists. It's been a wonderfully (in part) helpful book for me to read in a situation qua "house" like the present one however —Jeeze how mankind stands it at all I don't know—it never occurred to me that consciousness itself could be of any aid, quite the contrary, and let alone a goal, "Man forget yourself," having been too often my motto, but I feel for the first time he may have been right. All aboard for the good ship Solipsism, boys, in short, and don't forget your sea boots. . . . Our little ship Solipsism, for which we've already secured passage by down payment of $100, is Italian, of the Costa Line, takes 12 passengers (of which we still hope you may be one) and would appear to leave sometime between September 1 and 6: with this in view, unless we have to take a later sailing or the ship itself, which is bound for Genoa or Naples or both, be otherwise delayed, we

would arrive in New York the night of the 25th of August—D.V., and hope to God at least to see you then. Best love from us both.

Hasta la vista,

Malc

To David Markson

[*Postcard from Milan, 1954, remainder of date illegible.*]

Bang!

Malcolm

To Signor and Signora Giorgio Monicelli*

Villa Margherita
Mazzaro
Taormina, Sicily
[*1954*]

THE MEANING OF THIS LETTER IS, despite my occasional irrelevant poetics, I love you and DON'T WORRY!
Beloved Giorgio and Daniela:
For Christ sake don't pay too much attention to the damnfoolish compilation of self-pity sent you day before yesterday, save to the proof of affection to yourselves contained therein. (I *had* to show I *had* written you.) The situation is certainly a pretty perilous one, psychologically (and physically) but perhaps not half so perilous as my braggadocio made out. As far as the leg was concerned apparently it decided to heal itself as if overnight, for I walked some miles on it today without undue trouble. My fear of its reinfection being apparently due to the horrible pain caused by leaving a Band-aid on too long. So I removed it—I mean the Band-aid, not the leg—and God help me if it doesn't appear healed (touch wood). Or almost. The weakness continues, but even here I seem to be regaining weight, and becoming my abnormal deranged fat self again, under the influence of vast quantities of Gorgonzola cheese and mineral water (the water always being relatively mineral of course). But not all my

* Monicelli was Lowry's Italian translator.

braggadocio can remove the perilousness of Taormina as a place to live in—especially here, where there are ten abysses round every corner. Enough of this. The mystery to me is how even Ulysses, reputed for his aplomb and cunning, could ever have been seduced by imaginary siren voices emerging from a barren island on which you can't even land—even though we half live on it—and which is inhabited by nothing but a few dwarf cactus and three wild constipated goats, driven mad by the noise of the traffic to Messina on the coastwise road and that of the coastwise train. The weather is bloody awful, the Mediterranean here—final humiliation—continues to be almost unswimmable in—Margerie, poor gal, has another bad throat, snow falls on Calabria, we are served in this house by a male Neanderthal orangutang in a flapping overcoat with a forehead like the infant Mozart and a female gorilla with a heart of gold and a mind that thinks of nothing else, unless it is food, most of which is inedible. If Western civilization began here, all I can say is it should not have been difficult to predict long ago how it would end.

Margerie has just said that she would rather be asphyxiated than frozen (though what usually happens is that you are both) so I have just called for the brazier which will arrive with a lemon on top. Meantime you can see that I *have* rallied à la Stendhal, so don't worry.

It seems terribly impolite of me to take it out on poor Sicily but all I can say is that Sicily is certainly not Italy—in fact they hate you worse here than they do us, which is saying something—and that you have my permission to give Scotland a beating any time you want to, Scotland, which is not England, and I say this as a descendant of Robert the Bruce (though it is true he had many descendants, most of them, like doubtless me, illegitimate). What arouses my ire about this island, though, is partly no doubt of course occasioned by a mixture of compassion and envy. The life of the Sicilians seems to me hopeless beyond hopelessness and everything bad in it of course washes into Taormina, where the majority seem not human beings at all, but vultures preying on the tourists. But how do they get up and down the hill—and what fabulous hills, and how sing doing it? How preserve a certain stern autochthonous beauty in their native culture?

How did Pirandello, Verga, ever first draw breath in such a place, which is not only improbable but to my mind impossible, a fantasy God, if He ever created it, should have forgotten, or tried to have forgotten, that remorseful man. Margerie of course thinks its romantic: I think the only beauty it possesses is that of death and dead it is—

yet the people are not. Or not yet. Or not quite. As it stands it is a hideous travesty of our old life where life was yet uncompleted and the great trees still stood—who is to blame? I asked the priest, who runs the local cinema (where we saw *Quo Vadis*) and all he said was "Sprechen Sie deutsch?"

It all would seem to me to represent an almost incredible anomaly of the modern world that makes me feel like parodying Eliot—strength without courage, fortitude without guts (for all the Sicilians seem to understand is brute force and shouting)—all of which is very different (though it may be similar after all) as "strength broken by strength but still strong," as a friend of mine once wrote about Canada. A mixture of the Isle of Man, Acapulco and Liverpool. God help us all. Margie's southern tradition, though, is in full buzz: they are nearly all slaves (I don't overlook the fact that I am one myself) and if you don't treat them as such they won't respect you. There is much love and tragedy in this, but I won't go into it any more. I went and took a look at D. H. Lawrence's house and disrespected him for having taken it, I'm afraid—even though I cried—I think it was on March 30th, 1930, and I'd just come out of a cinema in Cambridge (which was out of bounds) when I heard he was dead.

Basta! Basta! Basta!

Pazienza! Pazienza! Pazienza!

Publish, though, what I have said neither in the streets of Tyre nor in the by-streets of Ascalon. Do not either (even if you already have) mention this ordeal to the good Eric Linder.* For, apart from anything else, he will—good soul—worry. Mention it not to Harold Matson and also to Innes Rose who will, good fellow though he is, then mention it to the Caspian Sea, out of which you know is no outlet, and so poor Otto will just go round and round and round. . . .

Neither mention it to Garzanti. Or mention it to yourself. Emped-ocles is finally becoming a bore.

Love,

Malcolm

* Lowry's literary agent for Italy.

PART XI: *1955–1956*

PART XI: 1953–1956

To David Markson

Dear old Dave:

I am terribly sorry I haven't written. Partial explanation is a p.c. that should arrive about the same time as this.

I am struck dumb by your news of Jim Agee's death: something goes fast out of your life when a man as good as that dies, even though people of worth are dying like flies these days, I can only think, to armour the dead.

All my best love to Scipio and Kitty: their wedding invitation, to hand, has arrived just about in time for me to give them a Christening present—please convey my apologies and congratulations (it is terribly hard for me to write at all at present).

Sicily—or at any rate Taormina—is a first-rate disaster: the noise so appalling I have to wear ear plugs all the time, which is causing one to go deaf (as well as blind). I fear you would like it.

Margie sends her love. As do I. I can't send you any good news so get busy and send me some. We depart for England soon. Robert Haas of Random House was here, but by bad luck I missed him. I heard roundabout that he spoke very well of me which I count damned sporting of him since I am 99 years behind in fulfilling my contract.

Our maid's daughter had a child the other day: the father and mother get married next Monday. I am thinking of forbidding the banns: apart from which the *Volcano,* though translated into Italian, is apparently in potential trouble with the Vatican: so it hasn't come out, the only thing that has being our dinner, from the ice box, which a neighbouring cat has learned how to open. Let her have it!

Sursum corda!

Malc

To Albert Erskine

Brook General Hospital
Ward H (neurosurgical)
Shooters Hill Road, Woolwich
London, S.E. 18
[July, 1955]

Dear brother Albert:

I would appear to be here, Margie likewise, but in another ward, F.2; fortunately we can see each other. It is an extremely good hospital, and everyone is very kind indeed, and one eats (I speak for myself, not Margie, who can't eat at all) like a horse: this is a ward more or less entirely devoted to people with brain or skull injuries, or to the post-operative recovery of such, so that the reaper is omnipresent but it is by no means grim for all that, in fact I spend most of my time shirtless on the cricket pitch in the dew. Briefly the news: it was for a time thought possible that sundry past injuries and fractures or what not might have damaged a tricky area of my brain but despite some still perplexing symptoms it seems this isn't so; therefore, though I have been x-rayed and probably will be again to determine whether an operation is necessary, so far as I can tell I'm not going to be operated on, or at least not yet, and even if so the thing would be a minor one. (I'm having one for haemorrhoids, though I hope that's not where I keep my brain.) Touch wood. The most trying symptom has been eyesight, which has been on the blink (sick transit!) since the beginning of the year, and in fact occasionally so bad I thought I was losing my sight altogether, moreover I had dark thoughts that my childhood trouble* was recurring on another plane or to blame: not so, it is just, some experts say, the usual weakening of the muscles behind the eyes that can occur at my age. So I am now bespectacled, for reading, which would scarcely be a unique state were it not that the whole thing is so maddeningly inconsistent. Sometimes, especially in sunlight, I see worse with spectacles than without and by electric light print sometimes will blur or black out altogether: then for a while I'll see perfectly again; much the same too with my physical well being: I lost 42 lbs. in a couple of months in Sicily, but back it all seems to have come here in a fortnight, I'm half sorry to say. Needless to say all this has not been too good for work, with poor Margie out of commission altogether quite impos-

---

* Lowry was nearly blind for four years.

sible. This must be only about the third letter I've managed to complete this year, if I manage to complete it and—beautiful petard!—things are not rendered any easier by the fact that I can't read my own ex-handwriting, or only with great difficulty. By the time you receive this we'll both have been in here a month and probably will have at least another month to go. What is wrong with Margie no one as yet has fully determined but she is certainly damned sick, in fact a great deal sicker than I am: both of us take some grave delight in that they are feeding her paraldehyde as a sedative, though her problem is certainly not an alcoholic one (nor is mine, though I must say I feel I could use a paraldehyde and splash sometimes). Both of us have been under medical care a good deal longer than we've been hospitalized and the former doctor forbade me to write (especially on the *Gabriola* theme), supposing this to have been possible, or even think of writing until things were much better sorted out than they were: the present treatment so far as I'm concerned has had as its aim my resumption of the Work in Progress but I have to write off much of the last 18 months as a dead loss, I fear. Today the necessary MSS has been teleported to me again and sits glistering by my bedside in the ward (where my neighbour died last night to the accompaniment of "Wabash Blues") waiting for me to bash into it once more, which I mean to do as well as I can, starting immediately, though things are bound to be delayed, not least because of typing, moreover what with this eye business I have to revise entirely my method of writing and in fact generally reorient myself to it—it's been hard for me up to now sometimes to hold a pencil at all for more than 5 minutes at a time. Needless to say I feel badly not to have delivered the goods, some goods, long ere now, it was a great pity for me we had to sever the umbilical cord with Random House at the time we did: moreover I got very discouraged, not only by the reception but by the lack of a word from anyone in regard to what small things I did publish: both "The Bravest Boat" and "Strange Comfort" have become classics in French and Italian and the latter is in an anthology of *Best English Short Stories* of all time and so on. I have read aloud parts of *Gabriola* with great success too when in Taormina, which may mean something. But a truce to this. Should I kick the bucket, or the project seem really hopeless, it is arranged that the money so far advanced will be paid back to you: as things stand I can keep our heads above water without aid; I don't want to assume failure in advance, to complete things or to engage myself in extraneous projects in *order* to pay you back now. I

[381]

hope the situation may be still as it was, that the clock was stopped when it was stopped, and that I may have time, no matter how much I've lost or how tardy I am, to catch up now. It would remove a major source of emotional tension (a commodity I'm not allowed to indulge in) if I could feel this were so. I believe I can make the grade though luck has been consistently against me and us so far and I don't have any right to make any promises save that I'm going to TRY, after so long silence and limbo. A letter to Mr. Haas (to whom please convey as much or as little of this as you think fit), who was in Taormina and who was kind and sporting enough to speak well of me there, I heard, though unfortunately I didn't meet him, accompanies this, which please give him if you think it right, and if not not. Another strange casualty is my English grammar: a total amnesiacal loss, but I don't think a very serious one. All the best love from us both as always, with the utmost affection,

Malcolm

To James Craige

[*London*]
September 12, 1955

Beloved Jim:

Have never stopped thinking of you or the beach.

Please give my best love to all, especially Downie, the gang and the rest; and the good Harvey.

My inability to reply has been due—tell Downie, for I value his letters more than I can say—to my eyes failing. Faltering and recovering. I go in hospital for a brain operation thing tomorrow: (But UP UP UP FROM THE FLOOR. That's the way). Margie 2 days later. Don't think it serious. There has never been a moment when I have not thought of you all with deepest love.

Malc

P.S. And tell Downie's Dorothy not to get the big head. I made it to Barnet once alas in 1 hr and ¾. We shall all rejoin each other.

Love,
Malcolm

To David Markson

The White Cottage
Ripe, near Lewes
Sussex, England
February 21, 1956

Dear old Dave: A thousand thanks for your many deeply appreciated letters (which is an understatement) to us both: I'll just have to start again as a letter writer since I'd never catch up were I to try to reply in detail: one inhibiting factor among others has been the defection into defectiveness of my eyesight: a confounded nuisance. But I'm back on the work in progress again and again thanks for your encouragement. It seems to me you need some in kind: why not set yourself for a start the one goal of *finishing* the *Satevepost* story as they want it—you can always alter it afterwards if you want— and getting paid for it? You have Fitzgerald and Faulkner as precursors. If you can get to England you can come and work here—a delightful old place, and we can start a mutual aid society. There's a fine old pub too with an 120-year-old German jukebox that plays 18″ brass records. Hudson lived hereabouts. Henry James' ghost prowls not far. So does that of almost every other writer you can think of, for that matter, and though something similar might be said of Greenwich Village as from the White Horse to the White Cottage might be a palpable step. Meantime I drink Cydrax (Cider's nonalcoholic little sister) and behind a Melvillean boskage ponder the usage of the introverted coma. Wish you could find a *P.R.* with the "Bravest Boat" in it—of June 54?—and I'd love to read the New Writing. Please send us the good word and all best love from Margie and me.

Malc

To James Craige

The White Cottage
Ripe, near Lewes
Sussex, England
[April, 1956]

My very dear Jimmy:

This is just a short note that is intended to reach you for your birthday and simply to say many very happy returns of the Day—probably it won't get to you in time, its being Easter time—and a very Happy Easter too!—but still the thought is the same. I have heard from both Downie and Harvey that you have been in hospital for which I'm very sorry for I know how you hate that, but I hope you will now, or very soon, have left all that behind, and be back at the dear old beach again. (I too have been in hospital, twice since being in England, but am better now.) Though we like this place quite a lot, please don't think we have abandoned Dollarton, we have not, and think of it constantly, and of yourself, and miss the old times, but it seems better for reasons of health to stay where we are just at the moment, though the beach will always be home. Please give my best love to Downie, to whom I am writing, to Harvey should you see him, and of course Whitey. I am copying out some poems for you by John Clare an English poet (1790–1860) who reminds me of T. E. Brown somewhat and which I think you will like, so you will have another letter from me soon. Get better soon and God bless you.

Love,
Malcolm

To Clarisse Francillon

The White Cottage
Ripe, near Lewes
Sussex, England
April 21, 1956

Clarisse darling:

We are at the above address, scarcely a stone's throw away just across the Channel, quite near Newhaven, to which a boat used to go from Dieppe. I am dying to see a copy of *Lunar Caustic* in your translation—could you lend me the *L'Esprit* with it in, and I'll send them back, for it will be ages otherwise before I get them from Matson. Also I am longing to know how it went over in France and what people thought of it, including you, as you know I haven't let it be published yet in English! Many congratulations on your novel, and the short story for the *Mercure de France*. How are you and what is your news? I am not much changed, save for a long flowing white beard and the fact that I am ruining my health drinking large quantities of non-alcoholic cider: also I am working hard. Is there any chance you can pay us a visit sometime? We could put you up and would love to see you. We live in an ancient cottage in an ancient village, where there is not even a village idiot, unless you count myself. But it is really a beautiful place. Margerie sends her best love, as do I.

Malcolm

To David Markson

[The White Cottage]
[Spring, 1956]

Dear old Dave:

Just a note, between paragraphs, to thank you very much indeed for sending the *Partisan Review*. I'm very fond of the old "Bravest Boat" though I have never managed to ascertain what anyone thought of it, if anything, in the U.S.* *Lunar Caustic,* by the way, is appearing serially in the French mag. *L'Esprit* in Paris. I think you would be enchanted with this place to which a visitor came the other day asking to see the room (here) where her grandmother was at school in 1830: must be ghosts here, gol durn it, though we ain't laid none yet. House was built in 1740. Margie is having a wonderful time with the garden, as am I, she planting seeds destined to be glowing hollyhocks, I sowing sweetpeas—4 seeds in each hole—"one for the rabbit, one for the cow, one for the fieldmouse, and one to grow," as they say here, while meanwhile I weed sentences full of contorted lousewort which I lay neatly in rows, for use later no doubt. Though we miss the water-bourne bounties and forest and sea and mountains drama of old Dollarton at times, without abandoning our forest

---

* Since Lowry's death, the story has been anthologized many times.

home we nevertheless have a good feeling of temporary home here at least and are having a great deal of fun while at the same time living quite cheaply, compared with American standards. Margie's in the best health I've seen her in in years and myself in good form too albeit bearded like the bard and despite having fallen painlessly and soberly out of a train the other day while reading a book. I don't have any other news, save this, culled from a Government paper: In the Nuts (unground) (other than Groundnuts) Order, the expressions nuts shall have reference to such nuts, other than groundnuts, as would, but for this Amending Order, not qualify as nuts (unground) (other than groundnuts) by reason of their being nuts (unground). Tell me news of the *Satevepost* story, your health, your plans—other work, your comedies and dramas (or I shall have sended a boy to have founded out, señor, whether you are not making more tragedies). Best love from us both,

Malc

To Harvey Burt*

> The White Cottage
> Ripe, near Lewes
> Sussex, England
> [Spring, 1956]

Dear Harvey:

Thank you from our hearts for the wonderful letter. But to reply briefly and to point since time is so short. I think your young married couple—he the teacher and actor—sound a good thing for the house and the house for them. The important thing is to have someone who'll both live in it and love it during the summer (I can't think too far ahead) and perhaps part of the autumn and at least drop down to see it during the winter. With this in view I feel the more things of mine, ours—books, for example—that are left there the less desolated it will look, also *feel* from this end, not to say be for you in other ways more convenient: the less desolated it will be from your point of view too. Also one has to make clear they have no actual responsibility for anything of mine, in case some such feeling as this should be a deterrent. As for *My Heart's In* . . .†—well, all

---

* Schoolteacher and summer neighbor of the Lowrys.
† *My Heart's in the Highlands*, the Lowry boat.

this is left to your heart and discretion. You make our hearts feel better about it all, however: and again, thank you from them. There're a few important points to bequeath to any possible temporary successor, I mention, partly because they are even more valid to anyone not living your more specifically Conradian existence on the beach: first, though it may look like a Pig-in-a-poke (and indeed is—in a spiritual sense) to hang on to the "mink's house" next door your old one is virtually a necessity to any married or indeed unmarried couple if their lives are to be tenable as ours; I'd hate to see that big cedar come down between the houses or imagine any other horrors that could happen otherwise. (To me, too, childish though it may seem, there is the pier, which we built, which I cannot imagine myself living without, even if it isn't there or myself am dead.) Then there is the old pier: it can be a delight to a swimmer. Please give it a long counterbracing master building look at least before you should leave, cast some Harveyian architechtonic charm at it, some spell against teredos, and tell your descendents to cherish it (even if in its absence). Finally there is much of love about the place that will surely come to any lover's aid, especially in such strange seasons as autumn and winter and early spring: in your most knightly fashion I commend you to pass such words down to whom it may concern, (even if necessary in the accents of Sir Walter Scott). Finally there is the question of the MSS. Leave 'em lay where de Lawd hath flung them. That is to say, use your discretion about this. Books—again, as I say, largely these will be better, I think, where they are more or less: wherever they are. All we'd like ourselves in Europe, if you can somehow manage it, are two magical books, both in bad shape, and written apparently by one Frater Achad. One is called *Q.B.L.*, the other *The Anatomy of the Body of God*. They are books about the Cabbala. Another very small book is a copy of Melville's *The Confidence Man,* if you can slip that in anywhere: it's scarcely larger than a pocket book. *The Melville Log* and the Daumier your guests might like to look at, in fact they might be an added attraction. It is a blow that Jimmy won't be there, but give him our best love should you see him: he thinks very highly of you. I reiterate the names of the two possibilities we had in mind, if anything should fall through at the last moment. Gene Lawrence, 2233 McPherson Ave., S. Burnaby. Or Bill and Alice McConnell—Einar will know where they are now.

You say you think you're gaucho. If that means left, as I understand it to do, let's hope we both are so far gauche that we're right.

If I'm to understand that it means provincial, you are the exact opposite, in my opinion, as I was reflecting only the other day, treading Raleigh's walk in The Tower of London.

~~~~~~*

Do they still come homeward? And the mergansers? And—Ah pardon me thou bleeding piece of earth! I would rather have spoken that line (and that we had erected that outhouse) than have taken—perhaps—Dollarton. God bless!

<div align="right">

Love from us both,

Malcolm

</div>

To Harvey Burt

<div align="right">

[*Summer, 1956*]

</div>

Thank you, dear old Harvey, for the more than bravest boat. It is truly a work of art and great kindness, and if I look at it long enough maybe I can forget the poor shack being hurled out of the window, though that was a great work of art too, and heartbreaking that it had to happen, especially after all the love you put into making it.

I am writing without my glasses so the contours of this note may be a little awry. Also I am very tired: I cannot believe our poor pier has been swept away: that pier, that gave so much happiness to many and us, *was us* in a sense; we risked our lives building it, especially on the further reaches you never saw, where there was a 35-foot perpendicular drop on to the granite and barnacles if you made a mistake: nobody could understand how it survived so long, not even engineers, and it was nicknamed "The Crazy Wonder" on the beach. Ramshackle from certain angles though it was, and the handrails puerile (but oh the washing hung out on the line there, like great white stationary birds beating their wings against the gale). Margie and I built it together with practically no tools and I am broken hearted it has gone.

<div align="right">

Malcolm

</div>

* Lowry-drawn seagulls, used in many of his letters and manifestations of a happy frame of mind.

1955–1956

To David Markson

Ripeness is only the beginning or the Shape
in the Haunted Rectory
The White Cottage
Ripe, near Lewes, Sussex
[November, 1956]

Dear old Dave:

I haven't not written out of negligence or lack of affection but
Margie has been in hospital for the past month and very ill indeed
for much longer: very worrying, but I've been expecting it for some
time. She has had a complete nervous collapse, can't speak, scarcely
walk, anything, and I'm not allowed to see her as yet. They keep
her asleep mostly and she can read no letters at present, but her
address is St. Luke's Woodside Hospital, Ground Floor West, Woodside Ave., Muswell Hill, London N. 10 and if you dropped her a
note she'd have it when she comes out of her Rip van Winkle snooze.

Anyhow while she is away I am living on an absolute incontro-
vertible wagon in a rectory haunted by a phantom billiard ball that
bounces down the stairs at midnight and working like hell and seeing no one (apart from the billiard ball of course). I think the pictures of yourself and Elaine are marvellously happy and Elaine wonderfully pretty. Perhaps you look a shade Mephistophelian though, if
very fit and all a-taunto. I think your chain-gang haircut is only
justified should you swim. All right then, swim. I have a greatgross-
father beard—don't know what you would say of that: I have taken
to saying "beaver" in a loud tone to unshaven people who are about
to say it to me.

I believe Israel's action in invading Egypt, as well as England's, to
be thoroughly justified, and admirably courageous, though I seem to
be in a minority of one. England is in an unbelievable turmoil, with
riots in the streets, and they are burning the Pope for some reason
in effigy this afternoon in Lewes near here, together with Anthony
Eden, which seems to me very confusing. I shouldn't wonder if it
makes my billiard ball so nervous it starts going upstairs. Some of
Eden's reasons for taking action seem a little screwy but all in all
I continue to feel the VIII chapter of the *Volc* to be redeemed. But
I don't think anybody's existence should depend on oil and if it
does, they should do something about it. Don't mention the "war"
if you write to Margie. Gloomy Sunday in Hungary too and have

you ever heard the Robeson record of *Gloomy Sunday:* it's the only truly tragic song I ever heard. But all manner of things will be well soon here—at least with us. I am studying your story in the *Satevepost.* I think it would make an admirable film, please tell me where they made you alter it: I suspect they've made you make a grammatical mistake at one point. We may be film magnates together yet: a producer has just paid me $500 for a 6-months option on the *Volc.* And just as Margie went into hospital there was a note (which Fitzgerald would have appreciated) just arrived re Selznick offering some hope re our M & M version of *Tender Is the Night* for Frank. We are very proud of your story and boast of knowing its author: I really mean this in case you think I'm being ironic. Give Elaine my and our best love—and now to go off and make both yourselves happy forever and aye as I'm sure you will.

Bless you both.

Love,

Malc

To Dr. and Mrs. E. B. Woolfan

The White Cottage
Ripe, near Lewes
Sussex, England
November 13, 1956

My very dear Priscilla and Bert:

You must by now have received my cable and fearing that it may be anything but self-explanatory, and thus may be adding unnecessary anxiety about Margerie to your feeling of deep loss and sorrow—in which I deeply share and participate and for which I express my profoundest sympathy as well as I can, in the words that are nonetheless heartfelt for being platitudinous—at Mother's death, I'm writing this that will have to do at the moment (even though it does not of course do and can be nothing but inadequate) also as a vocal expression of Margerie's grief and solidarity with this, but the situation about *her* is roughly this: first let me assure you that there is nothing greatly to worry about. She has however been in hospital in London for about a month, during which she has had the best of care (and has been for the most part even very comfortable, she assures me, and with a private room of her own), but has also for the latter part of this time been mostly asleep, under deep and continuous sedation, more or less, from which she emerged a few days ago into a routine of glucose, insulin, massive doses of vitamins and so on. But on top of this she has not been allowed to see anybody or receive any news of the world outside—and God knows what news it has been—until a few days ago, as I say, with still a ban on any personal news of a disturbing nature, when she emerged from this Ripvanwinkledom, feeling and sounding better than she has in ten years. All this however as a result of a kind of cumulative nervous upset and anxiety and tension evincing, as its most hospitalizable and aggravating symptom for her, a colossal stammer which practically prevented the poor girl from talking at all coherently: from all this (there turned out nothing organically wrong) I'm delighted to say that she's almost completely and miraculously recovered, and she was to come home, and may still do so, next Friday, *une femme nouvelle:* on the other hand there had to be an agreement between all con-cerned that I would absorb all shocks for her in the meanwhile, good or bad (for example I wasn't able to tell her there is a serious pros-pect of the *Volcano* as a film—and please don't mention this either outside the family; if it comes off I want to get Margie in on the script), and there was a tacit understanding as to what the nature of that bad news might be, so that, suspecting with some sudden second sight, just at the moment I was going to forward the two letters, that this might be this news, or something like it, I felt mor-ally obliged to break the law against tampering with Her Majesty's mail, and thank God opened them, with some misgivings, I admit (that you were kept in the dark at first was to spare you anxiety, and of course Mother, when you already had enough). But there was no reason she couldn't have written you the last day or two, giving you her good news. Even as it was, having, tragically, read Mother's letter first, with its cheerful tone and splendidly courageous outlook, I was tempted to post that on to her as good news and scrupulously keep yours at first I thought unopened till after her return when she was stronger, and then I read its deeply sad contents and had to make my decision not to send either letter, or impart that news, until I'd consulted with her doctor. I immediately phoned the sister at the hospital to get the doctor, who was away, to phone me, which he'll do tomorrow morning, with his opinion on how best to break the news to her or even for a while not at all. It was terrible to speak to Margie on the phone with her in such high spirits about coming home and myself with this black tidings I dared not impart in my pocket. So there the matter rests. And apart from this, and the world, things have rarely looked so good for us. I'll keep you informed. Deep sympathy and love to you both,

Malcolm

P.S. Darling Prissy do not blame yourself for having written on top of all your poor woe. If anyone is to blame it is I, for not giving you the lie of the land before, though I don't see how I very well could. Have you any liquor in the house? I am tee-total these days but I think you better have a good slug. Mother would be the last to mind.

P.P.S. Nov. 14. Dear Bert: The doctor has just phoned me long distance to say that he's returned from an important conference especially to break the news himself, myself having supplied the details, so that the hospital, where she may have to stay a little longer, can absorb the initial shock. I, Prissy, will now forward your letters which now can afford only relief at how splendidly you took care of her, and Mother's happy outlook at the end. Your very affectionate brother,

Malcolm

To David Markson

The White Cottage
December 11, 1956

(Letter from Margerie Lowry
with interpolations and P.S. by Malcolm)
Dear Elaine—and Dave—
Bless you both for your letters. Here I am again, feeling fine and all a-taunto. I was furious at being ill. God how I hated it! So I marched into the hospital, fell flat on my face, flat out, opened one eye half way and hissed: Now do whatever you have to do as quickly as possible and I'll cooperate. So they did and I did and it was unpleasant but worth while. Basta!
We are impressed, entertained and delighted, Dave, about Oedipus. Malc immediately made up one blurb after another, each wittier than the last and we roared and rolled in the aisles. Seriously though, cheers, darling, cheers. (I don't see why Margerie should find it necessary to write a blurb about my wit however, if any.)

And the apartment too—my dear Elaine, what is in store for you I know only too well. Are you going to do it yourselves? If so I can only quote Malc's timeless remark when we had gazed, silently, for some minutes at the celebrated ceiling of the Sistine Chapel. "Margie," he said reverently, "do you remember when we painted the ceiling of the shack?" (There she goes again: timeless because witless, probably she means.)

Did he write you from the vicarage? I hope so. He has a new title now: Saint Leon of Ripe. (She knows I wrote you from the vicarage, which was a rectory.)

The chaps who want to film the *Volcano* are (1) a Mr. Nichols (why *Mr.* Nichols?) who's made so much money on T.V. he now wants to make a serious film (why shouldn't he make money if he wants it?) and (2) José Quintero, director of the current O'Neill, *Long Day's Journey*, who, it seems, has long cherished an ambition to direct the *Volcano*. This is still only in the family, as it were, because we haven't signed yet but it looks as though we would any day now. And this morning came a letter from Alfred Knopf, Jr., who claims he's been trying to find Malcolm for years and wants to do a reprint of the *Volcano* for his Vintage Books. (Lion Books please note. Lion Books please note.) He says he finally located us through Jimmie Stern, though it was the wrong address and only reached us by luck. Meanwhile my beloved old demon just tosses these missives at me and says yes, that's fine, now I must get down to work. (Just too bloody nonchalant for words.) And he's writing as he hasn't done since he finished the *Volcano*, which is the best news of all. (Except that he hasn't finished the *Volcano* yet.) Love to you both,

Margerie

P.S. All the very best love to Elaine and yourself! Interpolated remarks were not exactly due to irritation, rather to ebullience. Or perhaps I felt she wasn't taking your Oedipus break seriously enough, that really is a crazy opportunity to do something real cool, when one thinks of it, besides you've probably got as long as Sophocles had to get Tiresias in training for Melbourne. Have you got your Cocteau's Machine Infernale well oiled? sleeping with Yeats under the bed? In Cocteau the Sphinx falls in love with Oedipus, and then eats him, I think; I forget but anyway it's mighty powerful stuff. And I really did have a blurb all written out for you, but I've lost it so I'll have to make up another one. All power to you anyway. We are having a grand life now and I am working like absolute sin on *Gabriola* with which I have completely fallen in love but I am managing to eat it a little more than it eats me so far. Back to work now, boys and girls. Whales! Inlets! The Towering Rockies! Glittering Lakes in an Evergreen setting on the—sorry, I forgot. Sphinxes! Jackals! The Seven Against Thebes! the man woman! Anubis! All the glory that was Greece overturned in this pulsating drama of a mother's love that triumphed even beyond the grave to give psychoanalysis its proudest name! THE STORY *BEHIND* THE FREUD LEGEND.

M.

MARKSON

ΣΟΦΟΚΛΕΟΥΣ

ΟΙΔΙΠΟΥΣ

'ηΤΕΚΝΑ, κάδμου τοβ πάφαι νέα τρφη—

SEE Kingly pride dragged in the dust by the claw-footed Desert Bosom! See the Burning Demon that strikes her blow by night! The Sphinx humbled! What did Nasser's mother really look like? You'll find out when you see Oedipus confronted by the Lion-Faced Lady! What is behind the Greek attitude to Cyprus and the Western Powers? You'll discover when you read this torrid drama of the Son-Husband Wife-Mother Relationship embroiled with the madly jealous all-Egyptian Lion-Woman in Eternal Sexagon! See the young Oedipus and the Lion-Faced Lady! See the Sphinx feeding! How the Young King saw the riddle of the Sphinx and what he did about it! HEAR THE FIRST AND MOST SEXUAL QUIZ ON EARTH! At all Vista-Vision Book Stores.

Several Drachmas.

PART XII: *1957*

PART XII. 1937

To George Sumner Albee*

The White Cottage
Ripe, near Lewes
Sussex, England
March 17, 1957

Dear George Albee:

Thank you very much for your generously worded and warm-hearted letter. What you say about *Under the Volcano* is tremendously encouraging, even more so, and not without its gratifying ironies too, in that it was anything but a success here in England, so much so that my mother, whom I had deceived for years into thinking I was writing a religious book like Butler's *With Christ at Sea,* or at least some sort of Anglican or even Methodist-cum-Swedenborgian *Bildungsroman,* only the second syllable of which was apparent from the reviews, said she simply could not endure reading their harsh criticism, and she though having a kind heart was quite a tough old lady, as befitted the daughter of the skipper of a windjammer from whom she would have doubtless heard some harsher criticism still, had not the good mariner been by this time at the bottom of the Indian Ocean, whither he had followed the windjamme in question. All was made well when my wife (herself American) when she visited England showed her some of the more sympathetic American reviews —including that very one which maybe put you off—so that this kindness, however undeserved, as I must gratefully say of yours too, had its pragmatic value in that my mother would otherwise have died in the unhappy belief (for old ladies are liable to set as great store in the literal interpretation of reviews as of Gospels, without finding it necessary to investigate the original text) that I had accomplished nothing whatsoever, since other work, so far as she was concerned, had for years been locked up in the strong square walnut desk of my deceased father, where for all I know it still remains. Even more depress-

* American novelist

o

ing was its reception in my then adopted city of Vancouver, Canada (whose literature I had had the childish dream of enriching with some well-chosen words), who described the matter variously as ". . . these turgid pages . . ." ". . . not improved by being written in the style of Conrad at his worst . . ." ". . . volcanoes erupt for no reason, what is it all about?" Or even, witheringly, ". . . typical of the 'new school' of American delinquency and sadism," or, patriotic-ally, "This Consul should have been sacked before we reached page 5." So much for local boy makes good in his home town. On all the more grateful ear then, fall your own kindly words, including those of the kindly action in writing to Sam Rapport: here, however, friendly coincidence appears to have come into play, because at about the same time you were doing that, Alfred Knopf, Jr., was writing to me asking if he could republish it in Vintage Books. Imagine my pleasant surprise at this honour after ten years even though I had to say—as to you regards Rapport—thank you but I thought not, as I believe Random House had a lien on the work: however meanwhile Random House had apparently given their per-mission to Knopf, so that it looks as though Knopf will reissue it fairly soon in that edition. But I thank you for the thought anyway.

Meantime, what is life like in Cuba? I am curious. I read of revo-lutions, counterrevolutions, and *borrachonazis* in the zócalo. I hope sincerely that such has not disturbed the peace or person of yourself and your good wife in Playa Veradero. I have once been in Cuba, for the space of about an hour, having set foot upon your soil in a place named something like Camaguay, from a plane flying from Haiti to Florida, about ten years ago, in fact about a week before *Under the Volcano* came out in America. I gained less idea of Cuba, however, probably, than those to whom my wife and I sent postcards thence, the airport being little more than a well-stocked bar in the middle of a limitless desert. And I also had a strange friend who once invited us to live in the Isle of Pines (though not—or not then anyway—in the Convict settlement) where, he assured me, a fortune was to be made out of marble, although he did not state what was to be done with the marble, and I very much fear, not having heard from him since, that a tombstone may have been contrived out of that same marble for himself. On the other hand I have an impression that Cuba must be a marvellous place in which to live, and pursue the Better Life, the Better Thing, and indeed celebrate generally the Life Electric: such at least would seem to be confirmed by Hemingway's attachment to it, and since you live there yourself too (as did my father, from time to time, in Havana) perhaps you'll tell me how you find it. In England, even as I write, there is a feeling not so foreign from that of your revolutions, counterrevolutions, and *borrachonazis* in the zócalo, though on a somewhat more polite and (perhaps) bloodless scale, though nonetheless bloody in other respects since we appear heading, unless some wisdom stops it, into a General Strike of catastrophic proportions. I was a schoolboy here during the last General Strike in 1926 and naturally regarded it as being a great deal of fun, but there is in fact no fun about it, labour troubles here having no relation to those in the rest of the world, and but remote similarity to those in America, and being based upon a huge implacable hatred and desire for revenge upon one class by the other, indeed the desire for revenge is really mostly on one side, namely Labour's, nor does the fact they've already had all the revenge possible without cutting their own throats seem to make any difference, when there's a chance to get some more, and they don't give a damn what happens to the country in the process: since the fact is that Labour is for the most part unblushingly reactionary while the Conservatives are relatively revolutionary the only thing that one could do, if one doesn't like the Conservatives too well either, is to put one's school cap back on and read Wordsworth, or perhaps Henry Adams, until it all blows over. Meantime it is likely that no contribution will be made to human freedom.

Meantime too I had a letter coincidentally from our friend Anton Myrer himself: I thought *Evil Under the Sun* was a splendid book, and I'm very glad to hear he's got another one on the way and am much looking forward to reading it. And have just written to tell him so. We had a publisher in common for a while, prior to which I had the pleasure of reading *Evil U.T.S.* before publication, and indeed wrote an eulogy of the same to the publishers in question, who prior to that had been largely responsible for the publication of the *Volcano:* but I think *Evil* did not have the same luck.

Tell me what I should know of your own work, and where I can get it. Both in Canada and here, for long periods, it has been all but impossible to keep in really close touch with American literature, for reasons of embargo and one thing and the other, so that I am ashamed that your name alone is familiar to me, and this perhaps for the wrong reasons, as I am sometimes congratulated or the reverse for the work of Robert Lowry, which I think is good for that matter, although I fear him to be dead too, or even worse, though I hope better. But don't be so down-hearted because you're going to write a funny book. I hope to do so myself someday. In fact, damn it, I thought *Under the Volcano* was funny, in parts anyway. Please thank your wife very much for liking it—my own wife joins me in sending you both kindest regards.

Sincerely,
Malcolm Lowry

To Viscount Churchill*

The White Cottage
Ripe, near Lewes, Sussex
April 4, 1957

Dear Peter:

It† seems to me excellently written, with a fine choice of the right clear vocables, and uncle Hugh a genuine delight throughout, and the thing preserves interest and vitality all the way through, with humour and nostalgia intermingled in the right proportions, while uncle couldn't be better or more endearing as I said before. The writing seems to me, though, a thought less careful after the first four pages, albeit it recovers again after that and the points I pick you up on are in any case minor—ah, the ands, the ifs, the buts, the howevers. As Flaubert—wasn't it Flaubert?—said, is there never an end to this tyrannical prose? Nonetheless one has to drive in one's finishing nails accurately or chinks appear in the corners of one's style; I might as well add that you seem to me to have achieved a good and individual one. Please excuse my writing in pencil but I can't write with the family pen (I feel perhaps one should spend one's days "making" or "mending" pens in this Mrs. Gaskell type of atmosphere).

p. 3. (middle and bottom) "thought about" and "go on," end two sentences: there's absolutely no objection to this *here,* and I just mention it as something to "think about" or "go on" for I think you tend to overdo this sort of construction elsewhere which gives the same effect as if it were incorrect, which of course it is not.

p. 4. (top) I'm very shaky about the rule but shouldn't it be "about *his* having tamed wild animals?"

p. 5. (bottom) I don't see why you shouldn't say "he broke loose," especially since you have a "had" problem here and top p. 6.

* Writer and journalist, cousin of Sir Winston Churchill.

† Manuscript of *All My Sins Remembered: The Autobiography of Lord Churchill,* published March 1965, by Coward-McCann in New York and Heinemann in London.

p. 6. (bottom) Query—commas after uncle Hugh and greyhound (if you omitted these deliberately that's different).

p. 7. (middle §) Margie noted this but I think I agree—seems a bit choppy even if you want to vary the rhythm. I append Margie's solution but I feel there now may appear something confused in the thought. "Not being that kind of snob" doesn't apply directly to being "not much given to thinking things out," on the other hand the latter is presumably included as an Edwardian characteristic: however the implication could be that had your mother been given to thinking things out she would have arrived at a point of social disapproval (which, not being that kind of snob, she wouldn't have arrived at)— pay no attention to this, you probably take care of it by using the "and" after "spirit" and hence cancelling the modification of the rest of the sentence by the "although"—*this way madness lies*, but I'd wanted to change the order in your sentence and I see I can't do it. Herewith Margie:

You could see she thought it silly or perhaps a disgraceful episode: there may have been a girl in the act or something. I thought of that later. It was not just social disapproval on my mother's part—although she was fully Edwardian in spirit and not much given to thinking things out—she was not that kind of snob.

And me:

You could see she thought it a silly or perhaps disgraceful episode —there may have been a girl in the act or something, I thought of that later—but it was not just social disapproval on my mother's part, although she was fully Edwardian in spirit and not much given to thinking things out, she was not that kind of snob.

I fear I haven't improved matters but perhaps you can make something better out of both of these. I deprived you of that last sentence by *itself* to prevent your ending on "out." See below.

Ibid (How I have always loved the word Ibid.) And the very last sentence in the same § as above seems a bit ill balanced and non-euphonious:

Her hopes had not been so well realized in the matter of her two eldest brothers who had further disappointed by dying young and leaving Hugh head of the family, so that this circus business seemed like a bad beginning better not spoken of (sic.).

(I think something like this—though you may want to put back the "as" before "head"—brings out your meaning better too, for after all the so-called bad beginning is in the past, and moreover isn't a bad beginning in *fact* exactly, I mean not in the conventional sense

SELECTED LETTERS OF MALCOLM LOWRY

in your mother's view, and the "like" I feel deconventionalizes it somehow, but the main trouble is the rhythm of your sentence; I'm not sure that "eldest" is correct either unless more brothers were concerned, shouldn't it be elder?) Ibid (very bottom): Stop me if I'm wrong but shouldn't it be, after all that, "*were* all part of it." If uncertain you can dodge the issue by using "seemed part of it."

p. 8. Both Margie and I felt something wrong at the bottom, which starts "He did not feel any promptings," which is clumsy, while "All of which accounted for why" is a good ending to a poem, but not a good beginning to the next sentence, at least not without putting "most likely" between commas though your trouble's elsewhere, I think: maybe the subject "Hugh" is too far away from the "why," too far *down* the sentence. In the next sentence Margie questions the "It" as a correct apposition for "All of which" but I think this is O.K. as a substitute but the trouble certainly does carry through the construction of the sequence over to the top of p. 9. where all in all one finds oneself with too many "gettings," and there's a monotony in the governing propositions, a plague of "fors"; the earlier problem I think can be solved simply by transposing the subject to an earlier position and using more commas etc. viz:

He felt no promptings to hide his light under a bushel. All of which accounted, most likely, for why Hugh, instead of growing fat as a racehorse owner, and getting his sporting reputation that way, as other Englishmen did and do, was always spending large amounts of violent and dangerous energy, as well as a great deal of money. It accounted for his hunting the Quorn Hounds himself instead of leaving that to a professional huntsman, for jumping big Leicestershire fences, so big that they were photographed afterwards by horse enthusiasts, for getting himself knocked out by famous boxers, going on safaris, and arctic hunting trips, where he would become snowed in for half a year, and on top of it all, every so often, flower in button-hole, cigar in mouth, for leading in a Derby winner.

(I hope not too much charm is lost in this way, but it may be a basis to go on—you still have two "gettings" as it stands: if you could sacrifice "growing," you could make one "getting" do double duty, i.e. instead of "getting fat as a race horse owner, and his sporting reputation that way etc." Also you could say: "becoming snowed in for half a year," if you don't like "where he would become" and "on top of it all," etc. But it's all too easy to lose the spontaneity of the thing tinkering around in this way: still you have to do a bit here, I think. Fortunately a sentence itself will cry uncle, so to speak, when

[402]

it's had enough, and though it may still look full of derangements, by
that time it's probably immortal.)

p. 10 (top) Margie criticizes the sentence beginning "I watched as the
international crisis" etc. I rather like the unusual construction—the
only thing is you have an unconscious rhyme in crises and surprises
—do you care? I don't.

Ibid. Youthful hanger *on* would finally be *on* not to say years went
on—watch this.

Ibid. (bottom) *"as it might be* by anyone these days," or "as it might
have been" etc. (otherwise the second "bought" is not properly understood in the passive) with the money.

Ibid. (last words) are O.K. but I'd look through and back and see
you don't do it too often—as I said—or it seems "conscious" or,
conversely, careless (if also "better not spoken of" end of 7 "that he
was accused of" Bottom 4) even when, in fact, it's more grammatically
correct to end with a preposition. It's a case of pure Gallic superstition having become ingrained in the language so that one might as
well seem to be flouting it with effect, I guess.

p. 13 (bottom) would be leaving . . . to be eyes . . . would be told, in
the same sentence.

Ibid. Type error. For "play with with" read "play with them." But
don't forget you have another "with them"; and also a "with suspicion." (Note: Not merely English but perhaps *all* children should be
eyed with suspicion whom there is any danger of having to play with
with with.)

Ibid. (Still at bottom) Comma after yellow cars too or none at all in
sentence. All this I find delightful and excellently written: Margie
likewise.

16 (top) Another "get away from" as ending. Not necessarily to alter
but simply to watch.

I like all this very much: I'm afraid I can see a bit here, quoted in
Time, beneath your portrait: "Glittering saddles and unmilitary
positions in the heather" or: "Gipsies and devilish ponies" or "They
gave the Kaiser a quieter pony than the rest."

17. Margie notes lack of verb in The incredible house etc. sentence. It
seems to me O.K. because there's a sort of implied exclamation point
at the end. Maybe there's something in the punctuation that could be
bettered though, likewise in previous sentence, which causes the sense
of lack.

19. (top) And certainly something amiss in the punctuation here,
which makes it look a bit like a poem by José García Villa:

I doubt though that Hugh, unless perhaps at the very end, etc.
Ibid. (last sentence) Margie suggests there should be some punctuation in this last sentence, a comma after "child," perhaps, but in my
opinion this would involve logically other balancing commas (after
"Hugh," after "winter,") which might spoil the unit of the sentence,
which *as* the last one perhaps has a beauty and extra-authority of its
own, by virtue of not being punctuated at all, and for which it has its
own license as a coda. As a coda it moves me as it is, but if you didn't
intend it as such maybe Margie's right.

I hope some of these reactions may be of some practical use, if their
somewhat gloomy grammarian nature does not give much indication
of the real pleasure reading the excerpt gave me. I look forward to
seeing more. Meanwhile I have another reaction to report which
came to me (while, dear Joan,* dipping my Plymouth Rock one day
into my tea) about the story you told of visiting the Lord Chancellor.
It occurs to me that this, much as you told it, could form the basis of
a really profoundly excellent short novel—I imagine it should be
short, not more than about 210 pages because you have the temptation
of too much material to draw on—which as a project is always a useful
thing to have up one's sleeve when discussing matters with publishers
(in fact you can make it two things to talk about, as you said, and
imply a sequel), entitled something like Missing Peer, or maybe better
Lost Peer, or more euphoniously still The Lost Peer. The story as you
told it is full of wonderful touches, the taxi driver who you felt
ought to know exactly about such objectives as the Chancellor, and
how to get there and did, the irrelevant conversations that nonetheless seemed so quintessentially English, the glossy unlikelihood of the
Lord Chancellor himself resembling a cross between a stockbroker and
Michael Arlen, but who nonetheless too is the Chief Equity Judge in
England—the significance of Law in this (though the Law is talking
about being stuck in the lift), the sense of the House of Lords being
above the law, or a law unto themselves, the dichotomy of the
spiritual need to participate, but of being American, yet at the same
time being not merely English but at the very centre of history, with
the superb symbol just thrown in, of the Thames flowing immediately
below, seen through the big windows. It isn't the Kafka-like element
of this which mainly appeals to me—though that may enter in or
contribute—it is the fact that, in the matter of establishing the
universality of your principal character (who could be a projection of
any or all sides of your many-sided self and simultaneously quite

* Viscount Churchill's wife.

[404]

distinct from your autobiographical self, etc.). In establishing this despite the apparent esotericism of your *mise en scène*, you are ex officio (which I hope to explain) more than up on Kafka, in fact the main battle of such a novel is already won at the outset. On second thoughts it's too complicated to explain why a peer of the realm, especially a missing peer, should seem more of a universal figure than a land surveyor, but one main point is that no one believed for one moment that Kafka's K. had ever surveyed any land, or ever had the remotest intention, let alone capability of doing so, whereas no one will doubt that your peer is a peer, which somehow renders his quality of being missing that much more human and dignified. In short, as a Much in Little, it has everything—there is the universal need for participation, to belong, yet the ennobled position of the protagonist, which might seem to disqualify him from *universality*, on the contrary makes him everyman too, in every man's eyes, testifies to the uniqueness of the individual—peer is also a highly ambiguous word, by the way, which can even mean comrade, if you want it to. What is more, you have the individual vis-à-vis the group, vis-à-vis the law, divine and human, but also he is a maker of the law himself, or ex-maker of the law, or law unto himself, and certainly squelcher of the law, or potentially to be so once more. So then there is the suspense!—Will he be able to take his seat, or won't he? You can be sure that this question will come to symbolize something of vital concern in the reader's life. There is great opportunity for splendid humour and sadness here, I feel. The piece could end perhaps with the hero's taking part in some fantastically involved debate in the House of Lords itself, either upon a subject of deadly seriousness of vital importance to mankind, or upon one of correspondingly little importance, yet whose very negligibility is almost sublime, or it could be upon some legislation pertinent to himself, in which he is obliged through honour to take a standpoint detrimental to his own aims, or vice versa (though one draws the line at some final debate on a capitalist punishment where he is an abolitionist who perhaps inadvertently has meanwhile committed a murder). On top of all this you have, presented to you on a platter, the situation which Henry James, if I'm not wrong, always thought of as the most essentially dramatic one, yet never succeeded in carrying off emotionally himself, namely the return, after many years, of the wanderer to his own country. But here you have another turn of the screw, not only in that your protagonist has become an American, but that America has come to represent to some extent, rightly or wrongly, and on several planes, the forces of reaction, contrasted with which even the most diehard Toryism exemplified in the House of Lords—not that your protagonist is necessarily even a conservative—sometimes seems liberal, "democratic." As against this there is his justified pride in his aristocratic heritage, and so forth. One doesn't stop there: there's always the suggestion in James that the American finally represents some down-to-earth autochthonous force of nature, a finer fresher thing morally, alongside the calculating essentially moribund European who, while taking the other in, always tends to look down on his "grass roots" values. Now, by gosh, when the last old sourdough has traded in his divining rod and gold sifting pan for a geiger counter, and conservation itself has a positively revolutionary aspect, the grass roots are sprouting in the House of Lords, so to say—and none of this by any means obvious, or cut and dried, and without ever losing sight of the conflicting pathos and humour in the situation, nor, visually, ever of that grand view of the Thames, below the big windows. And very grand and beautiful is the book, likewise, in which you can draw occasionally, but sparingly, from the material in the autobiography itself, particularly the postillions in short yellow jackets and beaver hats on p. 14—a masterly American thought to have in the taxi, for instance, while journeying in more humble mode toward the Lord High Chancellor, Keeper of the Great Seal, Privy Councilor, prolocutor of the House of Lords and what not—or better, a bit later, in retrospect—or p. 15, the dramatic Gothic appearance of some equivalent of Lowther, the Castle, and so on, all of which nostalgias would be highly accentuated by the double-barreled doubly transatlantic nostalgias of your lost and found hero. Don't let such a notion distract you from the work in progress, but I can't help counselling you to keep it in mind for some future date, or rather don't keep it in mind, rather forget it, and remember it when you wish to, and dig it up then, if you wish to, for it strikes me that all this presurmise of your own work is slightly forward, even a bit assuming and possibly mistakeable in the sense that in my enthusiasm I have suggested a kind of book you may dislike. On the other hand I can't apologize, for I was so smitten by the conviction that you do have a book there, after your conversation of the other day, that once I'd started to write about it to you I couldn't stop or let my words tail off unconvincingly in a fog of Cydrax fumes. Moreover I felt the more inclined to mention my strong impression because I feel you are uniquely equipped to write such a book and indeed nobody else but yourself possibly could write it. So you must forgive me. Don't bother to answer this letter either, which is far too long, though a pleasure to write; but to answer it is another matter. I just spoke on the telephone with John, who seemed in very good form, and has just burned Mr. Connolly in the *New Statesman,* though I don't know yet on what grounds. He, John, recently wrote a brilliant thing on Isak Dinesen in *Twentieth Century* which caused me to reread her *Gothic Tales* with profit, and indeed it was somewhat in the manner of one of those wonderful tales, a bit longer than the longest, and not so diffused through various narrators, and not so Gothic (though still Gothic), and with a certain advantage of contemporary realism, that my Plymouth Rock caused me to visualize your unborn opus, which would have the added advantage of taking you perhaps (ha ha) less than six months to write. At least in the first draft. Do I have anything else to say? Yes, Joan, a masterpiece culled from the paper, and copied from a government paper, so that it might be used in the aforesaid debate, Peter, in the House of Lords, in kindly derision of certain goings-on in Commons: it seems to concern certain nuts and runs: In the Nuts (unground) (other than Groundnuts) Order, the expressions nuts shall have reference to such nuts, other than groundnuts, as would, but for this Amending Order, not qualify as nuts (unground) (other than groundnuts) by reason of their being nuts (unground). And by the way did you ever notice that the Prince of Darkness, the Prince of Peace, and the Prince of Wales all lived next to each other in the dictionary? They do, anyhow. It was very good to see you both the other day, and the best love to Joan and yourself from us both,

Malcolm

To Ralph Gustafson*

The White Cottage
Ripe, near Lewes
Sussex, England
[April 29, 1957]

Dear Ralph Gustafson:

I'm very sorry to take so long to reply to your letter of March 12 but Jonathan Cape sent it back to Canada again, so that it had to get re-forwarded again from B.C. before I received it.

I'm very honored to be put in the Penguin though whether I qualify

* Writer and anthologist.

strictly as a Canadian is another matter though I like to think I do: under the old law I did, though I still have a British passport, albeit I took out Canadian papers, never decided on any final citizenship, so am classed as a Canadian resident. My wife and I lived there for fourteen years in a waterfront shack on Burrard Inlet which I still have that I loved or love more than my life and wrote—all my best work, as the saying is, there. I left in 1954 because of my wife's health but we hope to return. But I never became a Canadian citizen under the new law: nonetheless I've as much right to call myself Canadian as Louis Hémon had and I even wrote a Canadian national anthem, though nobody's sung it except me. I had a childish ambition—maybe not so childish—always to contribute something to Canadian literature though, and I wrote a book called *Under the Volcano,* which has become fairly well known, but which people seem to think is written by an American. Like all blokes in the throes of an anthology I suppose that you are persecuted by replies from contributors you want saying that they want you to select something else—of theirs—if possible *too,* and I do not want to torment you in this way but I am no exception, thinking I've done some things better than these two, but I'm proud you selected them anyway, though I thought a thing called "Sestine in a Cantina" (perhaps too long) and one called "Salmon Drowns Eagle" that I thought might have been suitable: and A. J. M. Smith printed another in his Scribner anthology called "In Memoriam Ingvald Bjorndal" that I'm fond of: when I say *I'm* fond of, I mean this literally, because very few people have ever expressed their opinion one way or another about my verse so any fatherly advice on the subject, no matter how devastating, will be very welcome to me: sometimes I think I've never been able fully to understand the most elementary principles of scansion, stress, interior rhyme and the like with the result, by overcompensation, that my poems such as they are *look* as though they had a kind of wooden monotonous classical frame: perhaps I have no ear (Birrell on Dr. Johnson: "He knew but one way of writing poetry, namely to chain together as much sound sense and sombre feeling as he could squeeze into the fetters of rhyming couplets and then to clash those fetters very loudly in your ear. This proceeding he called versification") but then I must have some sort of ear because I began life as a would-be composer of hot jazz, and what is more I think a good one. All this is very sad and complicated to me because I think of practically nothing else but poetry when I'm not thinking about my old shack on Burrard Inlet but *like* so extremely few poems of any kind by anybody that it seems to me I am maybe inhibiting myself from writing, either by some serious lack of judgement in regard to my own craft, or some fanatical narcissism or other that makes me set the touchstone impossibly high, as a result of which I am now writing a huge and sad novel about Burrard Inlet called *October Ferry to Gabriola* that I sometimes feel could have been better stated in about ten short poems—or even lines—instead: then again I have good judgement about other people's poetry when I can understand what they are saying, which isn't very often, so please tell me what I should read: I'd like to educate myself as a poet seriously, though it's getting a bit late in all conscience. Tell me of your own recent work: I like much all that I have read of yours.

Two wild western poets came to see my wife and I in the bush on Burrard one stormy night some years ago, and I enclose you some of the recent work of one, which seems to me—the typed ones—damned good. This fellow Curt Lang was scarcely out of his teens and he impressed me mightily as being a type I thought extinct: namely all poet, whose function is to write poetry. His address is Curt Lang, 517 Pine, West Montreal, Quebec. I think the written poem would be better without the *on retina* in the first line, and the final couplet is weak: but the other two have a kind of fury, and the architectural one at the end, a really terrifying quality, that seems to me very rare and original in a poet, whatever the merits of his typography or indeed however he means it to be printed: I do think he is worthy of inclusion, even if you have to kick me out, for he is a young bloke who could use and deserves that kind of encouragement in my opinion. (Not that I couldn't or don't, but I'm older.) The work of his friend on that occasion, whose name I've unfortunately mislaid, is also worth looking into: his name is Al something or other, but Curt Lang would put you on to his work which again impressed me by its originality, intricacy and power. He is an older poet who has published a chapbook or so, but both are well worth watching and he too is worth considering in my opinion but maybe you've already made your selection. I've met a lot of writers but I have rarely been impressed by such dedication on the part of anybody as these two, and as for Lang he might well have genius. (I hope these poems will cause you to drop a line to Lang anyway and if you decide to use any of them he could enlighten you as to the typography—or you him, but could you let me have them back eventually because I thought of sending them to Spender or somebody). Re my bad memory, I seem to recollect a misprint, if not two in "The Glaucous Winged Gull." A memory *stronger* than childhood it was meant to be, not *stranger* anyway, for what that's worth. Among your own admirable but lesser-known works did you not once write a story about someone climbing a building printed by Martha Foley in 1948?—horrifyingly good. I can still feel it. If you didn't write it please take it as a compliment that I thought you did.

Sincerely yours,
Malcolm Lowry

P.S. Did you ever come across the work of a man named Norman Newton? He struck me as an exceptionally promising writer, though I have not heard from him for many years.

P.P.S. We are going to live in the Lake District, in Grasmere, for a while not because it reminds one of Wordsworth so much but because if we half shut our eyes we may be able to imagine we're back on Burrard Inlet!

To James Stern

The White Cottage
Ripe, near Lewes
Sussex
[1957]

Dear Jimmy:

We looked for you all day through the storm but didn't even see a flash of lightning (though just now, a week later, I heard a great roar of thunder).

The poppies blew over in the bloody brood, however, and we still live in hopes you may be coming, as when a certain magician was thinking, the churchbells started, elsewhere, ringing, though I'm not quite sure who the magician was. I hope you didn't have any trouble with your car on that stormy day, on which I also received an extraordinary letter from Germany about the *Volcano* couched in terms rather more suitable to the young Hofmannsthal than to the Cydraddict of Ripe. I would be extremely glad of your translation. Don't be put off by the rumour of Cydrax either, as my other friends seem to be. There's plenty else in the house. I don't even drink Cydrax myself for that matter, not to any excess, that is: in fact remembering that Burton (not on Trent) somewhere said that borage was an aid to melancholy, and finding the garden full of borage, I have taken somewhat to borage: borage, I discover, on the contrary, *hugely induces melancholy,* so I can suppose only that Burton (not on Trent) meant that he found it an aid in *writing The Anatomy of Melancholy.* Well, life is full of little touches like that. Do let us see or hear from you soon. The phone number is RIPE 282. Everything you say can be heard next door by our landlady's sister, who just lent me *The Psychic Life of Jesus,* so don't say anything too metaphysical. For the rest I am doing a bit of fairly good work that is boring me to death but we do have—largely thanks to Margerie—a marvellous garden, in which everything is to be found in flower, except henbane, which is to be found in the churchyard. Drop along: and if you will, stay. In fact both of you stay. Let us hear. Love to you and to Tanya.

Malcolm

P.S. I forgot to say that the house in question (easily distinguishable over the foregathering gloom by reason of its two immense chimney stacks, pots, etc. etc.) is—in fact, indeed is—Rumplespiel—is—is, perhaps—indeed is—

etc.
Telegraphic address: Usher

To Ralph Gustafson

The White Cottage
Ripe, near Lewes
Sussex
May 23, 1957

Dear Ralph Gustafson:

Thank you for your kind and very encouraging note.* Also I'm pleased you liked Curt Lang's poems. Yes, by all means add your praise for the old novel: I'm honored you should give it. But of *Cain,* of which I can't find a copy, can't remember the title, and can't quite the meaning or intention—what does it mean? I mean I vaguely remember what it was *meant* to mean (and I also remember reading that poem—which was written in 1936, one of my first—to a girl, intending to cheer her up, instead she passed out), but does it *mean*

* See Appendix 9.

what it might appear to mean? Does it have any religious parallel or is it a kind of traumatic dislocation of pre-Judgement day? In any case can you improve it, for I do remember one thing in A. J. M. Smith's reprint of it which was a misprint, viz: it couldn't be *recommend the Pentecost* could it? which was printed, I must have meant *recommemorate*, though that can't be it either quite, or can it? And why the Pentecost too? I'm glad you liked it though, for I loved it when I wrote it, which was with something considerably worse than a hangover, in a million acres of cactus (but fortunately some tequila) in a Mexican pullman car called the *Aristotle*. "Lupus in Fabula" was written at the same *time* I wrote p. 88 of the *Volcano* (how good of you to spot the identity), in the margin of the MSS and was originally called "Xocxitepec," a better title, I think, but it was suggested by an article by J. B. Priestley on being followed in a dream by some beastie perhaps of the fifth dimension! But in *Cain* (or whatever title) I'm sure it *can't* be recommend. Yet what would I mean by recommemorate? Please help.

Sincerely yours,
Malcolm Lowry

P.S. I have just found the poem and surely *recommemorate* is better, though I still can't quite understand what I meant, albeit I do like it somehow and *recommemorate* is in the original so could you now restore it; if you cannot—improve on it. I see the point now, with my wife's help; the descent of the Holy Spirit on the Apostles. Maybe the punctuation is a bit screwy in places. What about "Pentecost" as a title?

Gratefully yours,
ML

HAPPINESS

Blue mountains with snow and blue cold rough water—
A wild sky full of stars at rising
And Venus and the gibbous moon at sunrise.
Gulls following a motor boat against the wind,
Trees with branches rooted in air;
Sitting in the sun at noon
With the furiously smoking shadow of the shack chimney,
Eagles drive downwind in one,
Terns blow backward,
A new kind of tobacco at eleven,
And my love returning on the four o'clock bus—
My God, why have you given this to us?

1957

I couldn't resist sending you this which I love and is about our old shack that we still have. I thought it might make a good resolution to the other two. Brother what a life that was, is.

To David Markson

Grasmere
June 15, 1957

Dollarton? That's what we thought but it's Grasmere where Words-worth designed the chimney pots and you may see de Quincey's room (smoking prohibited) in de Quincey's house to which, on payment of 1/6 you may be admitted on all days save Sundays as Wordsworth's cottage, which it was for 5 years. How goes *Swellfoot the Tyrant?* Your letter was melancholy, but cannot you *use* that very uncertainty as to one's ability as a strength? O'Neill (see *Long Day's Journey*) thought himself not much use as a writer too. Have you read *Isaac Babel?* You should. Do you know which stars are which and what bird is flying over your head and what flower blossoming? If you don't the anguish of *not* knowing is a very valid field for the artist. Moreover when you learn something it's a good thing to repossess the position of your original ignorance. Best love to Elaine and yourself from Margie and Malc.

To Harvey Burt

The White Cottage
Ripe near Lewes
Sussex
[June, 1957]

My dear Harvey—
We have not your new address albeit I hope it pleases you, and, whether or no, we may still have the privilege of staying with you both in some Metz of the soul, whether of good or even of damnation. I have some friends in Germany, notably a publisher, Klett, of Stutt-gart: should you be in that neighborhood of the Black Forest? Though I loved your description of Metz. And I am delighted that

you both were so happy there, as unhappy we missed the opportunity of all seeing it *zusammen:* but this was unavoidable. We went for a fortnight to Grasmere, and it is wonderful beyond belief: even the Ambleside golf course is only putted on by two curlews, leeches lurk for the gatherer still at the bottom of the tarns, and the loud old ferry no longer runs: children too, I am glad to say, seem less noisy than Wordsworth led one to believe they were, and we sat at the desk of the old man himself in Hawkshead, which is exactly like Tlaxcala in Mexico, examining the words mysteriously written thereon: W. Wordsworth.

> That, musing on them, often do I seem,
> Two consciousnesses, conscious of myself
> And of some other Being. A rude mass
> Of native rock, left midway in the square
> Of our small market village, was the goal
> Or centre of the sports; and when returned
> After long absence, thither I repaired
> Gone was the old grey stone, and in its place
> A smart Assembly-room usurped the ground
> That had been ours . .

He was too pessimistic: everything is the same, except the local bus, which in any case once ran into him.

> We rested in the shade, all pleased alike
> Conquered and conqueror. Thus the pride of strength
> And the vain-glory of superior skill
> Were tempered: thus was gradually produced
> A quiet independence of the heart . . .

Try though we might, however, we could not gain quite the same kind of quiet independence out of the silence of the new Laurie, the guardian of our Dollarton Grasmere, and, if I doubt not, of your own pinnace of peace of shining water, even while knaves and monarchs surely, not to mention queens, gleaming through the splendor of their last decay and unfading recollections, raged bitterly with keen and silent tooth all the green summer to forlorn cascades.

> The sounds of Westmorland . . .
> The creeks and bays . . .

And it is forgotten—or at least that's what they say.
No matter, my brother, thus oft amid these fits of vulgar joy, which

through all seasons on a child's pursuits (and I was about to get back
to Kyd the next moment by chance collisions and quaint accidents).

AND IT IS FORGOTTEN

I beg your pardon: I meant it wasn't. But hell, what shall I have to
say but:

> Uncouth assemblage was it, where no few
> Had changed their functions: some, plebeian cards
> Which Fate, beyond the something something something
> (I forget)
> And monarchs surly at the wrongs sustained
> Protracted yelling like the noise of wolves
> Or from the meadows sent on gusty days
> Beheld her breast, the wind, then suddenly
> Dashed headlong, and rejected by the storm.
>
> Ye lonely cottages wherein we dwelt
> A ministration of your own was ours
> Can I forget you, being as you were
> So beautiful among the pleasant fields
> In which you stood? Or can I forget
> The plain countenance with which
> You dealt out your plain comforts.

(at evening, when with pencil etc. etc. etc.)
Hell, I could record with no reluctant voice
God damn it Kyd, I didn't know how else to address you but in this
verdammit Norwegian.

M.

Note from John Davenport

[June, 1957]

Malcolm is buried in the parish churchyard. As he died so suddenly
there had to be an inquest: I have just heard the Eastbourne Coroner's
verdict:

Death by Misadventure.

APPENDICES

APPENDIX 1

To Malcolm Lowry

September 5, 1941

Dear Malcolm:
I have regretfully come to the conclusion that I am not going to find a publisher for *Under the Volcano*. It has been rejected by:

Farrar & Rinehart
Harcourt, Brace
Houghton Mifflin
Alfred Knopf
J. B. Lippincott
Little, Brown
Random House
Scribner's
Simon & Schuster
Duell, Sloan & Pearce
Dial Press
Story Press

I am sorry that I wasn't successful in placing it for you, and am holding the script here for your instructions.

Sincerely,
Harold Matson

APPENDIX 2

To Malcolm Lowry

July 31, 1945

Dear Malcolm:

Your novel has for me a peculiar fascination, sometimes aggravatingly. It is full of wonderful potentialities, in my judgement, but it needs a great deal of work to bring it down to size and proportion within the limits of its own worth. Perhaps I have become impatient with it and that may be the reason why this novel is much too long, and much too full of talk—for me.

But I wanted to find myself confirmed or wrong, and so I submitted it to Cap Pearce of Duell, Sloan and Pearce. I have just heard from him that he thinks the material should be placed in a "sharper and more dramatic form," and he doubts if it could have real appeal as it is.

Well, both he and I could still be wrong and I am submitting it to another editor immediately.

Sincerely,
Harold Matson

To Harold Matson

Dollarton, B.C., Canada
August 10, 1945

Dear Hal:

Please do not think me impertinent for what I am about to say, or think I'm trying to tell you your business, or any of those things: but please read carefully, with a detached and open mind, what I'm about to say, for I know it is of value to us all.

I can't help feeling, from your letter to Malcolm, that you haven't

[420]

quite grasped the nature of his book, and this is quite understandable, since it is seldom, I believe, that a great work of art finds its way easily. One possibly expects good books, even first-rate ones, to come one's way occasionally, but one does not expect one of the caliber of the *Volcano,* and why should one, for they come, if they come, very rarely indeed. I tell you without hesitation that the *Volcano* is such a book: one which will stand comparison with the past as well as the future. I have lived five years with this book in its present form; it has been as much a part of our lives as eating and breathing. I am not blind to Malcolm's faults as a writer. His astonishing awareness of the thickness of life, of the layers, the depths, the abysses, interlocking and interrelated, causes him to write a symphony where anyone else would have written a sonata or at most a concerto, and this makes his work sometimes appear dispersed, whereas actually the form and context have arisen so inextricably one from the other that they cannot be dissociated. Then too he is cramped, for instance, to some extent as a novelist by the subjective equipment of a poet, so that I doubt if he could ever be a great novelist of "character." And so on. But it is impossible that I could read this book a hundred times and still not, on rereading, find more in it, as if the thing were practically inexhaustible, if there were not that about it that was, to say the least, worth *publishing.* The *Volcano* is, actually, some sort of masterpiece, not just a thing of potentialities, and must be dealt with on that basis and sold on that basis, or not at all. If you choose to look at it on the surface as merely being the story of the last day in the life of a drunkard and his death, you are right too, since it is written on that level as well, and once in print will be doubtless read by many people on that level only with much excitement and enjoyment, since it is always dynamic and frequently hilariously funny (it is, in fact, on one plane a comedy, a sort of cosmic jape if you like). But it is a grave mistake to look at it *only* on this level and ignore the other levels on which it is written and its real meaning and meanings. Yet I feel that in your busy and hurried existence you simply may not have had the time to cope with this book at present as it should be coped with. And my only fear for the book is that very element of time which seems to rush on at such pell mell speed in New York that no one has time to read anything properly, with thoughtfulness, patience, a desire to have his imaginative life enriched, and at least some attempt at sympathy with the author's intention. But somehow you must find such a person, who loves literature for itself, and will not merely dash through the book or dip into it with an eye to its popular appeal. To tell Malcolm that it is too long or too full of talk is about as pertinent as telling Joyce or Proust that *Ulysses* or *Remembrance of Things Past* has wonderful potentialities but should be cut down to size etc. Or to tell Wagner that *Götterdämmerung* had some fine tunes but could never have popular appeal in its present form—which I have no doubt people did: for some reason the really unique work of art always arouses either outright antagonism in the first people who see it and before time has proved its place in the world of art, or, failing that, merely a complete lack of understanding. It is, perhaps, primarily a writer's book, and one which is likely to influence other writers and so filter down to the general public. Mind you, I'm not comparing Malcolm to Joyce or Proust or, say, Dostoevsky or Kafka or Melville in the sense of saying he is "like" any of them any more than they were like each other: each made his own tradition and is comparable perhaps only on the plane of outstanding importance.

The *Volcano,* as you know, is the first of a trilogy, the second of which is in progress (is, in fact, completed in a short form) and the third of which, as I told you last summer, was destroyed in our fire but which, in the course of time, will be rewritten, if not in its original form certainly in its original spirit and conception of its meaning to the whole. And now I put it to you squarely once more, Hal: in this book you have the opportunity of handling a work that is not merely a "good book" or even merely a first-rate one, but, it is at least arguable, is a classic of some sort, every bit as much as *Moby Dick* or what not, a milestone, if you like, and it is on this basis and no other that it must be dealt with, for, seeing its faults as we do and recognizing them, it has found its form, it is complete, Malcolm has found his style and come to maturity as an artist with it: it is finished. You may think that some of this smacks of the loyal little wife running to the defense of her mate, but I tell you this: that only a person whose whole existence *is* his work, who has dominated and disciplined the volcano within him, at what a cost of suffering even I do not wholly understand, could have written such a book.

From the sublime to the ridiculous: are Scribner's still extant? After having received from them some six or seven months ago the proofs of the *Shapes* (half corrected, half uncorrected) there has ensued another Great Silence, which was broken the other day, curiously enough, by a letter from a clipping bureau which informed me that "notices were appearing etc." Are they? And since, according to my

APPENDIX 2

contract, they must publish *The Last Twist of the Knife* this fall, do they plan to bring them both out at once? Or what? Would it be too much trouble for you to make one more effort to penetrate the mystery surrounding my mystery?

Cordially yours,
Margerie

APPENDIX 3

To Malcolm Lowry

Jonathan Cape
Thirty Bedford Square
London W.C.1
29th November 1945

Dear Malcolm Lowry,
 In the letter which you sent me with your manuscript there is the sentence:

But it would be heart-breaking to be told, when so much has been taken into account, that it should be couched in sharper or more dramatic form or something of that nature: it was created on many planes and everything in it, right down to the precise number of chapters, is there for a perfectly good reason.

Well, two readers have read it carefully, and I have read it also. The best thing that I can do is to send you a copy of one reader's report,* which seems to us here to crystallize most effectively and exactly what all three of us think about it. The question is, are you on reflection inclined to consider making the revisions which the report indicates, or, after thinking it over carefully, do you still feel about it exactly the same as when you wrote to me in August last? You no doubt have a duplicate of the typescript? I will retain my copy of the typescript until I hear from you.
 So that my letter should not appear ambiguous, let me say that if you decide to implement the suggestions contained in the report, I am prepared to say here and now that I will publish it and bring it out, I hope, sometime during next year. If you stand pat on your original declaration of last August that the book must remain exactly as it is, I will think again on the matter, but it does not necessarily mean I

* This report is unavailable for publication.

would say no. We feel here that the book has integrity and importance, but it would be a pity for it to go out as it stands, believing as we do that its favourable reception will be helped tremendously by the alterations. At the same time we believe that it would be considerably improved aesthetically if the suggestions in the report are carried out.

Yours sincerely,
Jonathan Cape

APPENDIX 4

FM 114 38
      ZG NEW YORK NY 19 1217P
MALCOLM LOWRY
DOLLARTON BC

HORRIFIED BY WHAT YOU TELL ME SHALL MAKE
THOROUGH INVESTIGATION AND WILL DO
EVERYTHING POSSIBLE TO MEET SITUATION COULD
YOUR WIFE SOON FURNISH COPY FOR LAST CHAPTER
THINK YOUR LETTER AMAZINGLY GENEROUS AND
TEMPERATE WILL WRITE YOU FULLY

                        MAXWELL PERKINS

                        SEPT. 23, 1946

MR. MALCOLM LOWRY
DOLLARTON
BRITISH COLUMBIA, CANADA

GREATLY APPRECIATE YOUR PATIENCE. HAVE SENT YOU
TWO COPIES OF BOOK AND DO NEED THE LAST CHAPTER.
FEEL SURE I CAN WRITE YOU QUITE FULLY BY TOMOR-
ROW. MANY THANKS FOR LETTER.

                        MAXWELL PERKINS

APPENDIX 4

To Malcolm Lowry

Charles Scribner's Sons
597 Fifth Avenue
New York 17, N.Y.
September 24, 1946

Dear Mr. Lowry:

Even now I cannot write you fully about this tragic episode. I shall be able to do so in a few days, not in excuse, but in explanation. When your first letter came, Charles Scribner was away, and after telegraphing you, I put it on his desk. After he had begun it, and had glanced at it here and there, he came into my office and asked me what I had discovered. He then said, "I'll go back and read the letter through, but it is too painful to read it." He agreed with me though, that it was an extraordinarily decent letter, and the forbearance of yourself and your wife has brought into this most unpleasant affair some element almost of pleasure.

Mr. X says he never saw the missing chapter. I had feared that since he seemed to think he had a free editorial hand—as the bill for corrections on *Shapes That Creep* indicates, and I enclose herewith a corrected royalty report since, of course, Mrs. Lowry should not have to pay for our corrections without approving them—he might have regarded the last chapter as superfluous, and deliberately omitted it. If his memory is right, this is not so, and it prohibits another possibility that occurred to me: the assembly of the signatures of a book is still done by hand, and occasionally a signature is omitted from some copies. I saw two or three letters saying that this book was not finished, and I turned them over to X, and even though he thought it was, it seemed to me possible that the last signature had in some way been omitted from every copy. But this could not be so. But even if your wife had somehow omitted it from the manuscript she sent us, the situation would be the same. For if we had sent her proofs, she would have discovered the omission. And we surely should have sent her proofs, by invariable custom. In fact, we almost always send first the galleys and then the page proofs.

Now as to what can be done: we have distributed about 3,000 copies, and we could not get them back, I am told by the head of the trade department. Many of them go out through jobbers. We have, though, 1,100 copies and we have forbidden any further distribution until we get a last chapter. We hope we may find a way, even though these copies are bound, to insert or add this chapter. We have also discussed the possibility of making some announcement that this chapter was omitted by error and that it is now available to anyone who asks for it, or that if they prefer, we shall supply them with a copy of the book containing it.

I hope you may be willing to let the matter rest at this point until the chapter comes, when we can see more clearly what will be practicable. But I assure you that we have every intention of taking every possible step to rectify our failure in so far as can be done, and to make restitution.

I have just talked with Mr. Matson to the same effect that I am now writing you. We did at least send him the author's copies of *The Last Twist of the Knife*. I think perhaps this was done because you were in Mexico at that time. I realize that you are entitled to a fuller explanation than I have given, but I must defer this for the moment.

Ever sincerely yours,
Maxwell E. Perkins

OCT. 7, 1946

MR. MALCOLM LOWRY
DOLLARTON
BRITISH COLUMBIA, CANADA

CHAPTER RECEIVED. WILL NOW STUDY PROBLEM OF HOW IT MAY BE USED. MANY THANKS. SHALL WRITE SOON.

MAXWELL PERKINS

To Margerie Lowry

October 9, 1946

Dear Mrs. Lowry:

I have never been more mortified than to learn of the very painful experience you have had in the handling of your books by one of our editors. I hope and believe that nothing of this kind has ever happened before or will occur again. Your husband has shown the greatest forbearance and patience in his letters to Mr. Perkins, and since Mr. Perkins, who is head of our Editorial Department, has had the matter in hand, I have not wished to complicate affairs. I believe, however, that it is only proper for me to send you a personal word of apology.

I believe Mr. Perkins has told Mr. Lowry that we have cancelled the author's alterations which, under the circumstances, should never have been charged to your account. I hear, also, that your final chapter has arrived and we will insert it in all copies of *The Last Twist of the Knife* which are in stock. This, I realize, is rather cold comfort to you as so many have already been sold, but it may be important in new editions or reprints of the story. I am also anxious to see that you do not suffer in any way through the fact that the sale of the book may well have been adversely affected by this omission. At present we have about three hundred dollars due you on the sales of *The Last Twist of the Knife,* after deducting the advance and some five hundred dollars on your earlier book. You are entirely at liberty to call upon this money any time you may choose without waiting for the period of accounting called for in our contract.

This is not a happy letter for one to write, but you have my sincere sympathy for the treatment you have received at our hands, and I assure you that I stand ready to do anything within reason to make amends. Your husband will soon be hearing from Mr. Perkins. Very likely you may never wish to hear the name of Scribner's again, but if you ever forgive us to the extent of sending another of your books, we will try to show that we are really responsible publishers.

Very sincerely,
Charles Scribner

To Charles Scribner

Dollarton, B.C., Canada
October 15, 1946

Dear Mr. Scribner:
Thank you so much for your kind and courteous letter. I realize that it must have been distressing to you to learn of the circumstances surrounding the publishing of my books by your firm. I have always considered Scribner's to be one of the finest of publishers and my husband and I felt certain, all during the time, that there must be unusual and extenuating circumstances.

P

Thank you for your offer concerning the advance money and also the consideration of a further book. These matters can probably best be dealt with through my agent when I have come to a decision concerning them.

Your letter and Mr. Perkins' communications have gone a long way in reestablishing my faith not only in Scribner's but in myself, which had become almost non-existent.

Yours sincerely,
Margerie Bonner Lowry

To Margerie Lowry

Charles Scribner's Sons
597 Fifth Avenue
New York 17, N.Y.
October 23, 1946

Dear Mrs. Lowry:

I sent you on Monday, in page proof, the last chapter for *The Last Twist of the Knife*. As soon as it comes back we'll print and add it to all the copies of the book that are accessible to us. And we'll have extra copies ready to send to anyone who may make inquiry. Now what else can we do to make reparations, for what we are doing is not very much?

As Mr. Scribner said, once this unhappy episode is closed, you will probably never want to hear our name again, but you and your husband have been so remarkably exceptional to the human race in general that I am taking the risk of sending you a book published on account of our centennial, *Of Making Many Books*. There are many people who, if they were in your position, would at last take pleasure in mutilating it, as we mutilated your book.

Ever sincerely yours,
Maxwell Perkins

P.S. What we would gladly do, since we cannot but believe that the sale of your book was injured by the omission of that chapter, especially after reading it, would be to add a thousand dollars to the advance against it. This would presumably offset any monetary loss. I do not know what else to suggest.

APPENDIX 4

To Maxwell Perkins

Dollarton, B.C., Canada
November 9, 1946

Dear Mr. Perkins:

I hope you won't think it boorish of me not having replied to your kind letter before, with its generous offer, or thanked you for the truly excellent, and at the same time frightfully funny, book by Roger Burlingame. These arrived at just one of those times: namely they coincided with not only the proofs of my last chapter, but with great titanic and extremely complicated lashings of galleys for my husband which had to be dealt with at once. My husband was so delighted indeed by *Of Making Many Books* that (a) it encouraged him to make some important corrections in his book we'd both otherwise have been reluctant to make and (b) I've had a hard time snatching it from him to read myself. But we have had to work literally day and night on his galleys to make a deadline, so much so that in dreams commas have wriggled round my ankles like tadpoles, even stinging me, colons have swollen up to giant size and hurled themselves at me, my husband heard the galleys singing out of tune, (but singing downwards instead of horizontally) and finally, as for myself, they had also a nasty habit of wrapping themselves around me like a winding sheet. So that your book, with its accounts of other such trials in other days, lent a lot of charm to our labours and provided a much needed obbligato thereto.

My husband says also to tell you, even though I wander from the point, that he is much moved to discover (which for some reason he had not known) that it was you who first perceived the extraordinary worth of Aiken's *Blue Voyage,* a book that not only had a tremendous influence upon him but which led to a lasting and valuable friendship. In fact we heard from Conrad A. only the other day. Malcolm says *Blue Voyage* was most unjustly and brutally criticized in England as in imitation of Joyce, which was so far from being the case that Joyce (as you doubtless know) was, largely on account of it, trying to buy "Osiris Jones" when he died, looking to that for fructification of his own work.

So much for that, although when we add to the coincidence of pressures that the whole district here including ourselves has been laid low with arsenic poisoning due to foreign bodies upon the local spinach, you will finally appreciate why I haven't answered before.

Though there is yet another reason: airmail has been held up due to storms and I seem temporarily to have lost touch with my agent. I can't make out if Hal is in New York or Christiania or where.

Now, as to my more practical answer. Well, oh Lord! how answer? Do I, Leacock-wise, dash the thousand dollars upon the ground, and then pick it up and dash it into my pocket? Malcolm says that could be regarded as a sensible course. But we both agree that in so far as we are all civilized, or for that matter even if we are not (for we ourselves live in the wilderness), if the matter is to be closed, it should be *closed*, that is, wiped out, as if not there (apart from which, in a bracket, it should be at least said that it was not *your* fault), an aberration, or an aberrant at least, such as any of us might have been capable of under anxiety, in short, forgiven and forgotten—if that does not leave me, which it perhaps does, looking unutterably smug. And if forgiven, how accept the thousand dollars? Or conversely, how not accept it? Moreover, the fact is I cannot either accept or not accept (according to my contract) without consulting Hal, with whom, as I said, I seem to have lost touch. I think the best thing is if you yourself consult with Hal Matson (if he is in New York) on the basis that so far as I am concerned the matter is closed, and that the thousand dollars more than adequately covers any monetary loss, which on the basis of the sale of *The Shapes That Creep,* and taking into account that *The Last Twist,* even with endings and all, is perhaps not so hot (though couldn't a fillip be given to its sale by some statement of the omission, as you earlier suggested, if not too agonizing?), it certainly does.

So far as concerns the rest, the statement "you will probably never want to hear our name again" if true, would, alack, probably work both ways. It is a fact that I do not want to go through "all that" again any more than you would want to go through "all this." But after all, there seems no reason to anticipate it.

As for myself, as a writer, I could and can go on writing mystery stories of a more or less first rateish, or even first rate, nature until all is blue: and here it is true I could have written you three or four better than the *Shapes* (which *is* good, and fresh, I think) already. But still—*cui bono?* And the more especially *cui bono* when you have rather more than a vague belief in your ability to play Hamlet. For one thing the material that gets wasted bothers me—something like putting flowers into a meat grinder. But probably, with any encouragement, I would write a few more in the coming years, if only to cut my teeth. I began to write mysteries in the first place with the definite idea of practice and discipline, feeling that the rigidity of the form would teach me to master my material, so that later I could discard this with at least the knowledge of what I was discarding. (I had another mystery two thirds written when our house burned down; my husband saved it, but I've never finished it, although I think it better than the other two.)

I have written one serious novel, *Horse in the Sky*, which it is no use my saying I wouldn't like you to look at because I would—it going without saying of course, in view of the obliquities, that all else be forgotten, should you find it hopeless. The situation in regard to this book is as follows: Jonathan Cape has conditionally accepted it in England, the conditions being that I want to make alterations in it and they want to see what they're going to be—the alterations pertain mostly to two chapters that I don't feel I've brought off in the way I intended them, and to a few small things like a trick I've rather overworked of ending a chapter with a single sentence on a separate paragraph. Malcolm says to tell you, should you see this book, that he considers his own influence, or the influence of others *on* him, *on* me, may have interfered here and there, to the book's detriment, with its proper accent. But however this may be (and I don't necessarily agree with him) I think you scarcely could fail to see a book *in* it, whatever your opinion of the use I've made of the material. I don't think it would be a waste of your time, even if all in all it is totally unfeasible for you to consider it, and I certainly would count it as a great favor if you would take a look at it, unless this should seem to come under Class X Division of Moral Blackmail, in which case don't, and please forget I even mentioned it. But to save you prior embarrassment at the mere thought of it, Cape's favourable judgement would seem to justify me in at least the suggestion. However, here again, I'm a little at sea (and this is another reason why I haven't answered your letter before) because I had only two copies (my own having become too mangled in our fire for any use); one is with Cape, and Hal has the other. I wrote Hal to send it to me as I wished to do some more work on it, but since I haven't received it perhaps Hal has done something else with it but at the moment I don't know what.

On the other hand, having found yourselves as a publisher (again forgetting all else) I don't think I'd count the labour worth the candle, for mystery stories alone, of going to all the trouble, or putting Hal to it, of getting another one. All that anxiety, for what? So, if I'm going to write or finish writing any more mysteries, I'd like to know if it strikes you as worth while, and when you'd like one, so that things may go not so much on crutches but a little more (as you might say) on skates. For I find myself, after a long period in which I was unable to write anything at all, even a letter, beginning to feel I can look at a typewriter with excitement instead of nausea. I did take quite a mass of excellent notes in Mexico last winter and I think there's a good mystery knocking around among them. Or should I try another straight novel? Or perhaps one should practise those scales awhile longer? Or perhaps the notion that they are, or ever were in the first place, scales, is an illusion. In short, although of course these are mostly questions no one but I myself can answer, finally, I feel that I am more in need, than of money, of some sound editorial advice.

One final small request. Would it be possible for me to have some author's copies of *The Shapes That Creep?*

Thank you again for your courteous letter and heartiest congratulations on your centennial.

Sincerely,
Margerie Bonner Lowry

To Harold Matson

Charles Scribner's Sons
597 Fifth Avenue
New York 17, N.Y.
November 15, 1946

Dear Mr. Matson:

I am sending you the amount due in royalties on Mrs. Lowry's account, according to the last royalty report, and the additional advance, after the necessary deduction for tax purposes, on *The Last Twist of the Knife.*

I am writing Mrs. Lowry now, and if we may continue to cooperate with her as publishers, we shall certainly make every effort to do it as we should.

Ever sincerely yours,
Maxwell Perkins

To Margerie Lowry

Charles Scribner's Sons
597 Fifth Avenue
New York 17, N.Y.
November 15, 1946

Dear Mrs. Lowry:

I called up Harold Matson and found him, and he had heard from you. I told him that I thought that, if only for our own sake, we should add a thousand dollars to the advance on *The Last Twist of the Knife*. He said he thought we should, and so I am now sending him a check for that, with the unfortunate deduction of $150 which we have to withhold for your taxes. At the same time we are sending him a check for $523.42 for royalties due according to the last royalty report.

Yesterday I called him about *Horse in the Sky*, but he had returned the manuscript to you, and I think it would be just as well—though I am most impatient to read it—if you made any revisions that you want to make. You would make them anyway, and they might as well be made now, especially as time will be saved by it. Maybe I ought not to attempt any word of what we call "advice" until I have read that, but I do not think there is much in detective stories alone, and though I understand the discipline you have got from them, I think you have probably had enough. I know of one writer who I am almost sure could have been a novelist of note, and wanted to be, who got so caught in the artifice and plot of the mystery story that when she tried to break loose with a novel, though it might have sold, it had all the qualities of the popular magazine serial. She could not break loose from the formula. I had to tell her this, and she decided not to publish the novel. I am afraid she never will write a novel. So I think that one can go on too long writing detective stories with a view to discipline. On the other hand, you certainly have a great aptitude for it, and it seems a pity not to finish the one that was two-thirds done, and perhaps you could alternate the Mexican one with novels. Mexico is now an interesting field, and fictionally rather unexplored.

I was amused about your getting entangled in the galleys, for I have seen it done in my own family. Some people just cannot handle them, and yet I have often thought that it was the best way in which to read a book. You don't have to keep turning pages, but just moving the galley up, and then when one is done, putting it at the bottom without even moving your eye. Now the Book-of-the-Month Club judges refuse to read galleys at all, and we have to make up all the books that go to them into pages—in fact, into a sort of bound book. So that leaves me in the great minority.

It is curious you brought up *Blue Voyage*. No, it was never an imitation of Joyce. Conrad had been investigating the vein in which it lies long before Joyce. I suppose it might have been influenced by *Ulysses,* but I never thought of it that way. Way back in his beginning he had been conscious of what Joyce later became conscious of, because of the events in his life and the revelations of modern psychology. He never was an imitator, nor could have been. But what was curious about *Blue Voyage* was that when it came here I was greatly excited, and was only troubled because it seemed unfinished. So I wanted to talk to him. I went to Boston on various business, and could not run him down until the end of the day, and then by phone. I told him how great was our interest, but that it seemed to me unfinished. From his response, I saw that he thought I meant that the ship ought to get to port, or something like that. He said he didn't see how anything could be more completely finished, and asked if we wanted it. I quickly thought even if it is a fragment, to my way of thinking, it is amazing, and we'll take it at that, and I said so. I was troubled about it though—until a few days later his agent brought in the last third, or perhaps the last quarter. In other words, they had done to us in a sense what we did to you. They had mislaid what made it seem to us unfinished. Conrad was naturally perturbed about this, but he loyally stood by his agent nevertheless.

Matson said that he would be willing that we should see *Horse in the Sky* when you are ready to send it, and so I'll wait for that, with appreciation of your kindness.

Ever sincerely yours,
Maxwell Perkins

To Margerie Lowry

Charles Scribner's Sons
597 Fifth Avenue
New York 17, N.Y.
November 19, 1946

Dear Mrs. Lowry:

I just dictated the enclosed literary note, and it needs editing, but will get it in the advertising department, but substantially this is what we shall send out to several hundred papers the moment we have copies of *The Last Twist of the Knife* with the final chapter. I suppose if we were really honest, we would put the word "crimes" in place of "errors."

We are supposed to have copies within a week, and I'll send you six.

Ever sincerely yours,
Maxwell Perkins

Through a curious combination of errors on the part of the publishers, one leading to another, *The Last Twist of the Knife*, by Margerie Bonner, was published without the last chapter in the first printing of the book. The mistake was not discovered for some time, but as soon as it was, the author rewrote the last chapter and supplied it, and copies of the book containing it are now available and will be exchanged for the imperfect copies on request. Anyone wishing to acquire the last chapter by itself, for the sake of discovering how the mystery was fully and finally worked out, may receive, free of charge, the last chapter printed separately from the book.

APPENDIX 5

To Albert Erskine

January 6, 1947

Dear Albert:

I had no idea, when I spoke to you about my difficulty with the first pages of *Under the Volcano,* that it would end by overwhelming me as it has. I read the last pages with a sense of dread and vision, as if I had come to the last act of a great tragedy. The book obviously belongs with the most original and creative novels of our time. I feel like paying homage to Lowry—all the more because there is such clear evidence in the book of deliberate self-mastery. His ability to convey in a single texture the different levels of consciousness and the effect upon them all of the Mexican landscape as a stage of the human soul seems to me one of the most remarkable achievements in modern fiction. But I think I understand as well that this is not only a profoundly sustained history of a man's disintegration, but also a positive statement in defense of basic human values and human hopes: and that it is in the best sense a novel of the politics of men.

I hope the book will get all the appreciation it deserves.

Yours,
Alfred Kazin

To Albert Erskine

February 11, 1947

Dear Albert:

I couldn't after all find a copy of my letter, but I think the following, replacing "and here I return to the words intensity," etc., will fix it:

"I am particularly struck by his achievements in intensity and momentum. Few novelists today, even those most to be respected, show anything like his interest and ability in either."

I'm sorry not to review this book, I would really like to, a great deal. But if I don't dodge things I'd like to do—to say nothing of things I don't—I'll never get any writing of my own done.

Hope to see you soon. And I look forward to an evening with you, Lowry, and Jimmy Stern.

Best regards,

Jim [Agee]

APPENDIX 6

To Malcolm Lowry

Columbia University
New York
May 10, 1947

Dear Mr. Lowry:

I'd have to be much more insensitive than Nature has made me if I weren't touched and moved by your long letter of inquiry concerning my review of your book. For an injured author you were extraordinarily forebearing, generous, reasonable. Your statement of facts and your inferences carry conviction, and I wish that I could feel differently about your novel—that I could feel about it, say, as I do about its author on the strength of this one letter.

My review was no doubt too brief and I accept your estimate that it was too scornful. With the best will in the world I could not find your work other than derivative and pretentious: it is that combination of misdeeds that aroused my scorn. But I am free to admit that I may be entirely wrong in this judgement. In fact, you have an array of critical talent on your side which makes my cavil negligible. Since I truly respect the capacities of your applauders, I hope for your sake and theirs that as regards *Under the Volcano* I have made a mistake.

The mind being what it is, however, the only way that I can genuinely come to recognize my error is by re-reading your book at a later time. This I intend to do, and in the interval you will probably have persuaded me of your powers by a fresh work.

In any event, I would have you believe in my heartfelt good wishes.

Sincerely yours,
Jacques Barzun

APPENDIX 7

To Malcolm and Margerie Lowry

Metro-Goldwyn-Mayer Pictures
Culver City, California
May 19, 1950

Dear Friends:

Please forgive me for not writing sooner, but I have hoped that time and thought would release my tied up tongue and heart. I have not felt this way since my first reading of *Volcano*. On those rare occasions when I read something as brilliant, original and artful as your script, I am so humbled and awed that written words come only with the greatest difficulty. There is so much I wish to say, but they are things that are much more easily said in a small room or on a long walk. I have read many scripts and seen many pictures, but never before have I seen writing so purely cinematic. The impact of your work was much, much greater than that of the novel. It goes devastatingly deep, and its direct filmic evocation of life's complexities is magic and miraculous. I have the feeling that everything that has been thought, written and recorded on and about film is preparation for and prelude to this creation. The only other person who has read it is Christopher Isherwood, and he will be writing you separately. He shares in every particular my feelings.

On the practical side I am still too stirred up to take an immediate step. The fact is that I have made a film—a small one and not bad. I am working on another, *The Case of the Journeying Boy* by Michael Innes. This is a little bigger, and I know will be much better. In the queer Hollywood scheme of things for me to presume that Metro would now permit me to do a film of this proportion is doubtless ludicrous. It is also difficult to imagine a studio such as this understanding such a project. However if you will give me a little more time to think it out and consult with others more professionally experienced, I shall attempt to work out a plan of presentation.

[441]

I am more touched than I can ever convey by your doing it for me. I am deeply appreciative and respectful of your affection and trust, and believe me, I will do everything I can from this day forward to realize our hopes.

Ever,
Frank [Taylor]

To Malcolm Lowry

6227¼ De Longpre Ave.
Los Angeles 28, Calif.
4 June 1950

Dear Malcolm Lowry:
This letter has been owing a long time, and it now has to be paid (in at least a first installment). Very grateful to Frank for increasing my debt by letting me read your multiplication of *Tender Is the Night*. The only thing I want to say now—for it now seems dimly likely that we may meet some day not too far off—is that you did not waste your time in putting an amazing film on paper. Frank is determined to take a next step with it, somehow. And soon, too, for M.G.M.'s antagonisms toward the novel may not be as deep as they once looked to him. I have several other joys in it as it stands—now—on paper, but I agree with you that the first consideration now is how to get it off the paper onto film.

If you're looking for more super-coincidences, you've provided one in your notes—for I don't see how you could have known that Welles once wrote a Marlow-eye-based screenplay on *The Heart of Darkness*. And by the way, in your unwritten preface, please don't mix up the 2 Mankiewiczes—they're pretty different.

This is not the fan letter that I thought it was going to be, but please take it for that.

Sincerely,
Jay Leyda

To Malcolm Lowry

333 East Rustic Road
Santa Monica, California
June 12, 1950

Dear Malcolm Lowry,
    I have been meaning and meaning to write you ever since I finished your wonderful script, an insult to call it by that name, there ought to be another, new one for it, made specially. It so happened that I had read the novel, for the first time, not long before. It impressed me greatly, of course. But I'm not trying to flatter you when I say that your version of it was a complete revelation of new meanings and of a greatness which was certainly in the book somewhere, but which you made evident. When I'd read you, I was really haunted for several days by the greatness of the themes. It has every bit as much right as Dreiser's to be called *An American Tragedy*—and all your changes and developments on Fitzgerald fill it out and add significance to it. But why do I drool on like this? Quite simply said, it is a master-piece—a new sort. I wait to see it filmed, of course—but equally I want to see your full script published with all your notes and com-ments—would New Directions do this, for instance? It *ought* to be printed as well as played, because much of it is for a mental theatre like Hardy's *Dynasts*.

Well, congratulations!
Christopher Isherwood

To Malcolm Lowry

April 18, 1951

Dear Malcolm:
    Thanks a hell of a lot for your card about the story* and for liking it even if you'd liked it only half as much as you do. It means an awful lot to me that you really seem *excitedly* pleased over it—and being an artist you'll know how much I mean that in that it wasn't mere child-ishness, or, if so, is a kind of childishness I am for. I felt and still feel happiness and excitement about something in it myself, and so, of

* *The Morning Watch.*

course, feel sad if any reader, or any perceptive reader, even if he likes it, doesn't feel that too. All the more because, barring a very few short things, and a few articles here and there, it's all I've ever done that I really mainly feel well about. So I am very happy and grateful to you and Margie.

I'm ending nearly six months' stay out here mainly involved revising a script I wrote last summer of Creves *Blue Hotel,* and writing (with Huston) a script of *The African Queen.* I love script writing. I also loved what little I got a chance to read of your great job on *Tender Is the Night*—because besides every accomplishment of insight and atmosphere, you're of course one of the maybe dozen really original, inventive minds that have ever hit movies.

I also got a coronary thrombosis but, thank God, it has not made an invalid of me—I'm only supposed to be careful and moderate and am trying not yet successfully enough to learn how.

I'll be going back home soon but rather hope and expect to work out here a few months each year—so I also confidently hope and expect, God knows quite when, to get up and see you both.

My love to you both, and again deepest thanks.

Jim [Agee]

APPENDIX 8

To Harold Matson

Harcourt Brace and Company, Inc.
383 Madison Avenue
New York 17, N.Y.
December 11, 1951

Dear Hal:

I have been very much impressed by the manuscript of Malcolm Lowry's stories, HEAR US O LORD FROM HEAVEN THY DWELLING PLACE, which you have been good enough to let us see. "Through the Panama" and "The Forest Path to the Spring" are excellent, and so are the two Roman stories. "In the Black Hills," which one might call a "Western," is one of the best stories I've read in a long time. Altogether it's an admirable collection, and one which whets the appetite for the dozen or so additional stories which Mr. Lowry describes in his notes at the end.

The outline of the long work-in-progress, THE VOYAGE THAT NEVER ENDS, promises what might be the most important literary project of the decade. The sequence of six novels described by Mr. Lowry is fascinating. Of the first novel discussed, LUNAR CAUSTIC, he states that "a first draft . . . has been written." Is there any possibility of our seeing this draft in the near future?

We ask to see this novel because, naturally, we should like to work out a publishing and financial program for the whole body of Mr. Lowry's work. He has many admirers here, and indeed friends. Alfred Kazin is on our staff as literary adviser; Catherine Carver, who helped put UNDER THE VOLCANO through the press, and had correspondence with the author about many textual points, is a member of our editorial board; James Stern and Jay Leyda, two of our authors for whom I have been editor, are devoted to Mr. Lowry and his work. I tell you all this so that you will appreciate the nature of the background against which his books would be published here.

We are most grateful for your courtesy in showing us the stories and the prospectus of Mr. Lowry's novels in progress. We should very much like to work out a publishing program, and we should appreciate your communicating our desires in this regard to Mr. Lowry.

With best wishes,

> Sincerely yours,
> (*signed*) Bob
> Robert Giroux
> Editor-in-Chief

To Malcolm Lowry

> *30 Rockefeller Plaza*
> *New York, N.Y.*
> *December 13, 1951*

Dear Malcolm:

With the arrival of HEAR US O LORD FROM HEAVEN THY DWELLING PLACE, and your letter of November 23 requesting that the manuscript go to Erskine immediately, I had no choice but to examine the Harcourt situation as an immediate problem and there, face to face with a decision, I found Harcourt asking to be given fair consideration for their legal rights and their moral rights, too. Harcourt would not simply bow out; to the contrary they regard themselves as able to offer you as much, if not more, than another publisher. I had no choice but to observe their option rights in a regular way, and I submitted the manuscript. There was nothing to be gained by showing it to Erskine, only time lost. One way or another we had to deal with the Harcourt obligation first. Enclosed is a letter from Bob Giroux, the editor-in-chief.

Malcolm, you must understand I have no personal preference between Random and Harcourt (at the moment I happen to have more clients placed with Random than with Harcourt, but next year it could be different). I do think that with Giroux' letter you should give consideration to the possibility that Harcourt may offer you the kind of publishing you desire and deserve.

Let us assume that editorially you could have a satisfactory relationship with Harcourt: What kind of a financial program would meet your requirements? Is the first draft of LUNAR CAUSTIC available?

In haste to report this to you, I'll not now deal with other matters. Do you want to wire me, collect?

Yours,
Harold Matson

To Malcolm Lowry

30 Rockefeller Plaza
New York, N.Y.
January 14, 1952

Dear Malcolm:

By any chance have you heard anything further from either Klett or Herr ten Holder? I've not heard from either one, ever, regarding the picture prospects for UNDER THE VOLCANO.

In the meantime, I've not attempted any direct communication with either Klett or ten Holder. I must say that this whole tangle seems very unlikely of a profitable outcome, in my judgment, and I wonder if it's worth pursuing unless there's something persistent and definite forthcoming from Klett.

I've been meaning to get on to Peter Lorre as a first move in attempting to unravel the tangle. This I shall do right away.

I'm sorry that I've been so long in getting around to this problem, but it's one that I've been putting aside, frankly, in favor of what seemed to be more urgent and more prospectful undertakings. I know that in poverty 50% of something is more than important and that a hungry man is not so concerned with what might be his rightful share of that loaf of bread as he is with any share. But it's not been my experience that deals which are all snarled up with irregularities ever come to anything.

Would you have any objection to my writing direct to Klett, asking him the simple question of what has become of his interest in the film possibilities of UNDER THE VOLCANO.

This has been an unusually busy and confused post-holiday season, and it's not been possible for me to get together with Bob Giroux. But I expect to find him available this week.

Have you heard anything further from Correa regarding your forthcoming royalties? It takes a long time for money to clear from France, as another client of ours well knows, as he is just now receiving some money he has been waiting for for at least ten months.

Just this minute Margerie's letter arrived, and I'm glad to know that you are in Vancouver and warm quarters. I'm glad that you're writing to Giroux direct. He wants to establish a good editor-author relationship, and I believe he's the man to hold up his end.

I'll answer Margerie's letter tomorrow.

Best wishes to you both.

Yours,

Harold Matson

To Harold Matson

1075 Gilford St.
Apt. 33
Vancouver, B.C.
Canada,
Feb. 9, 1952

Dear Hal:

What's the word? We've been brought to a bit of a psychological standstill here by lack of news. The point is this: as soon as we were settled in the apartment Malcolm wrote a long letter to Giroux. Then, working like inspired demons, we made a copy of Malc's two versions of *Lunar Caustic* (which you remember Giroux asked to see) together with a long and detailed account of what he intended—or suggested —doing with it for the final version, and another very long letter. *This we sent airmail on January 21.* So far we've had no reply to either and don't even know if the MSS reached him—partly sent to have a copy of the material in safe-keeping—though Malc asks me to say he definitely did tell Giroux he needn't be in any hurry to answer.

It was a terrific wrench for Malcolm to leave Albert—he is devoted to him, as an editor and a friend—and it's really necessary to establish some contact with Giroux or he can't well go on *in vacuo,* as it were, at least at this moment, it being a kind of hard turning point. Malc is truly eager to establish the best kind of relationship with Giroux and Harcourt Brace, but I know you'll understand our anxieties. We try to think he may be out of town, or heaven forbid, ill, and of course he's a busy man with a lot on his mind etc. etc. But then your letter of January 14 said you would be seeing him that week, and no word since from you. . . . Well, you see how it is. I hope we're not being too temperamental in worrying about this. Still, it has now been two months since you wrote us that Harcourt Brace wanted to hold Malc to his contract with them and included the very encouraging and heartening letter from Giroux. We had even believed that before now a new contract, at least as touching *Hear Us O Lord*, would be signed; (albeit we appreciate the complications that might surround the complexity of the whole bolus). And, as I say, we had hoped by now Malc might have heard from Giroux personally, though appreciating that the turn of the year is a hard time. Tambien, in your last letter of January 14 you said you were writing me tomorrow—or what was then tomorrow —and seeing Peter Lorre right away. Malatesta? To date we ain't heard. No doubt you would have written had you heard anything, but in our new inflated economic element (where we shall have to stay until April 1) even the welcome $375 doesn't go on forever, the prospect of the French money taking ten months, all these prospects twitter like birds round the prospect of Malc's English holdings heading straight for the ash-can, as he puts it, so I can't tell you how glum it is at this distance to send letters off into the blue, have no reply, not know what's happening, and so on. So please let us have word, even if you think we are forward, or if there is no word. I'm sure once we know a bit more clearly where we are we will cease to be such a problem to you and ourselves. Love from us both, and once more a thousand thanks.

Yours,
Margerie

To Harold Matson

Harcourt, Brace and Company, Inc.
383 Madison Avenue
New York 17, N.Y.
March 10, 1952

Dear Hal:
The enclosed letter to Malcolm Lowry was a hard one to write, and I'm sincerely sorry that we don't see the way clear to continuing with him. This then is formal notification of our decision not to take up the option contained in our contract.

Sincerely yours,
(*signed*) Bob
Robert Giroux

To Malcolm Lowry

Harcourt, Brace and Company, Inc.
383 Madison Avenue
New York 17, N.Y.
March 10, 1952

Dear Mr. Lowry:

It is painful for me to report that we have decided against making an offer on LUNAR CAUSTIC. I wish the decision were otherwise, and I want to say that this decision in no way reflects on the quality of the manuscript which you were good enough to let us see. There is fascinating material here, and it is clear that the place of the finished book will be important in your long work-in-progress. Financial considerations, rather than literary ones, have led to our decision. Since we do not see the way clear to advancing further money for the two years which would seem to be the minimum period of guarantee, to allow for practical results, it is best for us to withdraw from the picture without further delay. I regret this personally, because I believe that our relationship would have developed even more pleasantly than it began. And if the relationship must terminate on what is after all a publishing decision rather than an editorial one, I certainly hope that it may do so with no ill feeling on either side. I shall always be an admirer of your work, and in every way a well-wisher.

Sincerely yours,
Robert Giroux
Editor-in-Chief

APPENDIX 9

To Malcolm Lowry

2 *West 67th Street*
New York 23, N.Y.
May 2, 1957

Dear Malcolm Lowry,

I don't see why not—in fact you are Canadian, if it's loved that much, and Canada's certainly in your poems, at least I see it there. "Canadian resident," British subject—doesn't matter much against that—though, for my anthology purposes, I collect, have to, Canadians. Hope you'll be back on Burrard Inlet. I remember Grassmere —years ago, bemused, I sought Willie Wordsworth—and ended up not with daffodils but a fine water colour by Ruskin. His home broken up, the maid had grabbed all his sketch books and, having a postcard shop at Coniston, was tearing them up leaf by leaf and selling the sketches at 10/– a throw. You may run in to one of them.

I've added "Cain Shall Not Slay Abel Today on Our Good Ground" (right title?) to your other two I've put in the anthology. All right? I've corrected "stranger" to "stronger" in the 2nd to last line of "The Glaucous Winged Gull." I remember your poems in the *CPM* when Earle Birney was editing it—the magazine was never so good before nor since—though I don't see it now. "Lupus in Fabula"—those last two terrible (good) lines came straight from p. 88 of *Under the Volcano* didn't they? Can I add my praise for that novel? Wish I had that prose fluency of yours. I've spent the past two years—no, more like four—on a novel out of the Eastern Townships of Quebec (where my roots are) and I still don't know what I've got. I have to give it another revision I'm told. Perhaps it's no good. As soon as I finish this Penguin Book of Canadian Poetry I'll try to get back to it —if it lets me. I've held up a book of short stories meanwhile on the advice of publishers—*after* a novel, you'll sell more copies, et cetera. They were wrong. I should have had it out. I'm older than the stories now. Yes. I wrote that one of the building being climbed and the young bitch of a sadist watching below. It came out in *The Atlantic Monthly* ("The Human Fly") and was picked up by Martha Foley. I've just finished another story, "Shower of Gold," about an obsession to impregnate a cold bitch—beautiful, but cold. Norman Levine (he writes good poems is now living in Brighton) suggested I send it to Pudney who does "Pick of the Year's Stories" or some such anthology. Do you know the series?

The dead give-away of yourself as a poet is the thinking that the novel could as well be got over in ten stanzas—or ten lines—of poetry. I don't think there's anything truer. I suppose that's one reason why I love the short story—far nearer to poetry. And anyway, wouldn't we all do nothing but write poems if we didn't have to eat and protect love? For myself I could almost do without the eating— well, perhaps not. I hadn't known the work of Curt Lang. I've copied out the poems you sent me (they're enclosed. Thanks). The last two lines of "Architectural" are first rate. But I rather am afraid the anthology is closed—it's indexed. But I'll write him. Many thanks for your being in it. I'm very grateful.

Sincerely yours,
Ralph Gustafson

To Malcolm Lowry

2 West 67th Street
New York 23, N.Y.
May 28, 1957

Dear Malcolm Lowry,

It's a plea for compassion for this wrung world—the Cain poem— that somehow, somewhere, there will be a recommendation to God's mercy for a renewal Pentecost for the oppressed—on the part of some long-lost ghost, on the part of the poets of God's mercy—who (with a turn of the poem) cry out to the world of no-compassion, there is no time, no time, at dawn is the reckoning and the last night is long. But the Cain poem is more than plea, it is an assertion that there must be, is, compassion lest we all perish, lest anguish be all, "life hears our prayer"—who are moral because we love life.

Forgive the transliteration. No more blasphemy can be done a poem than try to deal with it without the poetry.

I only do so—as the Cain poem strikes me—to let you know why the word "recommend" never bothered me when I read it for the Anthology. The word seems to run on—both ways—back to what is said, and forward to the end. I'll, of course, restore "recommemorate" if you wish—but I couldn't help send along this viewpoint first. "Recommemorate" would (presumably) mean "again celebrate"— which makes the action in a Pentecost return on the celebrant— shouldn't the action in Pentecost be distributed to those who are under compassionate consideration? namely, recommend to God's mercy the need of it?

Do I go afield? Please let me know—a word will do: yea/no—for the Cain poem is a beautiful poem.

As for a title—"*On Our Good Ground*" (???). That would establish the defiance, the *saevo indignatio* over the suffering in this world— which I sense as the driving motive behind the poem. Establish the fact that this *is* a good world—if it's left alone.

I fear I'll be getting over some pious moral impression if I go on— I don't mean that. I only mean the poem is rooted in life. Let me know.

I wrote to Curt Lang at the address you gave me—but my letter was returned, addressee unknown.

Very many thanks for your response—it's good to hear from you. The anthology is about done—but being held up by the delay of publishers who own copyright—I can't index until they reply. But I can always catch the word-to-be-changed in the proof.

Yours,
Ralph Gustafson

The above doesn't get over to
you the emotion I feel reading
the poem. Please assume it.
R.

INDEX

INDEX

INDEX